CAESAR & THE ASSASSIN

Managing Celtic after Jock Stein

Billy McNeill & Davie Hay with Alex Gordon

CESAR OR CAESAR?

Before you start reading this book we thought we'd try to clear up the Cesar v Caesar debate. Alex Gordon actually covers this in Bertie Auld's book, A Bhoy Called Bertie, which was published in 2008. Billy McNeill was named Cesar after the actor Cesar Romero. Apparently, Romero was the guy who drove the Rat Pack around, that is Frank Sinatra and so on. As Billy did the same for the likes of Paddy Crerand, Jim Baxter and Bertie, he was given the nickname Cesar. So Cesar was the original nickname for Billy McNeill and Jim Black opted for Cesar rather than Caesar in the Hail Cesar autobiography of Billy McNeill, published in 2004. However Bertie Auld insists the players called him Caesar long after they stopped using Cesar and this evolved nickname obviously was a reference to the Caesar as in the Roman Emperor. Billy stature was obviously growing in the dressing room for both Celtic and Scotland! Bertie wrote something along the lines of 'Well, who would you want to be called after? A Roman Emperor or a Grade B list actor?'

So, both CESAR and CAESAR are technically correct. It's really up to you which one you prefer to use. We decided to let Billy McNeill decide and these days he prefers Caesar, who are we to argue? Thus the book is called Caesar & The Assassin and not Cesar & The Assassin. We hope that you enjoy reading it.

Celtic Quick News, 2014

CAESAR & THE ASSASSIN

Managing Celtic after Jock Stein

Billy McNeill & Davie Hay with Alex Gordon

Published by CQN Books, Quick News Media Limited, Glasgow
Copyright Quick News Media, 2014.
All rights reserved.

First published in the United Kingdom in 2014 by CQN Books
ISBN 978-0-9928828-1-5

A catalogue for this book is available from the British Library

Design and typeset by Suzanne Waters (CQN Magazine)
Printed in the UK – Print and logistics by Tony Warrington
Edited by David Faulds

Special thanks to Paul Brennan, Jim McGinley and all the contributors
on www.celticquicknews.co.uk

CONTENTS

BIBLIOGRAPHY

BACK TO PARADISE
(Billy McNeill with Alex Cameron, Mainstream, 1988)

HAIL CESAR
(Billy McNeill with Jim Black, Headline, 2004)

THE QUIET ASSASSIN
(Davie Hay with Alex Gordon, Black and White, 2009)

*Please note that both Cesar, Billy's original nickname, and Caesar, the one he prefers, are both correct. Jim Black decided to opt for the former whereas for this book I have gone with the latter as that is Billy's preference. Who would argue with such a Celtic legend?

DEDICATION

This is for Billy McNeill and Davie Hay. Two wonderful friends, two excellent men and two genuine Celtic legends.

ACKNOWLEDGEMENTS

Gerda, my long-suffering wife, who was always there to lend inspiration and support. And provide the odd bacon butty for much-needed sustenance during twelve-hour shifts.

The CQN team – Paul Brennan, David Faulds, Jim McGinley and Tony Warrington. David deserves a special round of applause for his outstanding dedication to the project from day one. Pleasure to work with such devoted followers of such a wonderful football club.

Thanks, of course, to Celtic supporters worldwide. Keep the faith.

PROLOGUE

Once Celtic Football Club casts its beguiling spell, it has the capacity to hold an enchanted individual in its net of wonder forever.

Echoes of the past resound around one of sport's most celebrated citadels. Heroes are made and hearts are broken; reputations are chiseled into history and dreams are dismissed for all time. Pleasure can often be peppered with pain. You need to be a strong, unremitting character to survive the relentless demands of such a colossus. A mental toughness is an urgent requirement while a glorious yesterday constantly demands a successful today.

There is unstinting adulation when the trophies are in bountiful supply. Failure, though, can engage merciless criticism. Expectations are high. Malfunctions are often brutally appraised. There is no hiding place. To perform in such a demanding environment is not so much a test of nerve, but an examination of a backbone. There are two such passionate personalities who understand these essentials better than most.

Billy McNeill and Davie Hay.

Both were blessed with a fierce rage for perfection as they wholeheartedly embraced the tradition of a proud and unique football club. Neither required an attitude adjustment as they answered the clarion call from this most celebrated and illustrious of sporting institutions. Irrespective of past sorrows, the affection for Celtic Football Club will never desert them. As players and managers, they engaged the many and varied confrontations with a verve and vigour expected of men in their position. McNeill and Hay refused to indulge in the superficialities of life. Not for them the whims, caprices and foibles of the conceited. If either possessed an arrogant, egotistical outlook, their disguise was perfect.

In short, they were men's men. And Celtic men at that.

They were euphoric in triumph, frustrated in stalemate and despondent in defeat. As managers, theirs was an extraordinarily emotional time at Celtic; the men who took it in turn to be in charge as the club embarked upon the post Jock Stein era. It was one of the most turbulent and remarkable periods in the club's history. It was exhilarating, exhausting, entrancing and exasperating in equal parts.

Billy McNeill, more famously known by his team-mates as Caesar after the Roman Emperor than Cesar after a Hollywood movie actor, took control of team matters as the legendary Jock Stein's successor in season 1978/79. In truth, it was not an enviable task. How does one replace the seemingly irreplaceable? Thirteen tumultuous years came to a halt with the same proud individual in the dug-out. However, for four years, there was another man making the important team decisions; Davie Hay, also known as the Quiet Assassin.

The sacking of this particularly honourable individual was a sad and sorry one in the lifetime of the club. There can be no argument he was treated extremely harshly, shabbily even, by a misguided board who blithely and naively ignored the urgency of a reality check. One year after delivering the Premier League championship, Hay was handed his P45 in deeply embarrassing and ignominious circumstances. A dignified man was stripped of the job he loved. Billy McNeill returned and the entire chapter was an utter, shameful shambles. It was all done with tasteless, indecent haste. There was no need for it. I defy anyone to even attempt to understand or defend how the decision-makers at the time went about their business.

Undoubtedly, the unhappy situation created friction between two strong characters. Nowadays, thankfully, there is a concentrated fellowship between the pair. It's clearly in evidence. I was part of the Testimonial Committee when we were organising a well-merited Davie Hay Tribute Dinner at Celtic Park on April 10 2011. Glasgow businessmen David Hislop, Eddie Kerr and Brian Sweeney, who made up the four-man Committee, and I met Davie to discuss who he wanted invited to his top table. Without a moment's hesitation, the Guest of Honour nominated Billy McNeill. 'He's got to be there,' said Davie. Unanimously, we agreed. Billy was only too happy to accept the invitation.

A couple of years beforehand, I had co-authored Davie's autobiography, 'The Quiet Assassin', and, of course there was only one person I required to pen the foreword; Billy McNeill. I got in touch with Billy and a meeting was arranged. I pondered over an angle. I could have saved myself the time. Without preamble and unwaveringly assured, I was given the opening line which was superior to anything I was about to conjure up.

'Davie Hay was second best to no-one.' The words were out even before Billy had pulled up his chair. They were delivered in a genuine, heartfelt way; from one human being who knew precisely what it meant to manage Celtic Football Club. And lose that prized occupation.

Over lunch that afternoon, I believed we were obliged to talk about Billy replacing Davie. Once again, there was a prompt response. 'Of course, I took over as Celtic manager from Davie in 1987 and, as you might expect, it was very much a time of mixed emotions for all concerned. I made it abundantly clear that Davie had to be told before I would meet the board. I knew Davie thought along the same lines as myself that Celtic was our club. It didn't make it any easier that he was a decent guy and a bloke for whom I had a genuine fondness.

'There was a lot of unnecessary suffering all round at the time.

'I had telephoned him four years earlier to wish him all the best in the job when I moved to Manchester City. I had nothing whatsoever to do with Davie leaving Celtic and I know he realises that to this day. I would never have done that to him as he would never have done that to me. It's not in our natures. If you ever needed someone to fight your corner, I would have no hesitation in putting forward one name - Davie Hay.

'However, if any two people knew how much it meant to be manager of Celtic it was Davie and me.'

There is a genuine bond of friendship between the pair and I have been extremely fortunate to witness it first hand when there have only been the three of us in company. There is one almost tangible emotion, though, and it can be summed up in one word. Respect.

Uniquely, I believe, I am placed to discuss the merits of Billy McNeill and Davie Hay as exceptional human beings. Not as someone who has shared a dressing room, of course, but as a journalist of almost five decades. I will never forget the day I telephoned Billy a week or so after he had been summarily dismissed by Celtic in May 1991. It was a sad chapter in such a celebrated, medal-laden career at a club that would remain close to his heart despite the inestimable hurt. I was Sports Editor of the Sunday Mail at the time and was preparing for the new football season. As you would imagine, it's sensible to have something special to provide for the readers upon the advent of a fresh campaign. Billy McNeill was our something 'special'. I also had the distinct impression, at the age of fifty-one, he had no intention of looking out the pipe and slippers.

I was well aware that this living legend possessed an inquisitive mind and had always shown an interest in the media. One of his best friends, in fact, was the celebrated journalist Alex Cameron, a giant of the inky trade who was also well known for his television stints. I also realised Billy volunteered to spend time with the journalists on European trips and had a fair depth of knowledge of how the newspaper industry worked. I put in the call and asked Billy if he would like to join the Sunday Mail. I was greeted with the immediate response, 'Are you joking?' I emphasised that I was deadly serious and I thought his presence would be a massive plus factor for our newspaper

Also, I told him there would be no contract; he could leave us and go back to mainstream football as soon as he believed a suitable job was on offer. He was with us for a full season and no-one will be surprised to discover he was thoroughly engrossing company and an excellent professional. Billy went back into business before having a brief stint as director of football at Hibs and I have to say I missed our Saturday morning tete-a-tetes before he went off to deliver his informed opinion on whichever game he was attending.

It's a similar tale with Davie Hay when he left Dunfermline in 2005 at the age of fifty-seven. It was near-impossible to comprehend that no other club would come in for a manager, remember, who had taken Livingston, then in administration, to a sensational League Cup Final triumph over the much-vaunted young Hibs team - Scott Brown, Derek Riordan, Garry O'Connor, Kevin Thomson et al - only a year beforehand. Remarkably, the telephone in the Hay household was never activated with the offer of another job in top-flight football.

I got in touch with Davie with the offer of a lunch, mainly just to have a chat and see how things were progressing. I thought, if nothing in football presented itself, he might go back into accounting, the profession he abandoned to go full-time with Celtic in 1967. I knew his brother Brian had a practice in Glasgow city centre and I wondered if this was a possibility. Davie shook his head, that wasn't under consideration. I was surprised, though, when he expressed an interest in journalism. Again, just like Billy McNeill fourteen years previously, I had been cognizant of his closeness with the press, myself included.

By this time I owned a sports/news freelance agency in the shape of 7 Day Press, working out of offices in West Nile Street. After all the good and helpful things Davie had done for me in my profession over the years, the least I could do was open the door and help him to get comfortable with new technology. Again, as Billy did, he embraced the challenge with enthusiasm. I have to admit it was just a little bizarre sitting side-by-side at a desk with a Celtic icon clattering away at our respective keyboards.

Something had to open up and it did in the shape of a column with a Scottish Sunday national newspaper shortly afterwards. Davie would visit my office on Friday morning and I would 'ghost' his thoughtful and forthright comments. Naturally, he was never short of a sharp observation and wasn't afraid to air his views. In truth, it was an easy column to write because most of our thoughts were in tandem. Davie began making more appearances on satellite sports channels, most notably the now-defunct Setanta, and today he writes a very entertaining and authoritative weekly column in a Scottish evening newspaper.

In such privileged circumstances, you can become privvy to the inner thoughts of someone close to you. You are in full realisation you have earned their trust. As such, you know when they are wounded. More than most, Billy McNeill and Davie Hay played their part in the history of a very special football club. After Jock Stein, they were pivotal to everything that happened in thirteen emotion-shredding, rollercoaster years.

This the extraordinary story of two authentic Celtic legends - Billy McNeill and Davie Hay. Or, if you prefer, Caesar and the Assassin.

CHAPTER ONE
HAIL THE RETURNING HERO

The pulverising crescendo of acclaim had Celtic Park rocking to its foundations as uncontrollable waves of exhilaration hurtled towards the heavens. Billy McNeill, bursting with pride on the touchline, was leaping higher than he ever did when scoring one of his trademark spectacular headed goals. And no-one could blame him and no-one could begrudge him his gleeful indulgence on a truly memorable evening in Celtic's glorious history.

It was Monday, May 21 1979 and Celtic, playing for most of the second-half with only ten men following Johnny Doyle's dismissal, had just overcome Rangers 4-2 in a pulsating confrontation of almost unbearable tension to claim the Premier League championship. The East End of Glasgow was engulfed in joyous bedlam as the fans celebrated a most famous victory over their oldest rivals and fiercest foes. And also against mounting odds.

Picture the scene. Billy McNeill, only one week short of a year after taking over from the legendary Jock Stein, knew his Celtic team required to be victorious in the contest to lift the title. Rangers could play for a draw and, with two games left against Partick Thistle and Hibs, had the luxury of dropping a point from a possible four - as it was then - to be crowned champions.

A crowd of 52,000 crushed into Celtic Park to witness an encounter that was transformed into a rumbustious, rollicking tussle of the Glasgow titans.

Murdo MacLeod revealed that there was no special preparation for the Celtic players before such an important occasion. 'There was just the usual build-up. Big Billy knew how to motivate every player. He didn't go round us individually. He motivated us a team, reminding us of how far we had come and telling us not to throw it away. He got his message across.'

McNeill recalled, 'I did not expect us to be challenging for the title in my first season as manager. I thought it would be a gradual process and at the time I believed we would have done well getting a place in Europe. Remember, the previous season had seen my old club finish in fifth position, nineteen points behind Rangers. But here we were in a position of claiming the silverware in front of our own supporters. Suddenly, we were ninety minutes away from being acclaimed the best team in the country. I made a conscious effort not to put too much pressure on my players before the game. I thought they deserved the greatest of praise just for getting us into this situation in the first place.

'I stressed that fact to them when I spoke before kick-off. Big Jock would sometimes single out a player and say, "There's Wee Jinky, he's the man who's going to win it for us today. Give him plenty of the ball and we'll win." Now that would work okay with an individual like Jimmy Johnstone. In truth, it pumped up the Wee Man and he responded just the way Big Jock knew he would. We would be in the tunnel, waiting to go onto the pitch and Jinky would say, "Ye a' heard the Big Man - make sure you gie' the ba' to me." But that approach doesn't work with everyone. I was aware I had a lot of players with strength of character in our dressing room that night.

'I looked around me and I saw goalkeeper Peter Latchford, a laidback big guy with a great pair of hands. Brave and strong and a good distributor of the ball. Danny McGrain? He never needed anyone to motivate him. Danny was a manager's dream, a top-class professional of the highest order. Andy Lynch at left-back was a converted winger. He was neat and tidy, read play well and had a smashing left foot. Tom McAdam and Johannes Edvaldsson in the middle of the defence. They dovetailed brilliantly and really complemented one another's styles. I'm fairly certain more than just a few folk had thought I had taken leave of my senses when I converted Tom from centre-forward to centre-half only three games beforehand.

'I would like to think I could recognise a centre-half when I saw one - I only played over 800 times in that position - and I detected something in Tom's play that persuaded me to take a wee gamble. I inherited Tom after Big Jock had bought him from Dundee United the previous season. I realised he had only ever played as a targetman at Celtic, United and his first club Dumbarton. I could see he had a good leap. He could get up to great heights in the air and he had a superb header on him. You would be surprised the amount of people who believe they are good in the air just because they are tall. Okay, nine times out of ten they will get their head to the ball, but it's important what they do with it after that. Some just let the ball bounce off their napper and it goes in any direction. Tom had the ability to climb high and divert the ball into the right areas.

'I could see he was decent on the deck and wasn't afraid it to mix it with the opposition when he had to. He would chase back, too, in an effort to get in a tackle. I thought he might just fancy the ball coming towards him instead of him having to chase balls around up front. I played him in central defence in a game against Partick Thistle at Firhill at the start of the month. I fitted him in with Roy Aitken to his right and Murdo MacLeod on the other flank. We won 2-1 with goals from Davie Provan and George McCluskey and I thought Tom did reasonably well throughout.

'Tom seemed quite satisfied, so I thought I would keep the little 'experiment' going for the next match, away from home again against St Mirren at neutral Ibrox with Love Street undergoing renovations. It wasn't ideal, either, that the game was switched to a Friday night to prevent it clashing with the Saturday Scottish Cup Final between Rangers and Hibs due at Hampden. It was an usual kick-off time on an evening when your players are normally preparing for a match the following afternoon. I told the players just to think of it as a midweek fixture with the added bonus they would get Saturday off. That seemed to work a treat and we won 2-0 with goals from George McCluskey and my old Lisbon Lion mate Bobby Lennox, who had come on as a substitute.

'Let me make it clear that sentiment was not involved in Bobby being utilised by me in the twilight of his fantastic career. That never came into it. I thought he would be an excellent guy to have around in the run-in. I still knew he had something in the tank. He may not have been able to whizz around the way he did in his hey day, but even Bobby at half-speed was faster than a lot of people going full tilt. I put him on against Saints and said, "Go out there and put this game to bed." He didn't let me down. He came in at full-time and said, "Ach, you knew I would score, didn't you? I ALWAYS get at least one goal at Ibrox." I had to smile.'

Hearts, deep in the relegation dogfight with Partick Thistle, arrived in Glasgow on May 14 ready to scrap all the way. The Edinburgh side were on the precipice and it was between them and the Maryhill side to discover who would join the already-relegated Motherwell in surrendering their elite status. It was a dour contest with the Tynecastle outfit accepting at kick-off they had a point and they would do all they possibly could within their powers to hold onto it. A goal from Mike Conroy settled it for Celtic. At the end of the campaign, Hearts were condemned to the First Division.

Billy McNeill could also look at McAdam's partner Edvaldsson. 'Shuggie was a lovely big bloke. I suppose you could say he was bought to replace me after I quit playing following the 3-1 Scottish Cup Final win over Airdrie in 1975. Roddie MacDonald and Shuggie became the central defensive double-act after I retired at the age of thirty-five. I liked the big Icelander. He was quite an easy-going character and, of course, he was excellent in the air. He could use the ball, too, which was helpful.

'There was Roy Aitken, Murdo MacLeod and Mike Conroy in the middle of the park. They chased and fought for everything. Big Roy was always urging the team forward and, like Danny, he wanted to pin back our opponents right from the start. Mike was a good tackler and passer. He was a runner, too, always moving intelligently around the pitch.

'Then there was Davie Provan on the right wing. I paid £120,000 to land him from Kilmarnock, my first signing since coming back, and he was worth every penny. I remember sitting down with chairman Desmond White and the board on one of my first days. I was informed I had a budget of £200,000 to spend on new players. I said I needed more.

'Let's be honest here. When I walked back through those big front doors at the ground I couldn't believe how low the standard had sunk. I had teamed with players of quality, class and character, but I was deeply disappointed looking at the side which it was now my job to improve. Finishing fifth was not Celtic form. Kenny Dalglish had gone to Liverpool for £440,000, one of the biggest bargains of all time, Pat Stanton had received an injury in the opening league match which forced him to retire and Danny McGrain missed all but the first seven games. Parkhead was dead.

'I had arranged to take Jimmy Lumsden, of Clydebank, to Aberdeen to help Teddy Scott with the training duties. But it was obvious I needed him at Celtic much more, basically to play in the reserves and help bring youngsters along. He ended up playing in the first team. That's how drastic things were back then. So, I had to sit down with the board to stress that we needed to strengthen the squad urgently. When I was told I had £200,000 at my disposal I knew it would never be near what was required. I didn't hesitate to sign a cheque for Davie from Kilmarnock. I had seen quite a lot of him in action and I thought he had a lot of class. He moved well, struck a very sweet crossball and I knew he had the capabilities to make chances for the forwards.

'Another thing that I liked about Davie was his courage. Like Wee Jinky, he would attract some heavy tackling, but he had the grit and determination to always come back for more. I was talking to him once and he recalled his first meeting with John Greig. Davie, just a youngster, nicked the ball through the Rangers skipper's legs before sending over a cross. Apparently, Greigy, in a quiet moment, sidled up to Davie and said, "I think you would be better playing over on the other wing, son. Try that again and I'll break your leg." Needless to say, Davie ignored him.

'On the left wing against Rangers that night we had wee Johnny Doyle, who was a massive Celtic fan. I always got the impression Wee Doylie would have played for the club for nothing if he could have afforded it. Just as well the old Board didn't get to hear about such devotion! I also liked the look of a young blond-haired lad at Dumbarton. His name was Murdo MacLeod and I was told he was available for £100,000. The Boghead Park club were quite well-run and financially stable, as far as I was aware, and I was told to match their figure or forget it. As I had already spent £120,000 on Provan I had to go back to the Board and make the case for them to release an extra £20,000, so I could sign Murdo. I insisted we needed young players and, particularly, guys who could perform in his position. Thankfully, the Board eventually relented, I got the extra cash, Dumbarton were paid £100,000 and Celtic got a player who went onto give them fabulous service for nine years. I think they got their money's worth.

'Leading the line was George McCluskey and I had always admired him. He was a real talent. George had loads of skill, could dribble like a winger - in fact, I think he started his career on the flanks - and, boy, could he hit a ferocious shot. He was excellent at link-up play and combined well with the likes of Big Roy and Murdo coming through from midfield. So, I looked around the dressing room and knew I was looking at eleven players I didn't think would let us down. That turned out to be quite an understatement. Oh, and I can't forget Bobby Lennox. I named him as substitute and for all the right reasons. I was aware he would be turning thirty-six on his next birthday in three months' time, but that didn't matter a jot. I knew he had always looked after himself, trained well and I didn't see it as being a risk having him geared up and ready to go. Our fate was now in our own hands.'

Rangers, with redoubtable captain John Greig taking over as manager from Jock Wallace around the same time as McNeill succeeded Stein, had made up ground in the flag race after a dreadful start to the defence of their championship. Amazingly, the Ibrox side failed to win any of their first six league games with defeats from St Mirren, on the opening day of the campaign, and, importantly, Celtic 3-1 at Parkhead - Tom McAdam (2) and George McCluskey on target - while drawing with Hibs, Partick Thistle, Aberdeen and Morton. It took Greig until September 30 before he could celebrate his first league success as Rangers team boss with a 4-1 win over Motherwell.

Celtic, though, had allowed their main protagonists to catch up ground by going on a similarly awful run that saw them go seven games without a triumph from the start of October into the middle of November. The woe began at Aberdeen when McNeill's former club had a runaway 4-1 success. Dundee United continued the misery with a 1-0 triumph at Tannadice before McNeill's men had to settle for a point in a goalless draw against Morton at Parkhead. Hearts claimed a 2-0 win at Tynecastle and Motherwell took both points from a visit to Glasgow, winning 2-1. Significantly, a goal from Andy Lynch gave Celtic a 1-1 draw in the second Old Firm meeting of the season at Ibrox. Goals from new boys Provan and MacLeod earned a point in a 2-2 stalemate with Hibs at Easter Road before the spell was broken when a McAdam goal was enough to down Partick Thistle at Parkhead. 'It was far from title-winning form,' conceded Billy McNeill.

But, with ninety minutes of the season to go, Celtic and McNeill were on the threshold of lifting the most glittering prize of the domestic trophies, the league title. It was pure theatre as the final hurdle came into view. The fans of both teams were vociferous, as ever. They chanted confrontational hostilities in their matter-of-fact manner. They knew it was expected of them.

What they did not realise was that they were about to witness Old Firm combat of seismic proportions, an epic encounter between football's sternest adversaries. Billy McNeill put it this way. 'It was like a fiction-writer's dream.'

Half of Celtic Park fell silent as early as the ninth minute. Rangers had struck the first blow and taken the lead with an incredibly simple goal. John Greig had vowed to attempt to put his stamp on the team he inherited. Jock Wallace urged his players to perform with their sleeves rolled up, all flaring nostrils and a full head of steam. Greig, despite his somewhat less than skilful approach to the beautiful game as a player, adopted a more scientific, thoughtful approach. It was a dramatic change in style and Greig encouraged it especially after watching his side putting Juventus, laced with World Cup stars, out of the European Cup on a 2-1 aggregate. Also, it was good enough to give PSV Eindhoven their first-ever loss at home in European competition when the Ibrox men won 3-2 after a goalless draw in Glasgow.

So, Greig believed in bringing a more measured perspective to the game. And he was all smiles when Alex MacDonald gave Rangers the advantage. Greig switched Davie Cooper from the left to the right wing, clearly believing his ball-playing wide player would have more joy against Andy Lynch than he would on the opposite flank against Danny McGrain. So it proved when Cooper accepted a throw-in deep inside the Celtic half. With a swivel of his hips, he raced away from three defenders into the box. The alarm bells were ringing as he sized up the situation in the penalty area. Alex MacDonald, so often a dangerous, eager opponent in Glasgow derbies, had taken up a perfect position just inside the six-yard box. A deft flick from Cooper eliminated the Celtic rearguard and MacDonald, with almost casual ease, knocked the ball wide of the helpless Peter Latchford. It was executed with devastating simplicity. Early in the game, Celtic were up against it.

The scoreline didn't alter before the interval, despite the superhuman efforts of Roy Aitken, a real powerhouse on this occasion. Ten minutes into the second-half Celtic were severely handicapped after a moment of inexcusable foolishness from Johnny Doyle, possibly caught up in the cauldron of a powderkeg situation. Mike Conroy clashed with MacDonald as both charged into each other going for a high ball. Down went the Rangers midfielder, normally the snappy protagonist in such situations, and Edinburgh referee Eddie Pringle sought to have a word with the young Celt, clearly not intimidated by MacDonald's carnaptious reputation.

Unfortunately, as the match official had a cautionary chat with Conroy, Doyle, obviously frustrated, thought MacDonald was overplaying the dying swan act. What came next was totally ill-advised. He had a nudge at MacDonald with his right foot as the Ranger lay on the ground. Amazingly, MacDonald reacted swiftly by jumping to his feet to confront his opponent. It was quite a recovery. The referee missed Doyle's act of sheer folly, but, unfortunately for Celtic and the player, the linesman on the Jungle side had a good view. He signaled to Pringle and Doyle was immediately ordered off. Billy McNeill stood grim-faced as Doyle, in tears, raced past him straight up the tunnel, seeking solitude to reflect on his misguided actions which had left his team-mates with another mountain to climb.

The Celtic manager had a quick word with his errant player. 'I remember telling poor Doylie that if Celtic lost he would be in very serious trouble. I was furious because it had been stupid to get sent off, especially when we were in such a desperate situation.'

A pall of dread was very swiftly disturbed. Eleven minutes after his banishment, Doyle's reverie in the dressing room was mercifully interrupted as Celtic Park erupted in unconfined elation; a whirlwind of euphoria sweeping around one half of the ground. Celtic had equalised and it was all down to the rousing determination of Roy Aitken. The midfielder picked up a thoughtful clearance from Latchford, steamed straight ahead for twenty yards before finding the roaming Provan on the left. The winger picked out Aitken as he continued his run into the danger area, dropped a cross in front of him and the Celt took one touch before knocking it wide of the exposed Peter McCloy. It was a goal made and finished with the combination of stunning speed and accurate execution. Suddenly, once more, it was game on.

At this point, Billy McNeill made a monumental decision. 'Get stripped, Wee Man, you're on.' Bobby Lennox was ordered to join the fray as the Celtic manager made a brave, bold decision amid the pandemonium all around him. He sent on the veteran frontman for Mike Conroy. His reasoning was simple. 'We only had ten men, but we were still having the bulk of the play. I thought we could get away with two in the middle of the park, Roy Aitken and Murdo MacLeod, with Danny McGrain and Andy Lynch offering good support on the flanks. Davie Provan was moving around in a free role, pulling defenders all over the place. Plus I knew Wee Bobby could still sniff out chances. It may have been seen by some as a gamble, but I knew my old Lisbon Lion colleague wouldn't let me, the team or the fans down. I had every faith in him.'

Greig reacted swiftly to the substitution and made one of his own. He hauled off Tommy McLean, a talented little ball player swept into oblivion by the hurly burly all around him, and shoved on Alex Miller, an unspectacular, no-frills defender. The Rangers manager made no pretence; he was now playing for a draw.

Rangers, however, were rocking as Celtic continued to surge forward for the goal that would edge them closer to victory, the championship and a place in the following season's European Cup. Billy McNeill, of all people, knew this was where reputations were made. With sixteen minutes remaining, Celtic Park was a sea of green and white as the supporters hailed a second goal. The equaliser had been well constructed, but this was all about the quick-wittedness of George McCluskey. Aitken, in his haste to dig out a shot from under his feet, sclaffed the ball forward. It was way off target, but, as can so often happen, it transformed into a defence-splitting pass. The ball spun in McCluskey's direction and he struck it firmly on the turn. The sprawling McCloy had no chance as the effort zipped high past his flailing right hand.

Rangers had rarely troubled Latchford after the interval, the one-man advantage being rendered futile such was the aggression and driving force of the likes of the tireless and energised Aitken and MacLeod. Two minutes after McCluskey's penalty box improvisation, a hush descended on the Celtic end. Incredibly, Rangers, with so little of the forward play, had levelled matters. Davie Cooper dispatched a high left-wing corner-kick deep to the far post. Johannes Edvaldsson, heartily challenged by Derek Johnstone, didn't quite make the contact with his head he would have hoped for as he tried valiantly to clear the danger.

The ball dropped invitingly for Bobby Russell and, from an angle, he flashed a right-foot drive at goal. Latchford was helpless, and so, too, were three defenders close to the goal-line. It was a heart-stopping moment as the ball bounced towards its intended destination. It wasn't a precision effort from the Rangers midfielder, but he wasn't complaining as it struck the inside of the right-hand upright before crossing the line and strangling itself in the net. The Rangers fans, behind the goal, rose as one in delirium. Fourteen minutes to go. Could their favourites hold out? Would Celtic finally accept fate was against them?

Billy McNeill was never comfortable with the runners-up tag.

Inexorably, the clock ticked down; far too swiftly for Celtic and their anxious supporters. The manager exhorted his team from the touchline. 'Keep going,' he shouted. 'We'll win this.' Words in hope? Or desperation? Or inspiration?

Six minutes remained as the desperate Rangers rearguard clumsily attempted to clear a nimble right-foot chip from Danny McGrain. The ball was haphazardly knocked forward, a fifty-fifty between Gordon Smith and Roy Aitken. There was only ever going to be one winner. The Celt, brushing the Ranger aside with almost contemptuous effortlessness, burst onto the wayward pass and slipped a ball in front of the tricky George McCluskey on the right-hand side of the box. He shimmied one way, turned the other and removed the threat of at least three defenders in doing so. Sandy Jardine, on his weaker left foot, was dismissed. Suddenly, there was a clear sight at goal and, from an angle, McCluskey let fly with a vicious right-foot drive.

McCloy, who had only moments earlier defied Aitken with a flying save from a goalbound header, catapulted to his right to get a hand to the whizzbang attempt. The ball cannoned off his glove, ricocheted up and out. Colin Jackson, racing back to guard the line, couldn't get out of the way of the rebound. It struck him full on and flew into the net. Celtic were 3-2 ahead. Glory was at their fingertips. Could Rangers now respond? Could they show the mettle of their ancient rivals?

Billy McNeill still bawled instructions from the touchline, arms waving in every direction. 'It's one of those situations where you live or die by your decisions. I was well aware we had played practically half of the game with only ten men and my players might have been running on empty considering what they had already expended. But, as a former player, I was only too well aware you always get that little extra surge of adrenalin when you are so close to something good. It pumps energy into your limbs and I was in no mood to even attempt to shut up shop. That would have been dangerous against opponents who were a man up on the deal.'

With a minute to go, Tom McAdam played a ball out of defence. It fell to George McCluskey who turned it in front of Murdo MacLeod, rampaging, as ever, down the old inside-left channel. Davie Provan was clear on the left and Rangers were exposed, Sandy Jardine abandoning his right-back berth to add his weight to his attack. Menacingly, MacLeod brought the ball forward to the edge of the penalty area before clubbing an almighty left-foot drive of awesome strength. McCloy threw a hand at it, but he had no chance as the effort exploded behind him.

MacLeod, Provan and McCluskey danced with unbridled joy behind the goal as the shrieks of a delirious support punctured the night sky in the east end of Glasgow. Game over. It had been a head-on collision between two mighty teams on an evening that eventually and mercifully favoured the brave. This was not a triumph created by the silky soccer everyone knew a Billy McNeill eleven could produce. This was a Celtic victory from the heart. The Celtic manager admitted, 'We won that extraordinary match with sheer character and drive. It wasn't class that did it, but it was tremendous just the same.'

The fourth goal epitomised a game of bone-shuddering impact. Murdo MacLeod later confessed, 'I remember picking up the pass in their half. I knew it was late in the game, but I didn't know how late. There was a pass on either side of me with team-mates breaking forward. I just kept going. In an instant, I knew I was going to shoot, there was no chance of me passing. I thought to myself, "Hit this as hard as you can and, even if you miss, the ball will go away into the Celtic end and it will waste time." But I struck the shot really well and it went high and dipped over the keeper's right hand into the top corner. We all geared up to go again when the referee blew for time up seconds after Rangers had kicked off. I was the last Celtic player to touch the ball that evening. It was my best-ever night in football. I had a few memorable ones, but nothing ever touched that. No team could have stopped us even when we were down to ten men.'

Billy McNeill recalled, 'When Murdo got the ball I was screaming for him to kick it anywhere for safety. I just wanted to run the clock down. Murdo, of course, couldn't hear me through the din. Either that, or he decided to throw me a deafy. He decided to play safe. He hit the ball right into the roof of their net. That was the best place for it.'

McNeill can still smile at the immediate aftermath of such a thrilling confrontation. 'In the foyer, Jimmy Johnstone, Bobby Murdoch, Mike Jackson, Paul Wilson, Pat McCluskey, Benny Rooney and whole host of former players were dancing around in amazement. Jinky was as happy as I had ever seen him. They all looked as though they were celebrating playing in the game. That win meant so much to anyone with an affiliation for Celtic. I was so proud to have played a role in their happiness.

'Only moments earlier, our players had taken a more than well-deserved bow in front of the best fans in the world. They were our twelfth man that night as they had been on so many occasions in the past. Our will-to-win was backed up by the same sentiments from the stands and the terracing. It was a great night to be a Celt. I was standing on the touchline, feeling my chest swell inside my shirt, and I suddenly realised there was no sign of Doylie. Where was the wee beggar? Swiftly, I nipped back to the dressing room and there he was sitting alone in the corner. "Get out there," I shouted. "I don't think I should," he said. There were still tears in his eyes and I wasn't sure if they were with sadness over his sending-off or happiness at our victory. "Why not?" I asked. "You've played your part over the season. You deserve to be out there." Doylie looked at me. "You sure, boss?" I didn't answer the question. I practically booted him all the way up the tunnel and onto the pitch. He was a smashing wee lad. Of course, I was dismayed at his dismissal, but, on a night like that, who could have bothered making an issue of his misdemeanour? No, he had every right to be on the pitch with his team-mates that evening. He was well worthy of the supporters' applause.

'Doylie, apart from that momentarily lapse, had played really well for us throughout the campaign. He was a natural right-footed winger and had played all his career in the outside-right position for us and his previous club Ayr United. However, after I brought in Davie Provan from Kilmarnock, I knew he would be operating in the No.7 slot. I didn't want to lose Doylie's passion or commitment to the team, so I switched him to the left. He was never going to be a noted goalscorer, so that was the only position where I could play him. The Wee Man never grumbled, not once. He was just delighted to be playing for Celtic, HIS team.

'As I said, he was never going to win any goalscoring awards, but I told him not to forget a very important goal he scored against Dundee United when we beat them 2-1 at our place in late April. Jim McLean always set out his teams to frustrate and then they would hit on the break. They would suck you in and then sneak in behind you. So, it was always crucial to get the United manager to change his game plan and the only way you could do that was to get that opening goal and, suddenly, they were forced to open up. They were still in the title chase at the time and were always dangerous opponents. But Doylie got the first goal that afternoon and Andy Lynch slotted in a penalty-kick and the victory was ours. By the way, United finished third in the league that season only three points behind us, so that emphasises just how important that win was. And Wee Doylie played a blinder.'

McNeill also remembered an exceptional act of sportsmanship by opposing manager John Greig. 'He must have been hurting like hell. Everyone was aware that Rangers meant as much to him as Celtic did to me and yet he was one of the first in the Celtic dressing room to shake my hand and congratulate the players. It took a big man to do that and I'll never forget it. Greigy and I had our moments as players when we would snarl at each other. Those things happen in the heat of the battle. But a lot of people wouldn't have appreciated that we were actually good friends off the pitch. We met up regularly on the international scene, of course, and, as respective club captains, we were invited to so many functions together. And, when we became managers, it was the same situation. We got to know each other quite well. I really did appreciate that gesture. Would I have done the same had the roles been reversed? Who knows? I would like to think I would have done.

'I was just glad I wasn't put to the test.'

CHAPTER TWO
MISSING THE POINT

Precisely three-hundred-and-thirty-three days after Celtic Park was transformed once more into Paradise, Billy McNeill, sitting on the Dens Park touchline, buried his face in his hands. He could not bear to witness the horrors that were unfolding before his eyes.

Eight of the team that had blown Rangers away in the wonderful and unforgettable climax to the previous campaign were performing in the green-and-white hoops, but it was an entirely different story and a dramatically contrasting outcome. The stark scoreline read: DUNDEE 5, CELTIC 1. And any hopes of retaining the Premier League championship were fading fast with Alex Ferguson's Aberdeen poised to pounce.

Ironically, Billy McNeill's Lisbon Lions team-mate Tommy Gemmell was the Dundee manager at the time and he admitted he felt for his big mate. 'There were four of Celtic's European Cup-winning team in the respective dug-outs that afternoon. I had Willie Wallace as my assistant and John Clark was No.2 to Billy. We were leading 5-1 with nineteen minutes still to go and I knew there was no way back for my old club. I always warned everyone not to write off Celtic, but, on this occasion, there was no chance of a revival. Near the end, I nudged Wispy and nodded in the direction of Billy. I couldn't see his expression because his face was obscured behind his fingers and, of course, I was a little concerned. Wispy frowned. Our team were beating the champions by four clear goals and neither of us felt like celebrating.

'I have to admit I was embarrassed by the result. Even as the Dundee manager, I didn't like to see Celtic being turned over and that's what happened that afternoon at Dens Park. We needed a good result because we were fighting relegation. I knew just how much playing in the top division meant in terms of finances to our club and I was doing my damndest to keep us there. They were my priority; they paid my wages, after all. At the same time, though, I had a lot of sympathy for Billy. I didn't know what to say afterwards when we met in the boardroom. Billy came over and, like a true sport, shook my hand and said, "Congratulations, Tam, the better team won. I just hope that doesn't cost us the league."

'We had the usual wee blether between managers following a game and it was obvious Billy was hurting like hell. He actually apologised to me for his team being so bad. He seemed as embarrassed by Celtic's display as I was at the scoreline. "We've got Aberdeen at our place on Wednesday," he told me. "We have got to win that one now. Any slips and we're done for. Fergie will never let me forget it." He was lost in thought by the time the Celtic coach arrived to take the squad back to Glasgow. I saw him to the door and he shook my hand again. "Good luck with your own problems," he said. "That team doesn't deserve to go down." I could only wish my pal the best of fortune with the title. But I realised we had rattled his players more than a little. In fact, I would go as far as to say that was the most sensational result in Scotland that season. No-one saw it coming.'

On April 19 1980, Danny McGrain led his unsuspecting Celtic team-mates into some unwanted history - Dundee's biggest-ever victory over the Parkhead side on Tayside. From the thrilling encounter against Rangers at the end of last season, the Celtic skipper was joined by Peter Latchford, Roy Aitken, Tom McAdam, Davie Provan, Bobby

Lennox, Murdo MacLeod and Johnny Doyle. Alan Sneddon, Roddie MacDonald and Frank McGarvey also lined up at Dens Park. There was no sign of Andy Lynch or Johannes Edvaldsson, who had moved on, while George McCluskey, so instrumental in the comeback against the Ibrox men, was one of two named substitutes alongside Tommy Burns.

It was a dry, dusty afternoon, the sun hanging low in the sky, with the uneven playing surface displaying the wear and tear of a long, hard season. However, everything was going according to plan as early as the seventh minute when McNeill's men gained the advantage. Aitken, in his usual powerhouse style, won the ball in midfield, thundered forward, played a neat one-two with McGarvey and swept a low right-foot effort from eighteen yards wide of the grasping fingers of the diving Ally Donaldson. Alarmingly, Celtic took their foot off the gas almost immediately. They were well aware of their hosts' plight in the drop zone of the Premier League and may have expected to stroll to both points. Complacency may well have crept in and that can be an overwhelming enemy. It appeared, so early in the confrontation, the points were in the bag. Dundee had other ideas.

Iain Ferguson, a seventeen year old striker thrust into the top team by Tommy Gemmell, equalised with the simplest of opportunities. Erich Schaedler, the home side's left-back with the ability to terrify opposing defences with his awesome ability at throw-ins, demonstrated the art to absolute perfection in the fifteenth minute. He hurtled in a ball from the left wing which created chaos in the Celtic penalty area. Centre-half Roddie MacDonald, always more comfortable when the ball was in the air, looked alarmed as the object dropped at his feet. He panicked, mishit a clearance and it eventually fell to the unmarked Ferguson who fairly belted a howitzer-like effort beyond the motionless Latchford.

'I knew I wasn't taking a risk when I promoted Iain to the first team,' said Gemmell. 'I watched him in training and I was hugely impressed with his shooting power. He could give that ball an almighty whack and, as everyone will know, I was a big fan of giving the old leather sphere a dunt when I was playing. Iain was a cocky teenager and I liked that, too. He had the confidence to drill in shots from all over the place, any distance, any angle and I immediately told him he was in charge of penalty-taking duties. I fully intended utilising his strengths to the maximum.'

As luck would have it, Ferguson was given the opportunity to show his spot-kick prowess in the twenty-sixth minute. Again, a shy, this time from the right, caught out the Celtic defence. Ian Fleming fired a throw-in at Peter Millar, racing clear into the box. Danny McGrain, playing at left-back, spotted the danger just a shade too late and put in an awkward challenge. Millar went tumbling and referee Davie Syme, never a favourite among the Celtic support, didn't hesitate as he gave the award. In truth, it was difficult to debate the decision. Ferguson, belying his youth and inexperience, placed the ball and almost casually rolled it to Latchford's left as the keeper took off to the right. The warning lights were flashing.

Two minutes from the interval, the sirens were sounding. McGrain made a rare mistake after losing the ball in flight. His misdirected header went to Peter Mackie who chased the ball to the bye-line before deftly flighting over an inviting cross. MacDonald was leaden-footed and Ian Fleming - known as 'The Flea' for his fantastic leaping qualities - couldn't miss from smack in front of goal as he bulleted a header beyond the helpless Latchford.

Gemmell recalled, 'Ian Fleming wasn't particularly tall, but, my goodness, could he climb for a high ball. He was a bit like my old Scotland international team-mate Denis Law. Denis had that marvellous ability to appear to hover in the air before getting his head to the ball. Ian was similar although, of course, not quite in the same bracket as Denis. Actually, I changed Ian's role for the game against Celtic. I knew the strengths of Roddie MacDonald. He was at his happiest when he was challenging for headers. Like Big Billy before him, he won more than he lost. So, I devised a plan for Ian to play about fifteen or twenty yards outside the box. I wanted him to get up and knock the ball on. If

MacDonald came out to deal with this danger, then, obviously, he would leave a space behind him. That's where I wanted young Ferguson to make his presence felt. Sadly for Celtic, it worked a treat. I don't think the defence came to terms with Fleming's new role in my team.'

Billy McNeill knew he had to make changes at the interval to kick-start his side's urgently-required rally. Danny McGrain was switched to his more accustomed right-back role with Alan Sneddon dropping out. Murdo MacLeod was deployed in a more defensive left-sided position and Tommy Burns came into midfield. How would the revised formation fare? It began brightly enough and the play flowed towards Ally Donaldson and a goal just had to come. And it did in the fifty-eighth minute. At the other end. Erich Schaedler, unhindered once again, was allowed to surge forward and dink a dangerous ball towards the Celtic penalty area. Ferguson cushioned a pass in front of Eric Sinclair, a big, bruising, old-fashioned centre-forward, and he first-timed a vicious low shot from the edge of the penalty area past Latchford at his right-hand post.

Celtic were looking down the barrel of a sensational defeat. To compound a challenging situation, a fierce wind was whipping up and blowing full blast into the faces of the Celtic players. That was highlighted in the in the seventy-first minute when Latchford attempted to launch a clearance downfield. The burly keeper was well known for heaving kick-outs deep into enemy territory, but on this occasion the ball merely got caught up in the gusts, travelled about fifteen yards and came hurtling back towards the penalty area. Sinclair accepted the gift, rounded the perplexed goalie and rolled the ball in front of Peter Mackie who tapped it home from virtually under the crossbar. Game over.

Gemmell takes up the story again. 'I actually bought Peter from Celtic. When he first started to break through at Parkhead a lot of people were likening him to Kenny Dalglish which was a fair compliment. I watched him on numerous occasions and I liked what I saw. He was never going to be another Dalglish, that was certain, but he had a nice touch, a lot of energy and a good football brain. Once it was obvious that he didn't really have a future at Celtic, I made my move. I didn't have to break the bank to sign him and the lad was happy to come to Dundee with the promise of becoming a first team regular if he produced the goods. He had an excellent game against his old club that day. Maybe he was trying to prove something, but, for me, he was easily one of the best players on the pitch.'

Amid the carnage, MacLeod contrived to miss a penalty-kick, hitting a badly-directed effort straight at the grateful Donaldson. It summed up Celtic's day as they toppled to their worst league result since April 1965 when they went down to an identical scoreline at Dunfermline. With sublime irony, Tommy Gemmell played that evening, only four days after Jock Stein had masterminded the club's first trophy success in eight years with the 3-2 Scottish Cup victory over the same Fife opponents. Billy McNeill and John Clark were also involved in the humiliation at East End Park fifteen years beforehand.

Alex Ferguson, after watching his Aberdeen side beat Kilmarnock 3-1 at Rugby Park, could hardly believe the Celtic scoreline when it filtered through. Earlier in the month, the Dons had come away from Celtic Park with an invaluable 2-1 triumph. It was a game that see-sawed for ninety minutes before the points headed north. Drew Jarvie, a deceptively-quick raider, opened the scoring in the nineteenth minute when future Celtic player Mark McGhee rounded Latchford and set him up in front of goal. However, Johnny Doyle, with a slick back-header, grabbed the leveller four minutes later. Celtic Park was silenced in the fifty-sixth minute when McGhee fired in what proved to be the winner. An Ian Scanlon drive was blocked and the rebound fell kindly for the striker to blast a vicious effort beyond Latchford. Yet Celtic, unbeaten in the league at home up until that point, had the perfect opportunity to salvage their record. They were awarded a penalty-kick, but Bobby Lennox, such a natural goalscorer from open play, demonstrated again that he was no expert with a deadball. Bobby Clark easily saved his weak effort.

It was obvious, then, that Celtic would have to be wary of banana skins on the run-in. However, they just weren't prepared for the roof falling in on them at Dens Park. Alex Ferguson, always with a finger riveted to the pulse, realised Dundee were averaging just over a goal a game during this testing campaign and were most assuredly heading towards the relegation trapdoor. To take two points off Celtic and score five goals into the bargain put a massive smile on the face of the ex-Ranger. Now he would plot to maintain the misery the following midweek when he took his team to the east end of Glasgow. Aberdeen, in fact, had gone ten games unbeaten - seven wins and three draws - as they prepared for the confrontation which would go a long way to deciding the destination of the 1979/80 title.

Stevie Archibald was in rip-roaring goalscoring form for Aberdeen as they challenged for the flag. By the end of the season he had scored twelve goals in the Premier League and twenty-two in all competitions. Obviously, his threat was not lost on Billy McNeill, the manager who had taken him to Pittodrie in the first place. 'I was only at Clyde for a couple of months before I received a call at home from Jock Stein,' said McNeill. 'He asked me if I would be interested in joining Aberdeen. Ally MacLeod had quit the post to take over as the Scotland international manager. Big Jock was involved in everything back then. Chairman and directors at other clubs always went to him for advice. I told him I wouldn't hesitate in taking the job and the next thing I knew I was Dons boss. Just like that. The Clyde board understood and didn't stand in my way. However, even in that short space of time, I had been well impressed by one of their young players.

'Stevie Archibald was a born winner. You could play him anywhere on the pitch and he would guarantee you one hundred per cent every time. He had a great attitude. He even went into goal once when keeper John Arrol broke a leg in a match against Queen's Park at Hampden. Stan Anderson was the manager at the time, but he told me Stevie was in goal for over and hour as Clyde won 5-3. Apparently, Stevie made some brilliant saves and Queen's only made the scoreline more respectable by netting two goals in the last couple of minutes. Stevie, in fact, had been playing in midfield when I arrived. I knew he had had a stint as sweeper, too. His versatility was astounding. He always looked sharp, keen and eager, worked hard during a game and really put in some shifts when he was training. All in all, I determined to keep my eye on him.

'I knew Clyde, like every other club, could do with a cash injection and I wondered if I could tempt them to part with Archibald. I got in touch with the board, told them I could go as high as £25,000 and the deal was as good as done over the telephone. I had no fears Stevie would fail a medical. He joined me at Pittodrie and then became a real threat to Celtic in my second season as boss of the club. He had moved up front and was scoring crucial goals. He netted three against us in a League Cup quarter-final tie at their place. We played well, scored twice, but Stevie put a hat-trick behind Peter Latchford and lumbered the pressure on us for the second leg. We lost that one 1-0 and went out of the competition.

'So, I had a fair idea what to expect when Aberdeen came to town on April 23, four days after our debacle at Dundee. I had to get my players' chins off the floor. I told them these things happen in football. The unexpected is always just around the corner and we were caught cold at Dens Park. It was a freak result and I hope I don't sound churlish in saying that. That wouldn't be fair to Big Tam or his players. However, I just wished Dundee had saved their best performance of the season for someone else!'

Stevie Archibald, born and brought up in the shadow of Hampden Park in Toryglen, thrived on meetings against either of the Glasgow giants. 'Fergie really got us up for these games, particularly in Glasgow. He would go on endlessly about the West of Scotland bias and how Aberdeen were never given the credit they deserved. What we were achieving was dismissed because we were out of sight up in the north. Remember, this was all coming from a former Rangers player from Govan. But he really worked on your psyche. "The referee will give you nothing. He'll probably be a Celtic - or Rangers - fan. Don't let their players bully you. They think they can get away with it just because they play for the Old Firm." And so on and so on. By the time the kick-off came round you were raring to go, to get out there and do the business.

'Fergie had devised a way of playing against Celtic, especially at Parkhead where they were always expected to attack you. We adopted hit-and-run tactics. Our players would hang back and not chase lost causes into the Celtic half. We would wait and, as Fergie accurately predicted, a defender would give the ball away with a wayward forward pass. We would snatch at the opportunity and suddenly there would be a cavalry charge towards the Celtic goal. We did this time and again and Celtic never sussed it. Fergie would actually give you pelters if he saw you running around trying to close things down. "Let them give you the ball," he would say. Invariably, that's what happened. Once the ball was ours, we got going. Mark McGhee and I would normally patrol the halfway line and, as soon as possession was surrendered, we just bombed forward. The Celtic back lot would be exposed and we poured into the wide-open spaces. We did the same against Rangers.

'It was an amazingly simple tactic, but it always took our Old Firm opponents by surprise and on the back-foot. I know Dundee United played a similar system against the Old Firm, home and away. We were a bit more adventurous and could attack on the flanks where we had players such as Gordon Strachan, on the right, and Ian Scanlon on the opposite wing. They would get in good crosses and Mark, myself and the others would try to get on the end of them. But one thing was absolutely certain - we never felt intimidated when we played at Parkhead or Ibrox. Far from it. After Fergie had had his say we were all pumped up and couldn't wait for the action to start.'

It was a blockbuster of an occasion as the two best teams in the country locked horns on a balmy April evening, without a whisper of wind, in the east end of Glasgow with 48,000 supporters eager for the gladiators to emerge. It was perfect conditions for two teams who prided themselves in attempting to play real football. The first opportunity fell to Danny

McGrain, of all people. He burst forward as the Dons rearguard backed off. The defender carried on, dragging the ball to his left foot. Suddenly, an opening presented itself and the captain must have envisaged his name in headlines. Either that or he took a rush of blood to the head. Either way, he pulled back his left foot from about twenty yards and sent a wild drive curving about thirty yards wide of the target. In an instant, you realised why Danny only ever scored five goals in his twenty-year career at the Hoops.

Somewhat wryly, Billy McNeill observed, 'If Danny had a weakness in his game it was his final ball. Having got himself into a great position, Danny often didn't finish off the move as he would have wanted. He didn't score many goals, either, but he made up for that with his incredible appetite for the game.'

Archibald, who would join Spurs in an £800,000 deal at the end of the season en route to Barcelona, broke the deadlock with a typical poacher's goal in the eighth minute, but that was nullified almost immediately with a smartly-taken penalty-kick from George McCluskey. It was a night of high drama at Celtic Park and the tension was raw as tempers simmered. Andy Watson, a future Rangers assistant manager alongside Alex McLeish, incurred the wrath of thousands when he cynically hauled down Tommy Burns as he broke clear in midfield. Burns had been ordered off in a bad-tempered 2-1 Hoops' win at Pittodrie earlier in the season and this time he merely brushed himself down as the supporters bayed for referee Douglas Downie to take action against the offender. Watson was let off after a finger-wagging exercise.

The match official had the Celtic fans raging shortly afterwards when he awarded Aberdeen a penalty-kick. Midfielder John McMaster went down rather theatrically after an admittedly badly-timed challenge from Mike Conroy. Some you win, some you don't. Downie pointed to the spot. Gordon Strachan, who had irked the Celtic fans right from the off, was given the responsibility. He faced howls of derision as he stepped forward before slotting a measured attempt towards Peter Latchford's left. The goalkeeper read it perfectly, dived full-length, got both hands to the ball and pushed it round the post. Strachan, unusually, had nothing to say as he stood hands on hips, staring towards the heavens twelve yards from goal.

But the flame-haired extrovert still had the ability to rattle the cages of those congregated in the Jungle. Roy Aitken brought down Archibald right in front of the more vociferous among the home support. Clearly, it was a foul. There was the usual eye-balling between the Celt and the Don when Strachan arrived on the scene to violently push Aitken full in the back. Not the brightest piece of action against a bloke who was known to some as Crocodile Ardrossan and The Bear to others. There was the usual torrent of abuse aimed at Strachan and sometimes you got the impression this was oxygen to the wee man. Certainly, he wasn't a fan of being ignored. Downie booked him, but the player, face contorted in rage, continued to argue his case. A Philadelphian lawyer couldn't have got him off on this misdemeanour.

There were only a handful of seconds to go until the half-time whistle and once more Strachan took centre stage. Amid clamorous barracking, he pulled a ball down expertly with his right foot and slid a perfect pass into space behind Murdo MacLeod, the midfield man operating as a makeshift left-back. Stuart Kennedy, a pacy right-sided defender, galloped onto the ball before slinging over a beautifully-weighted cross to Celtic's far post. Alarmingly, there were three Aberdeen players with what appeared to be acres of freedom in which to operate. The Celtic back lot were eliminated completely with one soaring crossball and Mark McGhee was the first to react. Latchford tried valiantly to get across his line, but he had no chance as a raging header zipped low in at his right-hand post. Celtic kicked off and the referee instantly blew his whistle for half-time. It was as close as that.

Ear-splitting, booming shrieks greeted the second-half. The opening forty-five minutes had served up frantic, breathless action with no quarter asked or given. Billy McNeill knew Celtic's season was on a tightrope without a safety net in sight. 'Losing the goal bang on the interval was so unfortunate. One minute, it's 1-1 and you're thinking of what to say to the troops in the dressing room. Then it changes so quickly and so does your focus. Suddenly, it's a different game. I knew Fergie would want to win the contest. At 1-1, he would have been devising a plan to get another goal. At 2-1, though, it's all-change. Now he could have been thinking of holding onto what he had. So, you've got enough going on in your own head without wondering what is happening next door.'

Celtic continued to press early after the turnaround. George McCluskey, in particular, looked in the mood as he probed away at the Alex McLeish and Willie Miller double-act in the middle of the Dons defence. In the sixty-fourth minute, Aberdeen broke forward to score a third goal and, unfortunately, it was a personal disaster for the normally-reliable Latchford. A pass found Ian Scanlon wide on the left as Danny McGrain scampered back to cope with the threat and attempt to retrieve the situation. Scanlon, a totally unpredictable character from the hot-and-cold school of wingers, swung his left foot at the ball as McGrain lunged to intercept. Neatly, though, the Dons player pulled the ball back to his right. McGrain, off balance, tried once again to block any attempted cross. Scanlon, completely one-footed, dragged it back to his left before flighting one into the box.

It was the goalkeeper's ball all the way as it spun lazily in the air towards the back post. Latchford, with his usual confidence, left his line and leapt high to gather. Without warning, though, he lost control of the ball, fumbled it haphazardly and it dropped right at the feet of Gordon Strachan. Who else? Goodness only knows what the diminutive winger was doing in that position in the first place, but he didn't hang about as he stuck out his right foot and poked the ball into the empty net. An extended, doleful cry came from the Celtic support, completely drowning out the cheers of the visitors. Strachan ran away in crazed delight. Latchford could offer no excuse to his team-mates. He stood alone, a disconsolate figure. There is never a hiding place for the goalkeeper.

At that exact moment, the favourites for the title transferred from Glasgow to Aberdeen. And yet, at one stage, after Celtic had drawn 0-0 with their main challengers on their own ground on January 19, Billy McNeill's men were ten points ahead of Alex Ferguson's side. Admittedly, the Dons, after suffering cancellations due to a savage winter in the north, had three games in hand. However, Billy McNeill and his team looked to be on their way to a successful defence of their Championship as they entered February.

Unexpectedly, though, they surrendered a point in a 1-1 draw with Partick Thistle at Firhill on the ninth of the month. There was one minute remaining on the clock with Celtic leading through a Murdo MacLeod goal when the Maryhill side struck. Jim Melrose, later to join up at Parkhead, knocked one past Latchford to ensure a stalemate. McNeill, though, wasn't too despondent when he learned Aberdeen, too, had been held to a draw, 1-1 against St.Mirren where Gordon Strachan got their goal. It would be fair to observe that neither team was at full throttle around this period. Rangers? They were limping along, shedding points as manager John Greig continued to revamp their style of play.

Celtic made heavy weather of their next home game against Dundee in Glasgow. They gifted Tommy Gemmell's side the lead in the fifteenth minute - Jim Murphy the beneficiary - before two goals inside a minute from George McCluskey and Murdo MacLeod halfway through the opening forty-five minutes eased the tension. However, seven minutes from time Roy Aitken deflected an effort into his own net and Dundee took home an unexpected point. The look of apprehension on Billy McNeill's face at full-time eased when he heard the news the Dons had lost 2-1 at home to Kilmarnock. Sadly, it was merely a stay of execution. A week later Johnny Doyle got the only goal of the game in a dour encounter against Morton at Cappielow while Alex Ferguson fumed as the Dons could only draw 1-1 with Partick Thistle at Pittodrie.

It was March and McNeill and Ferguson were thinking along similar lines; they both needed extra firepower to pep up their title challenges.

Ferguson realised he was relying far too much on Stevie Archibald and Mark McGhee, with Drew Jarvie as back-up. Joe Harper had fallen foul of the Dons gaffer. The chunky frontman, who still holds the goalscoring record at the club with 205 strikes in his two spells, didn't fit into Fergie's jigsaw. Harper was a penalty box predator, but that was never going to be enough for his demanding manager. Harper was injured in November and didn't figure again that season. He played only one game the following term before quitting Pittodrie at the age of thirty-two. In his memoirs, Fergie later revealed, 'We wouldn't have won the league with Joe in the team.'

McNeill realised Bobby Lennox's fabulous career was coming to an inevitable conclusion. The onus was on George McCluskey to rack up the goals and the Celtic manager was given the opportunity to solve the problem with the news that Frank McGarvey had failed to settle at Liverpool. Anfield boss Bob Paisley had paid St.Mirren £270,000 for the lively little raider in May 1979. McGarvey went public with his dissatisfaction at hardly getting a sniff at a first team place. 'If you're not in the top side no-one wants to know you. I could by lying on the dressing room floor and people would just step over me.' Unsurprisingly, he slapped in a transfer demand. Paisley accepted it with a proviso. 'We want our money back.' McNeill was aware a bid of £270,000 would be accepted by the Merseyside outfit. So, too, though did a certain Alex Ferguson. He had managed McGarvey at St Mirren and remained an admirer. Fergie wanted the player for Aberdeen.

Now it was decision time for McGarvey. Out of respect, he met his old boss in a Glasgow hotel. Alex Ferguson, known to have an extremely persuasive tongue, put his pitch to the player. He underlined his plans for Aberdeen. Fergie genuinely believed they were the coming team and he would be delighted if McGarvey wanted to join in. One thing counted against the Dons chief and he knew it; McGarvey was a massive Celtic fan. He had never attempted to hide that fact, so McNeill was already a step ahead of his competitor. Fergie never wavered, though. He spent two hours with McGarvey, emphasising his ambitions for the future and the role the striker had to play. Unfortunately for Fergie, his words fell on deaf ears. McGarvey was on his way to Celtic to realise a boyhood dream.

Billy McNeill and the press gave the player the razzmatazz treatment on the day he signed and McNeill, privately, told friends McGarvey was the player he needed to retain the title. The frontman made a quickfire debut as he led the line against St Mirren at Parkhead on Wednesday March 12. A healthy crowd of 30,000 on a damp and cold evening welcomed McGarvey to his spiritual home and the aspirations of the support were high when George McCluskey rifled in the opening goal in the twenty-first minute. McGarvey, all hustle and bustle, would have reminded some of the home support of a young, enthusiastic Lou Macari with his selfless and tireless running all along the frontline.

Everything was going according to plan when Johnny Doyle doubled the advantage seven minutes after the turnaround. Celtic were coasting, but the Paisley Saints had determined they were not there as bit-part players in a Celtic celebration. There was dismay in the sixty-ninth minute when they were awarded a penalty-kick. They had rarely threatened Peter Latchford, but they had been thrown a lifeline. Dougie Somner, a big, powerful attack leader, was their penalty-kick expert and, to the consternation of ninety-nine per cent of the fans, he made no mistake with his slide-rule effort. To most, it looked like a mere blip and normal service would be resumed as swiftly as possible. Celtic, remarkably, found themselves pushed back and central defenders Roddie MacDonald and Tom McAdam were clearly rattled by the intrusion of a fired-up Somner. Six minutes after the penalty goal, it was all-square. Somner was again on target and the carnival atmosphere that had greeted new boy McGarvey was well and truly punctured. Celtic had to be content with a point.

Three days later it was an identical situation at Rugby Park. Incredibly, Bobby Street, a nippy front player, gave Kilmarnock a goal of a start inside sixty seconds. McNeill had decided to allow the same line-up the opportunity to atone for their lapse against St Mirren the previous Wednesday, but they still looked a little shell-shocked from that encounter. McGarvey, for his part, put in his usual effort, but no rewards were forthcoming. With five minutes to go, the scoreline remained the same. Frustrated, McNeill had thrown on ageing substitute Bobby Lennox in desperation. The Lisbon Lion snatched a typical effort with the Killie players already counting their bonus money.

The Celtic manager's foul mood was not enhanced moments later when he was told Andy Watson had scored a late winner for Aberdeen as they overcame Dundee United 2-1 at home. The Dons were due to play two fixtures in the space of four days as they fought to get through their backlog. They won them both, beating Dundee 3-0 and Morton 1-0. Who would blink first? Billy McNeill? Or Alex Ferguson? It was enthralling stuff.

Frank McGarvey scored his first goal for Celtic on Saturday March 29 as Hibs were trounced 4-0 in Glasgow. Three goals in a devastating six-minute burst flattened the men from Edinburgh. Bobby Lennox netted with a penalty-kick a minute after the interval and then Celtic went into overdrive with McGarvey (64), Johnny Doyle (67) and Roddie MacDonald (70) joining in. Even better news filtered through from across the Clyde - Aberdeen had been held to a 2-2 by a Rangers team that had been a mere irrelevance in the league race that season. Stevie Archibald and Drew Jarvie were the men on the mark to make sure of at least a point for the Pittodrie side.

Four days later on April 1, Celtic hoped for Aberdeen to be involved in an April Fool's Day foul-up when they travelled to Rugby Park to take on Kilmarnock. The Ayrshire outfit had made life tough for Celtic a fortnight earlier and there was always the possibility they may raise their game against the Dons. No chance. Alex Ferguson's side didn't need to extend themselves as they cantered to a routine 4-0 win, Mark McGhee getting one of their goals. Then came the crunch at Celtic Park where Aberdeen celebrated their 2-1 triumph and all eyes were on the Dons the following Monday when they faced a quick turnaround against Dundee. Ian Fleming, after his dynamic display against Celtic, looked as though he might stage an action replay with the opening goal in the third minute. Nerves were frayed in those occupying the red jerseys as it remained that way right up until the hour mark. Aberdeen had struggled to make any serious headway, but a penalty-kick was awarded and Gordon Strachan whacked it home. With fifteen minutes remaining, Drew Jarvie claimed the winner.

Many years later, Alex Ferguson, as the Manchester United manager, would famously be quoted as saying it was 'squeaky bum time' when things got this tight. The evening following his side's hard graft against Dundee, Celtic took on the other half of the Tayside double-act at Tannadice. It's no secret that Celtic rarely enjoyed playing against Jim McLean's Dundee United. There was always the belief that McLean adopted, maybe even revelled in, anti-football tactics. When Celtic came to town, United did nothing to entertain the supporters of either team. It would have been intriguing to see what would have happened if Celtic had ever adopted a similar spoiling system. The game would never have got started.

Billy McNeill could never fathom the negative thinking of his United counterpart. They were awkward opponents who hit on the counter-attack. And they were good at it. Well, after years of practice you might expect that. McLean drilled into his players what they had to do. They performed like robots and no-one questioned the manager's ideals. To speak up against Jim McLean was to banish yourself from the first team. So, United lined up in their usual formation when Celtic arrived that Tuesday night. Again, they proved to be a puzzle Billy McNeill and his players couldn't solve. Two goals from Davie Dodds and a single from John Holt gave the home side a 3-0 win. The wheels were coming off the Celtic bandwagon.

On Saturday, April 26 - only days after the 3-1 downfall against the Dons in Glasgow and with a mere three matches to go in the league run-in - the Celtic manager had to make some brave decisions for the home game against Partick Thistle. He had left Frank McGarvey out of his starting line-up against Aberdeen with the striker still trying to channel his energy in the proper direction and fit into the system. He got the green light to come back and play alongside George McCluskey against the Firhill side.

Centre-half Roddie MacDonald was struggling, too, and his nervy performances against Dundee and Aberdeen, with Peter Latchford being forced to pick the ball out of his net on eight occasions, meant McNeill wielding the axe. Tom McAdam moved to the main central defensive role with Mike Conroy coming in to sweep up around him. Johnny Doyle was also hit by a crisis of form and Tommy Burns was played wider on the left with Dom Sullivan, an £82,000 buy from Aberdeen a handful of games into the campaign, taking over in midfield.

Could McNeill and his players arrest the stumble with the finishing tape in sight? Coincidentally, another Lisbon Lion was in place to attempt to obstruct the progression of the Hoops. Bertie Auld was the wily, streetwise individual who had been in charge of the Firhill side since1974. He had led them to the First Division title in 1975 and his remit was clear. 'My job was to keep Partick Thistle in the Premier League. How we went about achieving that was left to entirely to me. Some fans didn't like the way I set up the side. it. I just asked them if they enjoyed watching their team in the First Division. That helped them focus.'

Thistle didn't win too many games, but, importantly, they didn't lose too many, either. By the end of season 1979/80, the Maryhill outfit were safe in joint sixth position alongside Morton in the ten-team league. They were ten points ahead of second bottom Dundee and eighteen ahead of doomed Hibs. Auld would never apologise for his tactics which were less than entertaining. 'I knew what my players could and couldn't do,' he said logically. 'I had no intention of ever handing the initiative to the opposing team. If they wanted to take points off us, they would have to earn them the hard way.'

Billy McNeill said, 'I knew only too well what Bertie would do against us at Parkhead. I didn't expect any favours from my wee mate. He would come and get every player behind the ball. With that in mind, I thought it would be better to have a couple of guys like Sullivan and Burns in the same line-up. They were both excellent passers of the ball and I told them to continually look for the runs of McCluskey and McGarvey. We had to occupy Thistle all over the pitch and do our best to destroy their game plan.'

It was scoreless at the interval with the visitors carrying out the strict orders of their gaffer. They defended in depth, doubled up on Davie Provan on the right wing and it was difficult to see where the opening was going to materialise to force them to come out of their shell. A minute after the interval, McCluskey gatecrashed the Alan Rough barrier to stroke in the breakthrough goal. Ten minutes later Tom McAdam showed the touch he had so ably demonstrated as a striker when he notched No.2. Jim Melrose put the jitters through the home defence when he pulled one back near the end, but the scoreline remained unaltered at the full-time whistle.

The priority now was to find out what had happened at Pittodrie where Aberdeen had been taking on St.Mirren. Could the Saints emulate what they achieved at Parkhead when they spoiled Frank McGarvey's baptism as a Celt? The Paisley side, managed by Alex Ferguson for four years before he was sacked in controversial circumstances in 1978, were heading for third position in the league, their best performance since the 1892/93 season. Doug Somner was also romping away with the top marksman award with twenty-five goals. The more optimistic among the Celtic contingent hoped for a Dons setback. The realists believed the men from the North had overcome too many obstacles to take their eye off the main prize at this late stage. The optimists were disappointed; the realists got it right. The Dons didn't falter as they annexed a solid 2-0 victory. Doug Rougvie, the barrel-chested defender who tackled like a combined harvester, netted a rare goal and Ian Scanlon got the killer second.

Three days later, still playing catch-up, Ferguson's men settled for a 1-1 stalemate with Dundee United at Tannadice with that man Gordon Strachan on the scoresheet again. The following evening it was Celtic's turn to take centre stage as they travelled to Dens Park, the ground where it had all began to unravel earlier in April. Billy McNeill's men clearly had a point to prove against a team that had by now lost its battle to preserve its place in the Top Ten. Mike Conroy and Dom Sullivan, two players who missed the 5-1 flop, claimed the second-half goals that gave Celtic a 2-0 victory.

The situation was now clear. On May 3, Aberdeen could clinch the title if they beat Hibs at Easter Road and Celtic surrendered anything against St. Mirren at Love Street. The Dons had by far the easier of the tasks, taking on a team already shredded of confidence in a campaign that saw them hurtle out of the top flight at the speed of light. The once-mighty Edinburgh outfit won only six times from thirty-six games and had been on the receiving end of a disastrous twenty-four defeats. They picked up a miserable total of eighteen points from a possible seventy-two. They were there for the dismantling. The Dons could smell blood and they went for the jugular.

Stevie Archibald, continuing to haunt McNeill, got the opening goal in the twenty-seventh minute and Andy Watson added a quickfire second. Surprisingly, it took the Pittodrie outfit until the sixty-sixth minute before Ian Scanlon walloped in the third. Mark McGhee claimed No.4 in the eighty-third minute and, emphasising the chasm in class, Sanlon brought down the curtain on a thoroughly professional job with the fifth two minutes from the end.

Ferguson had been fidgeting on the touchline throughout the game. He appeared more interested in what was happening at Love Street than what was unfolding at Easter Road. Furiously chewing gum and checking his watch every few seconds, he looked a nervous wreck. Fergie was on the cusp of something marvellous and who knew where such an achievement would take him in his managerial career? Ten minutes from time, with his team three goals ahead and coasting, Fergie's smile evaporated. He was motionless on the touchline. Celtic had been drawing 0-0, but he had just been informed they had been awarded a penalty-kick. The colour drained momentarily from his cheeks. There was the very real possibility of no title celebrations in the capital. Moments later, he punched the air in delight. Fans may have wondered if he was watching a different game.

The referee had, in fact, awarded Celtic a penalty-kick, but, on the advice of his linesman, changed his mind and awarded a free-kick on the edge of the box. The assistant on the touchline apparently had a better view of the incident than the match official. Drew Jarvie, a substitute at Easter Road, recalled, 'There was a young girl with a transistor at the back of the dug-out. She kept us informed of the score between St Mirren and Celtic. At one stage, we thought Celtic were leading 1-0. However, in the middle of all the furore and noise, we soon realised that was wrong. At the end, the boss did his famous victory jig.'

So, there were some mixed messages, but no-one was confused in Paisley. Celtic's league season petered out in a goalless draw, the sixth time they had failed to score in an unusual campaign. They had crossed the threshold of pain to win the title the previous season, but, to many observers, had surrendered it all too meekly.

Celtic missed out by a point. Billy McNeill said, 'We paid a heavy price for every mistake. We've got to make sure there is no repetition in the future.'

CHAPTER THREE
PATHS OF GLORY

It was a victory parade that was transformed into a violent procession. Alas, memories of the actual football and the fact Celtic had beaten Rangers 1-0 in extra-time of a thrilling 1980 Scottish Cup Final were buried under the debris of the madness that erupted at Hampden, the afternoon that will be forever remembered as the day drink-fuelled cretins went to war in an orgy of destruction. It was a black chapter in the history of Scottish football.

Sickening images of the brutality and savagery among the pitch-invading rabble scarred what had previously been an engrossing spectacle at the national stadium. Pictures of mounted policemen, batons drawn, charging into hundreds of battling hoodlums were flashed around the globe. It was a repulsive, disgusting finale, a revolting, nauseating climax to a grand sporting occasion.

What triggered the insanity that sad and unforgettable day?

Captain Danny McGrain and his cavorting cohorts had accepted the glittering prize and raced to the Celtic end to show off the newly-won silverware. It's a dreadful condemnation of sportsmanship if a triumphant team cannot rejoice in such a manner. Admittedly, the occasion and the celebrations proved too much for some Celtic supporters who came onto the pitch to join in. Their jubilation activated an invasion from the opposite side of Hampden, traditionally the Rangers end. Hooligans were hell-bent on interrupting the mini-cavalcade. That, in turn, sparked an angry reaction from the rival supporters. Then came the meeting of the mindless on the Hampden turf as punches were traded, bottles were thrown, kicks were aimed and horses randomly galloped into the warring throngs.

As ever, fingers of blame pointed in all directions once the impromptu battlefield was cleared. Who would take the rap? Television pictures clearly showed that only eight policemen were in attendance at the Celtic end a few minutes after the conclusion of the game. That total was woefully inadequate in the attempts to stem the flow of fans who wanted to bask in the unconfined happiness of their idols. Iain McKie was the Strathclyde Police Chief Constable who was in charge of operations for the Cup Final that day. He explained that the majority of his officers were outside the stadium by the time the game was over, adding, 'There was nothing unusual about that. It was standard procedure. Most of the trouble at Old Firm matches took place outside the ground; fighting, urinating in gardens and so on.'

Of course, on such occasions, politicians are always swift and only too happy to leap onto a platform to pontificate and give their thoughts of why such a dreadful happening should occur. George Younger, the Secretary of State for Scotland, couldn't possibly pass up such an opportunity to hog a headline. In a statement to the House of Commons, he claimed, 'It was drink and the action of the Celtic players that led to the riot.' No-one thought to ask Younger if he was, in fact, at Hampden that day.

Sectarian issues were once again brought up to which Celtic chairman Desmond White responded, rather haughtily, that he had checked his team's Scottish Cup-winning line-up and discovered it contained six Catholics and five Protestants. He added, 'The list of Protestants include our captain Danny McGrain.'

Once the wreckage had been cleared, Celtic and Rangers were both fined £20,000 and a total ban on alcohol inside Scottish football grounds was enforced. That is still the case to this day. So, it is a Scottish Cup Final that is remembered for all the wrong reasons, but, in a purely, footballing context, Celtic should be warmly and heartily congratulated for a well-earned, heroic triumph.

Let's set the scene for another gruelling Old Firm encounter at Hampden on Saturday, May 10 as the sun smiled on the south side of Glasgow. It was an extremely unusual situation; this was the last chance for one of the Glasgow giants, the teams who had dominated Scottish football for so long, to claim a trophy. Aberdeen had knocked both out of the League Cup, doing the hard work before being beaten 3-0 by Dundee United in the Final replay. Celtic, of course, had failed narrowly to retain the league title with the Dons snatching the flag by a point.

Now football's fiercest foes were poised for a must-win confrontation. Celtic went into the game in the realisation that, at worst, they would be involved in Europe via the UEFA Cup the following season. Rangers didn't have that safety net. They had to win to reach the Cup-Winners' Cup, their fifth-placed finish in the league ensuring European oblivion if they weren't successful. And they hadn't missed out on excursions into Europe since 1965.

Even before the tussle, Billy McNeill had massive problems. For a start, he didn't have a centre-half. The SFA had suspended Roddie MacDonald and Tom McAdam placing a heavy burden on the Celtic manager. As luck would have it, he had sold Johannes Edvaldsson to emerging NASL side Tulsa Roughnecks in February of that year. McNeill turned to Jim Casey, hardly a first team regular and a twenty-two year old who had never played in central defence. However, it appeared there was a curse on the No.5 position when Casey, who only made eleven league appearances in his three years at the club, twisted an ankle in training a few days before the Hampden showdown. The injury was enough to rule him out. 'I couldn't believe it,' said McNeill. 'Clearly, it was a critical situation.'

The Celtic boss looked at the players who were available. He raised an eyebrow or two when he settled on Mike Conroy, another twenty-two year old who had never figured at centre-half. And at around 5ft 9in he didn't looked properly equipped to deal with the aerial threat of Derek Johnstone. But McNeill, working mainly on instinct, still thrust the midfielder into the centre of his defence.

McNeill went with Peter Latchford in goal and Alan Sneddon and Danny McGrain on the defensive flanks. Roy Aitken lined up with young Conroy while Davie Provan dropped into a wide right berth in midfield with Tommy Burns and Murdo MacLeod taking the other two positions. Johnny Doyle, George McCluskey and Frank McGarvey completed the line-up. Bobby Lennox and Vic Davidson were on the substitutes' bench.

A crowd of 70,303 gave a noisy welcome to both teams as they took the field, the hostilities on the back-burner for the time being. It had hardly been a vintage year for the Ibrox side, John Greig's second campaign in command, but Billy McNeill knew they would still prove to be dangerous opponents. 'Always beware a wounded animal,' was how he put it. The thought of missing out on Europe was a genuine worry for the men from Govan. But, as well as Johnstone, they still possessed a lot of talent in players such as Davie Cooper, Sandy Jardine, Bobby Russell and Gordon Smith.

in the early moments, Latchford dealt with a snap shot from Smith. It took only four minutes for referee George Smith to issue his first caution, Tom 'Jaws' Forsyth going into the book for a reckless challenge. There was plenty of effort and endeavour from both sets of players as the game headed for the half-hour mark. MacLeod joined Forsyth in the book after an over-robust tackle. The darting, eager McGarvey looked Celtic's best bet for a goal as he made his menace known to Forsyth and Colin Jackson, Rangers' experienced central defensive pairing. A back-header from the £270,000 purchase from Liverpool caught Peter McCloy unawares, but the attempt slipped narrowly over the crossbar. Before half-time McGarvey had another strong shot on target well saved by the beanpole Ibrox keeper.

Conroy, quietly and efficiently, was doing a solid job in his new role with Johnstone making little impact on the rookie defender. The duel between football's ancient double-act continued in much the same vein after the turnaround. Astutely, Celtic were closing down the likes of Cooper and Russell before they could even attempt to pick out Johnstone with a high ball. Provan was revelling in his new midfield role, unburdened by the responsibility of having to hit the touchline every time he received a pass. He was meandering inside to great effect and the Rangers rearguard clearly hadn't anticipated the drastic change in his style as plotted by McNeill.

As the game edged towards the ninety minutes, McNeill and Greig both took a gamble. Bobby Lennox, at the age of thirty-six, was sent on for the tiring Johnny Doyle and Tommy McLean, a mere thirty-five years of age, replaced the largely ineffective John McDonald. Only a minute remained of regulation time when Rangers almost nicked it. Referee Smith was already looked at his watch when Cooper produced a quickfire strike that looked a winner. Latchford, though, was equal to the effort and dived magnificently to get a hand to the ball to turn it to safety.

Celtic realised how close they had been to surrendering the game and they stepped up a gear in extra-time. There was a reasonable claim for a penalty-kick when Forsyth pushed McCluskey, but the match official waved play on. Tension settled on Hampden as the game ebbed and flowed. McGarvey and Gregor Stevens were booked as the drama mounted. Both sets of players realised one mistake or one moment of inspiration would be enough to win it.

In the one hundred and eighth minute, the green and white half of Hampden burst into a joyous chorus. The deadlock had been broken and it had originally materialised from the highly unlikely source of Danny McGrain. Forsyth was guilty of a loose header out of defence straight to the Celtic captain about twenty-five yards out. Now Tommy Gemmell might have burst the net from that range, but McGrain's shooting prowess never quite matched up with that of the Lisbon Lion. Nevertheless, the full-back decided to have a dig from range. McCloy, in all probability, had it covered, but as he went one way, the quick-thinking George McCluskey instinctively stuck out a foot to direct the ball in the opposite direction. The 6ft 4in goalkeeper desperately attempted to change his body weight and threw a hand at the ball. He got a touch, but it wasn't enough to prevent the effort rolling into the inviting net.

McGrain laughed afterwards, 'It seemed to take an age to go into the net. I thought Big Peter would have thrown his bunnet to stop it going over the line.' And so a fine, hard-fought Cup Final had been decided. Celtic, to many onlookers, looked the hungrier of the two teams. McGrain won the Man of the Match award, but Provan had put in an extraordinary performance in a novel role and Latchford had looked safe throughout. Conroy? McNeill smiled, 'I knew I had a lot of doubters when I gave the central defensive role to Mike. For me, though, he emerged as the unlikely superstar of the game.'

Invariably, in any Cup run it is the glamorous Final that takes centre stage and the ties in reaching Hampden are often overlooked or forgotten. In the opening round, Celtic overcame First Division Raith Rovers 2-1 in Glasgow with strikes from Bobby Lennox and Johnny Doyle. The scoreline looked tight, but the corner-kick count of 16-2 in favour of the home side is a fair indication of the flow of play throughout the afternoon. Former Rangers reserve goalkeeper Murray McDermott was the Kirkcaldy side's star performer and he said, 'That was the game of my life.'

It was at the next stage that Celtic displayed the awesome character that was also in evidence against Rangers some three months later. Billy McNeill's side were paired with St Mirren, more than competent opponents and going exceptionally well in the league. Indeed, the Paisley side had beaten Celtic 2-1 in the league at Love Street two months beforehand. Remarkably, they continued towards that trend, watched by 32,000 fans at Parkhead where Frank McDougall gave his side an interval advantage. McNeill said, 'It was a display that was out of character for my players. They adopted a casual attitude and couldn't shake themselves out of it before half-time.'

With four minutes to go, Celtic were hurtling out of the trophy. They had pounded the Saints goal, but had received no reward. Suddenly there was a chance as Davie Provan broke clear to set up Murdo MacLeod and the sturdy midfield man steered a drive wide of Billy Thomson. Celtic lived to fight another day. That day, in fact, being the replay in midweek at Love Street. A crowd of 27,000 was shoe-horned into the old, ramshackle ground that had seen better days. Many others couldn't gain attendance as the game was a pay-at-the-gate affair. A certain Jock Stein, the Scotland international manager, even had trouble getting into Love Street that evening.

It had all the making of a blistering, Cup cracker in Paisley and the Saints were celebrating when Jimmy Bone, who flopped spectacularly at Celtic when Stein signed him for £25,000 from Sheffield United in 1974, sent in a looping header that flummoxed Latchford and dropped into the net. In one moment, Bone had equalled his entire tally during his only season at Parkhead. Bone celebrated as though he had scored the Cup winner.

The tie hadn't reached half-time when Celtic were left with ten men. Tom McAdam and Frank McDougall, two warriors on the pitch, tussled and the linesman flagged to attract the attention of referee Ian Foote. After a quick consultation, the match official pointed to the dressing room for McAdam while MacDougall was given a reprieve. It seemed a harsh decision, but, remarkably, the gallant ten pulled it back to all-square before the turnaround. Little will o' the wisp Johnny Doyle was the marksman to help relieve some of the tension in the dressing room at half-time.

'We didn't think the sending-off of Tom McAdam was fair,' said McNeill. 'But there was little point of complaining - it wasn't the time or the place. You've got another forty-five minutes around the corner and you've got to say all the right things to your players. I could see they were determined and, for some reason, I had a feeling they would achieve something in this game.'

McDougall, a striker with a fully-committed aggressive approach, was taken off injured after a challenge from Danny McGrain. The St Mirren attacker was clearly unhappy, made a few comments in the national press about the Celtic captain and provoked an official rap from the SFA. The drama continued when the referee awarded the Paisley side a penalty-kick. Latchford bravely beat out Doug Somner's first attempt, but the Saints striker followed up to rattle the rebound into the rigging.

The Celtic players, though, refused to lie down. They were drawing on astonishing reserves of courage as they took the game straight back to their opponents. Doyle was upended in the Saints box and this time it was McNeill's men who were presented with a spot-kick. Bobby Lennox, happily, made no mistake. An extra thirty energy-draining minutes on a heavy playing surface was the reward for an awesome display from the ten men in green and white.

They refused to be beaten on a powerful night of emotion and was Doyle on the trigger again to settle the argument with the Paisley outfit. It had been a rollicking, rousing encounter and a team filled with the spirit Billy McNeill admired so much. Interestingly, with the exception of the banned double-act of Tom McAdam and Roddie MacDonald, the other nine players on the Love Street pitch that evening picked up a winner's medal at the national stadium in May.

The other two Cup hurdles for Celtic en route to Hampden were shoo-ins in comparison. Goals from Jim Casey and George McCluskey eased them to a 2-0 win over Morton at Parkhead. Next up was the semi-final against Hibs, with George Best in the line-up. Billy McNeill recalled, 'Before that game, we went to Seamill and I had a real head-to-header with the players. I fell out with Tommy Burns, a player I admire on and off the pitch. He felt I was picking on him, which wasn't true. We won 5-0 with Bobby Lennox, Davie Provan, Johnny Doyle, Murdo MacLeod and Tom McAdam scoring the goals. We coasted through that game and Tommy came on as a sub for Bobby. My words had paid off.'

Now all eyes were on Hampden where Rangers were lying in wait. In the First Round, they had required a replay to beat Clyde 2-0 after drawing 2-2 at Shawfield. A Derek Johnstone goal gave them a 1-0 win over Dundee United at the next stage and they followed that up with a 6-1 hammering over Hearts in the quarter-final. Another goal from Johnstone was enough to defeat a strong Aberdeen team in front of 50,000 in the semi-final at Hampden. Johnstone was seen as the key man to Rangers' hopes of success.

However, a young man from Johnstone, in Renfrewshire, had other ideas. Mike Conroy was immense as he won his solitary Scottish Cup medal with Celtic.

CHAPTER FOUR
CORNERED
IN MADRID

Billy McNeill was positively seething as his deepest suspicions were confirmed. The Celtic manager, speaking to close friends and associates, cast doubt over the ability of Hungarian referee Karoly Palotai, the man in charge of the return leg of their European Cup quarter-final tie against Real Madrid at the Bernabeu Stadium on Wednesday, March 19 1980.

McNeill was always far too smart to point an accusing finger at the match official, but it was obvious he had misgivings about UEFA's appointment and he wondered if his team, two goals ahead after a glorious first leg in Glasgow, would get a fair crack of the whip when they played in front of 110,000 fans in Madrid. After ninety tortuous minutes McNeill had his answer. The mighty Spaniards emerged victorious by the required three goals and Celtic's hopes of a semi-final place were obliterated. Karoly Palotai, unwittingly or otherwise, certainly played a key role in the outcome of the tie.

The Celtic boss said, 'I remember talking to Bob Paisley, the Liverpool manager, before going to Madrid and he made the point that we would have difficulty with the Hungarian referee, especially as the game was in Spain. He was right. Palotai was as disappointing as the result.'

It had been goalless nudging towards the welcome break at half-time. In fact, Real Madrid could well have been in the position of being asked to score four goals to advance into the last four. In five minutes, George McCluskey, a scorer a fortnight earlier, was presented with an absolute gift six yards out with only goalkeeper Garcia Ramon to beat. Murdo MacLeod started the move with a run from midfield and a neat pass to Johnny Doyle, also a marksman at Parkhead. He picked out McCluskey, completely unattended with the home defenders AWOL, and a goal looked a certainty. The striker, though, looked as surprised as anyone in the capacity crowd to find himself in oceans of space in the danger zone. He snatched at the shot and his mishit effort meekly trundled wide of Ramon's right hand post. McNeill stated, 'If that had gone in, I'm sure it would have killed the game stone dead.'

The Spaniards realised Dame Fortune had bestowed one of her most gleaming smiles upon them. Frantically, they took the game to Celtic with the elastic-limbed Laurie Cunningham, like Peter Latchford a former West Brom player, seeing plenty of the ball. The winger roamed all over the pitch and made it impossible for someone to pick him up with McNeill refusing to risk man-marking the clever, astute England international. Chances were created, but, fortunately, Latchford was equal to the task. 'I was actually enjoying myself,' he said. 'Goalkeepers get days like that. The atmosphere inspired me.'

Vicente Del Bosque, the future World Cup and European Championship-winning manager of Spain, came the closest to equalising with a blistering drive from outside the box, but the Celtic keeper produced a majestic save. Juanito was next up to have a pop and once again the defiant Latchford gripped the ball confidently. Half-time was in sight when Palotai made a strange and, unfortunately, crucial intrusion on the proceedings. He punished Latchford for taking more than the permitted four steps while carrying the ball, the rule at the time. The goalkeeper was adamant he released the ball at the right time. 'I always counted the steps. One, two, three, four and then kick it or throw it. I counted them as usual in that game, but the referee made a very wrong decision.'

The resultant free-kick was blocked by the Celtic defensive wall and broke to Bobby Lennox who heaved the ball high into the third tier of the Bernabeu stand. 'I was trying to waste time as I knew half-time was almost upon us,' admitted the Lisbon Lion. Billy McNeill, patrolling the touchline, looked again at his watch. He was convinced the forty-five minutes had come and gone. Palotai waited for Cunningham to carefully place the ball on the right before the player eased a cross into the crowded penalty box via the outside of his right foot. It was an exquisite piece of skill and the ball took a devilish curve down on top of Latchford as he tried to come and collect while being barged by two robust Spaniards. It broke from his hands and Santillana managed to prod home while three Celtic defenders guarded the goal-line in vain. The match official blew for the interval as soon as McCluskey kicked off. Latchford was left fuming. 'I've no doubt it was a foul on me when the corner came in. They got away with it.'

Afterwards, McNeill, in the immediate aftermath of the game, said, 'I was wondering if the referee would ever blow for half-time. If we had cleared that ball I honestly doubt if he would have put the whistle to his lips. Certainly, it would have been more than interesting to see what would have happened if they had forced another corner-kick. I got the impression he would simply have kept playing on until they scored a goal. I mean that.'

It was a horrible time to concede a goal. The impetus switched to Real Madrid, who were probably convinced it was going to be their day after McCluskey's awful miss so early in the encounter. Eleven minutes after the turnaround and all Celtic's hard work in Glasgow evaporated when the Spaniards equalised on aggregate. Once again the strolling Cunningham played his part with an excellent cross from the left which was nodded back across the box by Juanito. Tom McAdam was caught ball-watching and was far too late in sensing the danger of the lurking

Uli Stielike. The astute German midfielder hit the ball as it dropped and Latchford was beaten low to his right.

McNeill said, 'At half-time in the dressing room, I could see from the expressions of our players after they had conceded the first goal. So, I had to work on building up their confidence by stressing how well they had done. Now, though, it was all-square and, as you might expect, the place was in uproar. Their fans were going crazy and they still had over half-an-hour to get another goal. We were up against it, no doubt about it, but I tried to get my message across to the players to keep their composure. We had to hold onto the ball to prevent them attempting to run all over us. Thankfully, the team settled and we started to play our passing game again.'

The Celtic players screamed beseechingly for a penalty-kick when they ball struck the hand of defender Benito. Palotai waved play on. McNeill wasn't surprised. 'The Real player clearly handled, but it was ignored. I had warned about this referee before the game and I wasn't best pleased to be proved right.' The Celtic manager was at pains to stress he did not believe the match official's fairness was in doubt. 'I just didn't rate him as a referee and, before the kick-off, I wondered how he would have deal with 110,000 fans trying to influence decisions.'

Central midfielder Jose Pirri, a road block of a footballer, almost gifted Celtic a goal with a wayward passback that had Ramon scrambling to prevent the ball crossing the line. The dream was over, however, when Real Madrid scored the winner six minutes from the end. In truth, the Celtic defence practically presented the winner to Juanito. Tom McAdam and Roddie MacDonald were both enticed towards the near post as Angel, Danny McGrain in his wake, came in from the right. Juanito, not the tallest player you'll ever see, was left unguarded by a careless back-four and he couldn't miss as the ball dropped on his head. He threw himself forward for maximum impact and once again the unprotected Latchford was left clawing fresh air as the ball screeched past him.

McNeill, clearly frustrated, knew it was all over. At the final whistle he applauded his disconsolate players off the pitch before waving to the 3,000-strong travelling support. 'We wanted to do it for ourselves and, of course, those guys up in the stands. I'm so proud to be Celtic manager. We've just been beaten, everyone is disappointed, but they're still chanting non-stop. Those people are what Celtic Football Club is all about.'

George McCluskey put it more succinctly. 'We were cheated over there. We were never going to be allowed to win in Madrid.' No-one in the Celtic camp even attempted to argue. One neutral Scottish journalist wrote, 'Real deserved their win, but they didn't do their sporting image any favours. There were three appalling fouls on Celtic players in the first minutes of the game, undoubtedly meant to be intimidatory and certainly referee Palotai was shockingly weak in taking no action against the offenders.' The author of those words was Hugh Taylor, a doyen of the written word who was the chief sportswriter at Scotland's mass circulation Daily Record, the biggest-selling newspaper in the country at the time. I was a colleague of Hugh and I can tell you he wasn't witnessing the spectacle in Madrid through green-tinted spectacles. Hugh was the most fervent Kilmarnock fan you were ever likely to meet.

Justice was seen to be done, though. Real Madrid were routed 5-3 by Kevin Keegan's SV Hamburg in the semi-final, conceding four goals in a whirlwind first-half of the second leg in Germany. Possibly, they had used up all their good fortune against Celtic.

However, before acrimony in Madrid came the applause in Glasgow. The ballot, of course, generated great excitement throughout the support and, in fact, Celtic drew in excess of £250,000 in gate receipts, a record at the time. Billy McNeill had a youthful squad, with the exception of the evergreen Bobby Lennox and dependable Danny McGrain, and he pondered if they were up to the monumental task of dismissing excellent opponents. In the previous round, they were one minute away from one of the most disastrous and embarrassing results in the club's history against the Irish minnows of Dundalk. Celtic had hardly looked exceptional as they clawed their way to a 3-2 win over the part-timers in the first leg at Parkhead. Roddie MacDonald, George McCluskey and Tommy Burns were on target against battling, game opponents who scored through Cathal Muckian and Mick Lawlor.

It was scoreless in the return leg with a minute to go when a Dundalk player, from practically under the bar, had a fresh air swipe at a crossball. If he had connected the odds were that Peter Latchford would have been beaten and, utterly unthinkable when the draw was made, Celtic would have been out of the tournament. There would have been no way back. The most relieved players on the Oriel Park pitch that night when Danish referee Henning Lund-Sorensen's whistle shrilled to bring a halt to the action were undoubtedly those from Glasgow.

And it hadn't been overly comfortable against the mysterious Albanians of Partizan Trivana. Over 25,000 packed their stadium on Wednesday September 19. It was extremely difficult for the reporters of the national press to obtain visas such was the suspicious natures of the hosts. Celtic director Kevin Kelly came to the rescue of one newspaper by filing a report from a telephone he had obtained from someone. Unfortunately, it didn't make happy reading - Celtic lost 1-0 to a dodgy goal from Agim Murati. Greek match official Nikolaos Zlatanos also enraged the visitors by ruling out a Vic Davidson effort after a neat cutback from Davie Provan. 'A baffling decision,' observed Billy McNeill.

The Celtic boss, predictably, was more than annoyed at the final whistle. 'I gave the players pelters. The goal we lost was diabolical and I told the defence I would have cleared it if I had still been playing. It came from a cross from the wing and both goalkeeper Peter Latchford and right-back Alan Sneddon swore the ball had swung a few feet out of play before coming back in again. Our back lot took their eye off the ball and fully expected to restart the game with a goal-kick. The quick-thinking Albanian obviously knew all about playing to the whistle. The ball dropped at his feet and he poked it over the line. I was fuming at my defence, but I accepted their reasons. These things happened all too often away from home in Europe.'

Two weeks later a crowd in excess of 50,000 was in attendance as Celtic tried to put the tie to bed. Danny McGrain joked, 'I think a lot of the fans turned out just to see what an Albanian looked like.' In fourteen minutes, the spectators would have witnessed that Albanians were, in fact, quite a happy race, even in the monsoon conditions of a raw night in the east end of Glasgow. Alan Sneddon misjudged the flight of a ball into the penalty area and managed to head an effort past his own open-mouthed keeper. McNeill recalled, 'Suddenly, the whole place went quiet. I don't think they had a single fan with them. Their players jumped about in delight to absolute silence. It was just a little bizarre.'

There was no need to hit the panic button. Celtic stormed back in tenacious fashion to score four goals in a blistering twenty-four minute spell. They could even afford the luxury of a squandered penalty-kick. Davie Provan, on a memorable night of twisting, turning and teasing on the touchline, set up the quartet of goals. In the twentieth minute, his perfectly-flighted free-kick was headed back across goal by Tom McAdam and his central defensive partner Roddie MacDonald arrived to nod the ball in from close range. Two minutes later Provan collected a short corner from Johnny Doyle, swung in another peach of a cross and Roy Aitken completed the job.

Celtic went ahead on aggregate on the half-hour mark when Vic Davidson knocked in a Provan corner-kick at the back post. George McCluskey was hauled down moments later and Swedish referee Lars-Ake Bjorck pointed to the spot. McCluskey took it and blazed wildly over the crossbar. A minute from half-time, Provan embarked on a mazy, mesmerising run which ended with another delightful, inviting cross and Aitken applied his Shirley Temple mop of curls to the ball and the bewildered Musta was beaten again. That completed the scoring and now there was the little matter of the draw for the quarter-final. And so Celtic were paired with Real Madrid and three hours of intoxicating football were about to be served up.

The Spaniards may not have been the team stuffed with legends such as Di Stefano, Puskas and Gento in their hey day as they dominated European football, but they were a high quality squad that was good enough to win their domestic league in fine style in the days you had to be champions of your country to enter the European Champions' Cup. Their progress through the first two hurdles had hardly been spectacular, though. They overcame the Bulgarians Levksi Spartak 3-0 overall fairly comfortably, but they received a real scare against Porto at the next stage. They lost 2-1 in Portugal and were nineteen minutes from exiting the tournament when Benito struck to level the tie on aggregate and they progressed by virtue of the away goal.

Celtic gave them the respect they rightly deserved. Laurie Cunningham was undoubtedly their most potent attacking threat. He weaved in and out from the wing, an intimidating presence with his marvellous ball skills. Billy McNeill's formation was built on a solid midfield of Roy Aitken and Murdo MacLeod while wingers Johnny Doyle and Davie Provan were in marauding mode. The Celtic manager emphasised before the players left the dressing room. 'This is a night for heroes. Go out and be heroes.'

The main talking points from a testing opening half came when Cunningham curled a wicked drive onto the outside of the post and Del Bosque appeared to handle in the box. Italian referee Riccardo Lattanzi was clearly unimpressed by the screams for a penalty from a frantic crowd of 67,000. Billy McNeill said, 'I told the lads they were doing well, but I asked them to up the tempo. I wanted them to get up the pitch that little bit quicker. I noticed, too, that Real were paying particular attention to Davie Provan. I'm sure they would have done their homework and realised he set up all our goals against Partizan Tirana. I told Davie to roam around and play wide on the left on occasion. I figured that might open up something for us down our right.'

Seven minutes after the turnaround, McNeill's prophesy proved sound. Alan Sneddon, an adventurous right-back, raced into attack. He jinked to go to the touchline, but turned inside before walloping a low left foot drive from just inside the box towards Garcia Ramon's goal. The keeper, as surprised as the rest of his defenders by Sneddon's quick change of direction, could only parry the ball as it dipped viciously in front of him. George McCluskey was onto it in a flash and drove the rebound into the corner of the net. The din was deafening, a sheer eruption of delight.

McCluskey thought he had doubled Celtic's advantage with a neat head flick past the keeper after a ball over from the right. The referee disallowed it for offside and TV later proved he made the correct call. However, it was extremely tight and on another night with another match official and it could have been a different outcome.

Sixteen minutes from time, Celtic did have the ball in the net again and this time there could be no argument. There was some tenacious play from Provan on the left in the lead-up. The winger actually gave the ball away with a slack pass to Cunningham. However, before the England international could get into his lengthy stride, Provan atoned with a well-timed sliding tackle, gathering the ball before dispatching a superb pass to the galloping Sneddon, once more in acres of space on the opposite flank. The Real defenders might have thought he was about to stage an action replay of the goal by cutting inside. This time, though, the thoughtful defender launched a high ball towards the back post. Ramon stood rooted to his line as two defenders moved to deal with the danger.

Johnny Doyle, never a great respecter of reputations, decided the ball was his as he careered forward. His timing was perfection itself as he soared high above the Real players and he made faultless contact with his forehead. The ball rocketed beyond the desperate keeper, arms thrown wide more in hope than anything else. The man in the Celtic dug-out would have been more than satisfied to have claimed that as one of his own. McNeill said, 'Wee Doylie was fearless. When he went for something he went in all guns blazing. Heading the ball wasn't his forte, but you wouldn't have known it with that attempt.'

The game ground to its conclusion with Ramon make a remarkable high-flying save to his right to push away a venomous left-foot drive from Murdo MacLeod. Celtic had to be content with a two-goal lead to take to the Spanish capital two weeks later. Alas, it wasn't to prove to be sufficient. It was a gallant failure that could well have been rewritten as one of glorious triumph. The fates, coupled with some odd decision-making from the referee, decreed against Celtic.

Billy McNeill made a telling observation at the end of season 1979/80. 'After the defeat from Real Madrid, we never recovered our league form and the season died a death for us, despite winning the Scottish Cup with a dramatic extra-time goal by George McCluskey. Frankly, I hadn't realised the impact losing to Real would have on the side.'

CHAPTER FIVE
TRIALS AND TRIBULATIONS

As ever, Billy McNeill had been refreshingly honest. 'It has been said that I was too hard on my players. If I was, it was the mistake of a young manager. I was still in my late thirties, but, at the time, I felt I had to be tough. Apart from Bobby Lennox and Danny McGrain, we had a very young side.'

The Celtic manager was reflecting on the previous season while preparing the team for the challenges and rigours of the 1980/81 campaign. Despite conceding the league championship to Alex Ferguson's Aberdeen, there had been no meaningful activity in the transfer market during the summer. The Scottish Cup had, of course, been won in extra-time against Rangers and McNeill had been left frustrated that his players had failed to receive the credit they deserved in the violent aftermath of morons masquerading as football fans staging an impromptu re-enactment of the Battle of the Little Bighorn at the national stadium.

Looking back, he said, 'We salvaged something from that season by winning the Scottish Cup, but perhaps we should have anticipated failure in the league. After my first term as boss, the team went on a sunshine holiday to Majorca. Neilly Mochan, our trainer, said to me, "Only one thing worries me, Billy. Maybe you've done too much too quickly. You weren't entitled to win the league." Those words came back to me.'

McNeill would never become famous for his complacency and he fielded a full-strength side against the part-timers of Ayr United in the now-defunct Drybrough Cup in Glasgow on July 27. He was eager to see his side hit the ground running. Instead, they hit the dirt. The Somerset side stunned the 16,000 crowd into silence by striking a goal three minutes from time to claim an unexpected 1-0 victory. Making matters worse, if that was possible, the winner came from a former Rangers player, Eric Morris.

Experienced campaigners such as Peter Latchford, Alan Sneddon, Danny McGrain, Roy Aitken, Murdo MacLeod, Davie Provan and George McCluskey were in the line-up. They had been part of a team good enough to overwhelm Real Madrid 2-0 in an epic European Cup confrontation the previous season, but they were incapable of seeing off a collection of free transfer journeymen. The rest of the formation consisted of Frank McGarvey, the club's record buy at £270,000 from Liverpool, emerging talent in the shape of a cheeky chappy by the name of Charlie Nicholas, Dom Sullivan, bought from Aberdeen for £82,000 the previous year, and Scottish Cup hero Mike Conroy. Youngsters John Weir, a hard-working midfielder, and John Halpin, a speedy outside-left, were introduced by McNeill as second-half substitutes against a team that had been bulldozed out of the top league only two years beforehand after winning a mere nine times in their thirty-six games.

A mortified McNeill apologised profusely to the fans. There was little doubt, though, away from the cameras and the microphones, he was livid with his players. 'It wasn't what I expected from a Celtic team. Not one that I managed or any Celtic team, for that matter. Okay, the players may still have had some rust in their limbs after a summer break, but, remember, it was exactly the same for the Ayr United lads and, as most of them were part-time, they wouldn't have had luxury of the month or so my players had to put their feet up. I knew one of the Ayr United defenders, as a matter of fact. He drove a taxi for a living and I realised he had had only a few days off over that period. You wouldn't have known it if you had witnessed his display against us.'

The league season kicked off on August 9 against Morton, the same first-day opponents as the previous campaign. Mystifyingly, the attendance was give as 20,000 - over 6,000 down on the previous year. And, like the opener in 1979/80, the Hoops had to rely on a single-goal victory. The team toiled from the start, but the generous Greenock guests presented them with the opening goal in the sixty-seventh minute when centre-half Joe McLaughlin and goalkeeper Roy Baines got their signals crossed and George McCluskey nipped in alertly to steer the ball into the net.

Pat Bonner, taking over from Peter Latchford in goal, didn't have too much to occupy him until the seventy-sixth minute when Andy Ritchie, the former Celt known as 'The Idle Idol' because of his aversion to hard graft, levelled with a guided effort into the corner after some nifty footwork inside the box. Only nine minutes remained when Murdo MacLeod lashed in the winner. It was one of those days Celtic were just happy to get the ninety minutes out of the way and collect the win. However, it was hardly a pointer of what was to come over the next thirty-five hurdles.

Frank McGarvey sparked to life a week later as Celtic thrashed Kilmarnock 3-0 at Rugby Park with the goals coming in a sizzling first-half. Dom Sullivan opened the floodgates with a neat effort in the twenty-eighth minute and, within sixty seconds, McGarvey had doubled the lead with a curling drive. In quickfire time, the contest was over when McGarvey ran free through a hesitant defence and left keeper Alan McCulloch helpless. The rubber-legged frontman took a knock on the ribs three minutes and had to be replaced. Charlie Nicholas came off the bench to make his first league appearance in the green and white hoops.

McNeill then readied his players for their first meeting with old enemy Rangers since the Cup Final riot. The Ibrox side had never won a Premier Division contest at Parkhead, but, once more in highly controversial circumstances, they achieved that feat against bewildered opponents who had dominated proceedings straight from the off. At 1-1, the game turned dramatically in the Ibrox side's favour. Eighteen minutes from time, a corner-kick from Davie Provan was cleared only as far as Murdo MacLeod. He wasted no time in bludgeoning in a ferocious effort that zipped low past Peter McCloy.

Referee Eddie Pringle, the same match official who had sent off Johnny Doyle against Rangers two seasons earlier, signaled a goal. The linesman flagged, but Pringle ignored him. Suddenly, he was surrounded by protesting Rangers players. He relented, had a word with his assistant and, remarkably, disallowed the goal. MacLeod hit this effort through a ruck of players, so there was no way he was offside. However, the linesman waved for McGarvey encroaching on play. It's worth pointing out, as the press did the following morning, that the Celtic striker was most certainly not interfering with play. It was a legitimate goal and there was little doubt Rangers, who had been on the ropes, received a large slice of good fortune.

That was the story, too, as early as the eleventh minute when a Tom McAdam header bounced back off an upright with McCloy rooted to the spot. It was something of a surprise that it took the home side until two minutes after the break to finally get the ball behind the Ibrox No.1. Dom Sullivan flighted over a ball from the right, Sandy Jardine miscontrolled it and Tommy Burns was onto it in a flash to sizzle one beyond McCloy. The Celtic fans roared for more. Just after the hour mark, Rangers stunned them into silence with an equaliser. Davie Cooper blasted a trademark free-kick at goal and the ball ricocheted straight to the lurking Jim Bett and he tucked it away with some aplomb. The Rangers fans were delirious and who could blame them? The occasion had been almost all one-way traffic and yet their team were level.

If the Celtic players thought they were hard done by at that stage, it was nothing to the way they felt with a mere eighteen seconds of the game to go. Willie Johnston took a throw-in on the left and chucked the ball to Alex Miller. No-one was unduly worried as the Ibrox defender scored goals as often as sightings of Haley's Comet. He took a touch and then struck a long-range effort from about thirty yards. Bonner looked genuinely startled. He threw a gloved-hand at the attempt, but the ball raged into the roof of the net. And that was that.

'It was an incredible shot from Miller in a game which we should have had well and truly wrapped up long before then,' summed up Billy McNeill. 'However, looking for positives, the players won't let the result upset them. I know they will continue to play methodically with the title our priority.'

Any hopes Celtic had of making an impact on the European front were obliterated by the first week in October. Once again, there were mitigating circumstances as the little-known Romanians of Politechnika Timisoara bundled their way through while winning on the away goal after the tie had finished 2-2 on aggregate. Chairman Desmond White, who normally displayed as much outgoing emotion as an exhibit at Madame Tussaud's, was raging at the end of the second leg. The reasons were not difficult to fathom; Celtic completed the fiery encounter with nine men after Roddie MacDonald and Frank McGarvey had been ordered off. The Romanians' goal nine minutes from time after a fierce challenge on Peter Latchford looked like a foul to everyone with the unfortunate exception of the match officials. The hosts also contravened the rules by having their team anthem blaring from the tannoys dotted around the stadium throughout the second-half.

Once again, no-one had seen it coming. McNeill's men coasted through the preliminary round of the Cup-Winners' Cup with a resounding 7-2 aggregate triumph over the Hungarians of Diosgyor Miskolc. Amazingly, it was goalless in the first-half in Glasgow before the roof fell in on the visitors. Frank McGarvey became the first Celtic player to notch a hat-trick in Europe since Willie Wallace against Irish outfit

Waterford in 1970. George McCluskey collected two and Dom Sullivan added another. Six goals ahead. Job done. Celtic could afford to lose 2-1 in Hungary with Charlie Nicholas scoring his first goal at that level. Maybe it was to be expected that there was little urgency about the Hoops' play as they strolled around in the sunshine in front of 8,000 mainly shirt-sleeved fans.

A six-goal first leg advantage wouldn't have flattered Celtic after their game against Politechnika in Glasgow. Charlie Nicholas was everyone's darling as he knocked in two first-half goals, making a massive impact during his debut season in the first team. His more experienced colleagues might have picked up a hint or two from the precocious Glaswegian, but a procession of opportunities were allowed to pass without any takers. Davie Provan missed an open goal after a fumble by the keeper and Tommy Burns rattled a vicious effort off the crossbar. Celtic were made to pay when the Romanians stole upfield and Pat Bonner was beaten by an angled drive from Adrian Manea ten minutes from the end. It was to prove to be an exceptionally costly lapse.

Celtic might have known what to expect before the game even started. Danny McGrain won the toss, but, incredibly, Greek referee Nikolaos Lagoyannis allowed the Romanians to take the kick-off AND choose ends. The visitors faced a fierce wind blowing into their faces throughout the first forty-five minutes. The outrageous antics of Lagoyannis continued in the seventeenth minute when Roddie MacDonald went for the ball after a fumble from keeper Aurel Moise. It was clearly a legitimate challenge from the big defender, but the referee stunned everyone by immediately pointing to the dressing room. MacDonald had company on his trek off the field with Manea also getting his marching orders for reacting violently to the so-called foul.

Lagoyannis continued to disrupt proceedings after the turnaround with Celtic holding onto their first leg advantage. The Greek booked Latchford for time-wasting - 'I had just picked up the ball and was looking for someone to throw it to,' said the keeper - and then, outrageously, allowed an effort from Politechnika to stand seven minutes from time. The Celtic goalie was clearly clattered by defender Dan Paltinisan as he went for a hopeful lob into the penalty area. The ball broke clear as Roy Aitken appealed for a free-kick. His words fell on deaf ears as the referee waved play on. Paltinisan managed to recover some composure before toe-poking the ball into the net. The woe did not end there, unfortunately. McGarvey, booked earlier, complained about a decision and that was enough to earn another yellow card and off he went.

Desmond White was animated beyond belief and he stressed he would be sending a strongly-worded protest concerning the bizarre performance of the match official. He said, 'The referee destroyed what should have been a keen and competitive match. It was never a dirty game. Also, the music throughout was illegal and inflammatory. The referee should have done something about that, too.'

The UEFA observer at the tie was Helmut Schoening, of West Germany. By way of explanation, he offered, 'Refereeing is a trustworthy job and I cannot discuss too much in public. But the referee obviously interpreted the game entirely differently from what you would expect in your country.'

Lagoyannis wasn't finished at the final whistle. He sent a report to UEFA that resulted in the club being fined £6,000, assistant manager John Clark banned from the touchline for two years and MacDonald and McGarvey suspended for two games and one game respectively for the following season. The suspensions were originally for three matches each, but an appeal saw them reduced. It was a very expensive last word for Celtic.

With Europe disappearing over the horizon, Billy McNeill, at least, could concentrate on the domestic trophies. Aberdeen had benefited the previous season by being knocked out of the UEFA Cup by Eintracht Frankfurt on a 2-1 overall score in the First Round. There is every chance, though, Alex Ferguson might not have seen the worth of the defeat at that precise moment.

Celtic's League Cup campaign had got underway in embarrassing circumstances with a 1-0 defeat from the part-timers of Stirling Albion at Annfield. After Ayr United in the Drybrough Cup, it was the second time McNeill had seen his team turned over by a team of butchers, bakers and candlestick-makers from a lower division. Lloyd Irvine booked his place in Stirling folklore by getting the game's only goal in the sixty-fifth minute after the central defence had failed to cut out a routine crossball.

McNeill had words with his players before they were allowed to go and shower. 'It was awful. We just couldn't get into our rhythm against opponents who were clearly up for this game. There is something about this ground. I never enjoyed playing at Annfield and good Celtic teams in the sixties used to get some strange results here. That's no excuse, we should have done an awful lot better.'

Unbelievably, Celtic were only four minutes from picking up their P45 in the League Cup in the second leg at Parkhead. Stirling Albion went two ahead on aggregate in the twelfth minute and Celtic were about to be confronted by their own 'Berwick Rangers'. Matt McPhee rocked the fans when he sent a twice-taken free-kick hurtling through the defensive wall and past the astonished Pat Bonner. It was Stirling's only shot on target all day. Desperately, Celtic needed an injection of pace, perception and power. Unfortunately, Jimmy Johnstone had left the club five years earlier.

Dom Sullivan got Celtic back into the contest with a crisp effort in the twenty-second minute and McNeill realised they had well over an hour to apply the killer touch. The pressure on Gordon Arthur, in the Stirling goal, was awesome as Celtic pummelled away at a defiant rearguard. It was getting frantic as the clock ticked down all too swiftly. Then there was a moment of inspiration from Sullivan as he picked up the ball outside a packed penalty box, weaved to his left, saw Tommy Burns coming in at pace, rolled a pass in front of him and his team-mate scorched a powerful drive away from Arthur. Burns was so relieved he raced straight to The Jungle and practically threw himself into the celebrating throng.

Whatever McNeill said at full-time, the players certainly took it on board as they went into the extra half-hour. He replaced George McCluskey, who had toiled from the start, with prodigy Charlie Nicholas. Mike Conroy came on for Frank McGarvey, who, like McCluskey, just didn't spark on this occasion and Tom McAdam left his central defensive berth to move into attack. It worked. Stirling, heroes all, were tiring and Celtic picked them off. Nicholas helped himself to two goals, Davie Provan knocked in one from close range and Burns added another. CELTIC 6 STIRLING ALBION 1 was the final scoreline on the day. However, for anyone who witnessed this match, it didn't come even close to telling the complete story.

Celtic won through the next two rounds of the tournament - Hamilton (7-2 aggregate) and Partick Thistle (3-1) - before being derailed by hoodoo team Dundee United, the trophy holders, in the semi-final. At that stage in November, after two back-to-back defeats from Rangers and Aberdeen, Billy McNeill had some big decisions to make. He felt seventeen-goal Charlie Nicholas was feeling the strain of playing too many games and was aware of the burn-out factor in a young player. Frank McGarvey had lost his sharpness and he, too, was dropped with Johnny Doyle and George McCluskey forming a new-look attack pairing. Mark Reid came in for his debut at left-back as Alan Sneddon made way and there was another surprise when John Weir was chosen ahead of Dom Sullivan in midfield. The Celtic manager decided it was time for drastic action in the midst of unsettling times.

It all looked like back-firing big-style in the first leg at Tannadice when United took the lead in the twenty-third minute after some faulty handling from Pat Bonner. A cross from Paul Sturrock was given the bar of soap treatment and the ball fell to Willie Pettigrew. He picked out the unguarded Eamonn Bannon and his first-time drive raged into the net. In sixty-eight minutes, McNeill made a double change with McGarvey and Nicholas replacing Doyle and McCluskey. Eight minutes remained when Nicholas rammed in the equaliser from close range after defender Iain Phillip had miskicked a Danny McGrain cross. Celtic could now look forward to the return leg in front of their own fans a week later.

There were no excuses from Billy McNeill for his team's utterly appalling performance at Parkhead. They were a goal down inside four minutes when Willie Pettigrew, totally unhindered, knocked a pass from Bannon beyond Bonner. United were playing their usual system, hiding and hitting on the break. Celtic struggled to come to terms with a tactic they faced every time the Tayside outfit were the opposition. The rain cascaded down from the heavens on a miserable evening in the east end of Glasgow. Nine minutes after the turnaround Jim McLean's men struck again and the tie was over. Another low cross from Bannon wasn't dealt with by a dithering defence and Sturrock gleefully powered a shot behind Bonner. Graeme Payne then struck the crossbar with a header and ten minutes from time Davie Dodds showed his diminutive team-mate how it was done by diverting in a cross from Sturrock. Sad to admit, but the 4-1 aggregate scoreline did not flatter Dundee United, who retained their trophy by beating city rivals Dundee 3-0 in the Final.

November, in fact, had seen Celtic put in some staggeringly awful performances. The parade of misery kicked off on the first of the month at Ibrox. Rangers had just been humiliated 3-0 by Third Division Chesterfield in the now-defunct Anglo-Scottish Cup in midweek and it was the general belief that they were there for the taking. Dom Sullivan had the opportunity to put them under the cosh inside thirty seconds when he got clear for a one-on-one with the stranded Peter McCloy. The Celt lacked composure and blasted the ball against the keeper's legs and the defence tidied up the rebound. It proved to be Celtic's best chance of a painful afternoon.

Colin McAdam, playing against his brother Tom for the first time, slammed in the opener midway through the first-half and John MacDonald added a second before the interval. It was all over by the time McAdam battered a header into the net from a Willie Johnston left-wing cross. A week later champions Aberdeen were in town. They had won a record three times at Parkhead the previous season - twice in the league and once in the League Cup - but could they manage to achieve a fourth on the bounce?

Like Rangers, the Dons were coming off the back of a midweek hiding after being thumped 4-0 by Liverpool in the European Cup at Anfield. Once again, though, Celtic failed to cash in on the frailties of their opponents. Alex Ferguson's smile was as wide as the Clyde as beanpole frontman Walker McCall, recently signed from American side Atlanta Chiefs, scored twice inside an hour and McNeill's men were sliding towards another defeat without managing to register a goal. The Celtic fans in the 29,000 crowd were far from impressed. The season was reaching a critical stage.

McNeill remained philosophical. 'I knew I had strong personalities in the dressing room. I also realised they were hurting and, like me, were absolutely desperate to turn things around. I looked at the likes of Danny McGrain, Roy Aitken, Murdo MacLeod, Tommy Burns, Davie Provan and Johnny Doyle. I could see that Charlie Nicholas was going to become something special and I had to be careful in the games in which he played. There was always something or someone to lift the spirits. For instance, no player gave me more enjoyment than Frank McGarvey. He was one of those delightful characters who brought fun to the dressing room. I'm not convinced that Frank knew what he was doing himself all the time, but he was a guy I liked to have around. He was always active and was a hard worker on the field. Basically, it was just a question of rallying the troops and picking ourselves up for what lay ahead.'

What lay ahead immediately was a game against Airdrie at windswept Broomfield a week after the home defeat from Aberdeen. The main focus for attention for the Celtic contingent in the 16,000 crowd packed into the tight, ancient ground was the home side's new goalkeeper John Martin, a part-time miner who, in his infinite wisdom, admitted on the eve of the game he was a big Rangers fan. His timing might have been better. As the Celtic fans taunted him, their team made life difficult by sticking four behind him in a workmanlike 4-1 win. Celtic were three goals ahead by the twenty-fifth minute with Aitken, McGarvey and Nicholas on the scoresheet. McAdam headed in the fourth near the end before Willie McGuire got his side's consolation bang on time.

Agonisingly, Celtic lost their fourth game out of six when St Mirren staged a last-gasp raid for a 2-1 win in Glasgow. It was one of those tough, no-nonsense, bruising tussles where you had to feel sorry for the ball that was black and blue long before full-time. All the goals came in a mind-boggling final, frantic six-minute burst. Lex Richardson gave the visitors the lead with a low drive after the defence failed to clear a lob from Peter Weir, the Saints' rangy left-winger. George McCluskey replied almost immediately with a penalty-kick after Tommy Burns had been hauled down. The Celtic fans thought they might have to settle for a point when full-back Alex Beckett connected with Tom McAdam's misdirected clearance from about twenty-five yards to thunder an unstoppable effort into the roof of the net. This was far from championship-winning stuff from Celtic.

Next up was a visit to Tannadice before the month was out and the travelling support must have wondered what to expect against Dundee United. Extraordinarily, Celtic produced from nowhere one of their most outstanding performances of the campaign as they turned the tables on the rivals who had hammered them in Glasgow earlier in the month. It was a scoreless stalemate at half-time, but McNeill's half-time pep talk worked wonders as the players came out for the second period displaying vigorous intent.

Tom McAdam headed past Hamish McAlpine just before the hour mark and John Weir made it 2-0 with a good run and finish in the seventy-eighth minute. It was to prove to be his only goal for the club. Just before full-time, United captain Paul Hegarty, normally so reliable, lost his bearings and turned, fully thirty yards out, to rifle a passback low past a startled McAlpine. 'Spot the looney,' chanted the Celtic fans, rather unkindly. It ended 3-0 and once more the focus was on the possibility of getting back into the title race.

Celtic scorched into December with three quickfire victories over Partick Thistle (1-0), Hearts (3-2) and Airdrie (2-1). However, Billy McNeill was well aware that the litmus test was just around the corner; Aberdeen at Pittodrie before the world said farewell to 1980. The Celtic boss recalled, 'I stressed the importance of this game, that, in fact, it could hold the key to our entire season. We were out of Europe, Dundee United had beaten us in the League Cup and you were never sure what the draw would hand you in the Scottish Cup. Right from day one of the campaign, winning back the championship was our priority.'

Pittodrie was barely playable, the pitch covered in silvery frost as the biting wind whipped around from the unforgiving North Sea. Unusually, McNeill opted for a defensive formation with a midfield three of Roy Aitken, Mike Conroy and John Weir. Ball players Charlie Nicholas and Davie Provan were left to shiver on the bench. The Dons got to grips with the treacherous conditions a lot quicker than their opponents and Gordon Strachan, in particular, was pirouetting around with delicate ease.

In only nine minutes, Strachan struck a fine corner-kick, the lanky Walker McCall jumped to flick the ball down to Alex McLeish and the future Rangers and Scotland manager couldn't miss from close range. His defensive partner Willie Miller claimed a second just before the interval . Strachan was again the architect with a sweeping ball to Ian Scanlon on the left. He drilled in a shot that Bonner couldn't hold and Miller played a captain's part to snap up the rebound and fire into the net. A minute after the turnaround the Celtic keeper mishandled a high ball from the right, it fell to Scanlon who whipped it low across goal and McCall stabbed it in from close range. Strachan then rattled in a penalty-kick before sub Nicholas got his side's consolation in the seventy-second minute. The defeat left Celtic trailing the Dons, who also had a game in hand, by three points at the halfway stage.

It was not a pleasant journey back to Glasgow for the vanquished troops. Billy McNeill made sure of that.

CHAPTER SIX
HE CAME TO PRAISE CAESAR

Billy McNeill was in no mood to take prisoners. 'I was forced to question the desire of my players. Did they believe the display against Aberdeen was acceptable from a Celtic team? Were they content to be second best?

'Ironically, I had been in this precise position only two seasons earlier. It was the same opponents, the same stadium and, sadly, the same scoreline. Aberdeen gave us a wake-up call in October 1978 in my first season back. I was very angry back then and I matched that emotion on this occasion. It had been an unacceptable performance from my players and I had to drive home that it would not be tolerated. Basically, as I had done a couple of years earlier, I had to ask the guys if they thought they were good enough to represent Celtic. I had to spark a reaction from them before it was too late.'

McNeill's stinging words hit home with remarkable impact. His players then embarked on a nine-game winning sequence that saw them victorious through January and February with the run only coming to a halt on the last Saturday in March with a draw against Aberdeen. It was a fabulous response from the Celtic players. The manager's tongue-lashing on the coach back to Glasgow from Pittodrie had the desired effect. 'I guess I got the response I was looking for,' said McNeill.

Celtic, though, were on the back foot two minutes into their New Year's Day game at Rugby Park when Jim Hughes put Kilmarnock ahead. Thankfully, Frank McGarvey retaliated in the fourth minute with the equaliser and the striker staged an action replay just before the interval to get what turned out to be the winning goal. The usual pleasantries were exchanged between both sets of support with the Celtic fans singing, 'You're going down again' and the witty riposte from the Ayrshire faithful isn't really worth cataloguing. The Hoops followers, by the way, were bang on the money and Kilmarnock were relegated for the second time in four seasons.

Two days later, McNeill sent out an unchanged formation for an encounter against Morton at a wild, wet and windy afternoon in Glasgow. The elements did not deter McGarvey, who maintained the scoring form that had taken two points from Killie. The livewire frontman struck in the twelfth minute after keeper Roy Baines, who spent three years at Parkhead in the seventies, had pushed a Charlie Nicholas flick into the air. McGarvey, with his sharp penalty box predatory instincts, was first on the scene to head the ball into the net. Three minutes afterwards, Davie Provan added to the scoreline with a low shot after a Tommy Burns effort had been blocked. It was all over just before the interval when McGarvey finished off a sweeping movement concerning Burns, Provan and Nicholas. The 3-0 success pushed Celtic to within a point of Aberdeen.

Dundee United provided sterner opposition a week later when they arrived at Parkhead, but, on this occasion, McNeill dynamited their safety-first tactics. 'I told the players if we were serious about doing something in the league then these were the games we had to win. We had to take points off teams who would be there or thereabouts at the end of the season.'

A crowd of over 27,000 turned out on a cold, frosty afternoon and underfoot conditions were far from conducive to good football, but Davie Provan and Dom Sullivan turned on virtuoso performances on the dodgy surface. Sullivan paved the way for the breakthrough goal in the twenty-seventh minute with a diagonal pass to Tommy Burns. The predominantly left-footed midfielder foxed the United rearguard by feinting to go wide before turning the ball onto his right foot and delivering a wicked cross and Frank McGarvey bulleted the ball into the net with a ferocious header. Three minutes from half-time, Jim McLean's tactics were in shreds when goalkeeper Hamish McAlpine, who would play for Celtic as an emergency keeper on a tour of Switzerland in 1988, was wasteful with a clearance. Burns knocked it forward and Nicholas latched onto it before lobbing an effort over the stranded goalie. Ralph Milne made the scoreline a little more respectable with a consolation goal eight minutes from the end, but there was no way Celtic were in the mood to surrender the points.

McNeill and Co were determined to bring the month to a close with a one hundred per cent record and that was put on the line with a trip to the capital to take on Hearts at Tynecastle. The Edinburgh side were a mere shadow of the team that often provided stern opposition when Celtic were in town in the past. This was a different Hearts side, though. Celtic dismantled them with ease; McGarvey (31 minutes), Burns (50) and Sullivan (69) sharing the goals. One shrewd observation from the Press Box pinpointed the difference in class between the team thus, 'Hearts' biggest mistake was bringing a ball along for Celtic to play with.'

The Celtic manager observed, 'The team were operating as a unit and we had discovered a good balance. For instance, Roy Aitken was pulled back from midfield to play alongside Tom McAdam in the centre of the defence. That may have surprised some who thought we would lose Aitken's drive in the middle of the park. What they didn't realise was the aggression Roy would bring to the team by leading from the back. Dom Sullivan and Tommy Burns were adding a lot of poise and polish in the engine room and Davie Provan, Frank McGarvey and Charlie Nicholas were three of the most enterprising front players in the game at the time. Everything appeared to be dovetailing very well.'

Flurries of snowflakes welcomed the visit of Rangers on February 21; a brutal winter shuddering to a halt. Celtic went into the confrontation in the full realisation they had the wherewithal to kill off the Ibrox side's faint title hopes. A crowd of 52,800 braved the plummeting temperatures to watch the action. McNeill's men were huge favourites, but, as everyone knows, the form book flies out of the window when these two heavyweights enter the sporting arena. And so it proved once again when Rangers took the lead in the eleventh minute. The elegant Davie Cooper slung over a delightful free-kick and Derek Johnstone, as he had done so often in the past, was the first to react as he sent a header gliding past Pat Bonner.

The scoreline remained the same at half-time. McNeill went to work in the dressing room. 'I told them to continue playing in the same manner. The goal was a bit of a blow, but it was the only time they had threatened us. All the chances that were being put together from open play were coming from us. I couldn't see us going another forty-five minutes and not getting some sort of reward. I told the lads to be patient and be on their alert throughout.'

Three goals in thirty minutes turned the game on its head. In the fifty-seventh minute, Dom Sullivan had a shot blocked by a frantic defence and Nicholas, swiftly becoming a clinical finisher, was perfectly placed to tap the equaliser over the line. A green-and-white tidal wave continually flooded forward, but Celtic had to wait until the seventy-third minute before they scored again. Provan and McGarvey combined with some intricate inter-changing before the ball was swept in front of Nicholas. He took a touch, steadied himself and McCloy's worst fears were confirmed as the unerring drive zipped low towards its destination. Three minutes from time, Aitken, bursting forward as McNeill had predicted, stormed clean through and hammered a shot off the keeper. The relief didn't last more than a handful of seconds as the rebound went back to the charging Celt and he volleyed a vicious effort straight and true into the net.

It had been another eventful, momentous Old Firm occasion. Celtic were now four points ahead of Aberdeen and eight in front of Rangers, the Ibrox side's slight championship dreams well and truly buried after a well-deserved defeat. Billy McNeill positively purred afterwards as he gazed into his crystal ball. He predicted, 'The world is going to hear a lot more about Charlie Nicholas. I was pleased for him this afternoon because it's a big thing to score your first goal in an Old Firm match. He's done it now and that should remove any block.'

A week later, 14,000 fans were crammed into Cappielow, the decrepit old ground of Morton, to cheer on Celtic in their quest for the championship. The transformation since Billy McNeill's heartfelt speech after the Aberdeen game had been nothing short of astounding. Morton's tight, little pitch could often strangle the ambition out of visiting teams, but Celtic were in the ascendancy and playing with a terrifying conviction and unquenchable spirit. Just after the half-hour mark, they swept into the lead. A superb passing movement between the slick McGrain and Provan after a quick corner-kick presented a chance for Aitken. He nudged it on and McGarvey, beginning to show the form that persuaded McNeill to shell out a Scottish record transfer fee, whacked it home with obvious delight.

A minute before half-time, McGarvey sprung Morton's offside trap and staged a lung-bursting run from the halfway line before leaving keeper Roy Baines helpless with a blistering finale. Fifteen minutes from time, with the light beginning to fade in Greenock and the antiquated floodlights struggling to illuminate proceedings, Provan put his marker on the afternoon as he accepted a McGarvey pass and weaved his way towards goal before scoring nonchalantly. One of the biggest cheers of the day was reserved for a few minutes after the final whistle when the score came through from Pittodrie; Aberdeen had just lost 2-1 to St Mirren. Ironically, the winning goal was scored by Frank McDougall who would become a Dons player in the future.

The last time St Mirren had played at Parkhead they had returned to Paisley with both points courtesy of a last-minute whizzbang effort from full-back Alex Beckett. Before their return visit on March 14, they had made noises about the possibility of a similar outcome. It smacked of bravado and McNeill refused to be sucked into mind games. 'It was another game we had to win, as simple as that. We were playing well, had the fans behind us, home advantage and I had no fears we wouldn't perform against St Mirren.'

The encounter was played out in monsoon conditions, the players performing in an incessant downpour. A Frank McGarvey-inspired Celtic were three goals ahead by the interval and, yes, the Celtic support was indeed singing in the rain. Roy Aitken got the ball rolling with a neat head flick in the twelfth minute and McGarvey robbed Beckett of the ball before lashing No. 2 beyond Billy Thomson. Right on the half-time whistle, McGarvey scored what must rate as one of the best strikes of his goal-laden career. Without the trace of hesitation, and from twenty-five yards out on a heavy, punishing pitch, he swivelled and fired a devastating drive into the top corner of Thomson's net. It was a flash of genius.

The Saints' troubles didn't halt after a one-way procession in the first-half. Charlie Nicholas pounced to score two minutes after the break. Unfortunately, an overly-robust challenge from Mark Fulton left the teenage hitman writhing in pain and he had to be carried off with George McCluskey taking his place. Thankfully, the injury to Charlie wasn't as serious as first feared. Danny McGrain and Tommy Burns combined just before the hour to release McCluskey and he teed up McGarvey for his hat-trick. McCluskey decided to get in on the goal spree and added two more in the last three minutes. The first came from a neat pass from McGrain and then Burns did the spadework in the fading moments for the second. The Celtic fans were fairly ecstatic with what they had just witnessed, but just to put an extra spring in their step, the tannoy announcer told them Rangers had just lost 2-1 to doomed Hearts at Tynecastle.

A drenched McGarvey took a bow in front of the Jungle. He had scored a marvellous hat-trick - the second goal a certainty for the Hall of Fame - and had also hit the woodwork twice. He had now moved onto the twenty-five goal mark alongside Nicholas. Billy McNeill could afford to smile. Once again, he praised his big-money signing. 'In Glasgow parlance, Frank can best be described as a gallus individual, an infectious character with a droll sense of humour and a lively personality. His football is played off-the-cuff and he scores goals for fun. Football is a game to be enjoyed as far as he is concerned and his enthusiasm shines through. No cause is ever lost as far as Frank is concerned. He is prepared to run and chase all day long and he is also quick and sharp with complete faith in his ability. In short, Frank is a breath of fresh air to all of us because he is great for morale.'

Reflecting on the exhilarating display in awful conditions against St Mirren, McNeill said, 'We are playing like an early-season team. All the hard work the lads have been putting in recently is paying off. There's a great freshness about the side and I'm absolutely delighted at the way things are going. We'll continue to apply ourselves and we'll see what we can achieve between now and the end of the season.'

Four days after dismantling the men from Paisley, Celtic became Ton-Up Bhoys in a 4-1 thrashing of Partick Thistle at Parkhead. Dom Sullivan opened the scoring in the thirty-fifth minute with an unsaveable, pulverising effort from twenty-five yards to notch up the club's 100th competitive goal of the campaign. Firhill defender Brian Whittaker, later to have a brief spell at Celtic, was expelled from the field for stamping on Nicholas. Well, that was one way of trying to curb the menace of the youngster. A huge cheer greeted the re-appearance of Murdo MacLeod as a sixty-fifth substitute for Mike Conroy. The popular midfielder had been missing in action since injury sidelined him back in October. He marked his return with the second goal three minutes after trotting onto the pitch with a vicious dipping drive that left Alan Rough helpless. Four minutes from the end, MacLeod powered through and knocked in No.3 - this time with a cheeky effort through the legs of his international team-mate. McGarvey had been far too quiet, so he decided to take centre stage in the last minute when he took off on a mazy solo run before planting the ball past Rough. Donald Park was the Jags' consolation marksman. It was another crucial win for Celtic, lifting them six points clear of Aberdeen.

Broomfield used to be known as 'Battlefield' with bruising Airdrie teams over the years giving the impression they were quite happy to indulge in intimidatory tactics against luckless, trembling visitors. Their tight, little pitch was tailor-made for twenty-yard slide tackles and they had the defenders who indulged themselves throughout ninety rigorous minutes. Many of the supporters blended in with the thought process that their dilapidated, rundown ground should remain a fortress. Those 'fans' would spend ninety enjoyable minutes snarling at anything that moved, including their manager, their players, the opposition and the unfortunate newspaper scribes who were pitch-forked into their midst.

Celtic took on the heavy brigade a week after their eleven-goals-in-two games spree against St Mirren and Partick Thistle. Quite possibly, Frank McGarvey wasn't a devotee of Shakespeare growing up in Glasgow and might not have been aware of 'bewaring the Ides of March'. But the Celtic striker should certainly have been aware of the menace of Airdrie defender Jim March. Ironically, March got his marching orders in the month of March for an off-the-ball incident with McGarvey.

The uncompromising back-four operator had earlier gifted Celtic a penalty-kick after handling a corner-kick from Provan just after the half-hour mark. The confident Nicholas stepped up to take the award and was stunned when the keeper plunged to push the ball away. Unluckily for the Airdrie man, McGarvey, demonstrating his keen instinct once again, was first on the scene to hammer the rebound into the net. A sweet move involving Aitken, Provan and Nicholas set up MacLeod for what was to be the winner in the forty-sixth minute. David Thompson got Airdrie's solitary counter with a low shot in the seventy-third minute. Aberdeen were fixture-free that weekend as Celtic moved onto forty-six points after twenty-nine games, the Dons second on thirty-eight points with a game in hand. Rangers were now out of sight, ten points adrift.

Once again all eyes were on the east end of Glasgow when Aberdeen visited on March 28 and, as expected, it was a no-quarters-asked-or-given affair. Two determined sets of footballers faced each other and went about their business with a certain verve and gusto. Over 35,000 were at Parkhead to witness the duel of the giants. Celtic started brightly, but, agonisingly, found themselves a goal adrift in only eleven minutes. Andy Harrow, a striker just signed from Luton Town for £65,000, broke clear and plonked the ball in the Celtic net. It was as simple as that. One surge against the run of play, one goal. Alex Ferguson's tactics of never harassing the Celtic defenders had paid off yet again with possession being surrendered in midfield.

Davie Provan had the crossbar shuddering in the twentieth minute with a mighty whack and then Dom Sullivan passed up the opportunity of scoring against his former side as he sliced an effort round the post from close range. Undeterred, Celtic piled forward and in the seventy-fifth minute it looked as though they would get their reward. Dons skipper Willie Miller hauled down George McCluskey, just on for Charlie Nicholas, and referee Kenny Hope had no option but to award a penalty-kick. Celtic Park was hushed as Murdo MacLeod placed the ball on the spot. The midfielder with the explosive shot elected to place the ball, hit it without any conviction and goalkeeper Jim Leighton flopped on the attempt.

Celtic, though, refused to accept being second best to a team who were picking up the worrying habit of winning at Parkhead. With five minutes remaining, Provan unlocked the Dons back four with a teasing ball over the top and McCluskey's timing was perfect as he volleyed a drive past the despairing Leighton. Incredibly, Celtic had the ball in the net again a couple of minutes later when McCluskey thought he had scored the winner. The match official ruled it out for offside and Celtic's rage wasn't helped when TV pictures provided irrefutable evidence McCluskey was onside. It was a legitimate goal. The Dons escaped, but Celtic were still in control.

It had been a rough and tumble encounter and one newspaper put it thus, 'The Gunfight at the OK Corral was a bun-fight compared to this little shindig.'

April kicked off with a midweek visit from Hearts, a team which didn't have its sorrows to seek during a troubled campaign. Ruthless Celtic didn't offer a shoulder to cry on in another one-sided landslide. Billy McNeill's men finished the game as a contest with a pitiless display of unsparing emotion as they thumped in three goals in a whirlwind six-minute spell. George McCluskey got the ball rolling via the penalty spot in the twenty-third minute and, within sixty seconds, unfortunate keeper John Brough was in the back of his net again, the ball put there courtesy of Davie Provan. Frank McGarvey, almost inevitably, added a third before the half-hour stage.

Three minutes after the interval, McCluskey claimed the fourth before Murdo MacLeod came on the scene with two expert finishes in the sixty-second and seventy-fifth minutes. Unforgiving Celtic fans, remembering countless Old Firm occasions, mercilessly barracked ex-Ranger Alex MacDonald throughout the game. However, even at thirty-three years of age, the little midfield scrapper was still the Edinburgh side's best performer, which tells you all need to know about the calibre of those representing the Tynecastle outfit at the time. How the Jungle rejoiced in taunting this poor Hearts team with the topical chant of April Fools! It would be thirty-two years before Celtic bettered that winning margin when they ran amok in the capital, winning 7-0 in a Scottish Cup-tie in December 2013.

Partick Thistle were next to come into Celtic's line of sight with a Sunday offering at Firhill. Billy McNeill, despite the consistency and quality of his team, was far from happy. One newspaper had leaked a story about Everton showing an interest in Charlie Nicholas and the Celtic manager was fuming. The Goodison boss at the time was Gordon Lee and he was under massive pressure to deliver as the English season also came to a close.

McNeill said, 'It was inevitable that these stories would start to emerge, but it was far too early to start talking about Charlie and big-money moves to England or elsewhere. These things can turn a young player's head. It's a disruption, too, as far as the team is concerned and I didn't like the timing of the story. I know newspapermen have a job to do and I accept that. However, if they had been in my shoes, with Celtic closing in on a championship, they would have realised how unsettling these stories can be. I didn't know if there was even anything in Everton's so-called interest. Certainly, no bid was made, as far as I was aware. It was nuisance value and I'm glad to say it didn't affect the player.'

Bertie Auld, who would take over as Hibs manager in the summer of 1981, once again set up his Thistle team with defence as his main strategy. There was a blanket of red-and-yellow shirts in front of young keeper Dougie McNab, who was in for the injured Alan Rough. McNab was enjoying his fifteen minutes of fame - or seventy-eight as they case was - when Celtic were awarded a stonewall penalty-kick. Former Hoops protégé Frank Welsh upended McCluskey and McNeill's men were presented with ideal opportunity of unlocking a stubborn, rigid Thistle barrier. McCluskey's effort was far too direct and McNab saved with ease. Only two minutes were left to play when Murdo MacLeod, deputising for the suspended Danny McGrain at right-back, went on a foray into attack which ended with an inviting cross into the box and Tom McAdam ruined McNab's big day by firing in a header. It was Celtic's fourteenth win from fifteen games and Bertie Auld, no doubt disappointed with the end result, was among the first to congratulate his old mate Billy McNeill with a firm handshake and a pat on the back.

Auld recalled, 'I had told my players to expect Celtic to fight right until the end. If anyone knew about the spirit of the club it was me. In my playing days, we always fancied our chances of getting something even when it looked highly improbable. Also, we reckoned a goal in the last minute was better than one in the first. You get one right at the start and your opponents have eighty-nine minutes to get back at you. Get one with the last kick of the ball and there's nothing they can do. I was disappointed for my team, but, of course, I wasn't surprised by Celtic's attitude. I could see that Big Billy had installed some of the good old virtues into his team.'

Celtic required only two points from their remaining four games and the crown was theirs. The league fixture list had thrown up Rangers at Ibrox as their next opponents. However, a few days before that confrontation, Celtic had to face Dundee United in a Scottish Cup semi-final replay. McNeill put his usual spin on the situation. 'I had told the players that the title had to be our main target. That was our priority. But I liked the idea of a League and Cup double; name me a manager who wouldn't? I told my team to alter their focus for ninety minutes. Ibrox would still be there for us on the Saturday. Dundee United at Hampden on the Wednesday was the one that mattered at the moment.'

The Cup holders had coasted to within ninety minutes of another Final appearance at the national stadium. Pat Bonner had yet to concede a goal in the competition and, in truth, was rarely tested in the first three ties against Berwick Rangers, Stirling Albion and East Stirling. Ah, the romance of the Cup, I hear you say. There was fierce media attention on Celtic's first-ever visit to Shielfield Park on January 31 when the ballot paired the Glasgow giants with little Berwick. Of course, there was the inevitable comparison at the same crumbling, ramshackle ground in 1967 when Rangers, faced the Second Division part-timers. By coincidence, the Ibrox side were also Cup holders when they arrived for the tie that would live forever in Rangers history for all the wrong reasons. Berwick won 1-0 with a goal from Sammy Reid while Jim Forrest and George McLean were made scapegoats and never kicked a ball for Rangers again. And a giant of man with hands resembling bunches of bananas called Jock Wallace was in the opposition's goal that day.

Celtic had been forewarned, but history wasn't given the merest opportunity to repeat itself. Coincidentally, Berwick were also managed that day by an ex-goalkeeper, Frank Connor, who had spent two years at Parkhead at the start of the sixties and would return in the eighties as assistant boss to Davie Hay. But that's another story for another chapter. Charlie Nicholas - now known in the Press as 'The Cannonball Kid' - banged in the opening goal in the nineteenth minute after sterling work down the right by Danny McGrain while Tommy Burns' header for

Billy McNeill shares a joke with author Alex Gordon – we thought about adding the caption "And then they said they were the same club!" but that would be naughty!

Celtic in the early 1980s and what a squad we had! From left to right – Frank McGarvey, Tommy Burns, Dom Sullivan, Mike Conroy, George McCluskey, Graeme Sinclair, Tom McAdam, Davie Moyes, Pat Bonner…

...Peter Latchford, Roy Aitken, Charlie Nicholas, Paul McStay, Davie Provan, Murdo MacLeod, Danny McGrain, Mark Reid and Danny Crainie.

DANNY McGRAIN - Celtic's captain and world-class full back. Respected sports journalist Hugh McIlvanney said this about this Celtic legend:

"Anybody who saw him at his best had the unmistakeable impression of watching a great player, probably one who had no superior anywhere in the world."

TOMMY BURNS – a very special Celtic player and a very special Celtic man. Celtic Wiki said that Tommy was "one of Celtic's favourite and most beloved sons! Through his career he was at different times a player, a manager and a coach at the club, and there was nobody to say a bad word about him on a personal level.

He truly was Mr Celtic personified."

ROY AITKEN – Feed the Bear would be the regular chant from the Jungle as Big Roy broke out of defence to menace the opposition. Stunning performances were aplenty from the Bear and in particular who could forget Roy Aitken driving Celtic to the championship in that amazing match in May 1979? Club captain after Danny McGrain retired, Roy Aitken is truly a Celtic great, playing with distinction in 667 matches for the club over 15 years and scoring 55 goals.

PAUL McSTAY – Paul was the finest Celtic player since Kenny Dalglish but unlike King Kenny, Paul stayed with the club as captain with hard times looming. The Celtic fans adored the player they called The Maestro and from the moment he scored his first goal for the club up in Aberdeen on a freezing cold day in January 1982, we knew we were watching a special talent. Cherished memory is hammering Rangers one midweek with both Paul and his brother Willie scoring in a 3-0 win. Paul McStay was a world class footballer.

MURDO MACLEOD – After 9 action packed years at Celtic, Murdo reluctantly left the club in July 87 to join Borussia Dortmund. Fate would have it that his German club would be drawn against Celtic shortly afterwards and it was a mark of the high regard that Rhino was held in that he received a hugely warm reception from the Celtic support. Years later when the King of Kings returned with Barcelona, his welcome didn't even match that which was afforded to Murdo Macleod that September evening in 1987. For his goal in the 4-2 game alone – he deserves his place as a Celtic great!

CHARLIE NICHOLAS – Champagne Charlie could and should have been a Celtic great. He had everything – except socks! He scored goals for fun in a very attractive Celtic side that was attack minded and great to watch. To leave that for "boring, boring Arsenal" seemed like an ill-considered decision by the young Celtic striker. Of course the club could and should have done more to keep him but his loss to the club also resulted in him failing to live up to the success in his early career at Celtic. Sometimes the grass isn't always greener.

DAVIE PROVAN – Along with Murdo MacLeod, Davie Provan was brought in as early singings when Billy McNeill took over as manager. Like Murdo, Davie Provan turned out to be a sensational piece of business by Caesar. With his socks at his ankles, Davie was a committed, talented and successful number 7, playing in 287 games and scoring 42 goals for the club and making hundreds more – the most memorable goal he scored was that spectacular, curling free kick in the 1985 Scottish Cup Final against Dundee United.

BRIAN McCLAIR – Billy McNeill, having lost both Charlie
Nicholas and George McCluskey, proved once again that he had the
knack of signing some really excellent players for Celtic. In fact the
signing of Brian McClair from Motherwell was something of a going
away gift as Caesar would be on his way to Manchester City as
Celtic's Board demonstrated how not to run a football club. McClair
was often over-shadowed by the more flamboyant Judas, but was
a really intelligent footballer and a crucial player for new manager
Davie Hay. He won both Scottish PFA Players' Player of the Year and
Scottish Football Writers' Association Footballer of the Year in 1987
before being allowed to leave for Manchester United, where Alex
Ferguson regarded him as his best ever singing.

JOHNNY DOYLE – Johnny arrived at Celtic in 1975 and was a popular player with the support who always appreciated his commitment to the cause and his pride in playing for the club he loved. Many will regard his header, when he rose above two big Spanish defenders to head the ball into the Real Madrid net as a special moment in the Celtic career of Johhny Doyle. The Celtic support was devastated when Johnny lost his life in a tragic accident at home in October 1981. When Celtic clinched the title the following May the Jungle reflected in song that we had "won the league for Doyle." That would have pleased the wee man.

FRANK McGARVEY - Frank McGarvey played 245 times for the club and scored 113 goals, the last one being the winner in the 1985 Scottish Cup Final. He left St. Mirren for a frustrating time in Liverpool before Billy McNeill brought him to Paradise. He was not only a goal scorer, he made plenty too – indeed Charlie Nicholas, George McCluskey and Brian McClair all finished season's playing alongside Frank, each as top goalscorers in Scotland. Frank did much of the dirty work for the Celtic attack. When he re-joined St Mirren and returned to play at Celtic park the Jungle reflected in song that "Frank McGarvey is still a Tim." He loved that!

DAVIE MOYES – became an important member of Billy McNeill's Celtic squad in the early 80s before Davie Hay allowed him to leave to join Cambridge.

GEORGE McCLUSKEY – was played for Celtic on 204 occasions and netted 78 times for the club. He starred alongside Nicholas and McGarvey and his goal in Amsterdam is a particularly fond memory.

TOM McADAM – Billy McNeill converted Big Tam from a forward to a central defender and he played there for a number of years without losing his scoring touch. His late brother Colin played for Rangers at this time and both set family loyalties aside to do their best for their own team.

PAT BONNER – Pat made his debut against Motherwell in 1979 and went on to play for the club in another 640 matches. He was in the Celtic goals for the vast majority of the games featured in this book. He also established himself as Ireland's No.1 and played in World Cups and European Championships.

FRANK McAVENNIE – When Frank McAvennie scored the last
minute winner in the 1988 Scottish Cup Final to give Celtic a double
winning birthday present, Billy McNeill punched the air with delight.
So did every Celtic supporter. For this Frankie Bhoy – we will
remember you!

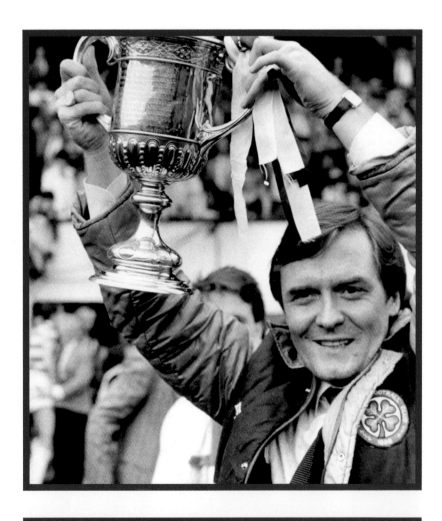

DAVIE HAY – some supporters still say that the man they call
The Assassin has been on occasion poorly treated by Celtic.
Celtic however remain Davie's team and he has as much passion
today for the club he loves as he did when he was picking up the
Scottish Cup in 1985 or winning the league in 1986 in the most
dramatic of situations. Big Billy calls it a fairytale – that day at
Love Street, Davie Hay understood exactly what Caesar meant.

the second goal was greeted with as much relief as delight.

On February 14, the Celtic fans might have turned up at Parkhead expecting a St Valentine's Day Massacre when Stirling Albion provided the opposition. Fate had decreed that the Annfield outfit, who had made such a nuisance of themselves in the League Cup earlier in the season, would get a second chance to create a sensation. Once again, they displayed stubborn resistance even after McGarvey had headed in the opener in the fourth minute. The goal deluge didn't materialise, though, and it was left to McCluskey and Burns, in the last ten minutes, to make the scoreline a little bit more emphatic.

East Stirling were the barrier to the last four and 18,500 fans were sufficiently interested to make their way to Parkhead on March 8. It didn't emerge as a game anyone would talk about in the future. Mike Conroy got his first goal of the campaign with a header in the twenty-sixth minute and MacLeod awakened the fans from their lethargy with a thunderous twenty-five yard drive that whooshed past stranded goalkeeper Charlie Kelly. Now Celtic could focus on Hampden where they were drawn against their old foes Dundee United, the team which ended their interest in the League Cup at the same stage in November. Strangely, with so many exciting individuals on show, the tie didn't ignite. Celtic were without the suspended Danny McGrain while Murdo MacLeod again deputised at right-back. Billy McNeill had to make another change when George McCluskey had to be withdrawn from action after taking a dull one and Johnny Doyle was introduced. Both teams cancelled each other out and McNeill refused to allow his team to be drawn into the cat-and-mouse tactics so beloved of Tannadice gaffer Jim McLean. A goalless stalemate was practically on the cards immediately the ball rolled off the centre spot at the kick-off.

After the inability of either team to score a goal in an hour-and-a-half on the Saturday, three were netted in a five-minute burst at the start of the replay. Unhappily, two were for the men from Tayside. Celtic were off to a flier in the fifth minute when John Holt handled a crossball and referee George Smith awarded the inevitable outcome. Charlie

Nicholas rolled the ball into one corner as Hamish McAlpine took off for the other. The celebrations on the sprawling Hampden terracing's had hardly time to quieten down when United equalised. Eamonn Bannon was unguarded at the far post as Paul Sturrock delivered a ball from the right and it was all-square in the ninth minute. Sixty seconds later, even the United manager - known to everyone as Glum McLean - had to smile. His side, astonishingly, were a goal ahead. Again the Celtic defence was all over the place as Bannon delivered a free-kick to the far post and centre-half Paul Hegarty drilled the ball beyond Pat Bonner.

With one minute to go until half-time, Charlie Nicholas, always eager, always dangerous, came to Celtic's rescue. McAlpine, harassed by the threatening presence of McGarvey, hastily fisted away a clearance and hoped for the best. The ball fell perfectly for the Celtic striker who drove a venomous effort into the gaping net. The game was finely balanced until fourteen minutes from time. Hegarty, a defender who had been converted from centre-forward by McLean, was the quickest to react when another dead-ball effort dropped into the danger zone. As others hesitated, Hegarty lashed out and the ball took the merest of touches off Mike Conroy as it zoomed into the net. Celtic were out. Unbelievably, United, after all their diligence and hard work against Celtic, contrived to lose 4-1 to a fairly mediocre Rangers team in the Cup Final replay after a goalless first game.

So, Dundee United had played a massive part in Celtic's 1980/81 campaign. Their role in the club's history for that particular season was not over yet. Before that, though, there was urgent business to be taken care of in the fourth Old Firm league meeting of the season at Ibrox on Saturday, April 18. Billy McNeill approached the game in a bold, cavalier fashion - he went without a left-back! The Celtic manager put Murdo MacLeod in the No.3 shorts, but the barrel-chested player known to his team-mates as 'Rhino', did not operate anything like a stereotype left-sided defender. Instead, he was released into his more recognisable midfield role. Afterwards, McNeill reasoned, 'I knew Rangers wouldn't play with a right winger. Tommy McLean was in their line-up, but, in his mid-thirties, I didn't think he would be asked to operate on the flank. I believed he would come inside and help out in their midfield. That left them with Willie Johnston and he operated on the left. Danny McGrain had returned from his suspension and he was in at right-back. I was quite happy with that situation.'

McNeill opted to bring back Roddie MacDonald into a central defensive role alongside Tom McAdam with Roy Aitken playing just in front of them. Rangers' battering ram of a centre-forward Colin McAdam had the ability to unsettle defenders as he rampaged around foraging for scraps. McNeill reckoned he had put out a line-up that would stifle John Greig's team while making sure the front two of Charlie Nicholas and Frank McGarvey were given decent service throughout. It worked a treat.

Celtic were far more composed and direct as they dictated the pattern of play. The only goal of the game arrived in the fifty-sixth minute and Charlie Nicholas' name was up in lights once more. Davie Provan and Frank McGarvey worked a neat one-two to give Nicholas a sight of goal. That was all he needed. He darted forward and sent a glorious effort past keeper Jim Stewart. At time-up, the Celtic fans were cavorting and cheering, 'We've won the league again' as their opposite number filed out in silence. Technically, Celtic still needed a point to make certain of the Championship although they were well ahead of Aberdeen on goal difference. It would have taken a disaster of seismic proportions for McNeill's men to fail to win their thirty-second championship.

However, one man who refused to celebrate the win at Ibrox was McNeill himself. 'The champagne is on ice, as far as I'm concerned. We haven't won anything yet, although, of course, we are in an excellent position. Let's talk about winning things when it is mathematically impossible for anyone to catch us. Then, and only then, will I talk about Championships.'

McNeill was a bit more forthcoming on the action he had just witnessed. 'I thought we played very well and were always in control of proceedings. I felt it was a one-off situation and that's why I made the changes I did.

They paid off and we deservedly won the game. Charlie took his goal brilliantly, but I was happy with the performances from all the lads. We can enjoy this win, but now we've got Dundee United at Tannadice on Wednesday and they've given us some problems already this season. So, I'll be looking at that one now we've taken care of Rangers.'

The Sunday newspapers were fulsome in their praise of Celtic's efforts. The Sunday Mail said, 'It was an Easter Parade of possession football which had Rangers pinned back almost monotonously in their own half.' The report went on, 'Rangers couldn't complain. They rarely troubled Celtic with their play. They couldn't produce the skill or the unexpected to pressure their opponents, spending most of the day defending desperately in their own half of the field. Right from the moment Nicholas tested Stewart with a low shot from twenty yards in sixty seconds it was a match in which Celtic were always likelier to succeed. They had more aggression and, on the day, more skill in individuals such as Nicholas, Provan, Aitken and McGrain. Technically, Celtic still require one more point to make the championship win official.'

In bold capital letters, the report concluded, 'BUT THERE'S NO WAY THEY CAN THROW IT AWAY.'

No-one was debating that very valid point. Not least the Rangers manager John Greig, who, sportingly, said, 'Celtic will get everything they deserve.' Celtic now had some unfinished business with a club from Dundee to take care of. Two pieces of domestic silverware had been swept out of reach of Celtic by Dundee United. It had annoyed Billy McNeill in the extreme, especially as both of the defeats were in Glasgow with their opponents scoring three goals in each game.

McNeill would never consider talk of revenge, but to people who knew him best he was absolutely determined to clinch the title at Tannadice. Celtic were due to face Kilmarnock, already relegated, at Parkhead the following Saturday and would have been off-the-scale favourites to triumph in that encounter. McNeill, though, only had eyes on United. He abhorred their tactics, especially as he rated players such as Paul Hegarty, Paul Sturrock and Eamonn Bannon so highly as skilled individuals. They were rarely let off the leash with Jim McLean in charge and that was never the way McNeill was brought up to believe how the beautiful game should be played.

'Wee Jim was perceived as taciturn and dour,' said McNeill years later. 'It was suggested that when United flew off to play in Europe, as the plane taxied on to the runway, a sign flashed up ordering that all smiles be extinguished! There was perhaps some truth in the claim that Jim rarely smiled or formed close relationships with his players and staff, but his achievements bordered on the unbelievable, given United's limited resources and geographical location. With two teams in the city drawing their fan base from a population of around 185,000, Dundee United commanded a fraction of the support enjoyed by the Glasgow giants, even during the club's most successful period, but few provincial clubs have ever come close to matching United's achievements under Jim McLean.

'I realise Jim was not everyone's cup of tea, but the fact remains that he made Dundee United Football Club. An illustration of how deeply Jim thought about the game was to be found one day when they were playing us at Celtic Park. When I was handed a copy of the United team lines I discovered that he had changed his line-up at least four times. The sheet of paper was full of scribbles. I could only assume that Jim had sat on the team coach on the journey from Dundee, constantly going over in his mind the different permutations we might adopt and how best he could combat the various threats we might pose. Yes, Jim was probably excessive at times in the way he disciplined his players and demanded the same level of professionalism from them that he himself strived to achieve, but I personally found him a decent enough individual. We never became close, but I have always admired Jim's achievements.'

At the same time, McNeill looked at the forthcoming game on Tayside and promised, 'We want to win this championship with a flourish. Celtic have a nice habit of doing things with a certain class.'

Jim McLean rarely praised his own team in public, so it is a collector's item to hear him going on record and lauding opponents. This unique event took place at Tannadice on a momentous evening on April 22 when the United manager applauded Celtic's third Premier League success in five years. 'I give Celtic all the credit for beating us well,' McLean said, almost in awe of Billy McNeill's team after a stunning 3-2 victory in front of 15,349 fans who were enveloped in their own green heaven long before the final whistle. 'With supporters like these, how can you fail to become champions? Yes, Celtic played exceptionally well, but their fans look as though they are part of the team. How can you let down these people, cheering you on from start to finish? Yes, these are real fans.' It was an extraordinary compliment from an individual not known to eulogise or lionise his own players or supporters. Yet Celtic earned a glowing tribute.

McNeill had demanded a triumph with a swagger and he got it that wonderful evening. The opening goal arrived in the second minute and was Celtic's eightieth of the campaign, another Premier League record. Davie Provan set it up with a cunning lob and Murdo MacLeod finished it off with a raging header beyond Hamish McAlpine. Willie Pettigrew equalised, but the night belonged to Celtic and, just after the half-hour mark, their advantage had been restored with a Frank McGarvey tap-in following a Provan corner-kick. On the hour cometh the man. MacLeod surged forward powerfully and pushed the ball to Tommy Burns. The midfielder turned two defenders, manoeuvred himself into a shooting position and blasted a ferocious drive into the roof of the net. The green and white ribbons were being looked out as United re-centred the ball. Paul Sturrock pulled one back near the end, but the singing, celebrating away support hardly took notice.

'It was a real gala night,' said Billy McNeill. 'I've praised our wonderful fans often enough, but they were exceptional that evening. Their support was almost overwhelming. They were there to see us win the title and I'm just delighted we delivered. As I usually do, I headed for the dressing room at the end to allow the players to take the plaudits. John Clark and I retreated down the tunnel, but, about fifteen minutes later, we were told to get back out on the pitch - the fans were refusing to leave until we took a bow. The players grabbed John and I and sat us on their shoulders. What a fabulous experience. You think you've sampled every emotion this great game has to offer then something like this comes along. It was just wonderful.'

A boisterous crowd of 23,200 were ready to party at Parkhead on Saturday April 25. The sun shone as the Celtic players, looking resplendent in their new all-white tracksuit tops, lined up before the kick-off against Kilmarnock. The Premier League trophy was about to be handed over to skipper Danny McGrain by Scottish Football League President Tom Lauchlan, who, as chairman of the Rugby Park club, could then take a seat in the opposition's directors' box to cheer on his team against the newly-crowned champions.

As so often happens on these occasions, the game hardly got off the ground. After all the razzmatazz, it settled into a fairly low-key affair. There was little tempo about the game from two teams at the opposite ends of the table; Celtic victorious at the top and Kilmarnock vanquished at the bottom. Davie Provan brought the fans to their feet in the twentieth minute, though, with a free-kick goal any Brazilian would be proud to claim as one of his own. Provan, Billy McNeill's first buy for the club from Kilmarnock two seasons earlier, placed the ball about twenty-five yards out, sized up the situation, waited for the referee's signal and then stepped up to create a thing of beauty. The winger bent the ball round the defensive wall and keeper Alan McCulloch could do little as the effort thudded into the net behind him.

The Ayrshire side, to their credit, kept plugging away and they got their reward just after the hour mark when they silenced the celebrating fans - well, at least, for a moment. Pat Bonner dived to push away an effort from John Bourke and eager youngster Ken Eadie followed up to claim the first of only four league goals he would score in his three years at the club. No matter. For a man who always wanted to do things with a touch of elan, Billy McNeill could still smile in the knowledge Celtic had lifted the trophy with a record haul of points, fifty-six and there was still one more game to go.

Lisbon Lion Tommy Gemmell watched the action from the stand and declared, 'This is easily the best Celtic team I have seen in years. I've been most impressed, especially since the turn of the year. When I saw Celtic last August they were playing as eleven individuals. Now Billy

McNeill has them playing for the team rather than for themselves. This is the most obvious improvement. I don't think they'll win the European Cup. Not just yet. But they are a young side. In three years they could be ready to emulate our 1967 team. In the meantime, it's vital they have a good run in next season's European Cup. A club of Celtic's standing must look further afield than Scotland.

'One good thing is that they are playing like a European side. They hold the ball well and try to play it to each other's feet. At top level, that's vital. You get crucified in Europe if you give the ball away. They could do with buying at least two experienced players, but not necessarily to go straight into the top side. But a few injuries and they could be in bother, especially with such inexperienced players as Pat Bonner, Mark Reid and Charlie Nicholas. You could also make the point there is no player in the reserves quite ready for European competition. But I like Celtic's balance. Murdo MacLeod really complements the ball players. It is crucial to have a ball winner who drives the game on the way he does.'

The last game was at Love Street on Saturday, May 2 and, sportingly, the St Mirren team applauded the Celtic players into the pitch as the curtain was about to be lowered on another incident-laden Premier League season. The charity from the Paisley players evaporated as soon as referee Andrew Waddell gave the go-ahead for the action to proceed. There was the little matter of a European place up for grabs as far as the Saints were concerned. They were neck and neck with Rangers for the last remaining spot in the UEFA Cup - and both teams started the day locked on forty-four points apiece. St Mirren went at Celtic like it was a Cup Final.

Billy McNeill's men weathered the expected early salvo and looked to be taking control until Frank McDougall netted the opener on the half-hour mark. A left-wing corner from Lex Richardson eluded Pat Bonner and the powerful frontman timed his run to the back to post to perfection before scoring with a simple header. Charlie Nicholas thought he had equalised when he turned a Frank McGarvey low cross over the line. Match official Waddell was satisfied it was legitimate and immediately started running towards the centre circle. However, a linesman waved frantically to attract his attention and, after a quick confab, the effort was ruled out, presumably for offside.

Saints made the most of the let-off and the busy Richardson eluded the Celtic back lot in the fifty-seventh minute to score with a well-placed header. Six minutes later, the champions were back into it with the rarest of sights - a Davie Provan header. The winger slipped almost unnoticed into the home side's penalty area and he took advantage after some intricate footwork from Tommy Burns on the touchline. Celtic went for the equaliser, but were punished yet again by a corner-kick with only one minute to go. Once more, Richardson swung the ball in from the left and McDougall knocked it past Bonner from ten yards. The keeper had every right to remonstrate with the men in front of him who were affording him very little protection at dead-ball situations.

The Paisley side took the points and then waited to hear what had happened at nearby Ibrox. The news came through that John Greig's men had snatched the UEFA Cup place with a 4-0 victory over Hearts. They were both level on points, but Rangers edged it on goal difference. Saints' superhuman effort was in vain. Surprisingly, this was Roddie MacDonald's last game for the Hoops as Billy McNeill sold him to the Tynecastle side for £40,000. Thus the tall centre-half celebrated winning the Premier League one season and kicked off the next in the First Division.

The Celtic manager was philosophical at the end. 'Our aim was to win the title and we've managed that. It's a pity our unbeaten league run had to end on the last day of the campaign. I can't complain, though. That's one defeat since December last year, a run of thirteen wins, two draws and now one defeat. If you had offered me that sequence on the journey back from Aberdeen after that dismal display, I would quite happily have accepted it.'

Love Street still rocked to the joyous anthems of the travelling support and one newspaper summed up, 'The Celtic fans were something else. They stood cheering their fallen idols well after the home supporters had departed. They seemed reluctant to accept their season was over.'

CHAPTER SEVEN
STRICTLY CONFIDENTIAL

Billy McNeill was doing his damndest to keep a secret from his players. It was May 15, the last day of the 1981/82 Premier League campaign and the destination of the title teetered in the balance. Celtic were playing St Mirren at Parkhead while Aberdeen were taking on Rangers at Pittodrie. The situation wasn't complicated; if McNeill's outfit lost by a single goal and the Dons won by five, the Championship was heading north. Simple as that.

At half-time it was goalless in Glasgow and, breathless with curiosity, the players wanted to know what was happening at Pittodrie. McNeill, of course, knew the precise details of what was unfolding in Aberdeen, but had no desire to put additional pressure on his team. He said, 'When the players came inside at the interval, they enquired about events up the road and how the Dons were getting on. I told them I hadn't heard and pointed out that it didn't matter, anyway. It was what we did on the day that would determine everything. We had our destiny in our own hands. I wanted them to focus completely on the second-half. As luck would have it, just as the players were preparing to go out for the second-half, someone on the staff came into the dressing room and said, "I see Aberdeen are beating Rangers 4-0." I could have strangled that guy!'

The position had altered somewhat. Celtic couldn't risk any sort of slip against the Saints. One mistake, one goal conceded, and Alex Ferguson's team only needed to add one more strike to their tally and the red and white ribbons would be on the silverware which would be removed from the Parkhead trophy cabinet. 'I could see my players looking at each other,' said the Celtic boss. 'I had to lighten the mood immediately. I chipped in, "Well, you didn't expect any favours from that mob from Govan, did you?" That did the trick. The players had a wee laugh and, shortly afterwards, they were back out on the pitch knowing what they had to do. And that was to win. Aberdeen could score ten and it wouldn't have mattered a jot.'

There had been some disturbing anxiety in Celtic's play in the opening forty-five minutes while the players chased consecutive championships for the first time since 1974. Billy Thomson, in the St Mirren goal, was performing magnificently as he went through an impressive acrobatic routine. After an hour, it was still scoreless, but Celtic kept their nerve and continued to take the play to their determined and committed would-be party-poopers. The burden for scoring goals had fallen on the shoulders of George McCluskey while Frank McGarvey and Charlie Nicholas were sidelined through injury. Young Danny Crainie was promoted from the reserves to play alongside McCluskey, but it was hardly an ideal situation.

In the sixty-third minute, in a typical surge from midfield, Murdo MacLeod powered forward, slipped the ball to Tommy Burns, by far the most majestic player on the field, and he set up McCluskey. The striker took aim and zipped a drive past the excellent Thomson into the far corner of the net. The relief was palpable. With the pressure easing, Celtic's fast flowing passing game came more into evidence. Davie Provan, all poise and grace, menaced on the right, MacLeod and Burns dovetailed imposingly and a young Paul McStay was looking extremely accomplished, too, with some subtle promptings. A second goal would go a long way to lifting the tension which was only too prevalent on the terracings.

Ten minutes after the breakthrough, Tom McAdam sauntered forward as Provan prepared for one his trademark deft corner-kicks. The ball was duly delivered, McAdam's timing was perfect as he headed past Thomson. Defender Davie Walker scrambled frantically on the line in an effort to clear the danger, but referee Eddie Pringle, in a perfect position, immediately awarded the goal. A whoosh of joy surged around the ground. Three minutes later and anything Aberdeen might be able to conjure against Rangers was rendered completely irrelevant. The elegant Burns swooped onto the ball in the middle of the park, breezed past two half-hearted challenges, rolled a pass to McCluskey and he cracked a left-foot drive past the despairing Thomson. Game over. Look out the green, white and gold ribbons. Let the good times roll.

A beaming McNeill immediately saluted the team's followers. 'These fans of ours are something special. I can't claim to have seen every set of supporters in the world, but ours are the best. All they want is the opportunity to display their feelings for this club and I'm so pleased for them that everything worked out perfectly.'

However, behind the gaiety, a worrying situation was beginning to develop. The Celtic manager appeared to be constantly at loggerheads with the board of directors and, in particular, chairman Desmond White. McNeill wanted to strengthen the playing squad, he was determined to take them to another level. White, a stubborn individual, was never a fan of writing cheques and wasn't quite in tandem with the ambitions of his team boss. Relations between McNeill and the board had been strained for some time. There had been an incident with a newspaperman, Gerry McNee, the previous season as Celtic prepared to fly from London to Hungary for their European tie against Diosgynor Miskolc. What had been a vitriolic verbal exchange, unfortunately, escalated out of control and, after a misunderstanding, McNeill admitted to throwing a punch at the reporter. 'It was a monumental error of judgement on my behalf,' admitted McNeill. The Celtic board collectively frowned when the tale was relayed to them.

The friction continued the following season and McNeill was becoming increasingly frustrated. He had spent wisely in bringing in players such as Frank McGarvey, Davie Provan and Murdo MacLeod in his first four seasons and he was continually identifying players he believed could perform key roles for the club in the future. I believe one of these players was Lex Richardson, the vibrant, lively little St Mirren midfielder. My information at the time was that the Paisley club would sell Richardson for £100,000 - the same fee that took MacLeod from Dumbarton to Celtic. The money was never made available and an exasperated McNeill failed in his pursuit of a player who always gave the Parkhead side a fairly torrid time when he was in opposition.

McNeill realised he would have to sell before he could bring in new players and he offloaded Roddie MacDonald to Hearts at the end of the previous season. He received £40,000 for the no-frills centre-half. During the summer, the Celtic boss paid an identical fee to take Willie Garner from Aberdeen to fill the gap in the defence. If McGarvey, Provan and MacLeod proved to be money well spent - a total of £490,000 - Garner was the complete opposite. The player, who had impressed McNeill during his brief stint at Pittodrie, turned into a one-man disaster area. He joined the Hoops on July 1 1981 and was an Alloa player by November 30 1982. In between, he played three games for Celtic - and the Glasgow club lost the lot.

Presumably, Garner never recovered from his debut where he scored TWO own goals as St Mirren won 3-1 in a League Cup-tie at Parkhead. McNeill kept faith in the new boy for the next match in the group section against St Johnstone at Muirton. The First Division side won 2-0. Garner then went into cold storage until a league game against Hibs at Easter Road on November 27. An injury crisis forced McNeill's hand, he had to play the central defender and the Edinburgh side celebrated an unexpected 1-0 success. That was the end of the line for Willie Garner and a future at Recreation Park beckoned.

Unfortunately, and against all odds, Celtic failed to qualify from their League Cup section which also contained Hibs as well as the teams from Paisley and Perth. The outcome in the kick-off against St Mirren was as disastrous as it was unexpected and Billy McNeill was not being unsporting when he observed, 'This is a result that must be considered a freak.' The 26,100 paying customers at Parkhead that afternoon would have undoubtedly agreed, even those supporters adorned in black and white. Celtic controlled the game immediately after it got underway and it was only a matter of time before they opened the scoring and Frank McGarvey duly obliged with a header just after the half-hour mark.

Two minutes later the Saints equalised and Garner's romance with his boyhood favourites was already beginning to fade. Frank McDougall tried a drive from distance that was more likely to worry the corner flag than Pat Bonner, but the new boy, eager to become an instant hit, threw out a leg in a desperate attempt to block the shot and merely sent the ball spinning into his own net. There have been better baptisms. It didn't get any better for the wretched Garner or his team-mates in the sixty-first minute when, incredibly, he staged an action replay. This time the struggling defender headed a Lex Richardson cross into his own net. I can only think of The Titanic having a worse debut. McDougall, with no assistance from Garner, settled the tie with a third goal nine minutes from time.

Tommy Gemmell, who had moved into the financial business sector after quitting as Dundee manager two years earlier, also undertook media work at the weekends where his colourful and incisive views were sought by newspapers and radio. The Lisbon Lion was in the stand that day and opined, 'There is only one thing Celtic can do about this game - forget it. I saw it myself and I still don't believe it. It was a freak result. (Gemmell was not to know McNeill had used the exact same word to describe the scoreline). For more than an hour, I was convinced Celtic were going to give St Mirren a pounding. They dominated the game, missed a lot of chances and saw a lot of rugged defending from their opponents and some excellent saves from Billy Thomson. What I didn't reckon with was the nightmare debut for big Willie Garner. Not only did he help two into his own net, but he looked ponderous and out of touch.'

Gemmell also added a note of caution. 'If I were Billy McNeill, I'd be looking for a bit more commitment from Charlie Nicholas. He didn't get into the thick of things enough for my liking and was deservedly substituted.'

Garner was still in the heart of the rearguard when Celtic travelled to Perth for the midweek tie against St Johnstone. Once again, Billy McNeill's men were tipped to win. Once again, they were on the receiving end of an embarrassing defeat. A crowd of almost 10,500 packed into tidy, trim Muirton Park to see how the Glasgow giants would react to the upset against St Mirren. Saturday's setback was replaced by Wednesday's woes.

Seven minutes from the interval, the outfit from the lower league took the lead from a youngster who was making a bit of a name for himself in Perth. John Pelosi squared a pass across the box and Ally McCoist prodded the ball past Pat Bonner from close range. Valiantly, Celtic tried to claw their way back into the contest, but McCoist was to figure prominently again nine minutes from the end. Danny McGrain was adjudged to have fouled the precocious twenty year old in the box. It seemed harsh, but substitute Jim Morton shrugged off any debate by lashing the award into the net. McNeill, understandably irritated, kept his players locked in the dressing room for an extended period afterwards. Grim-faced, he emerged afterwards to say, through gritted teeth, 'We've got much work to do.'

Garner's career in the green and white was already on the wane after a mere three hours of action. Tommy Gemmell's summing-up after the St Mirren defeat was proving to be spot on. He did look slow to react and even cumbersome in attempting to bring the ball out of defence. His distribution was suspect and it is still a mystery that such an imperious centre-half as Billy McNeill couldn't spot the imperfections in the graceless Garner.

McNeill was clever enough to coax or crack the whip in his efforts to extract the best from his players. It's more than likely he favoured the latter as he attempted to galvanise his team for the remaining four ties in the section. Only twelve points were up for grabs in a four-team group and already four had been carelessly shed. After only two games in the League Cup, Celtic were on thin ice. The players' response to their manager's persuasive demands was immediate and extraordinary. They walloped in seventeen goals - with the loss of four - as they wiped the floor with the opposition.

Hibs were first up on August 14 when 19,200 turned out to see if Celtic could transform their fortunes in a competition they once dominated - playing in fourteen successive Finals from 1964/65 to 1977/78 - and, in doing so, they got an early glimpse of a young centre-half debutant by the name of Davie Moyes who replaced the injured Tom McAdam during the action. Willie Garner was nowhere to be seen. Murdo MacLeod got the ball rolling with a vicious effort in the second minute and he added another after the hour mark. Charlie

Nicholas chipped in with two and the Easter Road side were well beaten. Veteran winger Arthur Duncan got their irrelevant counter near the end.

Ally McCoist was also on the scoresheet four days later at Parkhead, but that, too, was merely nuisance value as Celtic were already four goals ahead and coasting against St Johnstone. Moyes made his first start for the club with McAdam still struggling and impressed the fans with his steady, workmanlike performance. Up front, McGarvey got the opener in the seventeenth minute, Provan added a quickfire second and knocked in No.3 shortly after the turnaround. Nicholas notched the fourth and McCoist rolled one past Bonner twelve minutes from time. The effort was greeted with silence. The Saints had a sinner in Pelosi who was dismissed while his team were already trailing by three goals.

Such was the demand for the return game against St Mirren, that the Paisley club made it an all-ticket affair and 18,000 fans were in place for the kick-off. Celtic dismantled the opposition with McCluskey, in particular, in devastating form. Giving the Saints a taste of what was to come in the final league game of the campaign, the lithe, lively striker claimed a hat-trick while MacLeod fired in two. Ironically, the home side actually took the lead through a Billy Stark penalty-kick in the nineteenth minute before Celtic took exception to this intrusion. The shell-shocked Saints were due to play St Johnstone at Love Street in midweek and were still in pole position to qualify. McNeill said, 'I am convinced we are the best team in this section.'

Celtic travelled to Edinburgh on the Wednesday to take on Hibs while hoping McCoist and Co - what an intriguing thought - could do them a favour in Paisley. It was goalless at half-time in the capital before the home side's central defender Craig Paterson sparked proceedings to life. He netted in the forty-sixth minute and Celtic took total control after that. McGarvey levelled ten minutes later, sixty seconds afterwards MacLeod thundered the Hoops into the lead, before midfield sidekick Sullivan swept in a third in the sixty-fifth minute. The tireless McGarvey got a fourth twelve minutes from time. After claiming only one goal in their first two ties, Celtic had now collected a landslide in four. All eyes turned to Paisley. Would St Mirren trip up? Celtic's wretched start came back to haunt them; the Paisley side won 2-0 to go through by a point. Amazingly, Celtic were out.

Intriguingly, the champions were due to make a trip to Pittodrie and an early test of character against Aberdeen awaited them on the second game on the Premier Division fixture list. Alex Ferguson, do doubt, relished the opportunity to gain the upper hand so early in the campaign after his team's disappointment last time around. Before that meeting, though, Airdrie were due in Glasgow for the fanfare kick-off to the new league season. A crowd of 21,100 was in attendance to see if Celtic could continue their rollicking goal romps. They weren't disappointed.

Tommy Burns opened the scoring in forty seconds with the cheers for the unfurling of the flag still echoing around the stadium. Keeper John Martin punched away an inswinging corner from Davie Provan and the ball dropped at the feet of the smooth midfield man. Burns casually lobbed the gift straight back into the net. The supporters settled back and waited for the deluge, but the Celtic attackers were in an extremely generous mood and refused to pile on the agony. Making a mockery of how the contest was progressing, the Broomfield bruisers snatched an equaliser in the thirty-sixth minute. Danny McGrain bundled over Brian McKeown. It was a penalty-kick, no argument, and Sandy Clark thrashed the award into the net.

Billy McNeill had to sort out the mood of his players at half-time. 'I only had to remind them of the opening League Cup-tie against St.Mirren earlier in the month. We had dominated that match and lost 3-1. I told the players there was every chance it would happen again if we weren't careful. I reminded them that there were only three domestic trophies up for grabs and we had already forfeited our right to compete for one of them.'

McNeill's well-chosen words hit the target. George McCluskey rattled in one three minutes after the interval and added another later on. Frank McGarvey and Charlie Nicholas got on the scoresheet, too, and another from Clark for the visitors near the end didn't create a ripple. Now Celtic had a week to prepare for a trip north and another head-to-head with Ferguson and his highly-motivated team of players. They had been shredded 4-1 by Dundee United - the other half of the New Firm, as they were being called - in their opening day fixture at Tannadice. The infamous Fergie hair-dryer treatment could have made its introduction that day. If the Dons needed an extra edge for the visit from the team from the east end of Glasgow, it had dropped in their lap. They needed to respond swiftly.

And they did. They were a goal ahead inside two minutes while the 18,000 fans were still settling on the Pittodrie terracings. Danny McGrain got entwined with the awkward Walker McCall, a beanpole striker who was all elbows and knees, and the Dons forward went to ground. That was all referee Brian McGinlay required to put the whistle to his lips and blow for a penalty. A gleeful Gordon Strachan placed the ball on the spot, took a short run up, thrashed the ball past Pat Bonner and performed a perfect cartwheel to complete his celebration.

His antics weren't appreciated by one fan who managed to get through the police cordon at the Paddock End and to chase after the Dons winger. Thankfully, the intruder was apprehended before anything serious materialised, but Strachan must have wondered what it was between him and Celtic supporters. Ten months earlier, one got onto the pitch at Parkhead and made a beeline for the little flame-haired winger. Presumably, neither wanted an autograph. Strachan's grin was replaced by a grimace five minutes later when Celtic levelled. Aberdeen's much-vaunted central defensive pairing of Alex McLeish and Willie Miller were eliminated by a beautifully-flighted right-wing cross from Davie Provan and Tommy Burns stole in to zip a header past Jim Leighton.

Billy McNeill must have been purring at this stage as he witnessed some tantalising, intricate football from his team. Davie Provan was unstoppable and Frank McGarvey was chasing everything with his usual gusto. Tommy Burns and Murdo MacLeod were indulging in incisive thrusts from the middle of the park, the former supplying the silk, the latter the strength. Celtic looked comfortable at a stadium where things had gone dreadfully wrong in the not-too-distant past. Just before the half-hour mark, McNeill's men took the lead when a long ball from the ever-improving Mark Reid, a stuffy left-back, released the jet-heeled McGarvey. The Dons back lot appealed in unison for offside, but the sprightly Celtic raider had timed his run perfectly and he raced through to clip the second goal beyond the exposed Leighton. It was never easy to fathom whether the stone-faced Dons keeper was smiling or scowling such was his grim countenance, but, on this occasion, it might have been a fair bet he wasn't joining in the applause for a wonderful piece of judgement from his Scottish international team-mate.

Leighton most definitely wasn't happy nine minutes after the turnaround. MacLeod went on another stamina-sapping surge before setting up McGarvey and he sidestepped the keeper without too much difficulty and rolled the ball home. Celtic coasted after that and could even indulge in some eye-catching possession play as they shuttled the ball around with speed and accuracy. Afterwards, a sporting Alex Ferguson said, 'It must have been a great game for the neutral to watch - a match where both sides let each other attack and one with hardly a bad tackle. I don't know how many goals Celtic could have scored. We could have had a few, as well - not as many as them - but, in the end, we were given a comprehensive beating by a better side on the day. Now we are four points behind Celtic and that's a big gap.'

Celtic prepared for two vastly diverse challenges; Morton in the league at Parkhead and the visit of star-studded Juventus in the first round of the European Cup. McNeill, as ever, was forthright. 'I realise it's a cliché and I say it all the time, but I mean it. We have to take one game at a time. We've got Morton on Saturday and two points are at stake. They could be crucial at the end of the season. Then, and only then, should we turn our attention to Juventus. If we're caught looking too far ahead, we could come unstuck.'

Almost 20,000 fans watched as their favourites made hard work of overthrowing the men from Greenock. It took until the fifty-first minute for the apprehension to be lifted from the terracings. MacLeod, with another invaluable strike, steered a ball through traffic in a crowded penalty box and the Hoops were on their way. Seven minutes later McGarvey pitched over a high curling ball and McAdam rose with glorious confidence to glance a header wide of Roy Baines. The stress levels were raised a notch when Bobby Thomson climbed at the back post to knock in a header with seventeen minutes still to play, but Celtic saw it through to the end.

A relieved McNeill said, 'We didn't take the chances we should have, but the lads are only human. They must have had thoughts about the European tie and I can understand that to a certain extent. Looking on the positive side, though, they played some really clever football.'

Four days after facing Bobby Houston, Davie Hayes, Neil Orr, Jim Holmes, Roddie Hutchison, Drew Busby and the rest of Morton's honest collection of joiners, taxi drivers, plasterers and handy men, Celtic opened the doors for the soccer sophisticates of Juventus, a team consisting of such internationally-acclaimed football jewels as Dino Zoff, Marco Tardelli, Roberto Bettega, Pietro Virdis, Antonio Cabrini, Gaetano Scirea and a bloke from Dublin by the name of Liam Brady, a flamboyant individual who would become better acquainted with the east end of Glasgow a decade later. There was also an uncompromising defender by the name of Caludio Gentile who made a bit of an impression on Frank McGarvey.

Brady arranged for a coach-load of his family to travel from Ireland for the all-ticket encounter. He might have been slightly bemused when most of them turned up wearing green and white scarves. A crowd of 60,017 was in attendance, with fans forking out £6 for a seat in the upper stand and £2.50 for a place on the terracings. The referee was the experienced Charles Corver from Holland.

Juventus coach Giovanni Trapattoni, later to manage the Republic of Ireland, set out his team to stifle Celtic. Billy McNeill was prepared for his opposite number's cloak of defence. 'Giovanni is an old friend of mine. I first met him when he played for AC Milan against us in the European Cup in 1969. He had learned how to play football under that team's great coach Nereo Rocco, who was Italy's answer to Jock Stein. Not in the way he set out his team, but that he was very successful. Rocco always played hit-and-run tactics. His teams would soak up pressure for eighty-nine minutes, not even attempt to play football, and then hit you on the break. Bang! They've scored, you've lost and they're happy. It's their mentality. So, yes, I knew what to expect when the Turin team appeared on the pitch at Celtic Park.'

There was the usual huffing and puffing and Brady, that rare combination of invention and industry, was outstanding as he held up play and brought his team-mates into the game. He was the orchestrator in the middle of the park as Celtic stormed forward trying to ensure he saw as little of the ball as possible. They realised his left foot could wreak destruction if it was let loose. The only goal of a fraught confrontation arrived in the sixty-fifth minute and it wasn't the product of some fine, intricate football required to unlock the back door of an iron-clad rearguard.

Instead, Davie Provan slung over a dangerous left-wing corner-kick, Celtic's eleventh of the game. There was the usual jostling in the box, players being blocked and barged. The ball dropped to Roy Aitken who attempted a volley. It was charged down by the frantic defence, but dropped to the edge of the box where Murdo MacLeod was lying in wait. The midfielder sent a controlled first-time drive low into the corner well out of the reach of the diving Zoff. The Italians were rattled and Celtic went for the jugular. There was a remarkable incident near the end when Sergio Brio flattened George McCluskey in the box. Match official Corver raced towards the penalty spot before suddenly changing his mind while veering off back down the field waving play on. The Italians sighed with relief; they knew only too well they had been let off the hook.

The return was in Turin in a fortnight later and McNeill's plans were in tatters before half-time. 'I wanted the team to defend higher up the pitch. I didn't want us sitting back and inviting the Italians down on top of us. That would have been suicide. There was a heavy onus on Dom Sullivan, Murdo MacLeod and Tommy Burns in the middle of the park to make sure it was compact and we protected the ball. Davie Provan would be helping out and Frank McGarvey would have the main striking role with George McCluskey just behind him. We were missing the injured Danny McGrain, though, and, of course, his leadership qualities and experience would have been absolutely crucial in a game like this. These were the games Danny loved. He could organise things at the back and break swiftly, carry the ball deep into enemy territory when he saw the opportunity. No-one did it better than Danny. We had young Davie Moyes in at No.2 in his place and I knew he wouldn't let us down, but any team would miss their skipper on a night like that.'

Unfortunately, Celtic were punished in the twenty-ninth minute when Roy Aitken misplaced a free-kick on the edge of the Juventus penalty area. With his team-mates up in attack, the Italians broke at breathtaking pace.

Pietro Virdis accepted a pass and ran fully fifty yards before stepping round a clumsy challenge from Aitken, dragging the ball away from Moyes before firing a sixteen-yard drive at goal. Pat Bonner, easily Celtic's best performer on the night, got his left hand to the ball, but the power of the effort swept it high into the net. There was an incredible naivety about the players' inability to spot the danger when Virdis was allowed to race over such a length of the pitch without even the hint of a tackle. In my most vivid imagination I couldn't see Frank McGarvey being accommodated in such a manner by the Italians. More likely, someone would have gone to meet him when he crossed the halfway line and drop-kicked him into Row E.

Celtic's advantage had evaporated in a matter of seconds. Five minutes before half-time, they were deeper in trouble. Liam Brady's cross from the right wasn't dealt with properly and eventually the ball was headed down to elegant striker Roberto Bettega, who controlled the pass on his knee, swivelled and drilled a second goal into the net. The fireworks lit the evening skyline at the Communale Stadium as the 69,000 crowd celebrated. The Scottish champions were heading for the European Cup exit at the first hurdle. One observer noted, 'Referee Alexis Ponnet's interpretation of the laws varied to suit the Italians.' The draw had been unkind, to say the least. Serendipity must have been in a bad mood when Celtic's name came out of the ballot. Liverpool and Aston Villa, for instance, were paired with teams from Finland and Iceland respectively.

One Celtic player far from impressed by Juventus was Frank McGarvey, who, even decades later, admitted he would never forget both games. 'They did everything they could to upset us. Pulling your jersey was the least of it. Nothing was off limits. I was spat on, elbowed and their defenders were even pulling the hairs out of my legs. The worst, though, was when Gentile knocked me out. It happened during the first-half when we were attacking and the referee and linesman were following play. He just came up behind me and punched me on the head. I was unconscious. Our physio, Brian Scott, came on and brought me round with smelling salts. I was back on my feet and played on while the rough treatment continued.

'I was always very good with my discipline and I didn't respond to any of the fouls or the spitting. However, once the final whistle went I lost my head and went in search of Gentile. I went up the tunnel shouting for him and I was determined to land one on him for what he had done to me. It's the only time in my life I have ever reacted like that, but I was furious. As it happened, I didn't get to him, but that was probably the best thing because he was twice my size!

'The referee in Italy was from Belgium and all I'll say is that he was extremely kind to Juventus. I've never had a problem with hard tackling, that's all part and parcel of the game, but their challenges weren't exactly fair. Juventus was a team full of household names and about half of them were World Cup winners, but the referees in both games let them away with murder. Put it this way - their defenders, in particular, simply wouldn't have a career nowadays. The stunts they pulled back then would now be caught by the TV cameras, they would be pulled up and banned for it. Unfortunately, all those years ago, it was open season on us. It was obvious that they were desperate to win at all costs and they would stop at nothing when it came to putting you off your game. Juventus had a great team and I'm not saying their underhand tactics were the main reason we went out. But the aggregate score was only 2-1 for them and if the referees and their linesmen had taken action against the culprits then we would certainly have had a better chance of beating them.'

George McCluskey was also given the 'treatment' by the Italians. He recalled, 'Sergio Brio did a man-to-man marking job on me at Celtic Park. He just followed me everywhere. I thought I would be fly and wander out to the wing and create a big space, but he just came with me. He didn't bother about anything else. I tried everything to shake him off, but he wasn't bothered. He was obviously told to just mark me and that was it. And I found it strange. If I got the ball and turned and went at him, I could always beat him, but he's get an arm round me or foul me.'

McCluskey admitted he had been greatly impressed by Liam Brady. 'I thought he was the best in the world for going and getting the ball off the back four and then moving forward and getting it to the strikers. He was brilliant at linking the defence to the forward line. He would come deep, get the ball off the defence and then dribble through and link up with the likes of Roberto Bettega. And the fact that there were only three foreign players allowed in Italian sides at the time shows you how good Brady was to be one of them.'

The striker pointed out how close Celtic came to getting a goal in Turin that would have brought a famous aggregate victory. 'I had a chance at one stage when I managed to get free of Brio. Dino Zoff was about thirty-eight when we played them and I chipped him and the ball hit the bar. I was conscious of him coming off his line and I thought to myself, "He's that bit older, he'll not be that agile." I had realised he was like a cat when he was younger, but he was still very nimble against us. We weren't too far from knocking them out, though. If that chip had gone in, then we would have gone through. And that would have been us beating, basically, the Italian international team.'

Sandwiched in between the European tussles were two league games, crucially one was the first Old Firm confrontation of the season. Celtic were the opponents when Rangers decided to unveil their new £4million Govan Stand on September 19. Billy McNeill said drily, 'Let's give them something to remember.' The new stand was emptying before the final whistle with Celtic leading 2-0 and the points heading across Glasgow. It was an impressive performance from the guests and former player Paddy Crerand, who won a European Cup medal with Manchester United in 1968 a year after Celtic had shown the English how it was done, watched the game and made this sharp observation, 'I'll bet Tom McAdam and Roy Aitken didn't need to have a bath after that ninety minutes.'

Glasgow derby encounters are rarely that easy, but Celtic had bossed the match for a fair percentage of the ninety minutes and Pat Bonner was rarely troubled such was the domination of twin centre-halves Aitken and McAdam in front of him, Tommy Burns running the show in midfield, Davie Provan prancing all along the frontline and Frank McGarvey in super-charged mode in attack. Celtic's superiority was highlighted as early as the eleventh minute when Provan arced over a cross from the right and McAdam rose virtually unchallenged to head past the flapping Peter McCloy. Celtic continued to be the dominant, creative force and the frustration in the ranks of Rangers was evident as the crime count mounted and referee Bob Valentine was forced to book the quartet of Derek Johnstone, Tom Forsyth, Gregor Stevens and

Willie Johnston.

McNeill must have been tempted to put on substitute Charlie Nicholas as his team chased the killer goal, but he didn't want to disrupt the impressive flow of his team. The eleven who started the game were the eleven who finished it and the second goal duly arrived four minutes from time to trigger an exodus from the Rangers support who had seen their team taken apart. Forsyth fouled McGrain, Sullivan rolled the free-kick to MacLeod and he whacked it past McCloy. Game well and truly over.

McNeill declared himself 'satisfied'. The Celtic supporters declared themselves ecstatic. The trick was to keep the ball rolling against Partick Thistle a week later in another Glasgow derby; possibly less grand, but the reward of two points was the identical target. Dreadful, blustery weather made certain good football was virtually an impossible task. Celtic won 2-0, but at a terrible cost. Danny McGrain was carried off after a vigorous challenge from Donald Park and it was later discovered the captain had sustained a hairline fracture of the ankle. He would miss ten games in all, including, of course, the European Cup-tie in Turin.

Most of the play took place in the Thistle penalty area, as was expected. The activity in front of Alan Rough was so frantic, one observer said, 'It was like Glasgow Central Station on Fair Saturday.' This author has been there and, trust me, it did get a tad frenetic. So, the bodies were piling up in front of the very capable Jags goalie who appeared to reserve some of his best displays when facing the Parkhead men. He restricted Celtic to a 2-0 win. The keeper, known as 'Scruff' to everyone in the game, held out until the hour mark and then Charlie Nicholas knocked one in after some good work by George McCluskey. Eleven minutes from the end, McCluskey turned provider again with a cross into the path of Tommy Burns who turned it home.

Billy McNeill was pleased. 'In the circumstances, 2-0 was a good result for us. We created a lot of chances and Alan Rough had some tremendous saves and a little luck, which I have to say he deserved. Thistle played a frustrating game, but I'm happy that at the end of the day we managed to put two of the chances away. I wanted the players to give me a convincing win before they set off for Italy and that's exactly what they gave me.'

On October 3, three days after the disappointment of Turin, Celtic very quickly had to pick up the pieces against Dundee at Dens Park. And Billy McNeill, of course, still nursed feelings of abject disappointment and failure on this ground. Only four players remained from the wreckage of April 1980 - Roy Aitken, Tom McAdam, Murdo MacLeod and Frank McGarvey.

It was a determined set of Celtic players who took to the field against the promoted team, now managed by former Dundee United goalkeeper Donald Mackay, entrusted with the role after Tommy Gemmell moved on at the end of the 1979/80 season. The Tayside outfit made life difficult for the Parkhead side, but the points were safely deposited in Glasgow by the end of the ninety-minute head-to-head. Celtic had maintained their one hundred per cent record and had now clocked up seventeen goals in doing so. Burns, continuing to add a touch of arrogance to his undoubted composure, set up the opener for George McCluskey in the twenty-seventh minute. Celtic had to wait until just three minutes before the hour mark for the second. McCluskey combined with Dom Sullivan before finishing expertly once again. There was a small jangling of the nerves four minutes later when Pat Bonner failed to reach an Iain Ferguson cross and George McGeachie converted at the far post. McGarvey, almost inevitably, popped up with the killer third in the seventieth minute after a nice run and cross from Charlie Nicholas.

Former Dundee star Steve Murray, the cultured midfielder who cost Jock Stein £55,000 - a sizeable fee in 1973 - when he signed him from Aberdeen, took in the action and praised the Glasgow team. 'Entertainment-wise, it was Celtic who provided the thrills. They had forwards capable of taking on defenders and the underfoot conditions were perfect for that. There were no weaknesses in the Celtic side, which had a good blend and balance. Having said that, they did not play to their best, but even that was superior to what Dundee had to offer. Celtic have a great chance of winning the championship. Their biggest problem could be that they lack depth in their first team pool. If they get injuries or players go off form then they could have problems. George McCluskey stood out and was well supported by Frank McGarvey while young Davie Moyes showed a lot of potential.'

During the countdown to the meeting with their League Cup conquerors St

Mirren, Billy McNeill was having to deal with some more outside interference. While, quietly and determinedly, trying to loosen the purse strings in an effort to bring players to the club, the story had broken that Arsenal had taken a shine to George McCluskey, top league scorer with six strikes from as many games. Apparently, they were prepared to pay £400,000 for the player. Again, as with Charlie Nicholas and Everton the previous season, there was little the Celtic manager could do about it. 'My job was to keep the players' minds completely focused on Celtic. I always knew I was going to get all sorts of hassle elsewhere. Very quickly, I understood that was part of my job description. Frustrating, though.'

Highbury boss Terry Neill was, in fact, in the Love Street stand that crisp afternoon and his timing was perfect - McCluskey scored the winner in a 2-1 triumph. Nicholas was first to show, however, with the opening goal in the twenty-second minute, finishing off a sweet move put together by Burns and McCluskey. The striker claimed one for himself three minutes from half time when MacLeod picked him out with a raking pass, and from a tight angle, McCluskey clipped an effort goalwards. It looked as though it was going in under its own steam, but it got a nudge off Jackie Copland's knee before landing in the net behind a perplexed Billy Thomson.

Referee George Smith must have decided to enliven proceedings by awarding the Saints a penalty-kick five minutes after the break. A young Frank McAvennie went down when future team-mate Roy Aitken leaned on him and the match official, who gave Aberdeen a two-minute spot-kick at Pittodrie in September, once again wasn't slow in his decision making process. Ian Scanlon made his usual tidy job, leisurely placing the ball past Pat Bonner. Celtic then dug in for their seventh successive victory. It was the stuff of champions. Who could stop them?

Dundee United answered that one in the next game at Parkhead and referee Mike Delaney was criticised from all quarters for his part in the Tannadice's goal in the 1-1 draw. One newspaper reporter put it thus, 'The most outrageous goal of the season cost Celtic their one hundred per cent league record and had them playing throughout with a deep sense of injustice. Referee Mike Delaney and his standside linesman, John Reid, should avoid watching the game on the box. They will be embarrassed.'

So, what possibly could bring about the x-certificate rating from Celtic Park that would force the match officials to watch old favourites BBC's Sportsreel or STV's Scotsport through their fingers? In only two minutes, United were awarded a free-kick that was flighted in by David Narey. Ralph Milne blatantly handled the ball. It was such an obvious infringement that Roy Aitken, the closest Celtic defender to the United forward, immediately withdrew his challenge, expecting to hear the shrill of the referee's whistle. Everything switched to slow motion for a moment. Milne - obviously a devotee of the old adage 'always play to the whistle' - tucked an effort past the motionless Pat Bonner, who didn't see the point in getting his knees dirty. A strange, eerie silence enveloped the ground; 23,000 fans, friend and foe, struck dumb.

Was the referee going to allow the goal? Where was the lineman's flag? Suddenly, Milne was being congratulated by his bemused team-mates. It was an outstandingly bad bit of refereeing from Delaney. Aitken pursued him as he ran to the centre circle. The defender's protests were cut short as the match official, compounding his earlier howler, booked him and threatened to send him off if he continued with his appeal. Delaney's awful piece of misjudgment went a long way to stifling the entertainment value for the existing eighty-eight minutes.

Jim McLean, for once, beamed broadly on the touchline. His team, a goal ahead in the weirdest circumstances, could now shuffle into deep defence and attempt to hold what they had been gifted. It was something United did better than anyone else. Any fan in the vicinity daft enough to believe they would be regaled by a festival of football for the rest of the afternoon would have been better going to the local Roxy to be accommodated. United were only too happy to shut up shop. They weren't too fussy how they went about it, either, with Billy Kirkwood, Iain Phillip, Paul Hegarty and Davie Dodds going into the book. At least, the hapless Delaney could get something right.

An intelligent pass from the astute Tommy Burns, five minutes after the interval, found George McCluskey who tucked the ball behind Hamish McAlpine from a tight angle. Celtic virtually camped in the United half for the remainder of the afternoon, but, alas, Milne's bout of impromptu basketball early in the proceedings was enough to halt their winning sequence.

A week later in Edinburgh, a dark cloud settled on the Celtic players and it was little surprise that they under-performed as they lost 1-0 to Hibs. Johnny Doyle, their friend and colleague, had been killed only five days earlier in a freak accident at home. Billy McNeill said, 'We have all been saddened by the tragic death of Johnny Doyle. Johnny's enthusiasm and appetite to play at Celtic Park will be very much missed, but I can safely say that his love for the club and his very positive attitude will always be remembered.'

The only goal arrived on the stroke of half-time when Gordon Rae, already stumbling, was touched by Dom Sullivan. As the burly Hibs man sprawled on the turf, referee David Galloway was already pointing to the spot. The Celtic players, with obvious little heart for the argument, could only shrug. Newspapers the following day called the award 'soft'. Ally MacLeod swept the ball low past Pat Bonner. Celtic were given the chance to level matters six minutes into the second period. Tommy Burns went down under a challenge from his ex-colleague Alan Sneddon and the match official awarded another penalty. To be fair, that looked as much a spot-kick as the one Hibs received and another referee on another day would probably have waved both appeals away. Charlie Nicholas drilled his effort against Jim McArthur and the Hibs keeper made an even better save as Frank McGarvey tried to capitalise on the rebound. So, the unbeaten league run came to a halt in the capital. It didn't seem to matter among the players or the manager as the team coach whisked them back to Glasgow in the gathering early evening autumn gloom.

Celtic were conceding a colossal amount of penalty-kicks - or, at least, that's how the match officials were interpreting them - and Douglas Downie joined the brigade when he awarded a spot-kick to Airdrie after only five minutes a week after the Hibs defeat. Sandy Clark, an old-fashioned centre forward bereft of the talent of being capable of trapping a wrecking ball, rattled in the opener. Clark eagerly stormed around for the following eighty five minutes and upset McNeill's men to the extent Tom McAdam and Davie Moyes were both booked for fouls of the frontman. Charlie Nicholas was also cautioned for a tackle on Davie Thompson. That came as a surprise to everyone, the fact that Charlie ever bothered tackling.

Five minutes from half-time, Dom Sullivan equalised with a clever effort tucked behind young Airdrie keeper Alan Davidson, son of referee Bobby who was a figure of much derision from the Celtic following in the sixties and seventies. Dig out a DVD of Aberdeen's Scottish Cup Final win over Celtic in 1970 and all will be revealed. Referee Downie awarded a penalty-kick to the visitors in the fifty-sixth minute after Nicholas was bowled over by Norrie Anderson. McCluskey sent Davidson to his left and the ball in the opposite direction. In the fading moments, Mark Reid found Tommy Burns running free and he dinked a delightful right-foot effort over Davidson to complete the scoring at 3-1.

Celtic opted to play in a Testimonial Match for Ipswich Town skipper Allan Hunter at Portman Road a few days before the visit of Aberdeen the following Saturday. Some may have thought it odd preparation for such a vital game, but Billy McNeill still sent a full-strength squad to East Anglia. Around 5,000 fans made the journey south to swell the crowd to a total of 15,267. Goals from the firing squad of George McCluskey, Charlie Nicholas and Frank McGarvey gave the Glasgow side a 3-2 win. Genial Bobby Robson, the Ipswich manager, said at the end, 'These Celtic fans are bloody marvellous.' Hunter was more expansive. 'Down here, they talk about Liverpool, but they are not in the same class as the fans from Glasgow. Celtic have the best support in the world.' His co-central defender might even have agreed at the time, a bloke called Terry Butcher.

It was a bitterly cold November day, the unforgiving wind whipping viciously around the east end of Glasgow, when the Dons provided the opposition, content in the knowledge they hadn't lost at Parkhead since March 1979. All good things must come to an end and, thankfully for Celtic, they did that afternoon. The opening goal in the thirty-ninth minute was pure genius. Tommy Burns and George McCluskey combined to set up Frank McGarvey. Jim Leighton, undoubtedly, expected the striker to try to put his laces through the ball, that being the norm for McGarvey. The frontman, though, sacrificed strength for subtlety to propel a cunning left-foot effort from eighteen yards curling over the stranded keeper.

Eighteen minutes from the end, Neale Cooper would undoubtedly incur the considerable wrath of his manager, Alex Ferguson, for trying to be too smart in a vulnerable part of the pitch. He hit a sloppy pass, McCluskey seized upon it, took a few steps and belted an unstoppable twenty-five yard drive beyond Leighton. That was the second and well-deserved goal for Celtic. Gordon Strachan got one back with virtually the last kick of the ball, but his celebration, unlike the one at Pittodrie earlier in the season, was somewhat muted.

A week later, the Ambling Alp that was Andy Ritchie, a player Jock Stein later conceded was allowed to leave Celtic too early, put his old mates to the sword again, remarkably from another penalty-kick award, as he gave Morton a point at Cappielow. There were no complaints from the visitors. Pat Bonner pulled down John McNeil, it was a definite spot-kick and Ritchie tucked it away with only one minute left to play. The Celtic fans in the 14,500 crowd weren't slow to show their displeasure when Billy McNeill took off Frank McGarvey and sent on Charlie Nicholas around the fiftieth-minute mark. They saw the wisdom of their manager's thinking when a fit and fresh Nicholas went on a run before setting up George McCluskey for Celtic's goal in the fifty-eighth minute.

McNeill smiled afterwards, 'Managers aren't in the job as a popularity contest. You have got to make the changes as you see them and I thought it was time to introduce another element to the game. Frank put in his usual shift, I would expect nothing less, but I thought Charlie might just add a wee bit more guile. Happily, he showed that when he set up George, but until then Morton had been keeping us out of their box and we were being restricted to long-range shooting. I thought we would get more of a reward working the ball in and about their penalty area.'

The manager and his players weren't to know it, but Celtic were to play only three more league games until the turn of the year as Arctic conditions gripped the country in an unbreakable icy grip. One of the contests that did beat the freeze, however, was the second Old Firm league game of the season and 48,600 fans were in for a real humdinger when Rangers came visiting on Saturday, November 21.

CHAPTER EIGHT
TITLE TIGHTROPE

Davie Moyes, at the age of eighteen, wasn't the least bit fazed when Billy McNeill informed him he would be playing against Rangers at Parkhead on November 21 1981. Moyes, with a mere eleven first team starts behind him, assured the Celtic manager he was more than ready for the rigours of his baptism against Celtic's Glasgow rivals. His father, a Rangers scout, would be in the Parkhead stand that afternoon.

Winter's chill was invading the country; temperatures plummeted, cold winds shrieked, dark clouds gathered. But there were fireworks in a quite remarkable Glasgow derby, which left 48,600 fans spellbound and breathless after astonishing excitement. It was a game that see-sawed wildly and erratically throughout a pulsating ninety minutes. By the time the storm had blown itself out, six goals had been shared and Moyes, fairly dramatically for a teenager deputising for the injured Danny McGrain, had been involved in all of Celtic's three efforts.

Rangers, after being played off the park at their place in September, congratulated themselves on a point well won in the 3-3 draw at Celtic Park. It would be churlish to take anything away from the effort and endeavour served up by John Greig's side that afternoon. Mainly, they were playing for pride because any thoughts of a championship victory at the season's finale wouldn't have looked out of place in a fairy tale. They had won only five of their previous twelve league games and had lost to Partick Thistle (0-2) and Dundee United (0-2) as well as their Parkhead rivals by the same scoreline. They had also carelessly shed points in stalemates against Hibs (2-2), St Mirren (1-1), Aberdeen (0-0) and Morton (1-1).

And they couldn't have thought it was going to be their day at the home of their ancient foes when Tom McAdam opened the scoring in the third minute. Peter McCloy, in fact, had defied Celtic only moments earlier when he made a smart save from an effort from Dom Sullivan. That merely stalled the misery for the Ibrox men. Davie Provan swung in a corner-kick and new boy Moyes rose to head flick across goal. McAdam read the move superbly and was on duty in the right place to score. He wasn't picked up by the Rangers defence and couldn't miss from eight yards.

The Celtic end rose as one to acclaim the astute piece of play with some hard work on the training ground paying dividends. However, a silence swiftly descended only two minutes later when the Ibrox side levelled and, suddenly, it was the Rangers end's turn to celebrate. John McDonald picked out Derek Johnstone with a long crossball and he got up well to nod a pass into the path of Gordon Dalziel, who, like Moyes, was making his Glasgow derby debut. He was practically on his hands and knees, but he still managed to get his head to the ball to nudge it over the line. Five minutes played, two goals scored. What next?

Frank McGarvey provided the answer in the tenth minute when McNeill's men retaliated in the expected, time-honoured fashion. Provan carved open the Rangers left side with a searing pass to the sprinting Moyes on the right touchline. The defender took the ball in his stride before pitching over a deep cross into the Rangers box where it was met by McGarvey and his impeccable header looped over the frantic McCloy and into the net. Surely, Celtic wouldn't allow they opponents the opportunity to get back into the contest? Amazingly, by the twenty-first minute, Greig's men were 3-2 ahead.

Firstly, Dalziel picked out Jim Bett at the far post and his header swept beyond Bonner. Sixty seconds later it was bedlam in the Rangers end of the ground when McDonald scrambled in another from close range after the home defenders decided to take a nap. Billy McNeill admitted to being more than a little puzzled at the interval break. 'I thought we were playing well enough, but, unfortunately, Rangers looked like scoring any time they got into our box. I think they had three attempts on our goal in the first forty-five minutes and all three had ended in the net. I had to sort that out. On the plus side, I thought the midfield was doing well enough going forward, but I told them to remember their defensive responsibilities, too. Frank McGarvey and George McCluskey were playing well together in attack. I had every confidence we would score again.'

Six minutes into the second period, McNeill was proved right. Provan, once more, was the architect with a wonderfully precise corner-kick. Moyes challenged Johnstone and Colin Jackson in the air before knocking it down to Murdo MacLeod who thundered a drive of awesome power past McCloy. This was a meeting of the world's biggest rivals, often tagged the greatest derby of the lot and this one lived up to it. Importantly, too, it was played in good spirit. There were only two bookings - Rangers' Johnstone and Jackson - and, all things considered, that was more than acceptable. The main thing is those who witnessed the action actually talked about the football. There were no sideshows at the end of this derby.

Celtic actually won some silverware before their next match against Partick Thistle at Firhill the following Saturday. The Hoops picked up the Daily Express Five-a-Sides trophy at the Wembley Arena in midweek. They beat strong opposition in Watford (3-0), Ipswich Town (3-0), Manchester United (3-1) and Southampton (1-0) in the Final. The Celtic squad was Peter Latchford, Willie McStay, Danny Crainie, Charlie Nicholas, John Weir and Willie Garner. Maybe the bungling centre-half had discovered his forte. Still, not too many players can say they only played three first team games for the club, lost the lot and still picked up a winner's medal. Sounds like a good pub quiz question!

Once again, Jack Frost was doing his treacherous best to make the pitch virtually unplayable, but the game against Thistle still went ahead on November 28. Twelve thousand brave souls ventured out to watch the action and the Celtic fans were repaid with a solid, if unspectacular, 2-0 victory. George McCluskey got the opener in the twenty-fourth minute when he took a throw-in on his chest, shuffled his feet Muhammad Ali-style and then unleashed a twenty-five yard belter that Alan Rough barely saw. It was all over just before the hour mark when snake-hipped Davie Provan cut inside and fired low into the net. The Jags had their best effort near the end from a young red-haired darting imp of a striker. The unknown teenager turned and thumped in a ferocious effort, but Pat Bonner pulled off a fine save. The headlines would have to wait for Maurice Johnston.

The final league game of 1981 went ahead at Celtic Park on December 5 with an Arctic winter making its unwanted presence felt. Dundee promised to come and attack while looking for two points that would help them in their survival battle alongside Morton, Airdrie and Partick Thistle. It may have been their intention to take the game to Pat Bonner, but it didn't quite work out like that and they were trailing by three goals by the time Eric Sinclair netted a minute from the end. The game failed to catch fire in the first-half - hardly surprising considering the chilly surroundings - but Frank McGarvey got the ball rolling with the opener in the fifty-ninth minute and two goals in the final six minutes meant Billy McNeill's men would see out the year with a win. McGarvey scored again in the eighty-fourth minute only moments after Mike Conroy had claimed one with a vicious effort.

Celtic Park wouldn't see another league match until February 2 as games throughout the country were called off on a weekly basis. In quick succession, Celtic's matches against St Mirren, Dundee United, Hibs and Airdrie were wiped out by the weather. However, one fixture that got the go-ahead was the third Old Firm encounter of the campaign at Ibrox on January 9. Rangers' newly-installed undersoil heating had been operating at full-blast for forty-eight hours to ensure the playing surface was in reasonable shape for the 3pm kick-off.

Celtic had last played a competitive game on December 5 while Rangers were fortunate enough to have played fourteen days after that courtesy of their heating system when they beat Dundee 2-1 in Glasgow. Undoubtedly, they had the edge in match fitness and it showed only a few minutes into the game. The enforced inactivity hadn't sharpened George McCluskey's reflexes and he missed a sitter when he thumped a wayward drive into the side netting from close range. There can be no guarantee the Celtic striker would have scored a month earlier, but he would have been expected to hit the target, at least.

Celtic toiled after their month in hibernation and they paid the price when Rangers snatched the only goal of the game in the seventy-second minute. Pat Bonner pulled down Davie Cooper as he waltzed into the box and referee Brian McGinlay, correctly on this occasion, awarded a penalty-kick. Jim Bett tucked the ball into the right hand corner and the Parkhead men hadn't quite got off to the start they hoped in 1982. McNeill was philosophical. 'We can play a lot better than that as we have already proved this season.'

On January 16, on an extremely dodgy pitch, Charlie Nicholas suffered a broken leg in a meaningless reserve game against Morton. Billy McNeill made a startling confession. 'I criticised myself for playing him in that match at Cappielow. He had gone off form and I fielded him in tricky conditions to try to keep his form up. He broke a leg in an accidental collision with Joe McLaughlin. I saw another side of Charlie after that. He had come into the team and was the most prominent among the several youngsters whom we tried. He gave us confirmation that what we were trying at grassroots level was right and would be important to the club. Charlie was my first real chance to bring in an especially talented youngster. I could be accused of being that little bit slow in giving him his chance, but the truth is I recognised an outstanding talent and worried about the best time to introduce him.

'But Charlie possessed a tough streak and that showed after the leg-break. The injury was potentially serious and such a blow might have proved too much for some young players, but Charlie worked hard to regain his fitness and he returned fitter and stronger. That said everything about the lad.'

A week after Nicholas' accident, the Parkhead pitch was passed playable for the Scottish Cup visit of Queen of the South, but one end of the ground had to be closed because of burst pipes with the water quickly freezing over. Still, a crowd of 11,281 - with the princely gate receipts of £13,640 - watched Celtic stroll into the next round, winning 4-0. The biggest cheer of the day was reserved for the second goal scored by Danny McGrain. It was his first strike to hit the net in almost three years and it wasn't quite Tommy Gemmellesque, but he still lapped up the applause. His left-foot effort actually took a nick off a Palmerston defender on its way past keeper Alan Ball, but no-one was going to deny the Celtic skipper his glory moment. Frank McGarvey, George McCluskey, with a penalty-kick, and debut boy John Halpin notched the others.

Celtic brought the curtain down on the first month of the new year with a storming, well-merited 3-1 win over Aberdeen at Pittodrie. Again, Billy McNeill watched his side do it the hard way. They had lost a goal to the Dons in two minutes in their previous meeting. This time they conceded one inside sixty seconds. John McMaster set up John Hewitt who steered an effort wide of Pat Bonner. Hewitt was later signed by McNeill for Celtic in 1989 and made twenty-one appearances in three seasons. He didn't score a solitary goal.

His strike was the signal for Celtic to pile forward and Frank McGarvey had what one newspaper reporter noted as 'the sitter of his career' when he mis-kicked from two yards with Jim Leighton out of position. McNeill must have wondered if Dame Fortune was snarling on them when Murdo MacLeod pulverised a drive against a post and, shortly afterwards, George McCluskey did likewise with a free-kick. However, just before the interval Doug Rougvie, blessed with the subtlety of a train wreck and already booked for a foul on McCluskey, barged McGarvey in the back and referee Bob Valentine pointed to the spot.

McCluskey blasted in a ferocious effort.

Celtic were going for the win and MacLeod pointed them in the right direction with a free-kick special in the seventy-first minute. Paul McStay, only seventeen years old, emphasised his emerging potential by netting the third in the seventy-seventh minute. The gifted midfielder was almost nonchalant as he accepted a free-kick on the left, wandered through a couple of challenges and then flighted the ball high past Leighton. McNeill observed, 'That could prove to be a very important win come the end of the season. I was happy for everyone, but especially young Paul. He's a top prospect.'

Bertie Auld, after being enticed from Partick Thistle, brought Hibs to Glasgow on February 2 for Celtic's first league game at home in eight weeks. It was hardly a sensational homecoming. The Easter Road side, with relentlessly defensive efficiency, carved out a goalless draw in front of a crowd of 16,700 who were hoping for so much better. It could have been worse. With only eight minutes to go, Arthur Duncan, the Edinburgh team's speed merchant winger, was sent clear on a one-on-one situation with Pat Bonner. Thankfully, the young Irishman kept his nerve and saved at the feet of his rival.

It was Celtic's fourth draw of the season. Along with the previous twelve wins, McNeill's men were sitting on top of the table with twenty-eight points. Rangers, who had looked out of it at one stage, were dangerously close only five points adrift having played the same amount of games. Four days later, Murdo MacLeod was the star performer as Celtic won 3-1 at Dundee. The bitter eastern wind couldn't blow the gritty midfielder off course as he scored in each half while Frank McGarvey chipped in with another. Albert Kidd scored his side's late consolation counter. His goal wasn't quite greeted with the enthusiasm of the travelling support the way two efforts against Hearts would be acclaimed on a sunny afternoon on Tayside on May 3 1986.

Billy McNeill was delighted with his side's professional performance. 'I thought Murdo MacLeod was wonderful and he took his goals exceptionally well. Paul McStay impressed again. The kid showed a lot of class and style and I think I'll be right in saying he is set for a great future at this club.'

The feelgood factor hit the buffers as Celtic's Scottish Cup ambitions were buried at Pittodrie the following Saturday. Celtic hadn't qualified from their League Cup section, had gone out of the European Cup in the First Round and were now sent packing in the national cup competition at the second hurdle. Alex Ferguson had planned well for this tie and sprung a surprise by playing centre-half Alex McLeish in midfield. He wanted to take control in the middle of the park which his team had surrendered against Dom Sullivan, Tommy Burns, Murdo MacLeod and Paul McStay in the previous league game a fortnight earlier.

The aggressive McLeish, allied with the tenacious Neil Simpson, made certain Celtic would not luxuriate in possession in the midfield. It worked when John Hewitt got the only goal of a tense encounter in the nineteenth minute. Peter Weir curled in a left-wing corner-kick and McLeish charged in to challenge. In the ensuing melee of penalty box panic, the ball dropped nicely for Hewitt to hook over his shoulder and away from Pat Bonner. McNeill threw Roy Aitken into the midfield for the start of the second-half, but it didn't alter the scoreline. The nearest they came was when an effort from Tom McAdam came back off the woodwork. There was a nice touch from the Celtic manager as he congratulated some of his former Dons players at the end. He told them, 'Now go and win the Cup.' They duly walloped Rangers 4-1 in the Final.

Celtic were fifteen minutes away from a sensational 2-0 defeat from Partick Thistle at Celtic Park a week later. This was a Maryhill team fighting for survival in the Premier League and had just beaten Rangers 2-0 in midweek, the second time they had turned over the Ibrox side that season. All to no avail, alas, as they went down along with Airdrie at the end of the day. But against Celtic, they still believed they had a chance to remain in the elite. Midfielder Ian Jardine silenced the home fans in the 14,200 crowd with a twenty-yard free-kick that sizzled low into the corner in the fifty-second minute.

Maurice Johnston was the target for the wrath of the Celtic fans in the seventy-second minute when he appeared to go down far too easily after a challenge from Tom McAdam. Referee Willie Knowles bought it, gave the penalty-kick and Kenny Watson blitzed a powerful effort into the net. The player's antics, the award and the goal were met with howls of derision by the supporters. It was a sound that would avalanche around the ears of Johnston later that decade from the same set of fans.

Celtic's response was instantaneous as they netted twice in two minutes. George McCluskey blasted an exquisite low drive away from Alan Rough in seventy-five minutes and he set up the equaliser for Roy Aitken when he rounded the keeper and lobbed in a delightful cross for his team-mate to apply the finishing touch. Celtic, with thirteen minutes left to play, went for the winner, but the well-drilled Jags held out, mainly due to some heroics from the agile Rough.

Around this time, Hearts publicly applauded Celtic for their stance on £20,000 that was still owed on the summer transfer of Roddie MacDonald. The winter wipe-out obviously affected the finances of the Tynecastle outfit and they couldn't meet their financial commitment. They also owed money to Dundee United for the transfer of striker Willie Pettigrew and the Tannadice side were still pushing for a prompt payment. Celtic chairman Desmond White said, 'In view of these circumstances, we prefer to be a little bit generous in our dealings in these matters.' Billy McNeill must have been in urgent requirement of smelling salts when he heard those words from his thrifty chairman. For his part, Wallace Mercer, Hearts' vice-chairman, went on record. 'I am very embarrassed over the Dundee United situation and very grateful for the understanding attitude of Celtic Football Club.'

So, praise off the field, but little to earn a cheer on it as Celtic toppled to a 1-0 defeat from Hibs at Easter Road on February 27. Out of the Scottish Cup, a point shed against a team heading for relegation and now a loss against a mid-table Edinburgh outfit. Celtic were in danger of finishing the campaign with nothing to show for their efforts. If that had been the case they would have had no-one to blame but themselves. They just didn't turn up on this occasion. Gavin Rae scored with an eighteenth minute header and an out-of-sorts Celtic couldn't respond. Forwards Frank McGarvey and George McCluskey were starved of service in one of the team's worst performances of the campaign.

Celtic were toiling badly with the finishing tape in sight. They were the long-distance runner who had led from the start and now looked as though he had no energy left to get him to the first prize. Only 9,000 braved the vile elements for the game against Morton on Wednesday March 3, the abominable weather conditions driving people indoors. It was the smallest home crowd of the season and the lack of atmosphere did little to raise the tempo of a jaded-looking collection of players.

Billy McNeill could only wince on the touchline as his team squandered two penalty-kicks against a Greenock side who could only offer hard work as resistance. That commodity was enough to knock this Celtic side off its stride. Referee Kenny Hope awarded the home side their first spot-kick in the twenty-seventh minute and George McCluskey had the opportunity to soothe the nervous tension on and off the park. He recklessly and wastefully blasted over the bar from twelve yards.

Eight minutes from the end, there was a reprieve for Celtic and a second chance for someone to show their penalty-taking expertise. Frank McGarvey stepped up this time and could only look on in horror as Roy Baines dived to save his badly-placed attempt. Luck was on his side, though, as the ball came bouncing back off the keeper straight into his path and, on this occasion, the striker simply toed the ball into the inviting net. Former Celt Jim Duffy - Charlie Nicholas' best mate - was his team's villain on both counts when he downed McCluskey for the first award and Tommy Burns for the second. Conspiracy theories, anyone? Don't go there. Duffy came close to an instant dismissal with his vehement protests after the second award. If he was acting, Robert De Niro has a rival.

Ten days later Celtic rediscovered their goalscoring touch against

St Mirren at a windswept Love Street. Once again, master blaster Murdo MacLeod stepped up to be counted with two excellent strikes. He propelled Celtic in the right direction with a vicious volley in the seventeenth minute and had a shot blocked on the half-hour mark that rebounded for Tommy Burns to knock beyond Billy Thomson. Seven minutes later, Frank McGarvey crossed for Dom Sullivan to score the third and a minute from the interval George McCluskey got on the end of a Burns through ball to notch No 4. It had taken Celtic twenty-seven minutes to score four goals - a feat that was beyond them in the last four games put together. Go figure.

Frank McDougall, a self-confessed Celtic fan who appeared to take inordinate joy in scoring against his schoolboy heroes, pulled one back with a diving header shortly after the interval. Normal service was resumed when MacLeod whacked a fifth past Billy Thomson. McDougall completed the scoring with another header from an Ian Scanlon corner-kick. Billy McNeill was reasonably satisfied. 'We needed the win and 5-2 on the road is fairly acceptable. Hopefully, we can continue to build on this because, as everyone is well aware, we're getting to the time of the season when the prizes are being given out.'

Airdrie's dependency on the application of the physical in their outlook received its reward with relegation at the end of the season and Celtic helped them on their way with a 2-0 win in Glasgow on March 20. It wasn't a memorable performance from the champions who had Airdrie keeper John Martin, still proclaiming his love for all things Rangers, to thank for the opening goal in the twenty-first minute. He half-cleared a McGarvey cross and Sullivan pounced to score. Two minutes from the interval, Burns played a neat one-two with MacLeod and, as Martin raced from his line, casually lifted the ball over his head for Celtic's fiftieth league goal of the season.

Alex Ferguson's team were heavily committed to rearguard action when they arrived at Celtic Park on March 27. It was do-or-die for the Dons. Their manager knew they could not afford to lose, but he wasn't going to throw caution to the wind as he set out his team to search for a winner. The defence was so well organised to make it virtually impenetrable that one punter commented, 'Score a goal against that lot? It would be easier to get an each way bet on the Cambridge/Oxford Boat race.' Point taken. Or, more accurately, two points taken as far as Aberdeen were concerned.

There were two moments that turned the game around. The only goal of a dour contest and yet another botched penalty-kick from Celtic. Both teams were cancelling each other out until twenty-two minutes from time when Stuart Kennedy joined the attack. It took the right-back seven years to score eight goals for the Dons. One of that meagre total came at Parkhead and silenced the bulk of the 30,080 fans who witnessed it. Kennedy looked as though he was trying to pitch over a cross, but the ball spun crazily off his left foot, up into the air and caught Pat Bonner off his line. The ball sailed serenely into the net and Kennedy had the good grace to look ever so slightly embarrassed.

Not as red faced, though, as George McCluskey when he was presented with a penalty-kick with only a few minutes to go. Willie Miller was deemed by referee Douglas Ramsay to have pushed Frank McGarvey and McCluskey, at long last, could see the whites of Jim Leighton's eyes. Unfortunately, he could also see his knobbly knees and his thumping drive zeroed in on that part of the keeper's anatomy. The ball bounced away at a bizarre angle. Ferguson danced a jig on the touchline while McNeill buried his head in his hands. He had just watched the repeat of a horror show that had blighted his team all season; the complete inefficiency of players, totally unhindered, to score from twelve yards. He realised it could prove to be an exceptionally costly miss.

All eyes turned to Tannadice the following Wednesday where it was abundantly clear that Celtic could not afford to drop any points against the ever-dangerous Dundee United. Two goals from Tommy Burns fired Celtic to a deserved 2-0 victory in a bad-tempered affair. It was another win at a cost, though, with Frank McGarvey being helped off with a broken ankle after an accidental collision with goalkeeper Hamish McAlpine. McNeill groaned. First Charlie Nicholas, now Frank

McGarvey. His firing squad was being depleted just when he needed them most.

That was evident when Celtic travelled to Greenock on the Saturday to face a Morton team that had lost only twice at Cappielow all season. Teenager Danny Crainie was elevated to the first team and he scored his first goal for the club two minutes from the interval. Another point, though, was blowing in the wind when Andy Ritchie equalised in the fifty-third minute. It ended 1-1 and there was no time to draw breath with this game being the first of six Celtic faced in the space of twenty-one days as clubs throughout the land struggled to wade through the backlog of fixtures courtesy of a vicious winter.

Billy McNeill had to set out his team for the final Old Firm confrontation of the campaign without injured forwards Charlie Nicholas, Frank McGarvey and George McCluskey, the strike trio with sixty-eight goals among them. McNeill found himself with a gun largely firing blanks. For days, he pondered his final line-up. 'If you lose one player from a part of your team, that's bad enough. Losing three prolific goalscorers all at one time is unheard of. You can't help wondering if fates are turning against you in such circumstances.'

McNeill's solution to his lack of firepower was quite drastic - Tom McAdam was asked to lead the line for the first time since April 1979. Three years beforehand, McNeill had converted him into a more than reliable centre-half. Now he was asking him to go out and score goals against Rangers. Celtic were the walking wounded that day as Danny McGrain, Davie Provan and Tommy Burns were carrying injuries as they stepped onto a fiery pitch that was bare in places; evidence of a savage winter.

It was a day for the brave. Danny Crainie was making his Old Firm debut and, after only ninety seconds, he was dancing with delight in front of 49,144 fans, one half of the ground singing, the other half silent. Tommy Burns started the move with a delightful pass inside left-back Ally Dawson for Dom Sullivan, who was racing clear. He zipped one into the crowded penalty box, keeper Jim Stewart didn't collect properly and Crainie was in like a flash as the ball squirmed from his grasp.

It got better for Celtic five minutes after the interval and the goal was a scriptwriter's dream. Tom McAdam, the striker-cum-defender-cum-striker, got what proved to be the winner with a header at the back post. Rangers' rugged Northern Ireland international defender John McClelland went in 'like a can-can dancer', according to one newspaper report, as he needlessly fouled Crainie. Burns picked out McAdam with a cunning free-kick and Stewart was helpless.

There was a rally from Rangers and Derek Johnstone scored with a fierce volley fifteen minutes from the end, but there was no way back for the Ibrox club. How they must have hated the sight of Tom McAdam. The versatile performer only scored four goals all season - and three of them were against Rangers.

The following Wednesday, Celtic decimated doomed Airdrie 5-1 at Broomfield. The highlight of the performance was George McCluskey's goal - Celtic's third - in the fifty-sixth minute. He collected the ball just over the halfway line and hared towards John Martin. He swept past George Anderson and, without breaking stride, sent a raging twenty-five yard drive zooming into the net. Roy Aitken, Danny Crainie and Davie Provan also weighed in before a penalty was awarded near the end. After recent failures from McCluskey and McGarvey, Billy McNeill gave the task to young left-back Mark Reid. He fairly belted the effort into the net via the underside of the crossbar. If it had been a couple of inches higher, it might have clattered off the woodwork and rebounded all the way to Coatbridge. Airdrie were also awarded a spot-kick, converted by Sandy Clark to make the final scoreline an emphatic 5-1 for the visitors.

Celtic had to sustain the momentum and three days later Dundee, who had beaten Rangers in midweek, were the guests in the east end of Glasgow. Once more, Billy McNeill's men failed to convince for almost an hour. They were trailing to a simple headed goal from Jim Smith after the defence had failed to deal with a straight-forward corner-kick. The

Dundee player struck in the third minute and the 14,288 fans hoped for a swift reaction. It took an agonising wait until the fifty-seventh minute before their favourites levelled. Referee Kenny Hope awarded a spot-kick and Mark Reid kept up his one hundred per cent record by blasting past the keeper. Ten minutes later George McCluskey scored again to ease the tension. Davie Provan struck the third in the seventy-seventh minute, but Iain Ferguson pulled one back sixty seconds later. McCluskey finally settled things seven minutes from time. Four goals, two vital points, but McNeill knew his men could do so much better.

The biggest cheer of the day came when it was announced Aberdeen had lost 2-1 to a late goal against Morton at Cappielow. The signs were looking good.

Three days later, on a crisp evening at Parkhead, the troublesome Dundee United again provided the opposition. They provoked a far better reaction from the home side and McCluskey scored in each half while Provan claimed another with one of his trademark 'Brazilian free-kicks' - as they were now known - while Davie Dodds gave the side some comfort with a late goal in the 3-1 loss in front of 14,000 fairly satisfied fans.

Danny Crainie, displaying so much promise and potential, took centre stage when Celtic travelled across Glasgow to take on Partick Thistle at Firhill. McNeill's men won 3-0 in front of 18,000 spectators, but, to be fair, this was far from the one-sided affair the scoreline would suggest. The Maryhill side were desperately unlucky when the game was still scoreless. Kenny Watson hit the bar with Pat Bonner helpless and, shortly afterwards, Alex O'Hara struck a post. Celtic were riding their luck, but Crainie cracked the first past Alan Rough seven minutes after the turnaround to soothe the nerves of his more experienced colleagues. The livewire striker notched a second in the seventy-fifth minute and completed his first hat-trick for the club four minutes from time.

Billy McNeill's take on the game went along these lines, 'We knew we would have to earn everything between now and the end of the season.

Certainly, that was the case against Thistle. Yes, the final score may flatter us, but it is to our credit that we managed to overcome our poor form in the first-half.'

Privately, the Celtic manager would have been delighted. His team only required four points from their remaining four fixtures to retain their championship. A week later, the prerequisite total for looking out the champagne was cut to two. Celtic ran amok against Hibs, scorching their way to a 6-0 runaway victory. Bertie Auld's team was so inept, one newspaper reporter likened the contest to 'a group of Boy Scouts versus the SAS.' That's one way of putting it, I suppose. Tommy Burns got the show on the road with a memorable effort in the fourteenth minute. Davie Provan provided the pass and Burns added the sprinkling of stardust. The svelte midfielder was composure personified as he struck a twenty-five yard effort. Goalkeeper Jim McArthur afforded it the ultimate compliment by not even attempting to keep the ball out of the net. In an instant, he knew it was a goal as soon as it left Burns' boot.

McNeill watched contentedly from the touchline as his team swept Hibs away with some fabulous and pacy inter-passing as they swarmed forward into the danger zone. Three goals in just over twenty minutes sealed the points; Danny Crainie, Roy Aitken and Murdo MacLeod on target. It remained one-way traffic after the break, but Celtic settled for only two more goals, MacLeod and George McCluskey adding to the total. There was a huge roar from the 16,064 attendance, but, bizarrely, it was to salute a near miss. Danny McGrain, celebrating his thirty-second birthday, attempted to complete a wonderful afternoon with a cheeky back-header. The ball flicked over McArthur, once again striking an admiring pose, but the effort came back off the crossbar. Well, you can't have everything. One thing was certain, though, Celtic's points stipulation for the title had just been halved. What could go wrong?

Next up were St Mirren, the shock squad from nine months ago in the League Cup opener when Willie Garner still thought he had a future as a Celtic player. Billy McNeill's side had scored thirteen goals against the Paisley side in four games and realised the requirement on the May 1 Bank Holiday Monday meeting was just one goal while conceding none and the championship flag would be flying over the east end of Glasgow for a second successive season. A crowd of 27,395 rolled into Paradise fully in preparation of much signing and dancing. The wind and rain couldn't dampen their party spirits.

Celtic were also searching for their one hundredth goal of the campaign and were aiming to clinch the title in some style. Alas, stubborn Saints weren't reading from the same script, especially Billy Thomson. The goalkeeper was immense and the players in front of him, particularly central defenders Jackie Copland and Mark Fulton, were in no mood to be mere cannon fodder for the champions elect. Yet, Celtic started in a frenzy and looked as though they wanted to settle matters before the interval as they had done the previous week with Hibs.

Unfortunately, it turned out to be a frustrating day for the Celtic attack, particularly George McCluskey, so often the hero, but the main culprit on this occasion. The striker was wayward in his final attempts, his precision deserting him in his hour-and-a-half of need. And when he did manage to get something on target, Thomson, agile and reliable, was there to deal with the threat. It ended goalless and the champagne was put back on ice.

Billy McNeill wasn't quite pulling his hair out by the roots. He said, 'I wasn't displeased with the way we played. But we did allow frustration to take over after we had missed so many chances from a lot of excellent openings.'

Celtic now had two games in which to earn the crucial point. They were due to travel to Tannadice to lock horns once again with Dundee United on May 8 in the knowledge Aberdeen had just beaten St Mirren 5-1 at Pittodrie. That, in fact, was the Dons' sixth successive triumph as Alex Ferguson galvanised his troops as only he could after their nosedive against Morton on April 17. In rapid succession, the Pittodrie outfit had seen off Rangers (3-1), Airdrie (2-0), Dundee (5-0), Partick Thistle (3-1) and Dundee United (2-1) as well as taking five goals off St Mirren. They were due to meet the Paisley side again in the midweek at Love Street after Celtic's Saturday encounter on Tayside. It had been a magnificent effort from Fergie's side, but you had to ask if it was going to be a gallant failure. Celtic had the answer to that one. The Dons' final two games against St Mirren and Rangers would be rendered meaningless if the Hoops did the business at Tannadice.

The champagne, still on ice in the hamper, was heading back to Glasgow after a dreadful display against Dundee United, which wasn't helped by George McCluskey and Dom Sullivan limping off after taking some pulverising punishment from Jim McLean's men. Paul McStay and Davie Moyes replaced their injured colleagues in a bitter, bruising battle. A crowd of 16,779 watched the home side work their way to a 3-0 win. Celtic just didn't get to grips with their determined opponents on a day to forget. The defence had been conceding too many goals from corner-kicks to satisfy Billy McNeill and they lost another in eighteen minutes against United. Ralph Milne sent in an arcing effort, the defence was slow to pick up Paul Hegarty and he headed past Pat Bonner.

Murdo MacLeod hit the post just after the half-hour mark with a typical effort, but the game was slipping away from Celtic a minute after half-time when the nippy Paul Sturrock tried a shot from just inside the box. His effort looked like going wide, but it swerved slightly, hit the inside of the upright and rolled into the net. It wasn't going to be Celtic's day and that was underlined ten minutes from the end when Milne, a player who possessed blistering pace, raced through the defence to crack a third from eighteen yards past Bonner, who would have been forgiven for wondering if his team-mates were taking this match seriously.

Four days later, Aberdeen won 2-0 at Love Street with goals from defenders Doug Rougvie and Alex McLeish and the title was taken to the wire. Celtic needed to avoid defeat against St Mirren on May 15 and Aberdeen were required to win by a five-goal margin against Rangers. But that is where we came in. Billy McNeill's men won 3-0, Alex Ferguson's side triumphed 4-0 and the championship remained at

Celtic Park. The club may have stuttered a bit on the run-in - and there can be little doubt the serious injuries suffered by Frank McGarvey and Charlie Nicholas did upset the attacking flow of the team - but, in the end, the Premier League table showed they had played thirty-six games, won twenty-four, drawn seven and lost five. They scored seventy-nine goals while conceding thirty-three and had amassed fifty-five points, two more than Aberdeen. Celtic also had a superior goal difference of plus forty-six to the Dons' plus forty-two. Rangers were third twelve points adrift and Dundee United completed the campaign on forty.

No-one could argue the merits of Celtic's right to be crowned kings for a second consecutive season. It may also be worth noting that, quietly and away from the glare of the spotlight, the club actually won another piece of silverware, the Glasgow Cup. They contested the Final of this old trophy against Rangers at Ibrox on May 13. Billy McNeill fielded a young side with players such as John McGoldrick, Jim McInally, John Buckley, Ronnie Coyle and Jim Dobbin in the line-up. However, John Greig was clearly desperate to win the trophy and played experienced campaigners such as Peter McCloy, Tom Forsyth, Alex Miller and Tommy McLean against the Hoops rookies. He even put Davie Cooper on the subs' bench in case of emergencies.

The Celtic kids won 2-1 with goals from John Halpin and Paul McGugan. Rangers had to rely on an unusual source for their solitary effort. Alas, it was supplied by Willie Garner, sticking the ball past Peter Latchford in the seventy-second minute to level the scores before McGugan got the winner in the fading moments. Well, at least, Garner had added another medal to his collection along with his Five-a-Sides gong won earlier in the season. He could now tell his grandchildren he had prized mementoes to remind him of his brief spell at Celtic.

We do like a happy ending.

CHAPTER NINE
TROUBLE IN
PARADISE

It wasn't quite a 'back me or sack me' ultimatum, but Billy McNeill's very public pre-season proclamation emphasised the disturbing rift between the football manager and his obstinate chairman Desmond White and the inflexible Celtic board of directors. The bond between McNeill and the mulish powers-that-be was deteriorating at an alarming rate; animosity was tangible in a small, but important, corner of the east end of Glasgow.

Behind the scenes, the warm glow of a championship-winning campaign was already beginning to chill; there was the distinct pall of pollution in Paradise. According to McNeill, the board wanted to remove John Clark as his assistant. McNeill reacted to what amounted to something more than a mere request. 'At a meeting, Mr White said he wanted me to sack John Clark and appoint Frank Connor, who later got the job under Davie Hay. I had nothing against Frank and, having worked with him previously, knew his capabilities and his love of Celtic. I do, however, believe that a manager should be the judge of his working assistant.

'I asked for time to think, but my immediate reaction was to say no. I had a week's holiday in the west coast of Scotland which gave me the chance to ponder the whole scenario quietly. I decided that it was important for me to retain the right to appoint an assistant. So, I declined to do what I had been asked. I warned John what had been going on and he was naturally very upset.'

Celtic's jubilant supporters on Saturday, September 4, a fine, clear autumnal afternoon at Parkhead, were not aware that such friction had developed behind the doors of their cherished club. Their manager had revealed he had wanted to strengthen the squad during the summer break, but money had not been made available, despite a second successive title success. McNeill had brought in only one player - utility defender Graeme Sinclair at the cost of £60,000 from Dumbarton. The transfer, with all due respect, didn't exactly trigger a stampede at the turnstiles.

But on the opening day of the new Premier League season, all was sweetness and light as Liz McNeill, the manager's wife, unfurled the championship flag. At that precise moment, it would have been preposterous to even contemplate the campaign ending in bitter acrimony and savage mud-slinging. It was also well beyond the bounds of comprehension that McNeill would leave the club.

As the flag fluttered in the slight breeze, the Celtic players took a bow in front of a crowd of 19,122 and then set about kicking off their quest for points for the new season. New signing Sinclair was on the subs' bench. Dundee provided the opposition and the game, effectively, was over before the first-half was complete. It took the champions just over half-an-hour to open the scoring and the supporters must have thought they were watching an action replay of last season. George McCluskey shimmied past two defenders, slid a pass in front of Davie Provan and the winger rolled the ball wide of keeper Colin Kelly. It was the sort of neat, along-the-ground passing that had become synonymous with the team.

Four minutes from the interval, Provan, in tantalising form, tricked and teased his way past two tackles before setting up Roy Aitken with a precision pass. Aitken walloped the ball from ten yards with hammer-like force. Provan was graceful as he strolled around creating havoc, but the player who had entranced the watching support even more was eighteen-year-old Paul McStay. Such was his extraordinary vision, flawless passing, impeccable movement and exquisite judgement, it was obvious he would become a permanent fixture in the team. During the previous term, his manager had carefully chosen his appearances based on the opposition. That was no longer the case. Paul McStay had arrived and he was to remain in place for a further fifteen years.

Billy McNeill might have been in the mood to say, 'I told you so' to Desmond White and the board at Love Street the following midweek. Lex Richardson, the player he wanted to buy from St Mirren for £100,000 the previous year, had just put the champions under pressure with a screamer of a goal from twenty yards to give the Paisley side the advantage after only twelve minutes. Celtic toiled to get back on level terms, but they managed it via the penalty spot in sixty-four minutes. Charlie Nicholas tumbled under a challenge from defender Tom Wilson and got the benefit of the doubt from referee Kenny Hope. Nicholas dusted himself down before dispatching an unsaveable drive into the roof of the net. Remarkably, the charismatic striker got the opportunity to display his skills from twelve yards once more three minutes from the end. This time there was no argument about the worthiness of the award, John McCormack clearly handled a shot from Danny Crainie. Nicholas stepped back, tugged at the waistband of his shorts, moved forward and sent another shot into the net.

A few days later, Nicholas was unstoppable as he destroyed Motherwell at Fir Park. Celtic cantered to a 7-0 victory and cheeky Charlie claimed a hat-trick, his three goals coming after a devastating display of penalty box prowess. The home side had former Rangers manager Jock Wallace in the dug-out for his first appearance in front of the Celtic support since quitting Ibrox for Leicester City four years earlier. Ex-Celts Johannes Edvaldsson and Alfie Conn were in the Motherwell line-up. They must have wished they were still in green-and-white hoops after being swept aside by a Hoops hurricane.

Nicholas got the opener in the twenty-sixth minute and added two more in the final half-hour. In between, Frank McGarvey, Murdo MacLeod and Roy Aitken, with two, also made life a misery for Hugh Sproat, the rather eccentric Motherwell goalkeeper who attempted to antagonise Celtic by wearing a blue jersey while playing against them and, in turn, sporting a green top when he faced Rangers. Had he chosen to wear a red top against Nicholas and Co it would have matched the colour of his face at the end.

Long before the final whistle, the Celtic fans were in full throttle. 'Wallace for Rangers,' they sang in gleeful unison. At the end of the seven-goal embarrassment, Wallace didn't hide behind any gobbledygook phraseology attempting to justify the defeat. 'We were slaughtered,' was his considered opinion.

The sparkling early season form of Charlie Nicholas and Paul McStay had, inevitably, attracted the attention of clubs across the border. Arsenal were linked with the goalscorer and Manchester City liked the look of the playmaker. At least, no-one could fault their taste in footballers. A week later against Hibs in Glasgow, in only thirteen minutes, McStay had the bulk of the 16,371 attendance purring with delight as he pummelled a twenty-yard drive past the desperately-diving Jim McArthur. Bang on the hour mark, Murdo MacLeod sealed the points with the second, a cute lob high into the net when he spotted the keeper off his line.

In between the win over the men from Edinburgh and the meeting with Dundee United at Tannadice, Celtic notched a famous European victory by beating Ajax 2-1 after drawing 2-2 in the first leg of the second round tie in Glasgow. The Hoops fans in the 20,006 crowd packed into the Tayside ground were singing, 'When it's spring again, we'll sing again, 2-1 from Amsterdam.' And they continued in high spirits as their favourites raced into a two-goal advantage against a United team, who, coincidentally, had just returned from Holland following a marvellous midweek result after beating PSV Eindhoven 2-0 for a 3-1 aggregate success.

Paul McStay got the opening goal in the twentieth minute with a pile-driver from twenty yards. Powerful shooting from the edge of the box was becoming a forte of the youngster. A minute after the interval, Roy Aitken doubled the advantage when he completed a fine move with a clinical finish. Only fourteen minutes remained when Dundee United pulled one back. Pat Bonner failed to hold a Paul Sturrock effort and Davie Dodds pounced to knock the rebound into the empty net. Five minutes from time, the keeper had no chance as a Ralph Milne left-foot drive from the edge of the box ripped past him for the equaliser.

McNeill shrugged his shoulders at the outcome. 'You can never be pleased to surrender a two-goal lead, especially so late in the game. I thought we had done enough to win and they were looking a bit frantic in their efforts to get something back. Then they got a goal out of nothing, really, and that set them up for the charge to get the equaliser. We should have held out, but I have to say we did play some good stuff over the percentage of the game. We've got a point, but it should have been two.'

The Celtic manager and his players would discover at the end of the season just how crucial that salvaged point would be for Dundee United.

Tannadice was a sea of tranquility compared to the bedlam that ensued at Celtic Park a week later when Alex Ferguson brought his Aberdeen team to Glasgow. A raging Billy McNeill had a feud with referee Andrew Waddell that saw the manager banished to the stand, Danny McGrain was sent off for the only time in his career, Mark McGhee scored a goal for the Dons that was clearly offside - and Fergie's team went home with the points after a 3-1 win. Dull it wasn't in the east end of Glasgow that tumultuous afternoon.

Celtic were jolted when the visitors scored two goals in four minutes in the second-half. In the fifty-fourth minute, there was a dodgy penalty-kick decision when Mark Reid was adjudged to have handled a Peter

Weir cross. Gordon Strachan, rarely anonymous in this fixture, rattled the award into the net. Pat Bonner was beaten again shortly afterwards when McGhee squared a pass across the box and Neil Simpson banged it home. A fair percentage of the 29,733 crowd blinked in astonishment.

McNeill responded by throwing on an extra attacker in Danny Crainie while withdrawing Murdo MacLeod. Immediately, the bold move paid dividends. In the sixty-eighth minute, Davie Provan produced another excellent delivery from a corner-kick. Tom McAdam made contact to knock the ball back into the box and Charlie Nicholas was quickest to react as he hooked a drive on the turn past Jim Leighton. It was only justice for the young Celt because it looked as though he had earned Celtic a penalty earlier in the game after being scythed down by Doug Rougvie. To the dismay of McNeill - and the delight of Ferguson - the match official, despite being in a good position, waved play on.

Referee Andrew Waddell hadn't exactly endeared himself to the Celtic faithful at that moment and his popularity plummeted even deeper when he sent off captain McGrain. The right-back had picked up a yellow card earlier in proceedings after a tackle on long-legged left-winger Peter Weir, who was known to be a smidgeon theatrical when it came to falling over. McGrain went in with a rugged challenge and, once more, Weir went down as though he had been shot by an invisible sniper. Waddell hastily informed McGrain he would no longer being taking part in today's game. McNeill, on the touchline, was apoplectic.

For those who are not acquainted with this true legend of Celtic Football Club, Billy McNeill is a man of refined manners. However, by his own honest admission, he possesses a temper. And he looked fit to burst in this combustible situation. He confronted the referee on the touchline. It didn't make for good viewing and there can only be one winner in this situation; unfortunately that's the chap with the whistle. McNeill was removed from the touchline.

With three minutes to go, the place was in uproar. McGhee looked yards offside when he received a forward pass. There was no whistle, so, like any good professional, he carried on and plonked the ball behind the disbelieving Bonner. McNeill recalled, 'I was convinced their third goal was offside and I was also unhappy about Danny McGrain being red-carded. I questioned the validity of the penalty claim that allowed Aberdeen to go in front. The combination of emotions led me to challenge Waddell's competence and there is a famous photograph of the pair of us standing eyeball-to-eyeball at the side of the track. The scene took place in full view of the crowd and I was formally cautioned by the referee and sent packing. I was later fined £200 by the SFA and severely reprimanded. On reflection, it was a serious error of judgement on my part and I was none too proud of the way I reacted.'

Andrew Waddell, a pathologist by profession, is alleged to have remarked later, 'I would like to meet Billy McNeill one day in a professional capacity.'

Desmond White was not one bit impressed by the reactions of his manager during an admittedly stormy encounter when some of the refereeing decisions were questionable, in the least. Undoubtedly, though, that would be another black mark against McNeill's name during the ongoing behind-the-scenes infighting.

A week after the Dons encounter, the Celtic manager said sorry to the support in the match programme for the game against Kilmarnock on October 16. 'I know my behaviour will have disappointed you and I would like to take this opportunity to apologise to you all publicly.' But the matter wasn't done and dusted. Not by a long chalk.

It was time to get back to the actual football and McNeill was going through the agonies again when the newly-promoted Rugby Park side were leading with only twelve minutes to go. The game was played in monsoon conditions with the Celtic Park pitch swiftly turning into a mud-heap. A crowd of 11,063 hardy souls huddled in their overcoats and anoraks to witness Paul Clarke put the visitors in front with a header in the fifty-first minute. Charlie Nicholas appeared to take it as a personal insult. In the seventy-eighth minute, Davie Provan launched over another hanging corner-kick, Murdo MacLeod headed it down and Nicholas, despite the dodgy elements, kept his balance to perfectly flick the ball into the net. Six minutes from time, Nicholas repeated the feat. He was eight yards out with his back to goal, but swivelled with astonishing poise and, in the same movement, fired beyond Alan McCulloch. The heavens wept, but the fans went home happy and more than just a little relieved.

There was a solemn minute's silence at Cappielow on October 23 as a mark of respect for the passing of the greatest goalscorer in Celtic's history, Jimmy McGrory. The man who netted a remarkable 469 goals in 448 games from 1922 to 1937 and also managed the club for twenty years from 1945 until the arrival of Jock Stein in 1965 died at the age of seventy-eight on the Wednesday prior to the game. McNeill echoed the sentiments of many when he said, 'Jimmy McGrory was a lovely man. He was far too nice to have ever been a football manager.'

The game cried out for a memorable goal and Frank McGarvey duly applied the magic. There was no apparent danger in the twenty-second minute when he picked up a pass outside the box, but he turned swiftly and sent a scorcher raging past Roy Baines. Jimmy McGrory would have been proud to have put his name to that whizzbang effort. Charlie Nicholas rolled in a nonchalant penalty-kick six minutes before the turnaround after his Maryhill buddy Jim Duffy appeared to handle a crossball. Duffy was so enraged he was booked by referee Hugh Alexander for his vehement protests. Jim Rooney added a bit of pressure with a strike from twelve yards in the seventieth minute, but the points were safely heading home with the champions.

Next up was another epic encounter with Rangers at rain-lashed, windswept Celtic Park on October 30. The conditions were so bad, one reporter put it thus, 'Players attempting slide tackles were in danger of being left sitting outside the street.' The torrential outpouring from the swollen clouds in the dark skies circling Glasgow didn't deter 60,406 fans from turning up, a record league attendance in Britain for the season.

The Rangers supporters weren't bothering about the incessant bombardment of drizzle as they celebrated the opening goal in the sixteenth minute. Pat Bonner could, at least, apportion some of the blame on the constant deluge, but he didn't look too clever as Robert Prytz's left-winger corner-kick sailed towards the near post and he punched the ball straight into the net. His embarrassment was alleviated three minutes later after some tenacious play by Paul McStay in his own half. Determinedly, he won a challenge before releasing Murdo MacLeod with an excellent pass. The midfielder headed straight for goal and smashed in a shot that was deflected by the outstretched leg of Jim Stewart. The ball broke clear and McStay, following up his earlier pass, cheerfully side-footed the rebound into the net to mark the occasion of his debut in this famous old match.

Five minutes from half-time, Rangers scored again and once more Bonner and his back lot didn't look too inspirational. Jim Bett flighted over a straightforward free-kick into the box and Derek Johnstone rose to touch the ball onto the unmarked Davie Cooper who, from eight yards, looped a header up and away from the frantically-chasing Celtic keeper who finished up in the net with the ball for company. Back came McNeill's men in the sixty-sixth minute and Frank McGarvey, with a disguised shot into the corner, tied it at two-apiece after McStay sent him through with another glorious slide-rule pass. Three minutes remained when MacLeod claimed the winner. McGarvey started it with a ball from his own half to Charlie Nicholas who dummied Dave MacKinnon, MacLeod's cousin, and steered a pass across the mud to his hard-working team-mate. MacLeod's aim was unerring as he placed the ball behind the exposed Stewart.

Billy McNeill was all smiles afterwards and claimed, 'Paul McStay shone like a lighthouse.'

A newspaper scribe had another description. He wrote, 'McStay is the best thing to come out of Larkhall since the very first bus to Glasgow.'

Not too sure which is the bigger compliment, but one certainty was that Celtic were still top of the league, a point ahead of Dundee United who also claimed a late winner in their derby against Dundee. Matchwinner MacLeod struck two goals in the midweek European Cup-tie against

Real Sociedad in Glasgow, but the Hoops toppled out on a 3-2 aggregate after surrendering 2-0 in the first leg.

Billy McNeill had genuine concerns as he took his crestfallen troops to Dens Park for the next league outing. His players, however, rallied after the European disappointment. They were three goals ahead at the interval courtesy of strikes from Nicholas, with a penalty-kick, Burns and McGarvey. Two goals from Cammy Fraser might have taken the gloss off the scoreline, but the main thing was that the points were in the bag again.

Afterwards McNeill admitted, 'I had my worries going into this match. It is always difficult to guess how a team will react to going out of Europe. Our lads seemed quite determined to put it out of their mind and turned in a first-half performance that will be hard to equal. Having gone in 3-0 up after the first period, the players seemed to slacken off in the second-half and, of course, conceded two goals. It is perhaps understandable that they had become mentally and physically tired after our recent busy schedule, but they must learn that one hundred per cent concentration is required. The fright they got in this game will no doubt illustrate this to them.'

No such complacency was in evidence a week later when St Mirren came to Glasgow and were brutally dismantled by an unstoppable Charlie Nicholas who claimed a hat-trick in a whirlwind seven-minute spell. It was only mid-November, but the club's talisman had already racked up an incredible twenty-seven goals. Billy McNeill could already detect the unmistakeable sound of the opening of several cheque books from across the border. Nicholas was smack in the spotlight and he was loving every minute of it. So were the Celtic fans. Opposing defences didn't share in the overwhelming enthusiasm.

The only surprising thing about the game against the Saints was that it took Celtic twenty minutes to open the scoring. Billy Thomson had already been forced to make three super saves by the time Nicholas rattled one behind him from the penalty spot. It was the player's seventh success out of seven attempts. He looked unstoppable. Two minutes after the breakthrough, he smashed in another from the edge of the box and completed his hat-trick in the twenty-sixth minute with a header from a McGarvey cross. Just before that effort, he set up one for Tommy Burns. The bedraggled Paisley outfit went for the safe option after the turnaround and opted for damage limitation. They packed their box and got away with it until two minutes from time when Roy Aitken embarked on a solo attempt that saw him cut a swathe through the crowd in front of him before finishing with a well-placed drive from twenty yards.

Celtic went into double figures for their first two meetings with Motherwell, but there was to be no humiliation for Jock Wallace and his team when they visited Parkhead on November 20. A crowd of 14,963 had to be content with a 3-1 win for Billy McNeill's men. Former Hoops stalwart Johannes Edvaldsson, who was run ragged in the demolition job at Fir Park, must have been reacting to his manager's orders to make certain Charlie Nicholas wouldn't be allowed time or space to indulge his distinct brand of sorcery on this occasion. They jostled time and again and, afterwards, the Celt had the blood on his shirt to prove it.

There was no goal stampede on this occasion and, in fact, it took until the hour mark for Paul McStay to make an impact with another of his trademark long-range efforts that homed in on its destination with Hugh Sproat a helpless onlooker. Four minutes later Nicholas escaped his personal Iceberg to sizzle one low into the net and Tommy Burns gave the fans something else to cheer with a third seven minutes from time. Bobby Flavell got his side's consolation while a young visiting forward took the eye with some clever touches and good movement. The Celtic support would grow to appreciate Brian McClair in the coming seasons.

Alan Rough made his debut for Hibs when Celtic visited Easter Road a week later. The last time the Scottish international keeper had faced the Hoops, he was still with Partick Thistle and had conceded three goals the previous April at Firhill. Who says lightning doesn't strike twice? Celtic won 3-2 with Frank McGarvey netting two and Paul

McStay drilling in another. Gary Murray collected both goals for the Edinburgh club.

Celtic had to wait until December 11 for their next league encounter, a trip to Pittodrie to face Aberdeen. Thankfully, there was no sign of Andrew Waddell with Kenny Hope entrusted with the whistle. The game had an astonishing start - Charlie Nicholas was injured and required treatment after THREE seconds. Frank McGarvey took the kick-off, rolled the ball to his striking sidekick and in crashed Neale Cooper with a brutal challenge. Obviously, it was designed to soften up Nicholas and it was a 'tactic' favoured more than once by the Dons that season.

Thankfully, Nicholas was allowed to carry on after treatment from physio Brian Scott. The charismatic Charlie's route towards revenge was to play a major part in Celtic's opening goal in the sixteenth minute. Tom McAdam picked out Nicholas on the right and he whipped in a low cross that was dummied by McGarvey and rolled perfectly into the tracks of the inrushing Murdo MacLeod. He hit the ball on the run from twenty-five yards and it struck Dons skipper Willie Miller before flummoxing Jim Leighton and dropping into the net.

The Celtic fans were still acknowledging the goal when the home side levelled almost instantly. Gordon Strachan picked out Mark McGhee with a free-kick and, for no apparent reason, the Celtic defenders backed off a player who enjoyed a fair measure of success against them in previous games. McGhee was given time to turn, carry the ball and then tuck it away from the advancing Pat Bonner. Billy McNeill must have wondered about the validity of looking out his football boots and moving into central defence for the second-half.

The second and winning goal for Celtic came just before the hour mark and was all down to some ingenuity and improvisation from Davie Provan. His constant battles with man mountain Doug Rougvie, the Dons' rugged left-back, were features of Celtic v Aberdeen collisions and this one at Pittodrie hadn't deviated from the usual script. Provan was a dainty winger, but he was also the possessor of a solid backbone and refused to bow to any sort of intimidation from hardmen defenders.

Once again, he was up on his toes in an almost-balletic pose as he pondered the options in front of him. Rougvie, as ever, was showing him down the line where he normally lay in wait with a shuddering challenge to halt the forward's progress.

Provan nudged the ball in front of him, shaped to take off down the touchline as Rougvie prepared to sprint alongside him. In a flash, though, the outside-right, feinted right, switched inside and fired a left-foot drive towards Leighton from the edge of the box. It was a nice bit of impromptu footwork and it got its deserve when the ball struck Alex McLeish and completely wrong-footed the keeper as it zipped past him. It proved to be the match winner and, after the shenanigans at Celtic Park in the previous game, it could be claimed that Celtic might just have deserved a rub of the green in this encounter.

Provan and his team-mates were required to perform on a bone-hard pitch at Rugby Park the week before Christmas. However, there was anything but Festive Cheer in the cold, still Ayrshire air that afternoon. Kilmarnock knew they were up against it as early as the first minute when Provan flighted in a 20-yard free-kick. Alan McCulloch actually caught the ball, but, unfortunately for the gallant goalie, he was about two feet over the line at the time. Celtic had to wait until five minutes before the hour mark before they could add to Provan's unusual effort. The winger was involved once again as he tormented his former team-mates. He curled over a corner-kick and Tom McAdam met it solidly with his forehead and this time McCulloch didn't get anywhere near the ball. MacLeod set up McGarvey for the third and Burns battered No 4 into the net with his left foot after some great work by McGrain. Killie must have been fairly sick of seeing Celtic - that was now eleven goals they had conceded in three hours' of football against McNeill's outfit.

The Celtic manager was just relieved his team had won without any injuries on a dodgy playing surface. He remarked, 'It was a lottery out there. The players had no movement at all on those underfoot conditions. Thankfully, all my players came through unscathed.'

Charlie Nicholas was christened Champagne Charlie nine days later and this author has to accept some of the credit/blame for that moniker. As Chief Sports Sub-Editor of the Daily Record, one of my tasks was to come up with ideas to keep the sports pages 'fresh'. The action would always take care of itself, but a newspaper needed its own identity, a controversial columnist - and we had the best in Alex Cameron - and features, exclusive big-name interviews and such like to ensure your title continued as the market leader. I hit on the idea of 'The Golden Shot'. Let's give a prize to the first player to hit thirty competitive goals in one season, I thought. The rules at the time forbade the newspaper from offering a cash inducement, so bubbly it was. The winner could be a player from any division and the newspaper would run a weekly update on the progress of the prolific marksmen up and down the country.

I thought 'The Golden Shot' would be a reasonable feature that would keep going throughout the season. I reckoned without Charlie Nicholas. The competition was over and done with before the bells chimed to take us into 1983.

Charlie hit the magical thirty mark via the penalty spot four minutes from the break against Morton at Parkhead with Celtic already trailing to a Murdo MacLeod own goal. Murdo's mishap occurred on the half-hour mark when he lost his bearings during a melee in the crowded penalty box and toe-ended the ball past Pat Bonner. Perhaps it was a belated Christmas gift for the Cappielow side. They reciprocated with one of their defenders obligingly whipping the pins from Nicholas and the Celt sent Roy Baines the wrong way with the award. Cue giant colour photographs of Charlie with bottles of the fizzy stuff later in the week as he was presented with his Golden Boot award.

MacLeod scored into what was becoming his favourite net in the fifty-third, but this time it counted for Celtic. Davie Provan found him with a neat pass and the midfielder applied the finishing touch. Frank McGarvey's corkscrew runs had been posing problems for the Greenock side all evening and he got his reward by netting two goals before Mark Reid put the gloss on the performance with an angled drive that completely foxed Baines, who was clearly expecting a cross into the box. The scoreline of Celtic 5 Morton 1 sent the fans home happy.

Billy McNeill declared himself merely 'satisfied' as December faded to a close. The Celtic manager's emotional stance took a decidedly upward swing a few days later when he brought in the New Year by making history.

CHAPTER TEN
THE TITLE GIVEAWAY

Billy McNeill took his players across Glasgow for the traditional New Year's Day game against Rangers on January 1 1983 in the realisation no Celtic team had won that particular fixture at Ibrox since 1921. On that day, Celtic triumphed 2-0 with goals from Joe Cassidy, a player known to his team-mates as 'Trooper Joe' because he served in the British Army in the Black Watch (Royal Highlanders) 1/7th Fifth Battalion during World War 1 and won a Military Medal for his gallantry.

Times had moved on - off the top of my head I can recall man landing on the moon - but Celtic's wretched record still stood sixty-one years later.

However, on this afternoon, in front of 42,000 spectators, Tommy Burns and Charlie Nicholas illuminated grey, old Govan with performances of cocky assurance as McNeill's side carved out their own little piece of history on the battlefield of their fiercest foes. Rangers had no answer as they were pushed aside. To be fair, John Greig's side didn't let go of the points without a mighty struggle, but at the end the scoreline showed it was 2-1 in favour of the team from across the Clyde.

Burns, an elegant, strutting minstrel, and Nicholas, clever and sharp, were the architects, but goalkeeper Pat Bonner also deserved applause for his performance. The man from Donegal jumped and swooped throughout the ninety minutes and was desperately unlucky with the Rangers goal. Rival manager John Greig was so impressed he was moved to say, 'I have never seen Pat Bonner in such form. His was the display worthy of a World Cup Final.'

The one that got away for the keeper came in the twenty-fourth minute when John McDonald thought he had scored with a close-range header. Bonner stretched to his full 6ft 2in to push the ball onto the right-hand upright. So much for the luck of the Irish; the effort bounced straight to Kenny Black and the industrious little midfielder rammed the ball high into the net. Luckily, though, that strike was sandwiched in between two gems from the first-footing upstarts that day. The opening goal arrived in the thirteenth minute and was set up by an energetic run down the left wing by the rarely-feted Mark Reid. His well-struck low ball created chaos in front of Jim Stewart before it was prodded back to Paul McStay by Frank McGarvey and the youngster first-timed an unsaveable drive past the keeper.

The second from Nicholas was a typical piece of quick thinking allied with typical bravado. It came in the seventieth minute after he received a left wing throw-in from Murdo MacLeod about thirty yards out. With reassuring composure, he controlled the ball and eased away from Dave MacKinnon all in one movement. The fans, Celtic and Rangers alike, held their breath in anticipation. Craig Paterson came out of central defence to meet the Celtic intruder who jinked, stopped, took off again, leaving the centre-half in his wake before firing a glorious left-foot attempt at goal. Stewart seemed to be transfixed by the guile and trickery of the inventive forward. The keeper looked slow to move for the shot that whizzed over his head on its way to its true destination. In a moment of irresistible, off-the-cuff splendour, Nicholas banished sixty-one years of hurt into oblivion.

Burns, though, was the main man on an unforgettable afternoon, performed on a surprisingly good surface that suited Celtic's style of play. One reporter was moved to say, 'If Tommy Burns passed a bad ball in the whole ninety minutes I must have been blinking at the time.'

Hugh Taylor, a dear, old friend of mine and one of the finest journalists this country has ever produced, wrote in the London Times, 'It was fitting, perhaps, that Burns, a cool, elegant midfield player plucked from the school of Scottish football science, was voted the sponsor's Man of the Match. He brought distinction to this Old Firm game at Ibrox which, while exciting, was more red-blooded than a classic.'

Celtic's triumph widened the gap between themselves and Rangers to an unassailable thirteen points and the league was well and truly blown for the Ibrox side. Billy McNeill's team had played seventeen league games, won fifteen, drawn one and lost one. It was championship-winning form. But things can change so swiftly and dramatically in football. Two days later, Celtic took on Dundee at Parkhead and dropped a point in a 2-2 draw after coasting at two goals ahead for over an hour.

Billy McNeill was livid. His mood wasn't helped when Donald Mackay, his opposite number at the relegation-threatened Dens Park club, blithely admitted, 'We were so far behind Celtic, we could have taken the bus home at half-time.' The 16,615 fans were still discussing the merits of a wonderful victory in the Glasgow derby when Tommy Burns put the home side ahead in the twenty-fifth minute. It was a strike that would have been a contender for Goal of the Season in ANY season anyone cared to mention. Burns captured the ball in the middle of the park and ambled forward. He played a one-two with Paul McStay and then another quickfire wall pass with Charlie Nicholas. Before the Dundee defence had a clue what was developing in front of them, the classy Celt took aim and thumped a ferocious twenty-yarder beyond keeper Colin Kelly.

Nicholas' counter in the fifty-sixth minute wasn't quite in the same category, but no-one was complaining. Unusually for the cocksure striker, he mishit his shot towards goal. The fluffed attempt seemed to take Kelly totally by surprise and the ball crept under his body and over the line. It was just a matter of time before Celtic made things safe, thought their followers. There is little doubt, though, that the players took their foot off the gas. Some slack defensive play was seized upon by Eric Sinclair in the sixty-second minute and punished with a scoring shot from inside the box. Twelve minutes from time, quite remarkably, Dundee equalised. Peter Mackie, who seemed to enjoy playing against his old team, went for a wander down the touchline, slung over a cross to the back post - a problem area for Celtic all season - and Sinclair found himself in isolation to send a header past Pat Bonner.

McNeill cut to the chase. 'My players know that sort of display is unacceptable at this club. Frankly, I don't want to be associated with it. This is a dropped point that we can ill afford. If we play like that we will be punished at the end of the day.' Alas, prophetic words from the Celtic manager, as it turned out. There wasn't even the consolation of discovering Celtic were the best-supported team in the country with an average of 23,038 while Rangers were next on 19,677, Aberdeen on 13,281 and Dundee United on 10,187.

It was tense and towsy at Love Street on January 8 as the ball took on a life of its own as it was shuttled around in the wind, blown erratically off course as football and entertainment took a back seat to the elements. Pat Bonner was lucky if he was getting distances of up to twenty yards when was attempting to kick the ball downfield as the game developed into a farce. Thankfully, though, there was a moment of joy for the Celtic fans in the 14,748 crowd when Murdo MacLeod smashed in the only goal of the game against St Mirren.

It was Celtic's century of goals for the season and, despite the atrocious conditions, it was an effort fit to grace such a title. It came in the sixteenth minute when the pocket dynamo launched a vicious volley towards Billy Thomson's goal from all of thirty yards. The keeper didn't stand a chance as it erupted into the net. The goal was enough to give McNeill's outfit a 1-0 win, but the performance far from impressed the manager. In fact, the Saints' young bright spark striker Frank McAvennie missed a good chance in the second-half and Danny

McGrain played a captain's role by heading a Frank McDougall effort off the line in the last minute.

'That was too close for comfort,' observed McNeill. 'Having said that, I have played in conditions like that and strange things can happen. You try to keep the ball on the ground, but it just needs one rebound or bounce and suddenly it's up in the air again and the game is ruined as a spectacle. We're happy with the two points, though.'

Unfortunately, the wind was still whipping around forcefully and angrily a week later when Celtic visited Fir Park to take on a Motherwell side they had overwhelmed by seven goals earlier in the campaign. Maybe they should have kept a couple of goals for this encounter. They crashed to a 2-1 defeat and the severe gusts swirling around the trim, little ground playing a crucial role. The game was heading for a stalemate when the unthinkable happened. One newspaper reported it like this, 'With thirty-six seconds remaining, Stuart Rafferty crossed high from the left. Deceived by the wind, Pat Bonner came out too far, had to overstretch and couldn't hold the ball. It dropped kindly at the feet of Brian McClair and the man who hit a hat-trick against Rangers less than a fortnight ago did the trick once more.'

Once again, it could have been such a different outcome with Celtic taking the initiative in the twenty-third minute and good value for their lead. Davie Provan, yet again, provided the ammunition and Murdo MacLeod fired the bullet, a low drive that whistled past the diving Nicky Walker. Celtic's superiority wasn't mirrored in the scoreline at the interval, but the players would have been more than delighted if it had remained that way at the end. Two minutes after the turnaround, referee Louis Thow awarded the home team a penalty-kick after a hasty Paul McStay tackle on Tommy O'Hara. McClair stepped up to take the kick and made no mistake with a wicked drive.

There was an uproar not long afterwards when George McCluskey was brought down in the box by Brian Coyne, who had been on Celtic's books as a youngster. It looked a more plausible appeal than the one awarded to Motherwell, but, amazingly, the match official didn't want to know. Half the Celtic team surrounded referee Thow, but he waved away their protests before booking Frank McGarvey. The Man of the Match award went to Johannes Edvladsson and no-one was surprised that the man from Iceland revelled in the appalling conditions. You get days like that.

Celtic had now dropped three points from a possible six to Dundee and Motherwell, two teams in the lower reaches of the league. But Billy McNeill refused to push the panic button. 'We've got good players and I believe in them,' he said. McNeill decided to play all three of his main strikers - Charlie Nicholas, George McCluskey and Frank McGarvey - in an adventurous line-up for the visit of Hibs a week later. His bold move paid off with Celtic winning 4-1 and his prolific threesome sharing the goals. Worryingly, though, a trend was developing. The team appeared to lose focus after gaining the upper hand and they demonstrated their carelessness again in this confrontation.

Davie Provan was given a roving commission for this game - 'Pimpernel Provan' as he was christened in one newspaper - and he probed at the Easter Road backline for most of the ninety minutes. Nicholas got the opener in the fourth minute after good service from McCluskey. Two minutes from half-time Celtic threw a lifeline to their Edinburgh opponents. Pat Bonner mishandled a cross to create a melee of swinging boots and falling bodies in front of his goal. Tom McAdam, in trying to put the ball into the terracing, got his angles all wrong and booted his clearance high into the net. The Celtic fans in the 17,106 crowd were beginning to expect such gifts to rival teams.

Two minutes after the break, McCluskey stabbed in a close-range shot and the same player latched onto a sloppy pass-back by Arthur Duncan just before the hour mark, raced through, enticed Alan Rough from his goal-line and then floated over a cross for McGarvey to head into the gaping net. And it was all-action Frank who brought down the curtain on an enterprising second-half showing by running onto a superb through pass from Nicholas to squeeze a shot under the advancing Rough.

Celtic travelled to take on Dundee United seven days later and winced when they witnessed what the cruel winter had done to the Tannadice playing surface. It was black and mud-scarred, but Billy McNeill was swift to tell his concerned players, 'It's the same for both teams. Just make sure you adapt to it better than them.'

It looked as though the manager's words had hit their target when his players put together a rapid, crisp movement to open the scoring in the fourth minute. Davie Provan took a short corner-kick to Murdo MacLeod who stroked the ball straight and true to Paul McStay. Without breaking stride, the midfielder chipped a pass over the United back lot and Charlie Nicholas, running clear in keen anticipation, tucked away his thirty-fifth goal of an extraordinary campaign.

Pat Bonner then went through the hero and villain role most goalkeepers have to endure at least a few times during a season. In the fortieth minute, Derek Stark, the home side's stuffy full-back, ignored the scientific approach and applied the toe of his boot to the ball as he launched it out of his own half. The Celtic defence clearly expected the keeper to come and collect it, but Bonner, for reasons known only to himself, decided to remain on his line. Davie Dodds stole in to hit the ball on the drop and, in doing so, hauled his team back into the contest.

However, two minutes later the goalie redeemed himself with a fabulous penalty-kick save. Referee Eddie Pringle - and the majority of the 17,289 fans in attendance - couldn't fail to see Graeme Sinclair handling a bouncing ball. There were no arguments when the match official pointed to the spot. Eamonn Bannon hit it strongly, but Bonner moved cat-like to his right to get a hand to the attempt and shovel it wide of the post. Bannon looked mortified. And no wonder. Three minutes later he would have to explain himself to Jim McLean.

The best scoring opportunity of the second period fell to Celtic in the sixty-seventh minute when the debonair Paul McStay elected for power when he blitzed in a drive from outside the penalty area. Hamish McAlpine hadn't an earthly, but must have been relieved when he heard the mighty thud of leather striking wood above his head and the ball rebounding to safety. A point gained? Or a point lost? We would have to wait until the last game of the season for an answer.

Extraordinarily, Celtic lost 3-1 to Aberdeen in Glasgow a week later when, once more, it looked as though they were in the ascendancy. Charlie Nicholas put McNeill's men ahead before Eric Black became the first player to score a hat-trick for the opposition at Parkhead since Willie Johnston managed the feat for Rangers in 1968. It was a crazy state of affairs as Nicholas rolled the ball past Jim Leighton in the thirty-fourth minute after some good leading-up play between Paul McStay and Frank McGarvey.

With only one minute to go until half-time, that's the way the score remained. Sixty seconds later the Dons, in the most dramatic of circumstances, were in front. Black levelled in the forty-fourth minute with a simple effort and staged an action replay moments later when he headed in a Peter Weir cross. The Dons players danced with delight as they headed for the half-time oranges. The Celtic players simply looked stunned. Historians were scampering to discover when, if ever, an opposing team had scored two goals in a minute at Parkhead.

McNeill responded by shuffling his line-up and replaced left-back Mark Reid with George McCluskey, but it was to no avail. Black netted again in the seventy-first minute and the points were heading on the coach back to the Granite City. The result nudged Celtic off the top of the table for the first time in the vicinity of two years and Alex Ferguson must be complimented on getting his tactics spot on. There were gasps of disbelief when he left a fully-fit Gordon Strachan on the substitutes' bench and elected to go with a midline of Neale Cooper, Neil Simpson and Dougie Bell. There was skill within that trio, but there was also an abundance of steel. Fergie was prepared to tough this one out and he received his dividend.

It had been a bone-shuddering encounter and one reporter noted, 'Charlie Nicholas did score a cracker of a goal. But, over the piece, he failed to withstand some crunching tackles (not always fair) which came his way.' It seemed a reasonable summing-up of proceedings.

A crowd of 42,831 turned out for the game against the Dons, but only a fortnight later, that total had mystifyingly shrunk to 10,691 when Kilmarnock came visiting. Celtic cantered to a 4-0 triumph, but it had been a bruising, bitter battle where, interestingly, Murdo Macleod was in opposition to his brother Ally in the middle of the park. Brotherly love went out the window when Ally flattened Murdo in the twenty-fourth minute and referee Alister Hewitt awarded the inevitable penalty-kick. Equally inevitably, Charlie Nicholas drove the ball into the back of the net.

Paul Clarke, the Rugby Park side's burly centre-half, was obviously not a fully paid-up member of the Charlie Nicholas Fan Club and he threw himself into some reckless challenges on the fans' favourite. Nicholas' interest in the game was terminated in the sixty-fourth minute after another fierce tackle by Clarke. George McCluskey, on for Nicholas, got the same treatment and, after two bookings, Clarke was invited to take his leave of the proceedings. Frank McGarvey, with two typical opportunistic strikes, and Murdo MacLeod, with a net-bursting spectacular, piled on the misery.

One scribe described it thus, 'It takes time and a bit of courage to break down a defence which has the physique of a tug-of-war team or a bunch of Welsh front row forwards.' The Celtic players were happy to escape with the points in the bag and their limbs intact. No-one would shed a tear when the Ayrshire side disappeared from view at the end of the programme.

They would be joined by Morton who offered stubborn resistance a week later at Cappielow before being downed 3-0. The Celtic fans in the 8,500 crowd chanted for Danny McGrain to 'show us your medal' after the popular captain had been awarded with an MBE during the week. Well, at least, the supporters knew it couldn't possibly have stood for 'More Bloody Effort' from their wholehearted, one hundred per cent defender. Dom Sullivan, whose contribution in midfield was often overshadowed by the brilliance of Paul McStay and Tommy Burns and the endeavour from Murdo MacLeod, scored his final goal for the

Hoops when he gave them the lead in the ninth minute. He would be on his way on the completion of the campaign.

MacLeod walloped in a quick-fire second and McCluskey completed the scoring a minute from the end. Ironically, Morton keeper Roy Baines sponsored the match ball and got a good look at his 'investment' three times when he picked it out of the net. Billy McNeill had been pleased with his team's display on a spartan surface, but he was also impressed by young Morton centre-half Joe McLaughlin. He decided to keep the name in mind.

Two weeks later, Celtic stood on the banana skin that was Dens Park as they folded to a terrible 2-1 defeat. All the talk in the newspapers for a few days was centred around Charlie Nicholas. Would he go? Or would he stay? The charismatic youngster was coming out of contract in two months' time and there had been little sign of the Celtic directors making him an offer he couldn't refuse. Manchester United? Liverpool? Arsenal? The teams who weren't afraid to invest in strengthening their playing squad were apparently forming a disorderly queue as they attempted to lure the impressionable twenty-one year old to pastures new. It was turning into an unwanted and disruptive sideshow.

Billy McNeill urged his chairman and the directors to sort out the speculation and give Nicholas a new, enhanced contract. These were the days before Bosman transfers and, unhappily, the Celtic board chose to ignore the advice from their manager. They could smell money.

Under this suffocating cloud of speculation, it was hardly surprising Nicholas was far from his best on Tayside. By the thirty-fifth minute, the champions were two goals adrift against a line-up that was merely workmanlike. The descent began in the twenty-second minute when the normally sure-footed Tom McAdam miskicked a clearance downfield from keeper Colin Kelly. Eric Sinclair, who had scored twice in the draw in Glasgow in January, moved in, took control and released Albert Kidd who left Pat Bonner helpless.

Thirteen minutes later, with Celtic slow to respond to the danger signs, it was 2-0. Peter Mackie cut in, stuck a pass in front of Brian Scrimgeour and once again the Celtic keeper was beaten. McNeill, as anyone would understand, was furious. Roy Aitken got the message and surged forward in time-honoured style in the thirty-seventh minute to pick out Frank McGarvey and Celtic were back in the game. Unfortunately, that was as good as it got for the travelling fans in the 11,196 crowd. Another two points had been carelessly thrown aside. It was incomprehensible that Celtic should earn a solitary point from their last two clashes against the Dens side.

The players had an ideal chance to atone the following midweek when Rangers came looking for revenge. The Ibrox side had lost three times out of three in the previous Old Firm meetings and, although they were out of the race for the title, they were determined to put a dent in their old rivals' challenge for three-in-a-row. They took a point in a dour goalless stalemate in front of 50,939 fans. Peter McCloy, so often criticised, was their best performer with a string of superlative saves to deny Celtic. The best chance of the evening fell to the gifted toes of Charlie Nicholas. Sadly, he failed to make the most of the opportunity.

The Glasgow Herald reporter noted, 'In sixteen minutes, Celtic missed a great chance of going ahead. Sullivan robbed Redford in the midfield and sent McGarvey galloping down the left. When his low cross reached the near post, Nicholas was the first to it, but shot against McCloy. It was an uncharacteristic miss by Scotland's top scorer.'

The nearest Rangers came to breaking the stranglehold came when Sandy Clark, the bustling centre-forward newly signed from Airdrie, howled for a penalty-kick with Dom Sullivan and Murdo MacLeod close by. Referee Bob Valentine, quite rightly, waved away the appeal. In today's football, with TV cameras shooting from every angle, Clark would have been booked for simulation. It was a clear dive.

Ironically, Celtic went back to the top of the league on goal difference from Aberdeen despite conceding their sixth point from their last six league games. Billy McNeill wasn't being fooled, though. His team looked tired and, in particular, Charlie Nicholas, with so much happening off the pitch, who had lost his crucial cutting edge. Three days after the Rangers draw, Celtic shed another point in a disjointed display against St Mirren at Parkhead. In fact, McNeill's men must have been relieved to accept a 1-1 stalemate with the Paisley side after heading for defeat with only eight minutes remaining.

There was little doubt that Charlie Nicholas was going to wilt under the fearsome focus. Annoyingly, the stories were cropping up everywhere. Juventus? Inter Milan? Uncle Tom Cobley United? You name a team and they were now, apparently, about to buy Charlie. The player who had sparked right from the off and had already collected forty-two goals was out of touch with events on the field. It's hardly fair to heap the onus on the shoulders of a youngster, who, remember, hadn't even completed three full seasons for the club. But McNeill didn't have the playing resources to take Nicholas out of the spotlight for a handful of games and give him a rest in the hope he would return rejuvenated and up for the task of seeing Celtic over the line.

The defence's Achilles Heel of conceding goals at the back post was evident again in the sixty-eighth minute when Billy Stark flicked on a corner-kick and centre-half Mark Fulton could hardly miss from a few yards out. It looked like yet another costly lapse in concentration by the back lot, but they were thrown a life-line by Davie Provan. Mark Reid picked out the roving winger who cut inside before delivering a low angled shot beyond Billy Thomson. Celtic had now dropped four points in three games in a week. After twenty-eight games, Aberdeen were in pole position with forty-four points with Celtic, after the same amount of games, a point behind. Dundee United were third on forty-two points. This was not championship-winning form.

Charlie Nicholas was back in the limelight in midweek when he made his Scotland international debut and scored a magnificent goal in the 2-2 draw with Switzerland at Hampden. The world was sitting up and taking notice of the kid from Maryhill. Motherwell singled him out for heavy treatment in this next game at Parkhead, a 3-0 win for Billy

McNeill's men. Referee George Smith was one of the busiest men on the field that afternoon as he booked four Fir Park players - Bobby Flavell, Tommy O'Hara, Ally Mauchlen and Andy Dornan - while awarding twenty-eight free-kicks against Jock Wallace's side. With fame comes a price and Nicholas was stifled in this contest.

Willie McStay - brother of Paul - made his debut and saw Frank McGarvey give the team the lead in the seventeenth minute after latching onto a peach of a through ball from Danny McGrain. In thirty-sixth minute, McGarvey played a huge part in the second strike. He did some unselfish running on the touchline before zipping in a dangerous cross. Andy Harrow was the first to it, but, unfortunately for the defender, he sliced it high past his own keeper Nicky Walker. The goal of the day belonged to Tom McAdam when he unerringly volleyed in a left-foot effort following a Danny Crainie corner-kick ten minutes from time.

But most of the spectators wondered if the visiting players had been on a staple diet of red meat as they prepared for this challenge. One scribe wrote, 'Motherwell fought hard enough - maybe too hard at times - to upset the attacking flow of Celtic and I suggest if Jock Wallace doesn't get his men to cool it, he might find himself running out of players at the wrong time.' Interestingly, the reporter added, 'I was impressed with the determined play of young Brian McClair up front. He had a lot of success against the Celtic defence and was prepared to take them on himself.'

The loudest cheer of the afternoon came when the ancient tannoy system at the ground crackled to life to inform the departing supporters that Aberdeen had lost 1-0 at home to St Mirren. Celtic were league leaders again with forty-five points, one ahead of the Dons and Dundee United.

The Tannadice side were next to visit Glasgow the following midweek. It was all getting a bit frantic and 34,508 were at Parkhead to feel the tension. Flamboyant Manchester United manager Ron Atkinson was an interested, if unsolicited, spectator among the crowd.

It was as tight as a snare drum and it looked as though it would take an individual conjuring up an unexpected moment or magic or some unfortunate individual making an error. Paul Hegarty, normally so reliable, fitted into the latter category on the hour mark. Paul McStay delivered a probing pass, the Tannadice centre-half mis-controlled the ball, it rolled to Frank McGarvey and he seized on it with his killer instinct and flashed a drive beyond Hamish McAlpine. The United central defensive trio of Hegarty, Richard Gough and David Narey could only stand open-mouthed in astonishment while McGarvey took off to accept the plaudits from the adoring legions as Celtic Park rocked.

Old Trafford boss Atkinson was smiling twelve minutes from the end. He had arrived in Glasgow to see what all the fuss was about regarding Charlie Nicholas and he got a glimpse of it at that exact moment. McGarvey, always menacing, thrusting and exploring avenues where he could inflict damage, got a half-chance in a crowded penalty area. His shot was blocked and sped in the direction of Nicholas. In an instant, he killed the ball stone dead and, without as much as a glance upwards, lobbed the ball into a vacant space in the net. It was a sublime piece of cheek from the player and Atkinson would travel back to Manchester that night to tell his board the he wanted the player. So, according to the Press, did half of the teams in Europe. The main thing, though, was that Celtic were back on top three points clear of United and Aberdeen with only six games remaining. Now the team just had to make absolutely certain they managed to avoid that treacherous thin ice.

It was a bright Easter Saturday when Celtic faced Hibs at Easter Road and, unexpectedly, it turned into a roughhouse confrontation with ex-Celt Jackie McNamara - father of the former Hoops skipper of the same name - being ordered off. Pat Stanton, who performed briefly at Parkhead between 1976/78, had taken over from Bertie Auld in the Edinburgh club's dug-out and his order of the day seemed to be for his players to take no prisoners. Furious vendettas were being carried out all over the park and McNamara was banished after a crude lunge on Murdo MacLeod with only four minutes remaining.

What little football was on display came from Billy McNeill's side as they won 3-0. Charlie Nicholas got the opener in the sixth minute with a twelve-yard drive that took a nick off Gordon Rae on its way past Alan Rough. Davie Provan, playing with a swagger amid the flying challenges, got the second just before the half-hour mark with a chipped shot that Rough waved goodbye to as it soared into the net. The third from Nicholas was right out of the top drawer. He turned his former team-mate Alan Sneddon inside out with his quick feet before completing the solo performance with a devastating shot from the edge of the box that raged into the top corner.

Afterwards came the news that Aberdeen had lost 2-1 to Rangers at Ibrox. The title fight now looked like a two-way duel against Celtic and Dundee United, by one of football's little quirk of fates, Jim McLean's men were next up at Celtic Park on a brisk evening on April 20 where the stakes were at their highest. It wasn't quite a winner-takes-all situation, but it was as near as dammit. The game took off at breakneck speed and maintained the pace throughout an exhausting ninety minutes that must have drained the 23,965 fans as well as the players.

It wasn't the best of starts for the hosts - United scored in fourteen minutes and six minutes later Graeme Sinclair, playing at right-back in place of the suspended Danny McGrain, was forced to come off after a sickening clash of heads with Eamonn Bannon. Billy McNeill had to quickly re-organise and withdraw Murdo MacLeod to fill in at full-back, Davie Provan was required to slot into his vacant midfield spot and substitute George McCluskey went on in an attacking role. It wasn't an ideal situation, particularly when United had already exploited the Celtic defensive frailties with Paul Hegarty heading in at the far post from Bannon's corner-kick for the opening goal.

It took Celtic until seven minutes from the interval to get back on level pegging. Referee Davie Syme pointed to the spot after Derek Stark awkwardly barged into the back of Tommy Burns. There could only be one outcome and Charlie Nicholas drove in the equaliser for his forty-seventh strike of the campaign. However, United replied with a spot-kick of their own in the fifty-second minute when MacLeod tugged back Davie Dodds. Bannon, having missed against Pat Bonner in February, did a better job this time and sent his effort wide of the keeper.

The powderkeg went up two minutes from the hour mark. Richard Gough, who earlier been booked for a foul on McCluskey, was involved in a skirmish with Provan. Syme had a clear view of the exchange of niceties and cautioned both with Gough expelled for the remainder of the evening. Celtic capitalised with the equaliser in the seventy-third minute when McCluskey teed up Burns who drilled the ball behind Hamish McAlpine. McNeill's men went for the jugular, crowding forward in search of the winning goal.

Six minutes were left on the clock when Celtic were hit by the classic sucker punch by a team well versed in the tactic. Bannon eliminated several players with a searching pass to Ralph Milne who controlled it on his chest and then lobbed it away from Bonner for the winner. The ball entered the net to the sound of silence.

Celtic's crown was slipping. They suffered their third defeat in eight days when they met Scottish Cup conquerors Aberdeen at Pittodrie on April 23. A week earlier Billy McNeill's hopes of leading the team to the domestic treble perished at Hampden in the semi-final of the national competition. Celtic had eased through the opening three rounds with three-goal winning margins in each tie. Goals from Charlie Nicholas (2) and George McCluskey saw off Clydebank at quaint Kilbowie, McCluskey was on target again in the next round against Dunfermline with Frank McGarvey supplying the other two. There was a flashpoint moment in the quarter-final in the 4-1 victory over Hearts in a towsy affair at Parkhead.

Former Rangers winger Willie Johnston was sent off for the NINETEENTH time in his turbulent career after appearing to head butt Davie Provan following a throw-in on the left wing. Johnston pleaded his innocence, but referee Brian McGinlay, after a quick consultation with his linesman, wasn't dissuaded from flourishing the red card. Goals from Nicholas (2), MacLeod and McGarvey saw the Hoops safely through. One ex-Ranger who could afford a wry smile was Alex MacDonald, the one-time professional provocateur of the Ibrox side, who netted his well-beaten team's consolation effort two minutes from the end.

Having safely deposited the League Cup trophy in the silverware cabinet, McNeill was determined to do the domestic clean sweep. Those thoughts were obliterated against Aberdeen in front of 57,152 spectators in the semi-final at Hampden on April 16 when a controversial goal in the sixty-fifth minute from Peter Weir proved to be the decider. Eric Black certainly handled the ball on the edge of the Celtic penalty area on the right-hand side. Referee Alan Ferguson must have seen it and deemed it an accident as he waved play on. Black careered to the right, swung over a clever cross and Weir was all on his own at the back post to head the only goal of the game behind the exasperated and exposed Pat Bonner. How many crucial goals had the team surrendered in an identical fashion over the season? It was becoming the biggest flaw in the team's armoury.

Another talking point during and after the defeat was the non-appearance of Nicholas, who wasn't even listed as a substitute. Was he injured? Billy McNeill remained tightlipped. Had he been sold? McNeill could categorically deny that suggestion; not even this Celtic board would have considered selling their hottest property while two more trophies were up for grabs. There had been speculation of Nicholas breaking a curfew, but that was never confirmed.

The margins between success and sorrow in football are wafer thin and that was demonstrated in the matter of six first-half minutes against the Dons in the league encounter a week later. In the twenty-eighth minute, Murdo MacLeod picked up a full head of steam as he charged through the congested midfield. He unleashed a mighty effort that beat Jim Leighton, but the ball whacked against the crossbar and rebounded to safety. Six minutes later, Mark McGhee snatched the only goal to send Celtic despairingly to defeat.

Once again, the marking at the back post was lamentable and there is little doubt that Alex Ferguson would have zoomed in on that weakness. John McMaster sent over a left-wing free-kick into that vulnerable area and the intimidating Doug Rougvie got above any challengers to head down and across the penalty box. McGhee didn't connect properly, mishit the ball against a post with Pat Bonner scrambling. The effort bounced across goal, struck Roy Aitken and trickled over the line. A reporter described it like this, 'The strike was a untidy as an upturned ashcan.'

So, hardly memorable, but enough to create genuine consternation in the ranks at Parkhead. After thirty-three games, Dundee United were now on top with fifty points and Celtic were a point behind. The victorious Dons were out of it on forty-six, but they had still inflicted lasting damage on Billy McNeill's side. He tried to put a brave face on the situation. 'There are three games still to be played and, after recent events, anything can happen. We can only keep playing away, making sure we win and hope that Dundee United slip up somewhere. We're a point behind, but only a fool would dismiss us.'

Celtic got back to winning ways with a 5-0 success over Kilmarnock at Rugby Park. Three goals in the last fifteen minutes from Murdo MacLeod, who had previously netted in the first-half, Charlie Nicholas and Tommy Burns put a gloss on the final scoreline. Danny McGrain opened the scoring in the seventh minute after being set up by Nicholas. The fans in the 7,900 crowd in Ayrshire that afternoon witnessed McGrain's last goal for the club.

One reporter got slightly carried away in his match report. 'The Celts had back-up power, penetration, explosive speed, individual trickery, complex, but effective, teamwork and superb fitness. When Nicholas flashed into the game, Kilmarnock seemed blinded by his skill.' After that breathtaking tribute it was unfeasible to believe the team had been beaten three times in their previous three outings.

Celtic, simply, had to keep the momentum going and they stumbled through the challenge of Morton, already relegated, on May 7 at Parkhead with 12,610 in attendance. The sportswriter who was so entranced by their display at Rugby Park would have been hard pressed to shower this performance with fanciful expressions. In short, Celtic looked jaded. Goals from Roy Aitken, in the twenty-third minute, and Charlie Nicholas, from the penalty spot just before the interval, sealed the points. But it was far from impressive.

In the words of one scribe, 'The full-time whistle was a relief. Celtic will be disgusted with themselves. They should have hit a barrowload in this game, but their timing, passing of the ball and inability to control it under pressure, saw their attacking moves break down repeatedly. Maybe they were keeping their best stuff for Ibrox next week!'

Celtic made their way to Govan on May 14 while earnestly hoping a Dundee team that had beaten them on Tayside in March might be able to go up a gear again to prevent the embarrassment of their arch rivals United, from one hundred yards up the street, winning the Championship on their ground. Some hope. By the eleventh minute, United were two goals ahead with strikes from Ralph Milne and Eamonn Bannon and the news, via a handy transistor radio, was relayed to Billy McNeill. Twelve minutes after the breaking news from Dens Park, the Celtic manager had even more reason to be unhappy. Rangers were two goals ahead.

Davie Cooper whacked in a twenty-yard free-kick in the sixteenth minute for the opener and Rangers enjoyed a fair slice of good fortune when a shot from Davie MacKinnon, which was covered by Pat Bonner, took a wicked deflection off Sandy Clark and wrong-footed the keeper. McNeill winced. However, he had noticed the Celtic support were still in full voice, despite losing 2-0 and realising there were to be no miracles on Tannadice Street, although Iain Ferguson had pulled one back just before the half-hour mark. No-one seemed too interested in what was happening at Pittodrie where Aberdeen would eventually thump Hibs 5-0.

'I could sense the fans were in the mood to give us a rousing send off, come what may,' said McNeill. 'Everyone connected with Celtic was disappointed and the season had taken a downturn in April. We were on course for the treble and now it looked as though we would have to settle for being second best. That stuck in my throat. I tried to rouse the players in the dressing room. I told them, "Listen to that noise - that's our support. They're playing their part, it's time you played yours." I hit on the idea of sending the players out early before the start of the second-half. I wanted them to realise what Celtic meant to these fans. Sure enough, they didn't let me down. As the players knocked the ball about and waited for the Rangers lads to come out, our supporters started singing, as only they can, "You'll Never Walk Alone". The scarves were held head high and were swaying and the flags were flying. If that couldn't inspire a team then I haven't a clue what could. The players responded.'

By the seventy-third minute Celtic were 3-2 ahead and Rangers were on their knees. Charlie Nicholas kicked off the fightback three minutes after the interval when Dave MacPherson knocked Davie Provan to the ground as he spun onto a clever pass from Nicholas. Referee Brian McGinlay had no hesitation and Nicholas rolled it to the keeper's right as Peter McCloy toppled to his left. Just after the hour mark it was all-square. Provan curled over a left-wing corner to the near post and Roy Aitken flicked it across goal. Tom McAdam read the script perfectly and applied the finishing touch from six yards.

The Celtic fans were in full voice by the time Provan slung over a fabulous free-kick and Frank McGarvey nipped in before the stranded McCloy to bullet a header high into the net. Four minutes from time, Ally Dawson sclaffed a clearance high into the air and compounded the error by bringing down MacLeod as he latched onto the ball. McGinlay once more pointed to the spot and Nicholas placed it in the same corner as before although, on this occasion, McCloy got a hand to the ball, but couldn't prevent it from crawling across the line.

It finished 4-2 for Celtic, leaving them with four wins and a draw against their Old Firm foes in their five confrontations during the campaign. Dundee United won their first-ever - and so far only - Premier League title by grinding out a 2-1 win over their city rivals. It has never been recorded if Jim McLean smiled that evening, but his team completed the season with fifty-six points, one ahead of Celtic and the Dons with McNeill's side taking runners-up spot by virtue of a superior goal difference. Rangers, who would complete a miserable campaign with a 1-0 defeat to Alex Ferguson's outfit in the Scottish Cup Final, limped into fourth place on thirty-eight points.

Billy McNeill again sent his players out to take a bow in front of their adoring, vociferous support. Anyone dropping in from a distant galaxy would have been forgiven for believing the hordes in green and white were celebrating some sort of momentous trophy success. Sadly, it wasn't to be the case. The league was lost as the final curtain descended on a topsy-turvy season.

But the drama was far from over.

CHAPTER ELEVEN
SOMEWHERE OVER THE RAINBOW

Billy McNeill had won three Premier Division Championships and one Scottish Cup in his four years as Celtic manager. The League Cup - lifted six times as a victorious captain - had somehow escaped his grasp. Failure was never acceptable to McNeill. The situation would have to be rectified.

The quest for the silverware would kick off in bright sunshine at Parkhead on August 14 1982 against Dunfermline and the journey would be completed in a downpour at Hampden on December 4 against Rangers. There were ten ties leading up to the League Cup Final, nine victories and a solitary loss with a remarkable thirty-nine goals scored and five conceded. The signs were looking good.

Charlie Nicholas, who would become the phenomenon of the 1982/83 campaign, wasn't even in the starting line-up for the opening day clash against the East End Park outfit who were now languishing in the First Division. Frank McGarvey and George McCluskey got the nod from McNeill to lead the line and they repaid his faith by netting three of the six goals - McCluskey with two and McGarvey with the other.

Davie Provan also claimed two and Mark Reid launched a penalty-kick beyond Fife keeper Hugh Whyte, who was a doctor by profession. What he prescribed for himself after this nerve-shredding occasion is not known, but he may have had a disturbed sleep that particular evening.

One shame-faced Dunfermline player was leaving Celtic Park when he was pressed by young autograph hunters. He wasn't immediately recognisable, but the wet hair was a giveaway that he might just have taken a shower. 'Mister, were you playing?' asked an urchin, autograph book at the ready. The Fifer replied, 'I was on the field, son. I wouldn't go as far as to say I was playing.' Top marks for honesty.

Celtic had to settle for five goals in the midweek meeting with Alloa, their first trip to Recreation Park since 1955. At the kick-off, a rainbow arched over the ground that had seen better days. Billy McNeill must have wondered if there was a pot of gold - or, at least, a League Cup - at the end of it. It was a miserable evening for ex-Rangers goalkeeper Donald Hunter who looked jittery throughout. So riddled with nerves, in fact, that Danny McGrain even got on the scoresheet. The Celtic captain's big moment arrived in the thirty-fourth minute when Hunter spilled an effort from McCluskey and McGrain, in alien territory, fired the rebound straight back into the net. McCluskey had given the Hoops the advantage in twenty-six minutes and before half-time, Paul McStay and Mark Reid, with a penalty, had pushed the scoreline to 4-0. Tommy Burns sealed the win with a fine effort on the hour mark. There was still no place in the starting line-up for Nicholas.

Swirling rain greeted Celtic as they arrived in Arbroath for their next League Cup-tie. They had to work hard for their 3-0 win at Gayfield and that was mainly down to some heroic goalkeeping from David Robertson, who had been released by the Parkhead side as a youngster. He performed like a man possessed and Celtic went in all-square at the interval. The breakthrough came just before the hour mark when the bold custodian made his only mistake of the day. He misjudged a lob from Danny Crainie and George McCluskey headed in from close range. Charlie Nicholas, a substitute for McCluskey, shot under the keeper's body for the second in the seventy-fourth minute and Crainie wrapped it up with a header two minutes later.

The League Cup's latest format meant that the kick-off to the Premier Division season had been pushed back to September 4 as the Cup-ties came thick and fast during the month of August. Four days after Arbroath, Alloa provided the opposition and were swept aside 4-1. A crowd of only 6,100 bothered to attend the formality as Nicholas, starting for the first time, scored the breakthrough goal in the thirteenth minute. Lucky for some? Alloa went in level when Jim Gray rattled home a penalty-kick a minute before the break. MacLeod restored the lead in the sixty-sixth minute and Aitken and Burns, with goals within sixty seconds of each other in the fading moments, brought an end to the scoring. Reid should have had another, but almost splintered the crossbar with a wayward penalty-kick in the fifty-eighth minute.

Celtic were strutting along four goals to the good by half-time in their eventual 7-1 win over Dunfermline, once such fearsome Cup opponents, at East End Park. The Celtic supporters in the 7,100 crowd got their first glimpse of summer signing Graeme Sinclair who came on as a substitute for Danny McGrain, while youth team product Jim McInally made his debut at left-back. Mike Conroy, the Scottish Cup hero of 1980, also lined up for his last appearance for the Hoops before being sold to Hibs for £40,000.

Nicholas showed the sign of things to come as the months unfolded by taking centre stage with a four-goal haul, one a penalty-kick. George McCluskey, Tommy Burns and an own goal from the unfortunate Bobby Dall completed the scoring. Steve Morrison nicked a crumb of comfort for the Fifers. Billy McNeill was using the League Cup to bring in youngsters and John Buckley and Jim Dobbin were the next two starlets to roll off the conveyor belt when they made their first appearances in the 4-1 home win over Arbroath. The 5,202 supporters enjoyed what they saw of the fresh-faced kids. Buckley, a typical wily winger, caught the imagination while hard-working midfielder Dobbin scored the fourth goal. MacLeod, Nicholas and McCluskey made the home side comfortable at the interval before Dobbin's memorable moment in the fifty-fifth minute when he headed in a cross from McCluskey. Tommy Yule got the consolation for the part-timers.

Partick Thistle, newly-relegated from the previous season, were the quarter-final obstacle in September. Celtic romped to a 4-0 victory in front of 9,240 fans at Parkhead. The Firhill side could thank their lucky stars that Billy McNeill's men did not go into double figures. Aitken, Burns and Nicholas all hit the bar while overworked keeper Alan Rough pulled off blinding saves throughout the evening; three, in particular, from MacLeod, Provan and McCluskey. He had no answer, though, when Provan got the opening goal in the ninth minute. Celtic, amazingly, had to wait until ten minutes after the interval to notch another, Nicholas on target with a smart drive. MacLeod got the goal he deserved just after the hour mark and McGarvey completed the stroll in Celtic Park with the fourth in the eighty-fifth minute.

Two weeks later in the second leg in Maryhill, Graeme Sinclair made his first start as two goals from Nicholas and a single from MacLeod - a sensational left-foot long-range drive - sent Celtic through to the semi-final on a 7-0 aggregate. Nicholas, after being overlooked at the start of the competition, had now rattled in an impressive ten strikes to become a fixture in McNeill's frontline. Celtic, Rangers, Dundee United and First Division Hearts went into the ballot for the last four. McNeill's men were paired with the dangerous Tannadice outfit while the Ibrox side were handed the Tynecastle team that had been operating outwith the top league for two years.

At least, for the Celtic manager and his players, this was the opportunity to turn the tables on a team who had knocked them out in the semi-finals the last two times they had engaged in battle. Jim McLean took his men to Parkhead on Wednesday, October 27 for the first salvo in a bitter battle. It was the usual cagey stuff at the start, but Celtic managed the breakthrough six minutes from the interval when Derek Stark was adjudged to have pulled down Davie Provan. Referee Kenny Hope didn't think twice, but, clearly, McLean and Co were not travelling along the same thought process. After the usual protests, Charlie Nicholas clattered the spot-kick high past Hamish McAlpine.

And five minutes later, there was even more pain inflicted on the visitors. On this occasion, there could be no doubting the validity of the effort. Provan sent in a probing cross, Nicholas back-headed it and McGarvey, display courageous reflexes, threw himself between two United defenders to force the ball home. Five minutes after the interval, Celtic had a reasonable shout for a second spot-kick when Ralph Milne appeared to handle a shot from Provan. This time Hope was not convinced. The visitors' best opportunity was presented to Davie Dodds, but the lanky centre-forward bashed the ball against the crossbar to the relief of the home fans in the 19,149 crowd.

One observer from the Press Box noted, 'Paul McStay looked a veteran and certainly outshone all the other midfielders for creativity.' United had lost their first game in twenty stretching back to the previous season. They made all sort of noises about retribution on Tayside. And they kept good their threat. However, it was Celtic who were heading for Hampden just under a month later. United won 2-1, but McNeill had the satisfaction of seeing his side go through on a 3-2 aggregate after another torrid night of exhausting action at Tannadice. Celtic were looking good after the first-half where they refused to be drawn upfield by their rivals. McNeill's thinking was clear. 'We were two goals ahead, it was up to them to come forward and see what they had to offer.'

Everything was working well until seven minutes after half-time. Davie Dodds sent in a cross that was blasted goalwards by the ever-dangerous Paul Sturrock. The ball struck Pat Bonner and, unfortunately, rebounded straight onto Roy Aitken who couldn't get out of the way. The ball bounced over the line in slightly fortuitous circumstances. Jim McLean exhorted his troops to go forward and thirteen minutes later the tie was level. David Narey flighted in an inviting free-kick and Bonner seemed to hesitate. That was all will-o'-the-wisp frontman Sturrock needed to get into position to flick the ball home.

It was anyone's game at this stage, but United's eagerness back-fired in the seventy-eighth minute. John Holt, already booked, upended Tommy Burns with a tackle that wouldn't have looked out of place in that sport where they perform with an oval ball. Referee Brian McGinlay flashed another yellow and Holt was dismissed. It got worse for United with a mere two minutes remaining. Burns spotted a disguised run from Nicholas and pitched forward the perfect pass. The striker had only McAlpine to beat and he didn't fail. The ball nestled in the net and Celtic were in the League Cup Final for the first time since 1977/78.

Rangers lay in wait. The scene was set. John Greig's men had completed a competent two-game semi-final against Hearts, winning 2-0 at home and 2-1 away for a comfortable 4-1 aggregate. They had been unbeaten in the tournament with the only two blemishes being draws against Hibs in their section. They underlined their ambition, however, in the competition with a landslide 12-1 overall win against a wretched Kilmarnock in the quarter-final. With Hearts taken care of in the semi, it was now all eyes on another Old Firm encounter at the national stadium on Saturday, December 4.

The elements positively snarled on League Cup Final day. Raindrops the size of golf ball came hurtling down by the bucketload. The Celtic supporters, in the vast, exposed, uncovered terracings, risked hypothermia to cheer on their team. They were drenched but delighted at the end of a pulsating duel between the Glasgow giants. The crowd was reduced considerably to 55,372 due to repair work to the North Enclosure.

John Greig sprung a surprise when he signed former midfielder Gordon Smith on a loan deal from Brighton just forty-eight hours before the game. Temporary transfers, of course, are widespread these days, but they were rather unusual in the eighties. Greig, in fact, had sold Smith to the English club for £440,000 two years earlier and was happy to take him back for a couple of months. He went straight into the first team to face Celtic. It was an enterprising move by the Rangers manager, but it didn't pay dividends. Smith made only three appearances in total, didn't score in any, and was shipped off back down the coast with a runners-up medal in his pocket.

The League Cup Final was sponsored by a firm called Telejector UK, a first for the competition, and, by way of a bonus, they offered £20,000 for any player scoring a hat-trick and a further £10,000 for a team winning by four clear goals. Charlie Nicholas did his best to steer Celtic towards the financial bounty when he scored a splendid opening goal in the twenty-second minute. The strike owed everything to Nicholas' uncanny ability to size up situations in a flash in congested penalty areas. Davie Provan fed him a ball to feet and the Ibrox defenders expected him to take an extra touch. Without warning, the Celt stabbed out a left foot and propelled the ball low past Jim Stewart at his left-hand post. Some critics blamed the keeper for not reacting quickly enough, but the truth is the goal was all about Nicholas' hair-trigger thinking. To be fair to the Rangers No 1, Stewart didn't get the opportunity to set himself before Nicholas struck his unerring effort for his first-ever goal at the national stadium.

No-one even thought about blaming Stewart when Murdo MacLeod claimed the second goal nine minutes later. A platoon of goalkeepers couldn't have kept his effort out of the net. Provan, as ever, was involved with a low corner-kick on the right wing. Roy Aitken returned the ball to him and this time the winger pitched it to the far post. Tom McAdam climbed the highest to nod the ball across goal. Davie MacKinnon bravely threw himself in front of Frank McGarvey to frantically attempt to head clear. The ball sped to the edge of the box where MacLeod screamed at Aitken to leave it. MacLeod hit a ferocious first-time right-foot drive high into the top corner. If the net hadn't been there the ball might have ended in a street somewhere in Mount Florida.

Celtic looked in control, but, as we all know to our cost, bizarre things can occur in these Glasgow head-to-heads. Two minutes after half time, Rangers won a free-kick about twenty-five yards out following a McAdam challenge on Smith. Referee Kenny Hope signaled that it was a direct award and Jim Bett, with a lazy left-foot execution, lifted the ball over the defensive wall and past Pat Bonner, who seemed startled by the effort. It threw Rangers a lifeline on a day at Hampden where a lifeboat may have been more in calling.

However, McNeill's men remained unflappable. They looked the better team and might have had a third when a sizzling right-wing cross from Provan eluded everyone and MacKinnon had to indulge in some impromptu acrobatics to hook the ball off the goal-line. The referee's whistle shrilled and Celtic had won their first League Cup since 1974 when McNeill, coincidentally, captained the side to a captivating 6-3 success over Hibs. He applauded on the touchline as Danny McGrain went up to deservedly lift the trophy.

McNeill observed, 'The second-half was frustrating for us, but, to be truthful, it was never nerve-racking because we were still in control and Rangers did not create many chances, did they?'

With that, the Celtic manager went off to plot a clean sweep of the domestic silverware. Alas, things don't always go according to plan.

CHAPTER TWELVE
THE AMSTERDAM THRILL

There are some football games that are seared into the memory banks where they will forever spend a happy existence; unshakeable, wonderful, imbedded, frozen in time. The night Celtic beat Ajax in Amsterdam on September 29, 1982 is one of them.

They may not have been the extraordinarily gifted Dutch side of the early seventies that arrogantly swept aside all challengers as they dominated Europe for three successive years with Johan Cruyff striking up the band wherever they went on their majestic travels. However, the name Ajax still had a magical aura surrounding it and, naturally, they were still an excellent side with the same ideals that elevated them to a status above so many other clubs worldwide.

Cruyff and his talented entourage arrived in Glasgow for the first leg of their European Cup First Round tie on Wednesday September 15. They were ready, willing and able to put on a show for their Glasgow audience with a 56,229 all-ticket crowd turning out to welcome them. By the end of a scintillating evening, no-one felt short-changed - even if it did cost £2.50 for the privilege of standing on the terracing. The champions of Scotland and Holland shared four goals in a fascinating contest that thrillingly ebbed and flowed throughout the ninety minutes. The party got started almost immediately; the fourth minute to be exact.

Jesper Olsen, a darting, tricky customer, gave the Dutch the lead to silence the hitherto noisy crowd who just knew they would be entertained regally on this evening in the east end of Glasgow. Olsen, who would later to play for Manchester United, displayed mesmerising skills as he nipped in from the left leaving three defenders in his slipstream before sliding the ball between Pat Bonner and his near post. It was pace allied with precision and the home fans wondered, with a little fear and trepidation, if this was to be the agenda for the rest of the evening.

Ten minutes later the skies above Celtic Park were penetrated by the loud cheers of a happy, delirious support; Charlie Nicholas had equalised. The great Cruyff revealed his human frailties when he gave away a penalty-kick after a mistimed challenge on Tommy Burns who had just worked a quick corner-kick routine with Davie Provan on the left wing. Swedish referee Erik Fredriksson had no doubt it was a foul by the great Dutchman and Nicholas punished Cruyff's rashness with a sweet effort past keeper Hans Galje, who was an eleventh hour replacement for international No.1 Piet Schrijvers who was injured in the warm-up.

The Celtic fans could barely contain themselves on an evening when the air crackled with electricity and tension. They were breathless in anticipation, but there were frowns all round, apart from a small pocket of Ajax supporters, when the Dutch side went back in front in the eighteenth minute. Cruyff, possibly embarrassed by his rashness of only a moment or so earlier, demonstrated that he was still one of the most magnificent passers of a ball in the universe when he cushioned an Olsen cross into the path of Soren Lerby. It was sublime touch that carved open the Celtic back lot and Lerby, the Danish captain of Ajax, showed no little skill himself as he carefully dinked the ball high over Bonner. Would Celtic buckle? Not on your life. This was a Billy McNeill team with verve and drive.

Nicholas thought he had equalised after prodding the ball home following a goalmouth melee, but the match official ruled it out. If it was for offside, it was an extremely tight decision. Such was the frantic action, there wasn't time to dwell on the incident. Nine minutes after the Dutch side's second goal, it was all-square once again. Goalkeeper Galje thumped a clearance deep into Celtic territory that was met by the forehead of Davie Moyes, playing in central defence alongside Tom McAdam with the influential Roy Aitken missing. He powered the ball back into the Ajax half, Nicholas got the subtlest of head flicks to send Frank McGarvey clear. He made directly for goal, enticed Galje from his line before stroking the ball under him. Four goals inside the first thirty minutes with brisk, crisp passing the order of the evening from both sides. Celtic Park was illuminated by the performances of both sets of performers.

The scoring ended there, but there were scares for both teams before referee Fredrikssen blew for a halt to proceedings. The Ajax side, led by Cruyff, went to the centre circle to take their bow in front of the sporting Celtic fans who applauded them off the field. The Glasgow Herald's scribe in the Press Box figured without the fire and fervour of McNeill's men when he put together his match report. Clearly, he thought Celtic's European adventure for season 1982/83 only had another one-and-a-half hours to go before it would be extinguished. He wrote: 'Credit is due to Ajax for coming to entertain with open football rather than adopting the usual European tactic of holding out on an opponents' ground. Their reward looks like being a place in the draw for the Second Round after the return leg in Amsterdam in two weeks' time.' The Daily Record concurred. Their reporter's straight-to-the-point intro stated, 'Celtic will go to the Olympic Stadium in a fortnight chasing what appears to be a lost cause.'

Someone forgot to tell Billy McNeill and his players they were wasting their time. On a bright September evening, the Celtic players strolled onto the Olympic Stadium with 52,326 fans – 3,000 from Scotland - there to greet them. There was a strut in their proud march onto the field. If they were condemned men going to meet their grisly fate, they were going with gallant hearts. In thirty-three minutes they were ahead with a flawless piece of finishing from Charlie Nicholas. Cruyff couldn't have done better himself.

Paul McStay got the move in motion with a glorious ball across the park to Graeme Sinclair. The utility defender, playing for Dumbarton at Boghead Park only a few months beforehand, had been given the role of shadowing superstar Cruyff wherever he went. But he broke free of the defensive shackles to storm forward and burst down the left. He was stopped in his tracks by a slide tackle from a desperate Leo Van Veen and the ball broke to Roy Aitken, who transferred it quickly to Nicholas, who, with a delightful change of pace, skipped past two challenges before playing a swift one-two with Frank McGarvey and completing an admirable piece of quick thinking by lobbing the ball over Piet Schrijver. Quite simply, it was stunning in build-up and execution.

The scoreline remained the same until the sixty-fifth minute when Ajax levelled on the night with an odd goal. Soren Lerby attracted a posse of players to him on the left before a swift pass inside found the unmarked Gerald Vanenburg. He struck the ball with the outside of his right foot and Pat Bonner looked as though he had been caught in two minds with an Ajax attacker trying to get on the end of what looked like a cross. The forward didn't make contact and, before Bonner could get proper leverage to throw himself across his line, the ball found its way into the net. The Dutch were now ahead on the goals away rule. Celtic may have been forgiven for believing their moment had passed, especially after a header from McGarvey left Schrijver rooted to the spot, but, alas, clipped the crossbar and bounced to safety.

Cruyff, unwittingly, may just have done Celtic a massive favour with the clock running down. With five minutes to go, the great Dutchman, a true artiste of the sport, was substituted. As he walked off, he waved to the crowd and gave the impression the contest was over. Not with this Celtic team it wasn't. And Ajax would suffer the consequences three minutes later when George McCluskey, on as a substitute for the tiring Davie Provan, got the match winning goal.

Danny McGrain, of all people, tried his luck from about thirty yards with a shot that hardly got off the ground. McGarvey appeared to block the effort before shuttling it to Nicholas who knocked it in front of McCluskey. He dragged it to his left foot and shot across Shrijver into the far corner. The ball seemed to take an eternity before the net rippled. It hadn't been a formality for the Dutch, after all.

McCluskey recalled, 'That was a great result and a fabulous night in Amsterdam. I managed to get into their dressing room after the game because I was trying to get someone to swap jerseys with me. None of them wanted to do it. They all had their heads down. So, as I was walking out of the room, Cruyff was lying on the table getting a rubdown and he shouted, "McCluskey!" I stopped and he said, "I'll swap jerseys with you." It was just fantastic. The only thing was, I had to hold his cigarette while he took off his shirt. I couldn't believe it.'

Sadly, there is no happy postscript to this joyous little tale. McCluskey added, 'At home, we had an old coal fire with a big wire guard around it. When I eventually got home from Holland I headed to my bed. My brother John went to the five-a-sides and took the strip to wear and show it off to all his pals. Then he brought it home, washed it and put it on the guard - and burnt it! Needless to say, we didn't speak for a couple of weeks.' While the newspapers were waxing lyrical about his splendid winning goal, McCluskey had his own interesting take. 'I just wanted to get it on target. To be honest, I thought their keeper went down like a sack of spuds.'

McCluskey also revealed he might not even have been in Amsterdam that memorable evening. He added, 'I was carrying a wee injury and it was debatable whether I would travel or not. But Big Billy asked me to go, because at that time it was any two from me, Frank McGarvey and Charlie Nicholas to play up front. Among the three of us, we collected over one hundred goals that year; we were scoring a phenomenal amount of goals.

'When I came on in the second-half, I have to say the last ten minutes actually suited us because we were out of it and had nothing to lose.

The three of us were involved in my goal - Charlie got it, passed it to Frank, who passed it to me. I drew the centre-half and went by him. I struck it with my left foot and it went right across the box. I caught it sweet as a nut.'

If it was a fabulous night for scorer McCluskey, it was just as exhilarating for 'spoiler' Sinclair, given the onerous task of shackling Johan Cruyff for his eighty-five minutes on the pitch that evening. Years later, the player who had been performing in the Stirlingshire Cup only a month or so earlier told the Celtic View, 'As far as highs went, that was probably the greatest game I every played in. It was just an incredible experience.

'Big Billy was speaking about the tactics before the game. He came to me and said to my team-mates, "Sinky's going to be marking Cruyff." I think everyone must have thought, "What?" Remember, I had only been there six weeks. The manager insisted, "Even if he walks off the park to go to the toilet, I want you to go with him!" So, I knew specifically what I had to. I was nervous, but I was thinking, "Fair enough, I have to do it." Before the game, when the music is playing and the teams are lining up, it makes you get more nervous. You just want to get started.

'Big Billy just told me to stick to the task. We agreed there were times when it wouldn't work. But I knew how to man-mark people, so I just went out and did it. I had a good start to the game. I got a couple of good tackles in. I always tried to anticipate where the pass was going. I got a wee bit of confidence from it. The team started playing really well and I actually made some positive runs. Not everything was negative.

'Everything was going really well and then they scored a terrible goal. It was shocking. I don't think the guy, Vanenburg, meant it. It was a like a cross which he hit with the outside of his foot. I think Pat Bonner was unsighted and the ball just crawled into the net. But we weren't really deflated. I remember Big Roy Aitken saying, "We've done well, anyway, so if we go out we will go out with our heads held high." I had a run down the right-hand side and Frank McGarvey hit the bar. We brought on George McCluskey. He got the ball on the left hand side and he hit a good shot, a daisy-cutter, and it went in. There were only two minutes to go and I hadn't experienced anything like that in my life. It was just unbelievable. And then the whistle went and all the players were running about the park. We just had beaten an incredible Ajax side with the likes of Soren Lerby, Wim Kieft and Jan Molby. And, of course, Johan Cruyff.

'It wasn't as though we didn't believe we could win. It was just the manner in which we won that was so incredible. I was just running about daft. If someone could have pumped me up, I would have just floated away. Big Billy was going nuts, as well. I seem to remember going to the Celtic fans and the whole place was heaving. Our supporters were going wild. I had never experienced anything like that in my life.'

McNeill can laugh at the memory. 'I'm not sure if I was going nuts, but it would be fair to say I was exceptionally happy. A lot of people who should have known better had simply written us off. That was something that would always get my hackles up. It leaves you thinking, "Oh, is that right? I'll show you." And, of course, you have to get that through to your players. Thankfully, with this set of guys I didn't have to ever extend myself on that front. They had a lot of pride in their work and they would have seen a game in Amsterdam as being an ideal platform. It was a brilliant night and, yes, I joined in with the support. Why not? I may have been the Celtic manager, but I was always a Celtic fan. The draw hadn't been kind to us and that was the case in the next round when we were paired with the champions of Spain, Real Sociedad. They may not have had the glamour associated with Real Madrid or Barcelona, but there is no arguing with the league table and they had won the title, so that spoke volumes for their ability.'

Celtic travelled to San Sebastian in Basque country for the first leg on October 20 where a capacity 27,000 fans packed into the trim Arocha Stadium. Billy McNeill's side were looking very comfortable as they camped in midfield with Paul McStay, Roy Aitken and Murdo MacLeod policing matters while Charlie Nicholas and Frank McGarvey probed for openings through the centre. Everything was going like clockwork until two devastating pieces of ill fortune within the space of four second-half minutes. Striker Jesus Satrustegui had a pop at goal in the seventy-fourth minute. It looked like Pat Bonner's ball until the shot took a nick off Mark Reid to send the keeper scrambling. Too late, the effort crept over the line. The players were still cursing their luck when, remarkably, the Spaniards again scored with a massive deflection. This time winger Pedro Uralde shot and Bonner was moving to his left when it struck Aitken and changed course completely. The keeper valiantly tried to claw at it while still in mid-air, but he had no chance.

McNeill said, 'To lose one own goal is bad enough, but to lose two is practically unheard of. The annoying thing was that I could sense their players' frustration. We were matching them at every twist and turn and I would have quite happily settled for a draw and finished the business in Glasgow. And then, suddenly, it's 2-0 for our opponents in such a short space of time and you realise it's not going to be your evening.'

A crowd of 54,874 turned out at Parkhead on a crisp November 3 evening hoping to see Celtic overturn a Spanish side which, unusually, was not top heavy with big-name players. Their main personality was Spanish international goalkeeper Luis Arconada, who also doubled as their captain. He was rated as one of the best in the world and Celtic knew they would have to work for anything they got against him. A deflection or two would help, as well. No such luck.

Inside twenty-five minutes of the second leg in front of another all-ticket attendance, Celtic were required to score four goals to go through. The Spaniards struck with the Celtic defence hardly blameless. Lopez Ufarte, the winger who had played for his country during the World Cup Finals that summer, was given far too much time and space in which to ply his trade. When no-one came to challenge him, he set up an excellent cross for Pedro Uralde to head beyond Pat Bonner from close range. The keeper looked accusingly at Danny McGrain and he looked accusingly at Mark Reid and he looked accusingly at Tom McAdam. The Celtic fans just looked aghast.

They desperately needed a goal before half-time and Murdo MacLeod provided the lifeline. Davie Provan was brought down on the edge of the box and Belgian referee Alexis Ponnet awarded the free-kick. The winger rolled it back to MacLeod who rammed a twenty-five yard drive away from Arconada. Real Sociedad barely had time to re-centre the ball when the half-time whistle sounded. Billy McNeill had to get busy inside the next quarter-of-an-hour.

'That's a massive part of the manager's job, as far as I am concerned,' asserted McNeill. 'You have to think on your feet. We were playing well enough, but we needed to score three goals without reply within the next forty-five minutes or we were out. As it stood at that moment, our run was over before it got properly started. You've got to gamble on such occasions. I took off left-back Mark Reid and put on Tommy Burns. Graeme Sinclair was told he would have to combine his midfield duties with what was happening over his shoulder on the left. Sinky never complained. "Okay, boss," was all he said and I knew I could rely on him. So, the lads went out for the second-half and it was very much a case of win or bust. We had to give it our best shot.'

Real Sociedad made absolutely no pretence about how they would play in the second forty-five minutes. They practically abandoned any notions of attack altogether. It was defence-in-depth stuff and their back lot were quite happy to distribute clearances among the Celtic support in the stand or terracings. It wasn't pretty, but it was effective. MacLeod was Celtic's main threat as he continually attacked behind the main forwards Charlie Nicholas and Frank McGarvey with Amsterdam hero George McCluskey adding his weight as a late substitute for Davie Provan. Arconada made two excellent stops from MacLeod before the midfielder collected his second goal of the night with only two minutes remaining. It received a half-hearted cheer from the supporters who realised their team had reached the end of the road as far as Europe was concerned.

But they would always have the glory in Amsterdam.

CHAPTER THIRTEEN
FAREWELL CAESAR...
GOODBYE CHARLIE

It was a pleasant evening as sunshine bathed the small Irish town of Baleybofey in County Donegal. Around ten thousand excited fans squeezed into Finn Park, many of the supporters sitting on the touchline a few feet from the pitch. Finn Harps were playing host to mighty Celtic on Wednesday May 18, 1983 in a historic meeting of the teams. It was to be a memorable evening in more ways than one.

No-one in the trim, compact football ground realised they were uniquely placed to view the sun eventually going down on two legendary Celts. They were witnessing what would transpire to be Billy McNeill's last engagement as Celtic manager for four years. They were also observing Charlie Nicholas' final game as a player before abdicating to Arsenal a month later. Like McNeill, of course, he would return to Parkhead after a seven-year absence. Ironically, Nicholas signed off with a goal - his fifty-third of the season - in a 4-0 win over the Irish part-timers in a good-natured friendly.

However, amidst the sprinkling from the bright shafts of light, there was a lot more happening in the dark shadows off the pitch than on it in that cosy little neuk in Southern Ireland.

Billy McNeill vividly outlined the reasons for moving to pastures new in his excellent autobiography, 'Back To Paradise', which was published in Celtic's Centenary Year of 1988.

The skipper of the Lisbon Lions revealed, 'I never expected to leave the club. But a personality clash between myself and the late Desmond White, the club chairman, mysteriously built up. I am not saying I was right in everything, but I am still baffled and regretful that it reached such an extent that I had to leave. I am discussing this now as a matter of record. It would be dishonest in an autobiography to dodge an issue which was such an important milestone in my career. Happily, the situation has been resolved in the manner I always hoped it would be - by me returning to the club which has been such an important part of my life. The fact that I have been able to do so says much for the magnanimity and mature good sense of the directors.

'The story of what turned out to be my departure from Celtic began when I played in the first Glasgow Open Golf Championship at Haggs Castle. I was pleased at how good the tournament was for Glasgow which was my "adopted" city because, of course, I was born in Bellshill. Coming off the course, I was asked unexpectedly by a group of reporters about a move to Manchester City. The truth was I had been sounded out quietly, but had brushed the question aside without expressing any interest. So, I was taken aback that the Press had got wind of a private, and at that stage not too serious approach, although I could see it was to City's advantage to have it in the papers that they were enquiring about me.

'Two days later, on a Monday, I attended a meeting at Mr White's office in Bath Street. Most of the directors were also present. I went naively, thinking there was no major problem and certainly none which would lead to me leaving Parkhead. I had refused to comment on the City approach to the papers and was, therefore, shocked to see some of the headlines which included this one: "McNEILL DEMANDS A WAGE INCREASE." I never demanded anything. What I had done was ask the chairman twice if I could be included in a pensions scheme. I never received an answer.

'Quite a lot of my private business became public. The fact that I was being paid £20,000 a year and that I owed the club £11,000, part of an interest-free loan, was freely discussed in the media. The latter fact emerged in an official statement from Celtic. Some writers even pointed out that I was well down the salary scale in the Premier League. The Press were saying this, mark you, not me.

'At the meeting it was quickly clear that my future was secondary. The room was littered with Sunday papers and I was accused of making statements which I was required to deny. Since I had done no such thing, I pointed out that I couldn't be held responsible for the work of newspaper sub-editors. I did want my conditions improved so that I was at least in a comparable position to other leading Premier League managers. I certainly was not looking for fortunes and had not "demanded" anything.

'The media claimed that John Greig, Jim McLean, Alex Ferguson and Ricky McFarlane, at St Mirren, were better off. I have to be honest and say it got my back up that the meeting with the board had turned so badly against me that all they wanted were apologies for what had been reported. I felt I was being manoeuvred into a position where the chairman wanted me to walk out. I was shattered when I left that meeting.

'Pride has always been my spur. I don't like letting anybody down and I don't fancy being let down myself. I was asked to eat humble pie and I couldn't see that I had done anything, or said anything, to warrant this. I was never given the opportunity to spell out what I thought was reasonable by the way of a better salary scale. It seemed to me that Mr White wanted a parting of the ways. His mind was made up.'

As Billy McNeill has already pointed elsewhere, his chairman had also put it to him on another invidious occasion that he should sack his assistant, John Clark. It was clear bad feeling had been simmering for some considerable time between two headstrong characters.

McNeill continued, 'I wasn't even told the transfer fee paid by Arsenal for Charlie Nicholas. The chairman asked me to tell the Press that Celtic and Arsenal had "satisfactorily" agreed on a transfer fee, but he would not reveal the amount - even to me, his manager. I disagreed with the way the Nicholas transfer was handled, anyway. However, it seemed that my integrity was being questioned since I wasn't trusted with the information about the fee.'

The situation regarding Nicholas' transfer undoubtedly structured a permanent wedge between the pair. McNeill did not want to lose the player. If anything, he was looking to build a team around Nicholas, Paul McStay, Roy Aitken and Tommy Burns. He demanded a face-to-face with the chairman. McNeill recalled, 'I asked him why Nicholas had to be sold in the first place. I might as well have talked to the wall. The answer I got - if, indeed, you could call it that - was a rambling reply to the effect that Celtic had concluded a sound bit of business. That really annoyed me and I retorted, "Mr White, why has he got to leave the club?" The chairman said that was just the way it was in football and I snapped, "No, Mr White, that is the way it is at Celtic. "

'I then implored Mr White that if his mind was truly made up to sell our prize asset, at least make it a Dutch auction. By placing Charlie on the open market I reckoned we would receive a small fortune, but I was wasting my time. The board, or at least the chairman, had ruled and Charlie was going to Highbury because Mr White explained, Denis Hill-Wood, the Arsenal chairman, was an honourable man. What that had to do with it, I wouldn't know.'

Originally, Nicholas was in no rush to leave Celtic. Before he signed forms at Parkhead as a teenager, Ipswich Town manager Bobby Robson had offered him £4,000 as a signing-on fee. That was twenty times the amount Celtic had put on the table, but the player followed his heart and joined his boyhood idols. By his own admission, he hadn't made up his mind about staying or going when the 1982/83 season came to an end. However, fans at the 4-2 victory over Rangers at Ibrox that tumultuous afternoon were left with the distinct impression that when their favourite player waved to them at the end he was actually waving farewell.

The first offer to him from Celtic was a £300 per week four-year contract. Nicholas was well aware there were four or five players at Parkhead earning more than that. He knew, too, that players at Rangers, Aberdeen and Dundee United were on higher salaries. After a meeting with Desmond White, Nicholas had no doubt his future lay elsewhere. Belatedly, Celtic made a final offer, but the player wouldn't be swayed. The new contract was for £400 per week with a £20,000 signing-on fee spread over the four years of the deal. Nicholas' reaction was, 'By English standards, it was a lousy offer. Even in Scotland, it wasn't that bright.'

McNeill was certainly more clued up on the market value of Nicholas than his chairman. Manchester United and Liverpool also wanted the player and a bidding war among three clubs with secure financial resources would undoubtedly have seen the price pushed to seven figures. The Celtic manager was aware that Nottingham Forest boss Brian Clough had spent £1million on bringing Trevor Francis from Birmingham City in February 1979, the first deal of this magnitude between two English teams. In September the same year, Malcolm Allison ploughed £1.45million into Wolves' coffers to take Steve Daley to Manchester City. It was a British record transfer for all of forty-eight hours. Molineux gaffer John Barnwell added to the cash windfall from Allison and bought Scottish international Andy Gray from Aston Villa for £1.46million. All mind-boggling sums at the time. In October 1981, Manchester United manager Ron Atkinson raised the bar a little higher by spending £1.5million on West Brom's Bryan Robson.

Eventually, via the Press, McNeill would discover Arsenal had paid £650,000 for Nicholas. 'I had absolutely no fears that we would have got £1million for Charlie,' said the Celtic manager. 'I looked at what they were paying south of the border for players who were nowhere near the class or quality of our player. It wasn't just my opinion, either. Most people thought Charlie was worth at least the same as Trevor Francis, whose deal had taken place more than four years earlier. Taking the cost of inflation into consideration, Celtic could have asked for even more for their player. Yet they accepted £350,000 less than the market value for a young player who had his entire career ahead of him. Why? We'll never know.'

Nicholas, in fact, didn't even cost half of the gargantuan fee Malcolm Allison splashed so spectacularly and ill-advisedly on Steve Daley, a distinctly average midfielder who never won a solitary full cap for England. The rather staid and proper Observer newspaper, a few years later, summed up the deal as 'being the biggest waste of money in football history.' In fact, Daley was sold twenty months later to North American League side Seattle Sounders for £300,000, little more than a fifth of his original transfer value.

It was only too evident that the manager and his board didn't match ambitions in trying to bring players into the club. McNeill added, 'My position as manager was being usurped and this was underlined when I tried to sign Joe McLaughlin from Morton. Benny Rooney and Mike Jackson talked about £250,000 which I wouldn't look at. It was simply too much, but Morton needed cash and they were trying to get the best deal. Some time later Benny phoned me to say I could have the player for £85,000. This time I thought the price was right. With Morton's blessing, I established from Joe that he wanted to join Celtic rather than Chelsea, who were also in the bidding. I phoned Mr White, who said, reasonably, that he had to consult with the other directors. Eventually, Mr White came back with the news the board had turned down the idea of buying McLaughlin. I then spoke again to the player and wished him every good luck with Chelsea, for whom he has since been a very good player indeed.

'So, I was either being squeezed out or stripped of authority which would be unacceptable to any worthwhile manager. Mr White's parting shot was, "You can have further discussions with whichever club you wish." So, my days at Celtic were officially numbered.

'Soon afterwards, I met Peter Swales, the Manchester City chairman, in Carlisle. But, even then, I asked for time to have another chat with Celtic. He gave me twenty-four hours, but was on the telephone next morning trying to get a quick decision. I contacted Mr White, told him the exact position and asked if he had altered his thoughts. He came back offering to up my salary to £25,000, but insisting Frank Connor became assistant manager and that I retracted statements in the papers. Within a few minutes, I told Mr Swales that he had a new City manager.'

The situation, in fact, between the manager and chairman had deteriorated to the stage McNeill revealed he had previously twice offered his resignation, but White had declined on both occasions.

McNeill added, 'I tried to clear the air with Mr White, making the point that our troubles did not seem to be related to negotiations about either money or a contract. Mr White finally said that he felt I had "overplayed" my authority at times. The relationship between a manager and the chairman is very important and perhaps I should have tried even harder to ensure it worked at Parkhead. However, it was difficult to team up with Mr White. I asked him more than once if we could meet on a regular basis to talk about the running of the club and, preferably, away from Celtic Park, but this never happened. There should be a better understanding between chairman and manager.

'I admit I wasn't properly prepared for the Celtic job. It would have been better if I had been longer at Pittodrie. I tended to ride roughshod over things and maybe even people. More diplomacy was required from me. With hindsight, I can understand why Mr White was sometimes aggrieved. I even stormed out of a board meeting because the discussion became too explosive. To be truthful, I wasn't the easiest individual to get along with, but nobody could ever doubt that I wanted the best for Celtic. The Celtic board knew me well enough. I had, after all, been a player at Parkhead for eighteen years. I wasn't a new boy by any means. Throughout my career I've been fiery, but I've always aimed at being good for Celtic.'

In the midst of all the turmoil, it went almost unnoticed that a player who had scored eighty-three goals in two-hundred-and-seven appearances was leaving by the back door. George McCluskey was on his way to Leeds United. He later admitted, 'My biggest regret was that I had to leave Celtic. There was a lot of politics involved, but I would have been quite happy to have remained at the club. However, I was one of the lowest-paid players and I had been the top scorer the previous season. All I wanted was the same wage as the highest-paid - I didn't want any more or any less. I refused what I was offered.

'At that time, of course, there was the changeover with Billy McNeill and Davie Hay. Davie was absolutely fantastic with me and kept coming back with another offer from the board. I thank Davie for everything, but then Leeds came in. I said I would still stay at Celtic if the board made me the same offer as everybody else, but they wouldn't. That was regrettable as I would have loved to have stayed and played under Davie for a couple of years.'

So, Billy McNeill, the manager, Charlie Nicholas, the club's hottest property, and George McCluskey, a solid, honest professional, took their leave of Celtic in a summer of discontentment.

Davie Hay arrived as only the club's sixth manager in their ninety-five year history. He was following in the footsteps of Willie Maley, Jimmy McStay, Jimmy McGrory, Jock Stein and Billy McNeill. What lay in store for him?

CHAPTER FOURTEEN
FAREWELL CAESAR...
GOODBYE CHARLIE

'I have been very disappointed by the attitude of certain Celtic players. I can accept defeat if the players are trying and their sincere efforts still amount to a bad performance. That is understandable, it's football and it happens. But I will never tolerate players giving anything less that one hundred per cent in every game. To be a Celtic player you need a special commitment. A Celtic player is always up against it and he must be prepared to give absolutely everything to Celtic. He must be prepared to play until he drops for Celtic. Not for Davie Hay or anyone else, but for the club. We all know Celtic are different from the normal football club. Celtic are special and need special efforts at all times.'

Davie Hay, the new Celtic manager, was speaking from the heart. It was only his nineteenth competitive game in charge of the team in season 1983/84 and, clearly, painfully and abundantly, he had been far from impressed from what he had witnessed from his players in a 3-1 defeat against Aberdeen on a wind-ravaged Saturday at Pittodrie. It was the club's sixth match in what was swiftly becoming known as Black October. Celtic had failed to win any of the previous conflicts, losing two and drawing three. Now, on the twenty-second of that fateful month, they had sampled defeat on a third occasion.

Hay was livid. 'We collapsed in the second-half and these awful dips in form cannot be allowed to continue. Certain players, namely Davie Provan and Murdo MacLeod, have not given what is expected and, as a result, they will be dropped from the team for the next game against Hibs. If being dropped does not bring it home to players what they must do for Celtic, we must consider the possibility of letting them play their football elsewhere. No-one is assured of his place at Celtic Park. Every player must work for inclusion.'

Ironically, Provan and MacLeod, the players singled out for a special mention by a frustrated Hay, had been Billy McNeill's first signings for the club when he took over on May 1978. Reputations never meant a thing to Davie Hay. Possibly as a sideswipe at the perceived 'culprits', brought in from Kilmarnock and Dumbarton, he continued, 'Nothing is better than home-grown talent. That has always been the attitude I've known as a Celt. I now have the opportunity to bring in fringe players and one of the boys you can expect to see is John Halpin. He must take his chance and show me that he can hold his own in the first team.'

Nostradamus qualities were not required to fathom what had irked the Celtic manager way beyond his tolerance level. Celtic had under-performed against Alex Ferguson's side and, in truth, Hay was embarrassed. Hay and Ferguson may have been on the opposite ends of Glasgow's Great Divide as players, but, unknown to most, they were good friends and had a healthy mutual respect for each other. The Aberdeen manager would have realised it would have been sheer folly to adopt a condescending approach to his mate by close of play at Pittodrie.

Strangely, Celtic might have taken the lead in the tenth minute, but Tom McAdam's trajectory of the ball was just off kilter and his headed attempt clattered off the bar with Jim Leighton a spectator. To be fair, the Dons harnessed the conditions far better than their Glasgow rivals and deserved to take the lead two minutes before the turnaround when

Dougie Bell, who would never be famous for his acceleration, outpaced MacLeod on the wing before slinging in a cross that was buried behind Pat Bonner via the forehead of John Hewitt.

Ten minutes after half-time, Alex McLeish, almost effortlessly, rose to knock in another header and Gordon Strachan passed up the chance to pile on the misery when Bonner saved his penalty-kick after McAdam was adjudged to have handled the ball in the box. In the seventy-fourth minute, the cocky wee winger was put on the spot again after Paul McStay hauled down Mark McGhee. This time the midfielder made no mistake. Roy Aitken hit Celtic's consolation four minutes from the end. The Celtic fans in the 23,000 crowd weren't slow to express their displeasure. It was nothing, though, to what the players were about to face from their irate manager. MacLeod and Provan found to their cost that the new boss was a man of his word - neither was considered for a place on the substitutes' bench for the next game.

Davie Hay never shirked a challenge on the park. He was now demonstrating that identical steadfastness in the dug-out. As fate had decreed, he would face Rangers, and his old sparring partner John Greig, in two of his first seven games since replacing Billy McNeill. First up was the Glasgow Cup Final at Hampden on August 13, four days after beating Partick Thistle 2-0 in the semi-final at Firhill. That was Hay's first competitive game as Celtic manager and there was massive interest in how the supporters would react.

Desmond White and his directors had not been prepared for the backlash that came their way from furious fans over their shoddy treatment of Billy McNeill. To the board, he was an employee. To the followers, he was an icon. Hay was resolute before the game against Partick Thistle. There were no pleas to the fans to back him, no false promises. Basically, he just wanted to get on with the job. Half-time arrived in Maryhill and Celtic were leading 2-0 with goals from Danny Crainie and Brian McClair, McNeill's last signing for the club from Motherwell for £100,000. There were endorsing, encouraging cries of 'Davie Hay...Davie Hay' from the supporters.

The scoreline remained that way and the new man had the opportunity of winning some silverware two games into the job. Hay returned to Hampden where he had last performed as a Celtic player in the 1974 Scottish Cup Final. Jock Stein's men won 3-0 - and Hay was sold to Chelsea in the summer for £225,000 after a successful World Cup Finals with Scotland in West Germany. Big Jock and his board always knew when to sell a player; mainly when he was hot.

There was to be no dream return to the national stadium on this occasion, alas. Hay had resisted the temptation to buy a young Maurice Johnston from Partick Thistle. 'I reckoned I needed experience and I went, instead, for Jim Melrose. I paid £100,000 to Coventry City and I hoped he would score goals for us. The club had lost Charlie Nicholas and George McCluskey and it was obvious Frank McGarvey could do with some company in the frontline.'

Melrose made his debut for Celtic as a sixty-fifth minute substitute for Danny Crainie, but Rangers were already leading at that stage by a goal from Sandy Clark five minutes after the interval. The consensus of opinion among the 32,700 onlookers was that Celtic were the superior team, but Rangers got the goal. One Sunday newspaper reporter saw it like this, 'Celtic were so full of technical competence, they forgot Old Firm matches are never won by adoring glances. Celtic were by far the more skillful side, although in the absence of Charlie Nicholas, they were reminiscent of the guy turning up at the banquet without his false teeth. They were a team without bite.'

A week later, Hay kicked off the Premier League campaign with a victory and two points in a 2-0 win over Hibs at Easter Road. It was a solid rather than spectacular display from the visitors and the breakthrough effort came from Murdo MacLeod when he headed in a Davie Provan cross four minutes into the second-half. After an hour, Jim Melrose got off the mark in his Celtic career with a well-driven shot from the edge of the box past his old Partick Thistle chum Alan Rough.

Hay reflected, 'I did not feel any pressure. All the pressure was on the players. They were keen to do well and they succeeded in achieving that. I was pleased for the fans, too. I was very disappointed for everyone when we lost to Rangers last week. Remember, there have been big changes at the club, on and off the park. As far as the playing side is concerned, I realise there is still some way to go. However, I think this performance shows things are moving in the right direction. I put a great deal of importance on commitment and if our players continue to give the same sort of effort as we saw here at Easter Road, then we should do well.'

Billy McNeill's parting piece of silverware to Celtic had been the League Cup and Hay was determined to make certain it wasn't removed from the Parkhead trophy cabinet. He must have got a fright, though, when he took Celtic to their first visit to Glebe Park since 1950 for their opening tie in the competition against Brechin City. This was not an evening for footballing splendour. A connoisseur of the beautiful game would have been appalled. This was always going to be a scrap on a pitch that appeared to have last been rolled when Queen Victoria was on the throne. A crowd of 3,500 turned up to see what passed for entertainment. It wasn't pretty and Celtic had to battle all the way for a 1-0 success with Jim Melrose heading in a Danny McGrain cross three minutes from time. One scribe, with uncanny soothsaying qualities, wrote, 'The closeness of the result did nothing to convince the Celtic faithful who turned up at Brechin that Davie Hay is going to have an easy season.'

The return leg was at Celtic Park the following Saturday as the Scottish League continued to tamper with their own competition, making changes to the format almost every season. A crowd of 8,502 was in attendance, looking for an onslaught. Brian Whittaker, just signed from Partick Thistle, made his debut at left-back as the Angus outfit played their first-ever game in the east end of Glasgow. The best thing, maybe the only thing, you can say about this encounter was that the weather was glorious. The sunshine was relentless and the sweltering conditions may have been a contributory factor to the less-than-enthusiastic approach from the hosts or their guests. Unsurprisingly, it ended goalless.

Four days later, on August 31, Celtic faced Airdrie at Broomfield in midweek in another league Cup-tie. Hay must have wondered if he was witnessing a rerun of the Brechin stalemate. It was scoreless with only two minutes until half-time when Frank McGarvey, mercifully, ended the agony by blasting in the opener. Hay said, 'I was well aware that this ground seemed to present problems to even very good Celtic teams. I didn't feel we were being threatened, but, at the same time, I wanted my players to increase the tempo and add good finishing to our lead-up work.'

Under half-an-hour of the turnaround, Celtic had collected four goals with Murdo MacLeod (penalty), Davie Provan, Brian Whittaker and Paul McStay on target. The unfortunate Gerry McLaughlin joined the Celtic romp when he turned one past his own keeper and MacLeod could even pass up the opportunity of a second spot-kick strike near the end when John Martin parried his piledriver. The home side's moment of consolation came from Blair Miller.

Rangers arrived at Parkhead on Saturday, September 3 for the first Old Firm league confrontation, the Glasgow giants locking horns again with 50,664 fans in attendance. Referee Davie Syme hardly had time to blow for the kick-off when he was going through the same procedure to restart the game precisely thirty-three seconds later. Ally McCoist had put the visitors ahead before most of the Celtic players had even come close to touching the ball. Robert Prytz took a quick free-kick to send right-back Dave MacKinnon galloping down the touchline. He sent in a low cross and McCoist, coming in at top speed, walloped it first time from the edge of the box. Remarkably, the ball flew straight into the net through Pat Bonner's legs.

'Either that's the greatest and most accurate shot I've ever seen,' said one onlooker. 'Or that McCoist bloke is the luckiest wee player on the planet.' You pays your money and you takes your choice.

Thankfully, Celtic weren't in arrears for too long; seven minutes to be exact. Davie Provan floated in a free-kick, Frank McGarvey muscled his way in as ever and knocked the ball down to Roy Aitken who turned and whipped a fabulous drive away from Peter McCloy. The game was balanced on a tightrope after that, some players giving the impression the ball was a live grenade and getting rid of it as soon as it dropped at their feet. Old Firm encounters are not for the faint of heart, either on the field, in the dug-out or on the terracing.

With four minutes remaining, Paul McStay ambled forward and released Brian McClair who sent in a pinpoint cross. There was alarm in the Rangers penalty box as Tommy Burns and then Provan had efforts charged down. The ball eventually broke to Frank McGarvey and he pounced to stick it behind McCloy. There was no way back for John Greig's men. It was a landmark first Glasgow derby victory as a manager for Hay who enjoyed so many as a player.

The Ibrox side were pilloried in the following day's newspapers. The season had barely got underway, but already the knives were being sharpened for Greig. It was highlighted that this was Rangers' thirty-third meeting between the Old Firm since league reconstruction in 1975 and the Ibrox side had won only six to Celtic's sixteen. Furthermore, of the last twenty-one, the men from Govan had experienced only two triumphs and, in fact, had won only once at Parkhead over that eight-year period. The jungle drums were beating and the firing squad was on alert. Two months later they would be brought into action; John Greig was proving to be an easy target.

Four days later, Celtic were back in League Cup action and, after an initial hiccup, they coasted to a 5-1 win over Hibs at Parkhead. Over 11,000 fans watched Hay's side retaliate after allowing the Easter Road side to take the lead. Ironically, it was Mike Conroy, making his first return to Glasgow since his move to Edinburgh, who snatched the goal with a neat header from a Ralph Callachan cross in the forty-first minute. That stung the home side. Mark Reid, who had just come on for the injured Brian Whittaker, levelled when he latched onto a rebound and battered the ball behind Alan Rough. Just before the hour mark, Jim Melrose headed in a Davie Provan cross and shortly afterwards Reid claimed his second of the day via the penalty spot after Roy Aitken had been pushed in the box. Frank McGarvey, who had expended total energy and effort all evening, fired in the fourth from the edge of the box and Paul McStay netted a rare header from a McGarvey cross five minutes from the end.

'We're getting there,' said a fairly satisfied Hay afterwards. He knew there was more to come. It was back to points-collecting three days later as Celtic crammed another five goals into the opposition's net with a 5-2 triumph over newly-promoted St Johnstone. On this occasion, the team didn't require a goal deluge in the second-half to clinch the win. Jim Morton put through his own goal just after the half-hour mark and Jim Melrose and Tommy Burns added to the tally before the half-time whistle. Frank McGarvey claimed the fourth seven minutes after the turnaround and Burns got his second and Celtic's fifth ten minutes from the end. John Brogan stuck two behind Pat Bonner.

Davie Hay then prepared for his first-ever European tie as a manager when Danish outfit Aarhus visited Glasgow in the First Round of the UEFA Cup on September 14. Hay had done his homework and messages had been relayed that the opposition were a 'workmanlike' side. That summing-up didn't do the Nordic outfit justice. They were a controlled unit who indulged in possession football and were well equipped to frustrate the home fans in the 23,569 attendance. In fact, John Stampe had the ideal opportunity to silence the crowd in the twenty-ninth minute when Aarhus were awarded a penalty-kick. Spanish referee Augusto Castillo, rather harshly in most onlookers' eyes, pointed to the spot after a challenge by Willie McStay, who was playing in his first European tie. Stampe sent Pat Bonner the wrong way, but possibly justice was seen to be done as he also placed the ball wide of the target.

It had been a nervy moment in a game riddled with tension. The only goal arrived in the sixty-third minute when Davie Provan curled in a trademark corner-kick and Roy Aitken steamed in to power a header goalwards. Keeper Troels Rasmussen fumbled the ball over the line. No-one was complaining on the terracings as the keeper lay dejected on the turf. It didn't get better a fortnight later for the custodian in the Atletion Stadium as a Frank McGarvey-inspired Celtic romped to an exhilarating 4-1 victory. Murdo MacLeod swept a majestic effort high into the roof of the net from the edge of the box in the twenty-first minute to set the tone for the evening. McGarvey finished off a twenty-yard dash with a cunning lob over the stranded Rasmussen six minutes later. Roy Aitken and Davie Provan completed the rout after the interval with Willy Scheepers getting a late goal that offered some solace for the home fans in the 15,000 capacity crowd.

On September 17, Davie Hay made his first return to Fir Park since quitting as manager in 1982 after restoring Motherwell to Premier League status. However, sentiment didn't have a look-in as he put out an attacking line-up against the team who first gave him his chance in management. In five minutes, Celtic were a goal the good after a fast, flowing movement that began with Paul McStay latching onto a misplaced pass from left-back Joe Wark, feeding the ball to Brian McClair, also returning to haunt Motherwell, and he teed up Frank McGarvey to fire home. Second-half strikes from McStay and Tommy Burns secured a fine 3-0 victory.

Nineteen year old Brian McClair was beginning to win favour with the Celtic fans with his keen eye for goal, his clever link-up play and his all-round intelligence. He hit the headlines big-style with an extraordinary four-goal performance in the rampant 6-2 landslide over a Dundee team which had proved so troublesome at Dens Park to Billy McNeill's side the previous season. With Frank McGarvey injured, Davie Hay went with a new-look spearhead in McClair and Jim Melrose against the Tayside outfit.

Celtic, as appeared to be the norm, allowed their opponents to go ahead before they responded. This time it was Iain Ferguson who provoked the reaction with the opening goal in the nineteenth minute. The blond-haired youngster, introduced, of course, to the Dundee first team by Tommy Gemmell, would collect a second in the eighty-first minute, but, happily, the visitors had managed to hammer in six between his efforts. Tommy Burns claimed the equaliser just after the half-hour mark and McClair kicked off his one-man barrage by adding another shortly afterwards. In the space of twenty adrenalin-charged minutes, the youngster had knocked another three behind the luckless Colin Kelly. Melrose added the sixth ten minutes from time. Completing a miserable afternoon for the Dens Parkers, they had Cammy Fraser, later to join Rangers, expelled from the action near the end.

McClair may have thought a stunning four-goal haul would have ensured a first team place for the following game, but Hay underlined once again that no-one was guaranteed a spot in his starting line-up. The player had to be satisfied with a second-half appearance in the 4-1 win over Aarhus. The Celtic manager explained, 'Yes, I suppose that decision could have back-fired in my face. I had my team in my mind for the match in Denmark and I thought Brian would be more beneficial coming on from the bench, depending on how the game was running. It was my first away encounter as a manager in Europe, we were already leading 1-0 and I knew I had to get the tactics absolutely right.

'I was also aware that Danish football was at an all-time high. As luck would have it, their international team had won 1-0 against England at Wembley the previous midweek. Allan Simonsen got the goal and as a result Denmark qualified for the European Championship Finals in France the following year. So, a few of the Aarhus players had been involved in that historic victory and they reckoned they could overturn our advantage at their place. With all that in mind, I selected a line-up that could defend while hitting on the break. I wasn't looking to pull everyone behind the ball, but I certainly wasn't going to surrender possession anywhere on the pitch. We got it right on the night, thankfully. That was underlined by midfielders Murdo MacLeod and Roy Aitken getting two of our goals.'

Black October was lying in wait, though. On the first of the month, Celtic struggled against a competent St Mirren side and, after going a goal behind yet again, managed to scramble a 1-1 draw in front of 15,289 fans. A young Frank McAvennie was lively against his boyhood favourites, but it was another with Celtic allegiances, Frank McDougall, who scored once more against the Hoops. The heavily-muscled forward rose to an Ian Scanlon cross to bullet a header beyond Pat Bonner in the thirty-fourth minute.

Ricky McFarlane had just quit as the Paisley club's manager during the week to be replaced in a caretaker capacity by former Rangers goalkeeper Erik Sorensen. He made sure the team were well drilled in defence and Celtic knew they were in for a long road back to get something from this encounter. They had to settle for breaching the back lot just once in the sixty-fourth minute. Jim Melrose smacked one off the crossbar and Brian Whittaker followed up to force the ball over the line. The biggest cheer of the day was reserved minutes from the end when the tannoy announcer informed the supporters league leaders Dundee United had lost 2-0 to Rangers at Tannadice. Irony of ironies - Celtic fans applauding a win for the Ibrox side. United's loss put Celtic on top of the league by one point after six games.

A relieved Hay said, 'This was a match we should have won, but how can I complain when we've moved to the top of the league? We must all remember, however, there is still a long, long way to go. The reason we didn't get two points on this occasion is mainly due to Billy Thomson. I thought the St Mirren goalkeeper had a terrific game.'

Celtic were back in League Cup action in midweek against Kilmarnock at Parkhead where a disappointing crowd of a mere 5,485 turned out. The lack of atmosphere did little to raise the level of play and youngsters such as Willie McStay, Jim Dobbin and John Halpin seemed to suffer by the slightly surreal surroundings. Murdo MacLeod gave Celtic the lead with an unstoppable penalty-kick in the sixty-fourth minute to stir the support from their lethargy. A minute later, though, they were groaning when Brian Gallagher hit the equaliser. The performance bemused Davie Hay. 'We can do so much better than this. We just didn't get going, but I'll work on that.'

The players didn't respond to the encouragement of their manager in the next outing, a 2-1 slump against Dundee United at Tannadice.

It was a distinctly off-colour show from the visitors and, in the end, Hay offered no excuses. 'That just wasn't good enough. We let United control the flow of play for far too long. No-one can afford to do that in this league.'

Billy Kirkwood helped nudge the Glasgow side off the top of the table with a twenty-yard rocket after an Eamonn Bannon free-kick in the twenty-seventh minute. Another deadball effort from Bannon just after the hour mark presented future Rangers captain Richard Gough with a free header in front of Bonner and he couldn't pass up the gift. A goal from Jim Melrose six minutes from time failed to spark a spirited revival from the visitors.

It didn't get much better a week later when Hearts claimed a 1-1 draw in Glasgow. It was an encounter in which Celtic almost got completely lost in a maze of mistakes starting with a third-minute penalty miss from Murdo MacLeod when Henry Smith saved his effort. It didn't ease the pain that two former Celtic players, Jimmy Bone and Roddie MacDonald, were the Edinburgh side's top performers. Bone, who scored only one goal in his season at Parkhead after being signed by Jock Stein from Sheffield United in 1974, equalled that feat on this occasion while MacDonald was a rock in the middle of his team's rearguard.

Frank McGarvey gave Hay's men the advantage a minute before half-time when he wriggled his way along the eighteen-yard line before whipping a low drive that exploded behind the sprawling Smith. Five minutes after the turnaround it was level again when Alex MacDonald, the former Ranger who was still proving to be a wily customer when he was up against the Hoops, pitched a ball through the middle of the Celtic defence and Bone raced onto it to take advantage. Most of the 20,207 paying customers failed to be impressed.

Misery piled on top of pain as Sporting Lisbon won 2-0 in Portugal in the second round of the UEFA Cup four days later. Celtic could have no complaints at the final score. In fact, they escaped with a two-goal deficit. They were run ragged by a strong Sporting team almost direct from the kick-off and the central defence endured a torrid time against the tall, powerful and athletic Jordao. He rose, virtually unchallenged, to head the opening goal past Pat Bonner in thirty minutes. Celtic were on the ropes throughout and the only surprise about conceding a second goal was that it took the home side another thirty-eight minutes before the inevitable happened. Jordao, running at frightening pace, sped through to place a well-aimed strike wide of Bonner. Remarkably, the Portuguese took their foot off the pedal after that and that was good news for a shell-shocked Glasgow outfit. Older Celtic supporters had happier memories of Lisbon.

Hay cut to the chase. 'They gave us a doing, a real going-over. If I'm being honest, I was quite impressed by them. They had a good blend of skill and strength and used the ball very well. The atmosphere in the stadium was really good, too. It was just a pity the fans wearing green-and-white scarves and looking so happy were Sporting Lisbon's followers.'

After the team folded so unacceptably against Aberdeen at Pittodrie the following Saturday, Davie Hay could no longer remain silent. His players were not performing in the expected manner of Celtic professionals. Hay was forced to go public with his observations, but, make no mistake, what the manager said to the Press for public consumption was nothing compared to the stinging criticism of his players behind closed doors.

As promised, there was no sight of Davie Provan and Murdo MacLeod for the midweek League Cup-tie against Hibs at Easter Road. They had been unceremoniously dumped and Mark Reid and Jim Melrose were the substitutes. In front of 8,000 fans, Celtic once again failed to spark. They were a team playing without inspiration and were in grave danger of losing their way so early into the campaign. It ended scoreless and it could have been worse. Pat Bonner had to go down bravely at the feet of Bobby Thomson to save a certain goal late in the game.

Coincidentally, the Edinburgh outfit provided the opposition in the league three days later. Could Celtic stop the rot? October had proved to be a month of anguish and there were only two days remaining to stem the misery. Davie Hay brought back Provan and MacLeod and was delighted with their reaction to spending the evening in the Easter Road stand while their team-mates toiled to an uninspiring goalless stalemate. MacLeod hammered in two crackers and Provan claimed a single as Hibs were obliterated 5-1 in front of 13,777 fans. It turned out to be night and day in the quality of performances in such a short space of time.

Brian McClair also scored two - the first and last - and hit the woodwork twice. He claimed the opener in the eighth minute and it took the home side another forty minutes before Alan Rough was asked to pick the ball from his net again. Provan struck the second shortly after the turnaround and Brian Whittaker netted the third with an impromptu over-head kick. The left back raced to the Jungle to take a bow with a flourish. The fans lapped it up, but, most importantly, Davie Hay was not convinced about the player he had brought in from Partick Thistle earlier in the campaign. Hay was a hard man to please. MacLeod completed the scoring with two in the last ten minutes after Bobby Thomson had netted for the Edinburgh men who also had the rugged Gordon Rae sent off for one foul too many.

The focus switched back to Europe when Sporting Lisbon, so dominant a fortnight earlier in their Jose Alvalade stadium, were in Glasgow for the return leg. A crowd of 39,183 turned out to witness what emerged as one of the great European nights at Celtic Park. A certain Jozef Venglos, the Czechoslovakian manager of the Portuguese side, was introduced to the east end of Glasgow. It was to be a memorable evening for the thoughtful coach - for all the wrong reasons.

Davie Hay revealed, 'We hadn't put their Hungarian keeper under any pressure whatsoever at their place. I had received reports that he could be the team's weak link. I was told he tended to be showy and spectacular. I think it's known as making 'Hollywood' saves. I wanted to see how he coped when we piled down on top of him. I was determined to put him to the test. A lot of very good goalkeepers had gone weak-kneed when they sampled the special atmosphere of a European evening at Parkhead.'

After a whirlwind forty-five minutes, Janos Katrirz had been beaten three times and looked as though he had been hit by a bus. Celtic were heading for the third round. Tommy Burns headed in the opener from close range with the keeper flapping at a right-wing cross from Davie Provan. Katrirz didn't want to know when a corner-kick came swirling into his penalty area and Tom McAdam latched onto a half-hearted attempt at a clearance to blast a twelve-yard drive into the roof of the net. The Hungarian had no chance when Brian McClair embarked on a breathtaking solo surge coming in from the left and finishing off with an unstoppable angled shot. Sporting Lisbon players looked absolutely shattered when the half-time whistle blew moments later.

The first-half had been a relentless procession towards Katrirz. Jordao, a potent threat in Lisbon, was an isolated, exasperated figure in his team's non-existent attack. The Portuguese outfit had been taken apart by a devastating display from a Celtic team that fired on all cylinders. It must have been the only time in Celtic's history that supporters had been ecstatic to see a team wearing green-and-white hoops pulled apart in Paradise. Celtic, as the home team, were required to play in their change strip and they opted for the popular all-green strip that shimmered brightly under the floodlights.

Murdo MacLeod and Frank McGarvey cemented a marvellous 5-0 victory that had the Celtic fans dancing with delight. Brian McClair said, 'That game was my first European start. Everybody played so well. You just occasionally get games where everybody is focused. There just seemed to be quite a focused and humorous atmosphere on the bus and no particular nervousness. I think a lot of that stemmed from Davie Hay, who just told us to go out and play our normal game. The problem they had was that we started so quickly and so well. We were 3-0- up at half-time and when we scored again in the forty-seventh minute that was it all over.'

Hay recalled, 'That was such a wonderful night. Everything just clicked into place and the players deserved massive credit. They didn't ease up for a moment. We got a perfect start with Tommy's early goal and just kept going. We had seen how dangerous Jordao could be in Lisbon, so the main thing was to make sure we had plenty of the ball in their half and he was starved of service. I don't think he had a single shot at our goal. I can only remember Pat Bonner making a save from a free-kick in the second-half. Other than that, it was just an evening to savour.'

The Celtic manager was eager to maintain the momentum, especially with a meeting against Rangers at Ibrox coming up three days later. There had been ructions behind the scenes in Govan during the week. John Greig officially resigned, but there could be little doubt the Rangers boss was given little option but to accept his P45 and move on. Tommy McLean, brother of Dundee United chief Jim, was put in temporary charge. His timing could have been better.

Celtic won 2-1 and were in control for lengthy spells, despite losing Davie Provan early on after a dreadful double tackle from Dave MacKinnon and Jimmy Nicholl. Surprisingly, referee George Smith didn't take any action against either Ibrox offender. It was goalless at the interval, but Peter McCloy had been by far the busier keeper. Something had to give and it did eight minutes after the interval when Paul McStay picked out Frank McGarvey on the eighteen-yard line and he drilled a left-foot drive past the overworked Ibrox custodian. The goal that settled it arrived fifteen minutes from time when Tommy Burns, sparking with ingenuity as ever, played a swift one-two with McGarvey and strolled through the heart of the Rangers rearguard to roll the ball beyond the advancing McCloy. Sandy Clark got his side's consolation effort with only three minutes remaining, but a large chunk of the 40,000 crowd had already departed the scene by that time.

Amazingly, only a week after decimating Sporting Lisbon, Celtic couldn't score against Airdrie in a League Cup-tie in Glasgow. It ended goalless in front of a meagre crowd of 5,358 and there was little doubt the missing presence of Davie Provan, Roy Aitken and Paul McStay affected the flow of the team. The Broomfield side were quite content to play the entire game in their own half, limiting their input to the entertainment value to nil.

Hay said, 'It was quite a worrying state of affairs. We were struggling for consistency and there didn't appear to be a good reason for it. The players could hit the highs and dismiss a very good Sporting Lisbon side in Europe and pick up a win at Ibrox and then fail to overcome Airdrie. They were quite content to let us come at them, but it's our job to break them down.'

Murdo MacLeod led the way in the 4-0 win over Motherwell at Celtic Park on November 12. The midfielder gave the ball an almighty dunt from twenty-five yards and the effort screamed past the immobile Nicky Walker into the top corner of the net in the twenty-ninth minute. It was hit with such pulverising power, the ball was wedged between the stanchion and the crossbar. Pat Bonner rescued Celtic when he saved a penalty-kick from old Hoops favourite Johannes Edvaldsson after Willie McStay was adjudged to have felled John Gahagan. Brian McClair, looking more accomplished with every passing game, soothed the nerves five minutes from the interval when he ran onto a pass, rounded the keeper and knocked the ball over the line. Frank McGarvey claimed the third just after the hour mark and McClair completed a fine personal performance by outjumping Edvaldsson to head in a Tommy Burns cross.

No-one would have dared to predict the outcome of the next game against St Mirren at Love Street. Celtic were two goals ahead after nineteen minutes and contrived to lose 4-2. Hay hit the roof. 'Our performance was abysmal. For Celtic to build a two-goal lead then throw it away in such a manner is unheard of. We cannot afford to perform like that when we play Nottingham Forest on Wednesday night. If we do, there will be no chance of us making progress in the UEFA Cup. I'm sure the lads will pick themselves up after this defeat and turn in a more realistic performance.

'Recent games have seen us play brilliantly against Sporting Lisbon then poorly, like our recent match against Airdrie. We didn't start particularly brilliantly against St Mirren, but we managed to build up a lead before falling away. We cannot expect to play as we did against Sporting Lisbon in every game, but there is a standard below which Celtic should never fall. Certainly, we fell well short of that standard in this game.'

There didn't appear to be a shock around the corner in Hay's hometown of Paisley when Tommy Burns hit the opening goal in the ninth minute and Murdo Macleod doubled the advantage ten minutes later. Alarmingly, Celtic fell out of the game as the Saints came back at them. Stevie Clarke hit a long-range drive past Pat Bonner in twenty-five minutes, John McCormack levelled matters seven minutes later and Frank McDougall, a player who couldn't seem to fail to score when Celtic were the opposition, put the home side ahead just before half-time. It was an inexplicable turnaround in Celtic's form. Ian Scanlon hit the fourth two minutes from time as Celtic toppled to third in the league, behind leaders Aberdeen and Dundee United.

Nottingham Forest, double European champions in 1979 and 80, were next in line with Celtic travelling to a bitterly cold Midlands on November 23. The pitch was hard and frosty, underfoot conditions were crisp, and Brian Clough set up his team in his rather unattractive approach. His side was geared for hitting on the counter-attack, seeking to demolish their opponents with a sucker-punch. It was the system favoured by Jim McLean at Dundee United and, unfortunately, the negative thinking was bringing rewards via silverware, but it was also driving football fans from the terracings.

Celtic did most of the pressing at the City Ground where 32,017 fans - Billy McNeill included - crammed into the old stadium. There was a spillage of fans during the game as they poured onto the touchline, but it was no break-in. It was created by overcrowding and, thankfully, the situation was resolved fairly rapidly. The best opportunity of a chilly evening fell to the normally sure-footed Paul McStay. Only a couple of minutes remained when the midfielder found himself with only keeper Steve Sutton to beat as he got on the end of a right-wing cross. In normal conditions, Sutton wouldn't have stood a chance. As it was, he barely moved as McStay struck a venomous first-time effort from twelve yards that, unfortunately, rose inches over the bar and into the crowd behind the goal. Ultimately, Celtic's European hopes went with that miss.

It allowed Forest to continue their irritating, infuriating tactics in the second leg in front of a capacity 69,938 fans at Celtic Park. Clough's team contributed very little, sitting back and soaking up pressured while probing for openings in an exposed Celtic rearguard. Steve Hodge punished the home side's naivety when he got through on the right wing to slide the ball under Pat Bonner in the fifty-fourth minute. Typically, Celtic took the game back to the English side and, in the seventy-fourth minute, they paid the price when Colin Walsh knocked a simple one past Bonner. With ten minutes remaining, Murdo MacLeod fired in an angled eighteen-yarder past Hans Van Bruekelen, Forest's Dutch international keeper who had missed the first leg. Celtic still required a further two goals to get through. It finished 2-1 for Nottingham Forest.

Davie Hay had seen his side outplay the former European champions over two legs, have an incredible percentage of possession, but, in the end, they were still beaten and banished to European oblivion. Hay said, 'Clough's a genius. What more can I say? Only he could have managed that feat.'

Before the Forest disappointment, Celtic had played two games and won them both away from home. In the League Cup, on Wednesday November 30, a goal from Jim Melrose in the twentieth minute against Kilmarnock at Rugby park was enough to put Davie Hay's men through to the next stage, finishing on nine points with their Ayrshire rivals two adrift. In the league, four days later, Melrose was on target again as Celtic won 3-0 against St Johnstone in Perth, the last time they would play at Muirton Park. Jim Dobbin and Roy Aitken joined Melrose on the scoresheet.

Three days after exiting the UEFA Cup, Celtic were held to a goalless draw by Aberdeen in Glasgow. The Dons, who had won the

European Cup-Winners' Cup the previous season, had just returned from Germany after the first leg of their Super Cup Final against SV Hamburg. Alex Ferguson's side stifled the European champions at the Volksparkstadion and came home with a goalless draw. They adopted the same negative tactics at Celtic Park and obtained an identical result. Defences dominated the ninety minutes and there was little for the 25,867 fans to get excited about. It wasn't Celtic's day and Jim Melrose, goaded into a foolish act of retaliation, was sent off and would have to explain himself to the Celtic manager afterwards.

A week later Davie Hay handed new boy John Colquhoun, a right winger signed from Stirling Albion, his debut against Hearts at Tynecastle and he enjoyed a successful baptism in a 3-1 win. It was another solid showing from the Parkhead side and the only tremor came in the seventy-fifth minute when John Robertson scored for the Edinburgh outfit to bring the score back to 2-1. Brian McClair gave the visitors the advantage in the twenty-sixth minute and Jim Dobbin, looking a more than useful young midfielder, hammered in a second in the sixty-third minute. McClair hit the clincher nine minutes from time.

Just under 27,000 fans turned out on December 27 to witness a hard-fought 1-1 draw with Dundee United in Glasgow. Again, the temperatures had dipped frighteningly on a Festive encounter. Brian McClair followed on from his fine form at Tynecastle by getting the opening goal just on half-time, but Eamonn Bannon, who got plenty of penalty-kick practice against Celtic, equalised from the spot in the sixty-eighth minute and the game ground to a deadlocked conclusion.

On a howling, stormy Hogmanay in Edinburgh, Celtic brought down the curtain on an eventful 1983 with a 1-0 win over Hibs. A crowd of 11,234 braved the hail and rain to see John Blackley put through the ball past his own keeper Alan Rough in the seventy-seventh minute for the solitary goal that separated the teams.

Davie Hay wondered what lay in store in 1984.

CHAPTER FIFTEEN
SEASON OF
SECOND PRIZES

An aggressive winter growled and decimated football fixtures throughout the country as 1984 made a shivering debut. The scheduled third Premier League meeting of the campaign against Rangers - and Davie Hay's opportunity to lead Celtic to a hat-trick of triumphs over the club's fiercest rivals - was obliterated in the midst of the chaotic conditions.

Celtic were first foots to Motherwell on January 7 on a bitterly cold afternoon, the pitch bone hard. Bobby Watson, a former Rangers player, was now in charge at Fir Park following Jock Wallace's return to Ibrox in November after John Greig's exit. Motherwell supporters wondered if Watson would be eager to put his brand on the way the team played. Watson was an old-fashioned wing-half who could be termed, at best, ordinary. One unimpressed onlooker once likened his movement around the pitch to 'an elephant with cramp.'

Unfortunately, his Motherwell players came out the blocks at a ferocious rate against Celtic and were a goal ahead in the eleventh minute through Stuart Rafferty. Frank McGarvey responded with the equaliser in the twenty-second minute and it looked as though it was a belated Happy New Year for Hay and his players when Paul McStay hit a second ten minutes from time. But Andy Dornan nicked a draw with a goal a couple of minutes later. Stories in the morning Press revealed Inter Milan were prepared to pay £2million for McStay. Hay didn't bite. 'There are a lot of teams who would like to buy Paul. However, he's a Celtic player and he'll remain a Celtic player.'

Celtic were playing catch-up at the top with Aberdeen and the disappointment of an unexpected dropped point at Fir Park was softened somewhat by the news Alex Ferguson's team had drawn 1-1 with Rangers in Glasgow. All eyes were on Celtic's visit to Pittodrie on February 4, but before that game there was the little matter of a Scottish Cup-tie on thin ice against Berwick Rangers at Shielfield Park on January 28. Coincidentally, it was the precise date in 1967 where Rangers, then the Cup holders, hit a Titanic-like iceberg to sink without trace in one of the most incredible results in Scottish football history. Hay's take was fairly predictable. 'I told the players to forget all about the Rangers result because it would have absolutely no bearing on our performance. How could a game that was played seventeen years earlier have a say on this match? Nice bit of Cup romance for the newspapers to play around with, but we weren't interested in taking part. We were there to win - end of story.'

Brian McClair netted his first Scottish Cup goals for the Hoops with a strike in the fourth minute and a second just after the half-hour mark. Two late efforts from Frank McGarvey and Jim Melrose made certain there would be no sensations at Shielfield this time around. Now Hay could focus on Pittodrie.

It was always going to be a confrontation that would likely be settled by one goal. And so it proved. Unfortunately, for Celtic that effort came from John Hewitt who had a fair strike rate against the Glasgow team. A capacity crowd of 23,000 shrugged off the freezing conditions to see Hewitt seal the points in the nineteenth minute. Try as they might, Celtic could not get through the Alex McLeish and Willie Miller double-act that provided a formidable barrier in front of Jim Leighton. The Parkhead side were now six points behind the Dons.

A week later, watched by only 9,439 fans, Celtic beat St Johnstone 5-2 in Glasgow. Brian McClair and Murdo Macleod each scored two with Frank McGarvey chipping in with the other. Goals from Gordon Scott and Ray Blair for the visitors never threatened the destination of the points. Celtic had to hope Aberdeen would slip up against Motherwell who had given them such a rigorous test on their own ground the previous month. The Dons breezed to a 4-0 win. The games were coming thick and fast and three days later McGarvey claimed a double in the 2-0 victory over St Mirren. Once again, there was a poor attendance with only 9,835 sprinkled around the vast Celtic Park terracings.

Celtic then made their first trip in a decade to rickety Methil for their next Scottish Cup-tie against East Fife. The game, watched by a crowd of 10,000 which produced gate receipts of £18,000, turned into shooting practice for the visitors with Tommy Burns claiming two and Murdo MacLeod, Frank McGarvey, Brian McClair and new boy John Colquhoun chipping in with one apiece in the 6-0 win. East Fife players must have felt as though they had been armed with a toothpick to take on an army of Samurai warriors. The Fifers' young goalkeeper Gordon Marshall did his best to keep the score fairly respectable. Seven years later, Liam Brady would take him to Celtic.

Davie Hay's men faced a sterner challenge four days later in the League Cup semi-final when they travelled north for the third time in the season to face Aberdeen. Hay was well aware the other two confrontations had ended in defeat. 'It was absolutely imperative that we took something from this game,' said the manager.

Celtic, in fact, should have taken the lead inside a minute when Frank McGarvey, with just Jim Leighton to beat, completely fluffed his shot from six yards and the chance was gone. That was the Parkhead side's best opportunity all night. The nearest the Dons came to breaching Celtic's back line came when Gordon Strachan smacked a drive off the bar. It was a dour, old struggle between two heavyweights with neither willing to budge an inch. In the end, a goalless result was fair. 'People will say we now have the advantage with the second leg at Parkhead,' said Hay. 'The Dons have a good record in Glasgow, so no-one is taking anything for granted.'

Brian McClair scored his first hat-trick for Celtic the following Saturday as Hearts were overwhelmed 4-1 in Glasgow in front of a crowd of 17,950. The former Motherwell man didn't possess the same élan or poise or charisma of Charlie Nicholas, but he was swiftly building a rapport with the Celtic followers. While he knocked in three, John Coluquhoun netted another and looked like a good buy at only £60,000 from Stirling Albion. While Davie Hay's side were beating Hearts, Aberdeen were taking care of their Edinburgh rivals Hibs at Easter Road. They coasted to a 2-0 victory and the league championship silverware was beginning to move out of sight.

The picture became even more fuzzy the following week when Celtic were totally outplayed by Dundee United as they nosedived to a 3-1 defeat at Tannadice, a ground where they had suffered a 2-1 loss earlier in the campaign. Roy Aitken's goal three minutes from the end merely prevented the scoreline from looking too lopsided, but, in truth, this had been an extremely disappointing display. Eamonn Bannon, Billy Kirkwood and Davie Dodds were the home side's marksmen.

A week later, the grey clouds circling Celtic Park were transformed to an altogether brighter hue. Celtic were in the League Cup Final and Aberdeen had been vanquished in the east end of Glasgow for the first time since November 1981. A crowd of 41,169 made a lot of noise during a bone-crushing, pulverising skirmish that bordered on a fracas. Anyone witnessing this scrap would have been left with the distinct impression there was no love lost between two sets of warring footballers. They would have been right.

The game erupted in the fifty-fourth minute, with the tie scoreless, when referee Bob Valentine awarded Celtic a penalty-kick. Dougie Bell made what is commonly known as 'a forward's challenge' on a twisting, teasing Tommy Burns. Not skilled in the wiles of a defender, midfielder Bell lunged into a challenge that sent the Celt sprawling. The match official didn't hesitate for a moment and pointed to the spot. He was immediately surrounded by protesting Pittodrie players. There can be no doubt this was a ploy encouraged by Alex Ferguson. He worked on the principle that the referee might believe, in his subconscious, he 'owed' his team something and they might just get the benefit of the doubt next time around. That thought process followed the manager to Manchester United.

Valentine would not be swayed, however. Once the discord finally settled after an agonising wait of a couple of minutes, Mark Reid, the Celtic defender, ran forward forcefully and banged the ball straight into the net. Davie Hay was thirty-six minutes away from leading the club into a major Cup Final appearance in his first season in charge. The Dons rallied, as expected, and desperately tried to claw their way back into the contest. The nearest they came to overcoming Celtic's stubborn resistance came near the end when John Hewitt flicked in a soaring header, but Pat Bonner was alert to make a comfortable save.

Rangers, rejuvenated under Jock Wallace, lay in wait in the Final, due at Hampden on Sunday, March 25. Unexpectedly, they had dismissed last season's champions Dundee United in the semi-final. They earned a highly creditable 1-1 draw at Tannadice with a goal from new striker David Mitchell, a raw Australian who didn't attend to the refinements of the game, and triumphed 2-0 at Ibrox with efforts from Sandy Clark, another forward who didn't pay too much attention to the niceties of soccer, and Ian Redford, an elegant midfielder sold to Rangers by Tommy Gemmell when he was manager of Dundee.

However, Celtic had two engagements - one in the Scottish Cup and the other in the league - to take care of before they could focus on the League Cup Final. Davie Hay took the team to his old stomping ground at Fir Park for their quarter-final against Motherwell on March 17 and was determined to celebrate St Patrick's Day in a grand manner in front of a crowd of 14,795. The players responded and Celtic were three goals to the good by the time referee Davie Syme brought first-half proceedings to a halt. Mark Reid walloped one in to start the procession in the sixth minute. Tommy Burns netted a second just after the half-hour mark and Brian McClair added No.3 six minutes from the break. It was one-way traffic after the teas and oranges as Murdo MacLeod and Frank McGarvey got in on the act. McClair, revelling in playing against his former team, got another and the tie was brought to a 6-0 conclusion.

There was speculation once more in the media about Davie Hay being interested in Maurice Johnston, who had joined Watford for £200,000 from Partick Thistle in November 1983. The gallus Glaswegian was scoring goals for fun in England's First Division while swearing his undying love for all things Celtic on a daily basis. Graham Taylor, the manager at Vicarage Road, was exasperated to the point that he once said, 'I try to get Maurice interested in our next game and all he wants to do is talk about Celtic.' Hay, in fact, had kept Johnston on his radar since his first competitive game as Celtic manager in the Glasgow Cup-tie at Firhill back in August. His day would arrive.

Three days after the six-goal rampage against Motherwell, Celtic's hopes of a championship success all but evaporated. Once more, like Billy McNeill in April 1980, Davie Hay would be left with his head in his hands, sitting on the touchline at Dens Park. He had just witnessed Celtic surrendering a one-goal half-time advantage to collapse 3-2 against Dundee. Everything was going according to plan when Tommy Burns netted a minute from the interval, but, by the seventy-seventh minute, Pat Bonner had picked the ball out of his net three times and a shock defeat loomed large. Former Aberdeen centre-forward Walker McCall, the Peter Crouch of his day, had arrived on Tayside after a short spell in Hong Kong with a team called South China. How Davie Hay wished the beanpole forward had remained in the former British Colony.

McCall equalised in the fiftieth minute and six minutes later Ray Stephen fired the home side in front. As Celtic tried to regroup, McCall knocked in a third. Mark Reid offered hope with an eighty-first minute penalty-kick, but it was too late. At the close of play, the Hoops were once again trailing Aberdeen by six points. The race for the crown continued to be an uphill struggle.

However, the League Cup was there for the winning at the national stadium five days later. Davie Hay was squaring up to Jock Wallace for the first time as a manager. 'Actually, I liked Jock,' admitted Hay. 'I realise a lot of people might find that hard to accept or understand, two Old Firm managers getting on quite well with each other. At that stage, I hadn't met him too often, but, of course, he got the Motherwell job after I left, so we had a few things in common. His persona was that of a big, gruff bloke and I think he liked to perpetuate that image. There was a lot more to him that, though. Mind you, I still enjoyed gubbing him and Rangers when we met!'

Celtic made every mistake in the book as they lost 3-2 to their oldest foes in extra-time. They were trailing by two Ally McCoist efforts just after the hour mark and the second goal was typical of the x-certificate material on show from the Celtic defence at the national stadium that dismal afternoon. Rangers goalkeeper Peter McCloy possessed a booming kick and could easily reach opposing eighteen-yard boxes with his monumental clearances. In the sixty-first minute, McCloy prepared to launch another effort into orbit. Wallace would continually bellow from the dug-out, 'Get it down the park, Peter. Blooter it!' And ten times out of ten, that's exactly what the man known as 'The Girvan Lighthouse' would do as he cleared the ball like he never wanted to see it again.

Hay, on the other hand, would urge Pat Bonner to roll the ball and bring the back four and the midfield players into things as they built their attacks steadily. No-one had ever witnessed McCloy adopt this tactic. However, at that fateful moment during the League Cup Final, with Wallace issuing orders, the keeper prepared to shell another missile deep into enemy territory; his midfield being ignored once more.

McCloy gave the ball a ferocious dunt and it was up in the air for precisely four seconds. It bounced once when it fell to earth and Roy Aitken was caught running back towards his goal. Sandy Clark jostled with the Celt and managed to get his head to knock a pass sideways. Tom McAdam was sucked towards the ball and McCoist came in from behind the centre-half to hit a first-time effort at goal. It struck the out-rushing Bonner, but flicked up and over his body en route to the net. The Celtic defenders argued with each other and it looked for a split-second that Bonner and Aitken might come to blows.

One cloud-busting punt down the field, one header and one shot. Suddenly, it was 2-0 to Rangers and things were going their way. McCoist got the first goal on the stroke of half-time when referee Bob Valentine adjudged Aitken to have brought down Bobby Russell. It was in the marshmallow category, but the Dundee whistler was easily convinced. McCoist, with a lengthy run-up from well outside the box, tucked the ball to Bonner's left as the keeper took off for the right. A handful of seconds later, Valentine blew for half-time.

Celtic responded spiritedly to the sickening loss of the second goal. Six minutes later they were back in the game when Tommy Burns lobbed a cute free-kick over the Rangers defence and Brian McClair struck it perfectly as it dropped in front of him. His close-range right-foot shot left McCloy without a hope. The keeper continued his bombardment of the Celtic penalty area and on one occasion hit an effort that travelled the full length of the pitch before it was gathered by his opposite number. Overhead flying pigeons lived in mortal fear when McCloy was around.

There was only one minute to go when McCoist, of all people, clattered Murdo MacLeod from behind as a high ball arrived in the area. Absolutely no question about the referee's decision. Mark Reid was entrusted with the penalty-kick and the left-back didn't bother with finesse as he fairly leathered the ball straight and high into the net. The game was hauled into extra-time and with fourteen minutes gone, Rangers, quite remarkably, were awarded their second spot-kick.

McCoist tumbled as Aitken came in from behind and, once again, Valentine was easily persuaded to give the award. The Rangers forward took the same lengthy run towards the ball and he stroked it towards the same corner. Bonner wasn't fooled on this occasion and got down to his left to get his hands to the ball, but, unfortunately, couldn't prevent it from breaking from his grasp. McCoist, following up, couldn't miss from three yards. Afterwards, he said, 'There was so much pressure on me at that time. I was so low that Captain Nemo used to look down on me and ask if I wanted to come up and see him.'

Davie Hay refused to join in the after-match merriment. Clearly, he was unhappy. 'We were confident we would win. Not overconfident, of course, because that is not how any team can be in an Old Firm clash. No matter how much one side might appear to be in the ascendancy when the game comes long it's back to square one. So, while we had beaten them in two games in the league by the time this game came around, we knew it would be tough. It was. Probably too tough as we had six players booked. We didn't get much luck, but I'm not going to say that was the only reason we lost. The first penalty-kick award was a bit dubious, the second goal came from awful defending and the third came after Bonner had saved McCoist's second penalty-kick, but could only push the ball out and allow him a second chance. That was a sore defeat to accept, but football doesn't stand still. I knew we had Aberdeen at our place the following Saturday. And, to be honest, I thought the Dons had the strongest-looking team in the country at the time.'

The Dons had gone four successive games without conceding a league goal when they arrived in Glasgow. In fact, the last player to score against them had been Rangers' Davie Cooper with a penalty-kick back at Ibrox on January 7. So, once again, the Celtic players realised they would have to roll up their sleeves for another no-holds barred collision with the Pittodrie side. A crowd of 19,193 watched the spectacle and Hay admitted, 'I told the lads that anything we got against Alex Ferguson's team had to be earned. We couldn't expect any gifts from Willie Miller and the other defenders.'

The only goal of a determined, gritty contest came in the thirty-fifth minute and it was a fast-flowing move that momentarily exposed the Dons rearguard - and that was all Jim Melrose required to do his best work. Tommy Burns spotted the opening and threaded a pass towards his team-mate, who removed the Miller shackles for an instant and swung his right foot at the ball. Jim Leighton didn't stand a chance. Things were getting interesting at the Premier League summit.

On April 2, the McStay brothers, Paul and Willie, made history against Rangers in front of 53,229 fans at Parkhead. They both scored in the 3-0 victory over the Ibrox side and it's doubtful that remarkable feat will ever be equalled. Celtic, obviously still smarting from the League Cup reverse, rolled all over Jock Wallace's side. Paul McStay beat Peter McCloy with a twenty-yard effort in the thirty-first minute and Willie showed that anything his sibling could do, he could at least equal. He had to wait until the sixty-ninth minute for the landmark moment and, just to complete a very pleasant evening, Davie Provan, who had roamed around with purpose and menace right from the start, hit the third five minutes from the end. The Celtic fans leaving the ground were already in a state of euphoria, but their emotions were given a further boost with the message relayed over the tannoy that Aberdeen had dropped a point in a 1-1 draw at home to Hearts.

Unbelievably, Celtic then threw away a needless point in a scoreless stalemate against St Johnstone in Perth five days later. Before the game Davie Hay, who had been working without a contract, promised the fans, 'I'm staying on. I've started a big job here and I intend to see it through to the finish.' The League Cup was gone, but the Hoops still had a slim chance of the title and were due to play a Scottish Cup semi-final against St Mirren. So, there was hope. But, in front of 6,667 fans, Celtic, no matter how they tried, couldn't get the ball behind their old goalkeeper Roy Baines, who had fetched up at Saints after leaving Morton. On the same afternoon, the Dons struggled, but ground out a 2-1 home win over Motherwell.

Owen Archdeacon, a fresh-faced, leggy outside-left, made a goalscoring debut against Motherwell in a rearranged midweek league game at Celtic Park. Celtic won 4-2 with Brian McClair once again scuppering the hopes of his former team. He netted in each half with

Murdo MacLeod contributing a third before Archdeacon capped a fine first display with the goal that sealed the points a minute from time. John Gahagan and Graeme Forbes got the goals that made the game a little more nervy than it should have been. A disappointing crowd of only 5,673 bothered to attend, a fair percentage of the support already believing the title race was over.

Four days later, on April 14, Celtic were back at Hampden to take on St Mirren in the Scottish Cup semi-final. On the same afternoon, Aberdeen were due to play at Tynecastle against Dundee, now managed by Archie Knox, Alex Ferguson's former right-hand man at Pittodrie. The Dens Park outfit, who escaped relegation by only four points, had shocked Rangers in the quarter-finals. The first game had ended 2-2 on Tayside, but Knox's team turned the tables in the replay with a 3-2 win.

Two intriguing semi-finals, then, were on the cards in Glasgow and Edinburgh. Unfortunately, the infamous Hampden Swirl was much in evidence as a gale blew irritatingly through the old stadium. In front of 24,690 fans, Celtic were the first to show in the twenty-ninth minute when Willie McStay set up an opportunity for Brian McClair to blast past Billy Thomson. But the joy in the green and white ranks didn't last too long before Frank McDougall volleyed St Mirren back on level terms nine minutes later. Jim Melrose had a 'goal' chalked off in tight circumstances as the game developed into a midfield squabble. McDougall and Frank McAvennie were keeping the Celtic defence busy with their clever inter-changing. Only nine minutes remained when Tommy Burns, who had been a bright spark throughout, hit the upright with a strong drive. As Thomson struggled to get back to his feet, Paul McStay raced forward to control the rebound on his chest and fire an unstoppable effort into the net.

Celtic were in the Scottish Cup Final on May 19. Who would be there to offer opposition in their quest for silverware? Archie Knox made it extremely tough for his former ally Alex Ferguson, but the Dons struck first just before the half-hour mark with a goal from Ian Porteous and

Gordon Strachan wiped out any hope of a Dundee revival with the killer goal two minutes from time. Interestingly, Strachan had made it clear to Aberdeen that he would not be signing a new contract and would definitely be on his way at the end of the season. Bundesliga giants Cologne were confident they already had the deal in the bag, but Manchester United boss Ron Atkinson was sniffing around. Ferguson was far from happy at any interest in his little red-haired midfielder thinking he might become 'unsettled' with all the transfer talk while coming into a crucial period of the campaign.

St Mirren were Celtic's opponents again in the league only four days after Hampden and they were determined to avenge the Cup defeat. Ian Scanlon, an enigmatic and under-rated left-winger, netted in only three minutes, but Tommy Burns levelled in the thirty-first minute. Within sixty seconds, Scanlon had struck again to give the Paisley side the initiative. It remained that way until the roof fell in on the heroic Billy Thomson in the last fifteen minutes. Brian McClair levelled in the seventy-fifth minute and added a third seven minutes later. Graeme Sinclair scored his only goal for the club with four minutes remaining to bring down the curtain on a satisfying and well-earned 4-2 win. A year later Sinclair would be freed by Davie Hay and go on to join St Mirren. There is no happy ending to the story. Sinclair, who marked the great Johan Cruyff out of one of Celtic's most famous European nights, was forced to retire with persistent injuries at the age of twenty-seven.

Peter Grant, the Scottish Under-18 international captain, made a surprise debut for Celtic in their fourth and final Old Firm game of the campaign at Ibrox on April 21. It was a fiery, bad-tempered encounter that saw Jimmy Nicholl, Rangers' captain for the day, sent off for a deliberate and spiteful stamp on Brian McClair's ankle with the ball at the other end of the pitch. Unluckily for the Northern Ireland international defender, his act of folly was caught by Scottish Television's cameras and there was no case to argue as referee Hugh Alexander brandished a red card. It was Nicholl's farewell to Ibrox before he returned to Toronto Blizzard after his loan arrangement. There must be better ways of saying goodbye. Nasty isn't the way to go.

Rangers, with Davie Cooper in sparkling form, won 1-0 with a goal from Bobby Williamson, signed a few months earlier from Clydebank for £100,000. It came from a fifty-fifth minute right-wing corner-kick from the talented Cooper. Pat Bonner had just pulled off a breathtaking high-flying save to push away a dipping volley from Ian Redford on the edge of the box. Cooper's left-footed in-swinger was missed in the air at the near post by the Celtic defence, Murdo MacLeod was slow to react and Williamson attempted an acrobatic overhead-kick which took everyone by surprise, including Bonner, as the ball arrowed in on its target.

Celtic had their chances, notably in the first-half when Mark Reid found Frank McGarvey, in space in the box, with a nicely judged cross from the left. McGarvey hit it first time with his left foot on the turn, but Peter McCloy was alert and pushed the effort wide of the post. That was an excellent save by the veteran keeper, but he rode his luck after the interval when he instinctively stuck out a foot to divert a goal-bound drive from debutant Grant. Nicholl, who had already been booked for a rash and dangerous lunge from behind on Tommy Burns, then took his malicious brainstorm before the game limped to its conclusion. On the same day, Aberdeen won 2-0 at St Johnstone and the championship was moving out of reach and over the horizon.

Certainly, the fans believed there was no mileage in even daring to believe there was the possibility of a title party in the east end of Glasgow at the end of the season. Only 4,956 bothered to attend the match against Dundee at Parkhead three days after the Ibrox defeat. The lack of atmosphere gave the game the feeling of a pre-season friendly and there was even the bizarre twist of Celtic player Jim McInally playing against Celtic. He was on loan at the Dens Park club, but there were no clauses in the temporary contract preventing him from facing his parent club. Archie Knox, as he was quite entitled to do, played him in the dark blue at left-back. Celtic won 3-0 with goals from Jim Melrose, Brian McClair and Tom McAdam.

McClair claimed two in the 3-2 win over Hibs in Glasgow four days later.

On this occasion, 9,553 fans stirred themselves to watch the action. Davie Hay handed another debut to a youngster who had impressed, centre-half Paul McGugan getting his chance. McClair struck in two minutes, but that was nullified by a Ralph Callachan effort just after the half-hour mark. McClair was on target again two minutes following the interval for his thirtieth goal of the season - and the reward of a case of champagne from the Daily Record, the second successive Celt to bag the bubbly. John Colquhoun made it 3-1 on the hour before Brian Rice collected another for the Edinburgh men nine minutes from time.

Aberdeen had their sights on the main prize. In quick succession, they had beaten Dundee United (5-1), St Johnstone (2-0) and Dundee (1-0). They showed no signs of relenting. Davie Hay was correct in his judgement - they were the strongest-looking team in Scotland. Celtic travelled to Edinburgh on May 5 to face a Hearts side scrambling to win a place in the UEFA Cup. A crowd of 12,281 saw Tommy Burns give the Hoops the advantage on the stroke of half-time, but battle-scarred Willie Johnston, on as a late substitute, snatched the equaliser. Hearts won a place in Europe as Celtic were given the news that the Dons had just scraped a 1-0 victory over St Johnstone at Pittodrie. The champagne was being uncorked in the north.

Davie Hay paid £90,000 for Ayr United's old-fashioned centre-forward Alan McInally as he began preparing for the new season. He explained, 'I need options up front and McInally gives me that. He's tall and strong and can be used as a target man. At the moment, we've got Brian McClair, Frank McGarvey and Jim Melrose and they're not exactly in the skyscraper category. Alan will present us with the opportunity of an early out ball. We have got to give ourselves alternatives.'

On May 12, two goals in three minutes meant the points would be shared after a 1-1 draw with Dundee United at Celtic Park in front of 10,281 fans. Murdo MacLeod gave Celtic the lead in the seventy-fifth minute and Paul Sturrock delivered the quick-fire return. The following day, the Parkhead men managed to fit in a Testimonial Match at Old Trafford for Davie Hay's fellow-Quality Street Gang member Lou

Macari. A crowd of 40,140 - with an estimated 15,000 Celtic followers - turned out to witness a 1-1 draw with Manchester United. Arthur Graham, a massive Celtic fan from the sprawling housing scheme of Castlemilk in Glasgow, netted for United five minutes after half-time, but Tommy Burns levelled in the seventy-ninth minute. In a nice touch, Macari played in the red of the Manchester club in the first-half and the green and white hoops of the team closest to his heart after the break.

Six days after the razzmatazz of Old Trafford, Celtic were taking on Alex Ferguson's Aberdeen in the Scottish Cup Final. When Davie Hay agreed to become Celtic manager he delivered this message, 'Going home to Parkhead after almost ten years away was a special feeling for me, even though I recognised the pressures I was going to be under. The departure of Billy McNeill had upset the support. I had to win them over and I had to try to combat the menace of the New Firm, as Aberdeen, under Alex Ferguson, and Dundee United, under Jim McLean, had been dubbed. I also had to face up to the constant rivalry, which never diminishes between ourselves and Rangers. None of this would be easy and I probably put even more pressure on myself when I announced in a newspaper interview during the season that I would resign from the job if I failed to win a trophy. That was done in a bid to ease the pressure on the players, but it rebounded a little on me.'

So, Davie Hay had a fair idea how the Christians felt when they were introduced the lions in the colisseum all those years ago when he led his players onto the Hampden pitch for what became one of the most sensational, explosive and dramatic Scottish Cup Finals in the history of the tournament. The game wasn't helped by some erratic decision-making from referee Bob Valentine. It may have seemed odd, or even questionable, to have had the individual who had been in charge of an incident-riddled League Cup Final earlier in the season take charge of the Scottish Cup Final. Especially as one of the earlier participants, Celtic, had been involved in the previous Final and had felt aggrieved, with some justification, about a couple of the bigger calls.

Valentine didn't escape the spotlight in this one, either. Two massive decisions went against Celtic and pushed the trophy in the direction of the Dons. The opening goal in the twenty-fourth minute to give the Pittodrie side the advantage was blatantly offside. It looked bad in real time and it is even more glaring today in the reruns of the incident. There is not a shred of evidence Eric Black was in a legal position when he scored that goal. Sounds like a huge dollop of sour grapes, but there is no getting away from it, Dame Fortune smiled on Alex Ferguson's team that afternoon.

Gordon Strachan swung over a right-wing corner-kick as Alex McLeish got up to head the ball forward. The Celtic defence read the situation perfectly and moved out as a unit to leave Black in an isolated position, looking clearly offside. The Dons forward hooked the ball past Pat Bonner. There was astonishment throughout Hampden as the referee signaled a goal and the Aberdeen players danced with a mixture of delight and disbelief.

Not long afterwards, Roy Aitken was ordered off - the first player to be banished in a Scottish Cup Final since Rangers' Jock Buchanan in 1929. Once again, Hay was seething. Stewart McKimmie belted an effort from Murdo MacLeod off the line and his clearance flew straight to Mark McGhee in the old inside-right position. As he burst clear, Aitken came across to throw himself into a challenge. Certainly, it was robust and, without debate, would have merited a booking. But what happened next left a sour taste in the mouth. McGhee exaggerated the foul as he writhed on the turf. Aberdeen players swarmed around the referee, with Strachan the main protagonist, clearly advocating the removal of the Celtic player.

Valentine flashed the red card and off went Aitken. Murdo MacLeod was moved from midfield to take over the role as sweeper. The Final descended into a series of personal vendettas as players sought to right the wrongs, for better or worse. The game, as a spectacle, certainly suffered. Celtic pushed forward and there was the strange sight of Ferguson ordering his players back into defence on more than a few occasions. The game simmered until five minutes from time when Paul McStay nailed the equaliser. The Dons defence, for once, dithered in repelling danger and the ball broke for the midfielder to bury a sledgehammer close-range effort behind Jim Leighton.

Extra-time was required as a winner was sought. Celtic, with only ten men for so long, had fought like a team possessed. Would fortune favour the brave in the next thirty minutes? Eight minutes into the period, Dougie Bell, who had come on for Doug Rougvie, belted a shot from the edge of the box. Bonner stretched full-length, but couldn't get near it. The ball bounced off the junction of bar and post and rebounded to Strachan on the right. He tried to pick out Black in the centre of the goalmouth, but his elevation was just off. Black missed the cross, Bonner failed to get a hand to it, the ball fell to McGhee at the back post and he drilled it into the empty net. The villain of the piece in many Celtic supporters' eyes had won the Cup for Aberdeen.

It had been a volatile, bad-tempered affair and, in truth, the referee, Bob Valentine, had played his part in allowing things to get out of control. Two sets of players had set about each other with a frightening ruggedness and it was a surprise the casualty ward at nearby Victoria Infirmary wasn't utilised to host a couple of big-name guests for the evening. It was a pity that the so-called blue riband competition had been tarnished because there was little doubt that Celtic and Aberdeen were the two best teams in Scotland in season 1983/84. The Dons had two trophies - the league and Cup double - as their reward. Celtic, alas, had nothing. It had been a long, arduous and painful first season in charge for Davie Hay.

He looked back at the Cup Final. 'It was a game dogged by controversy and I remain angry at the way Roy Aitken was ordered off seven minutes before half-time. He was the first player in more than fifty years to be sent off in the Final and I still believe that the referee, Bob Valentine, allowed himself to be influenced by the Aberdeen players. The tackle Roy made was on Mark McGhee, a player I was later to sign for Celtic. I've never really talked to Mark about the incident though I know there is a bit of kidding among the boys about it. But Mark isn't one of the men

I would blame. He was hit and he went down and the referee awarded the Dons a foul. But as soon as the incident occurred, Bob Valentine was surrounded by Aberdeen players - all of them clamouring for Roy to be sent off. It was the kind of thing Aberdeen have perfected over the years. They do pressure referees. They do get fellow-professionals into trouble.

'I played the game hard. Tommy Docherty, of course, referred to me as "The Quiet Assassin" - though I don't know if I deserved that. But I didn't moan to referees if anyone whacked me. Football is a man's game and I think one of the worst crimes is trying to get a fellow professional into trouble. It was a part of the Aberdeen make-up, which I didn't like and I don't think too many people outside Pittodrie did, either. Roy Aitken was left with a blot on his record. It wasn't a happy day for the game when that happened and I hope the Aberdeen players who were responsible feel ashamed of themselves.

'After Roy went off, it was always going to be desperately difficult for us. We were already a goal down by then and with only ten men on the field it was an achievement to equalise five minutes from the end. Paul McStay scored then to give us another spell of extra-time in a Cup Final that season. Unhappily, the result was the same as first time around against Rangers and this time it was Mark McGhee who scored.

'That goal sealed a season of second prizes for us.'

CHAPTER SIXTEEN
THE PARADISE ROLLERCOASTER

As Davie Hay prepared for season 1984/85, his second as Celtic manager, his memo to himself was simple and straight to the point: 'Win something.' The previous campaign had promised so much and delivered so little. Or nothing, to be brutally accurate.

'I looked for at least one trophy in my first season,' said Hay. 'To be second in the league to an exceptional Aberdeen team would look impressive for any young manager in his first major job. To be so close in the two domestic Cup Finals and only beaten in extra-time in both might also be regarded by some as a reasonable campaign. But not when the club you are with is Celtic.'

So, Hay, at the age of thirty-six, embarked upon a new tilt at the silverware at home and abroad. The final whistle had blown on the early evening of May 19 as his players were presented with their Scottish Cup runners-up medals and the new Premier League obstacle course was scheduled for an August 11 kick-off against Hibs at Easter Road. There was much work to be done in between.

Hay looked to spring a surprise signing in the summer and had agreed to meet his former Scotland international team-mate Joe Jordan, who was up for grabs for £150,000 at Italian side Verona. Jordan, known affectionately as 'Jaws' because of his two missing front molars, was now thirty-two years old, but was hardly ready for his bus pass. The Celtic manager wanted to speak to him. 'I arranged to see him in the Grosvenor Hotel,' recalled Hay. 'I knew Big Joe had an affiliation with Celtic and I wanted to see how keen he might be to actually play for the club. We had a chat, but nothing came of it. Big Joe later joined Southampton and was there for three years. Who knows what might have happened if his career had led him to Celtic?'

On August 4, Charlie Nicholas was roundly booed and jeered every time he went anywhere near the ball as Arsenal played Celtic in a pre-season friendly at Parkhead. Hell hath no fury like a football fan scorned, indeed. The disappointment of the Hoops followers in the 23,000 crowd was starkly evident. In their eyes, Nicholas, their hero, had defected. Of course, they were never allowed to view the bigger picture.

It was another fixture designed to get the summer rust out of the limbs and Hay's team won 3-2 with goals from Brian McClair, Jim Melrose and John Colquhoun. Raphael Meade got the London side's first goal five minutes from the end and, mercifully, most of the supporters had headed for the exits by the time Nicholas did the unthinkable and scored against Celtic. And he came so close to missing. Pat Bonner pushed out his last-minute penalty-kick, but Nicholas couldn't resist the temptation of following up to clip in the rebound. It was his first goal at Celtic Park since netting a spot-kick against Morton on May 7 1983. On that particular day, you would have got good odds on Nicholas going such a lengthy period without scoring again at Parkhead.

Three days later, Brian Clough brought his Nottingham Forest team back to Parkhead for the first time since their 2-1 win in the UEFA Cup the previous season and the 16,000 fans yawned their way through a non-event. It ended goalless, but, at least, the Celtic supporters were now geared up for the real thing, the exciting start to the league conflict and a trip to Edinburgh and a meeting with Hibs, four fixtures that had yielded a maximum eight points while scoring eleven goals in the process in the previous season. Everything was prepared for a successful launch as the sun shone on Leith and a crowd of 15,495 waited for the action to begin. Tommy Burns, rather proudly, led out Celtic for the first time as captain in the enforced absence of Danny McGrain and Roy Aitken. Alan McInally made his league debut when he came on as a substitute for Brian McClair, but there was no sprinkling of stardust on this particular afternoon. The match slid silently to a scoreless stalemate.

A week later, Celtic had to be content with a share of the points in a 1-1 joust with Dundee United in Glasgow. The Tannadice side employed their usual, infuriating smothering tactics to stifle any adventure from their opponents. Celtic's cause wasn't helped when Jim McLean's team took the lead in the seventh minute through Stuart Beedie, a lively midfielder who cost £90,000 from St Johnstone in the summer. Seconds after his shot hit the net, the 19,000 fans could practically hear the noise of the United defensive door being slammed shut.

It would take something special for the re-enforced rearguard to be breached and, thankfully, Brian McClair provided that touch just on the hour mark. McClair was playing in place of the injured Paul McStay in midfield, which, unknown to most, was his preferred position. He picked up a loose ball in his own half and drove forward. The United defenders moved around to cut off a pass, but the adventurous McClair steamed ahead and completed a marvellous sixty-yard run with a crisp low drive into the net.

Davie Hay was well aware his players were failing to spark, the team had lost a bit of their gloss. That was emphasised when they were drawn to play Dunfermline in their opening tie of yet another new-look League Cup format. If Celtic lost at East End Park, they were out of the trophy without a safety net in sight. No second chances. And the Parkhead men were staring into oblivion for over an hour in Fife with the Second Division outfit a goal ahead and Celtic on the brink of embarrassing expulsion. They were trailing to a twenty-sixth minute goal from striker John Watson, who had cost Dunfermline £300 when they signed him from Hong Kong Rangers the previous year.

Brian McClair relieved the tension slightly with the leveller in the sixty-fourth minute and Alan McInally, now known as Rambo to the fans for his powerful forays, scored his first goal for the club with a header four minutes later. Amazingly, the home side came back and Watson, having the game of his life, equalised within sixty seconds. It was edgy stuff until McClair swept in the winner with six minutes to go. Celtic were through, but it had hardly been comfortable viewing for a fair percentage of the 9,000 fans.

Probably the last thing the Celtic manager needed around this time was a confrontation with Rangers, but the fixture list dictated that their next game was at Ibrox, the first head-to-head of the season. In actual fact, Jock Wallace's men had hardly got off to a flier, either. They kicked off with a goalless draw against St Mirren at Ibrox and toiled to a 2-0 win over Dumbarton at Boghead. In the League Cup, as Celtic laboured in Fife, Rangers were involved in something similar against Falkirk in Govan before defender Dave McPherson snatched the game's only goal. No-one, then, would have been unduly surprised that the Glasgow derby ended goalless.

One newspaper reporter summed up, 'A mixture of good goalkeeping and rank bad finishing saw to it that the scoreline would remain blank.' The nearest to a goal came from Iain Ferguson, Rangers' signing from Dundee, with a flick that was superbly saved by Pat Bonner. The only other occurrence that appeared to be noteworthy was the fact that the injured Paul McStay was replaced by his brother Willie. It would be fair to say there have been more lively local encounters. Over 44,000 viewers at Ibrox would undoubtedly have agreed.

The League Cup ballot for the next round dropped Celtic into another minefield. They were drawn against Airdrie at Broomfield and fire and brimstone would be the order of the day from the hosts. They never required to be pumped up for a visit from the team from Glasgow, but, on this occasion, Airdrie could smell victory in the air. Remarkably, they had beaten champions Aberdeen 3-1 in the previous round and they reckoned they could add Celtic's scalp. They were forced to have a swift revision of their ambitions after forty minutes when they found themselves three goals adrift.

Two goals in just over half-an-hour from Tommy Burns and Alan McInally had the visitors coasting before Peter Grant netted his first for the club. Brian McClair set it up with a good run coupled with fine vision and Grant did the necessary when he pushed the ball under the body of keeper John Martin five minutes from the interval. McClair helped himself to the fourth near the end as the Hoops cantered to a 4-0 success. A Press Box scribe put it thus, 'Tommy Burns was in his best form. Precise, aggressive and full of determination. He was the architect of this sound victory. He wouldn't grudge Peter Grant the honour of being named Man of the Match, though. The youngster improves with every game and certainly bristles with promise. And, of course, Paul McStay was there to add a touch of class when it really counts.'

Peter Grant was getting the hang of this goalscoring lark and he netted again in the 5-0 canter against Morton at Parkhead three days later. Frank McGarvey was outstanding and rattled in two before fifteen minutes were on the clock. He was slow compared to Brian McClair, though, who grabbed the first inside sixty seconds. Grant's big moment arrived in the twenty-third minute and McClair bagged the fifth in a runaway victory against the Greenock side.

Once again, though, Celtic were on their travels courtesy of the League Cup ballot. After Dunfermline and Airdrie, they were sent to Dundee United. A crowd of 21,182 crammed into Tannadice with hundreds more locked out. It was a tie that had caught the imagination and Davie Hay took his side to the City of Discovery in the knowledge he had yet to overcome Jim McLean as a manager. His time would come, but it wouldn't be the evening of Wednesday September 5. Again, agonisingly, a bout of extra-time saw a gallant Celtic side overcome and dispatched to the also-rans.

Eamonn Bannon, with an unbelievable success rate against the Hoops when it came to dead-ball efforts, kicked off the agony when the flighted in a free-kick with sixty-one minutes played of a tough, tense confrontation. The Celtic defence failed to deal with the danger and the ball was worked to Paul Sturrock who rifled an effort past Pat Bonner. The immediate response came from Brian McClair who thudded the crossbar with a fine effort. Davie Hay brought on Alan McInally for the tiring John Colquhoun in an effort to drag his team back into the contest. Only eight minutes remained when Paul McStay underlined his superior skills by skipping past two desperate lunges to pick out Rambo in the crowded penalty area and the burly forward knocked it over the line. Suddenly an extra half-an-hour was required. After the double Cup Final disappointment against Rangers and Aberdeen the previous season, would Celtic be spared anguish on this occasion? Football rarely does sentiment.

Two minutes into the extra period, John Clark, a substitute for Davie Dodds, was in the right place at the right time to condemn Celtic. Sturrock whipped over a low cross, Ralph Milne had a fresh-air swipe and, as luck would have it, the ball travelled across the box to Clark who rammed an unstoppable effort wide of Bonner. Celtic's players slumped to their knees. There was no way back. The club were out of a tournament and we had yet to complete a full week in September.

After the 1-1 deadlock with Dumbarton at Boghead on September 8, Celtic had won only one of their first five Premier League games, drawing the other four. No-one was required to inform Davie Hay that was far removed from championship-winning form. It was an all-ticket 8,416 sell-out at Boghead, Celtic's first-ever visit to the ground on Premier League duty. Davie Wilson, a former Rangers star of the early sixties, was the manager of the Sons and he had gained a reputation of winning the Ibrox side more than a few penalty-kicks with his tendency to fall over in the box when there was a stiff breeze in attendance. A bitter Aberdeen defender of the day once expressed his opinion on the lightweight winger. 'He once stubbed his toe getting on the coach outside Ibrox and earned a penalty at Pittodrie.' You tackled this guy within fifteen yards of the penalty area at your peril.

So, maybe it was no surprise that Dumbarton managed a point with a controversial penalty-kick on this particular day. Celtic were leading with a first-half header from Frank McGarvey. 'The referee, Ian Cathcart, changed all that with a penalty decision which goes straight into the doubtful category,' observed one Sunday newspaper reporter. 'Certainly, Joe Coyle dropped like a stone when Mark Reid stuck out a foot to tackle him. But I reckon the Dumbarton winger might just have taken off on an unassisted nosedive. Joe picked himself up, dusted himself off and gave Pat Bonner no chance with his kick.'

It was an unfortunate afternoon all round for Celtic when defender Graeme Sinclair, a former Dumbarton player, was hurt and had to be replaced by Reid. It was the injury that would force the premature end to Sinclair's career.

Brian Whittaker made his return to Celtic Park on September 15 with his new Hearts team-mates. The defender must have set some sort of unwanted record by being ordered off after being booked twice and sent packing - all in the space of THREE minutes. Whittaker came on as a second-half substitute for the injured Walter Kidd and his first action was to kick John Colquhoun. That earned a swift yellow card from referee Louis Thow. He followed that up with another reckless challenge on the same player. The match official was left with no option, but to banish the hot head. One reporter made the point, 'He hadn't even kicked the ball - just an opponent!'

His dismissal sparked a series of Hearts bookings with George Cowie, John Robertson and Gary Mackay yellow-carded in quick succession. It just wasn't the Edinburgh team's day - they lost 1-0 with Frank McGarvey heading in a Colquhoun corner-kick in the fifty-eighth minute.

A week later Frank McAvennie scored his first goal at Parkhead. It wasn't greeted with too much acclaim as his St Mirren team lost 2-1 to Davie Hay's side. There wasn't much on display to inspire the 12,550 crowd, but the stalemate was broken in the seventy-third minute when substitute Brian McClair, on for the injured Alan McInally, hooked a shot past Campbell Money after a Paul McStay effort had been blocked. John Colquhoun, fully recovered from his Whittaker ordeal, netted the second six minutes from time from a McClair pass. McAvennie got the Paisley consolation goal minutes from time with a header from an Ian Scanlon cross. It was met with a polite ripple of applause, but other efforts on the same ground in the future would provoke a more vociferous response.

Celtic came so close to letting a two-goal advantage slip in an extraordinary game at Dens Park. Mark Reid missed a penalty for the visitors - thumping a ferocious drive against the crossbar - and John Brown, at the other end, passed up a spot-kick opportunity for the home side when Pat Bonner kept out his effort. In the midst of all this reckless charity, Peter Grant, swiftly removing Reid as Celtic's penalty-taker, slammed in one from the spot in the twenty-first minute and John Colquhoun added a quick-fire second. However, the Dens Parkers clawed their way back into it and John McCormack left Bonner helpless with a scorching twenty-five yarder before the interval and Ray Stephen equalised on the hour mark. It was left for Tommy Burns to settle things when he burst through with nine minutes remaining to slide the winner beyond Tom Carson.

Aberdeen were the visitors to Parkhead on October 6 as 31,418 turned out to watch the champions against their main challengers. Alex Ferguson had to re-invent the Dons with Gordon Strachan (Manchester United), Mark McGhee (SV Hamburg) and Doug Rougvie (Chelsea) missing from his usual starting line-up. He had brought in two players from his old club St Mirren to replace Strachan and McGhee - Billy Stark and Frank McDougall, who had become a bit of a scourge of Celtic with a decent scoring record. Tommy McQueen, a neat and tidy left-back, arrived from Clyde to take over from the colossus known as Rougvie.

The Dons may have changed in personnel, but Fergie had kept them on track as far as the league was concerned. They arrived in Glasgow after eight games, having won seven and drawn one; the only blip being a goalless draw against Rangers at Pittodrie. They had also claimed six shut-outs in that impressive run. Davie Hay was under no illusions. 'You knew what you were getting when you played an Alex Ferguson team. They would be well-drilled, especially in defence, and would be physically challenging. You only had to look at their three guys in the centre of their defence - Neale Cooper, Alex McLeish and Willie Miller - and you were aware they would kick their granny if they needed to get a good result.'

Celtic broke the robust Red Line on the half-hour mark with a sweet three-man move. Murdo MacLeod sent in a deep cross, Brian McClair knocked it down and Frank McGarvey thumped it past Jim Leighton. Two minutes after the interval Fergie's men were level and McDougall had put his stamp on the proceedings yet again as he left Pat Bonner helpless with a vicious twenty-yard volley. The centre-forward, who thrived on the hurly-burly of the occasion, was then hauled down by an anxious Mark Reid and referee Bob Valentine had little option but to award a penalty-kick. Stark had taken over the spot-kick duties from Strachan, but was alarmed to see Bonner swoop low to his left to save his carefully-placed attempt.

Davie Provan claimed the winner ten minutes from time with another sublime free-kick. Alex McLeish fouled McClair twenty-five yards out; definitely well within Provan's range. He arced the ball up and over the defensive wall and high past the startled Leighton. One newspaper wrote, 'While Fergie must be furious at the loss of such a goal so late in the game, he cannot complain about the result.'

Davie Hay then played what he believed to be his ace card - he signed Mo Johnston for a Scottish transfer record fee of £400,000 from Watford. Actually, the Celtic boss might agree he got lucky. Dundee United gaffer Jim McLean had quietly knocked back a £300,000 offer for Davie Dodds the week beforehand. If he had said yes there is every likelihood Mo Johnston would never have been seen in a green and white jersey and history would have been denied one of the most sensational transfer tales of all time later in the decade. Hay made what he thought was a reasonable offer for Dodds and refused to up the ante. McLean, who could have given mules a lesson in stubbornness, stuck to his guns and the proposed move never got off the ground. Ironically, Dodds and Johnston would later become team-mates at Rangers, but that's another story. Hay kept the cash and a week or so later, bought Johnston.

'There was absolutely no problem in getting Mo to agree to join Celtic,' said Hay. 'Vice-chairman Jack McGinn, myself, Mo and Frank Boyd, his agent at the time, and a lawyer from Watford met for lunch in Langan's Brasserie in London. I got the impression that day that Mo would have happily paid the transfer fee himself just to play for Celtic. Before the lunch was over, the deal was done. As simple as that. Mo was overjoyed and couldn't wait to get started.'

Johnston made his debut the following Saturday, October 13, as Celtic left it late in beating Hibs 3-0 at Parkhead. A crowd of 27,865 was attracted to the game to desperately will the new striker, one of their own, they thought, to score a goal, but Alan Rough was to deny his international team-mate and former Partick Thistle pal a strike on his debut. The likeable big keeper made three splendid saves from Johnston, but had no answer to a Peter Grant penalty-kick eighteen minutes from time or a right-foot drive from Tommy Burns into the top corner or a typical Brian McClair effort.

One Premier League manager, wishing to remain anonymous, assured one newspaper reporter, 'Johnston's signing will be enough to win Celtic the title. Things are so tight at the top that a signing of this quality will certainly give them the vital edge.' We would see.

Davie Hay had reason to celebrate a personal first the following week at Tannadice, graveyard of the club's League Cup aspirations. Celtic overcame Dundee United 3-1 for the manager's first win over Jim McLean after sixteen months in the job. 'Aye, that was a long time coming,' beamed Hay. 'Well worth the wait, though.'

Mo Johnston played his part in the celebrations by netting the second goal which one scribe predicted would, 'surely be the first of many in the player's career at Celtic.' The striker's memorable moment came in the fifty-second minute when he directed a Davie Provan cross away from

Hamish McAlpine. An effort from Murdo MacLeod had given the Hoops the lead in the thirty-fifth minute after a well-worked free-kick with Provan and the wily winger set up Peter Grant for the third, a blistering thirty-yard piledriver in the sixty-seventh minute. Eamonn Bannon had given the home fans something to cheer with a fine twenty-yard effort in the fifty-sixth minute.

Celtic, though, were rattled by their European Cup-Winners' Cup 3-1 defeat from Rapid Vienna in midweek by the time they turned up at Cappielow for their meeting with rock-bottom Morton. Even at that early stage of the campaign, the Greenock side looked certain candidates for the drop. The torrential rain that Inverclyde can provide on an all-too-regular basis welcomed Celtic back from their fracas in Austria. Davie Hay, though, would never blame the monsoon conditions for the club's first defeat against Morton since 1979. In fact, he had flown to Austria that morning to have another look at his European opponents while leaving the first team duties to his assistant Frank Connor.

Celtic, as anticipated, took a ninth minute advantage when keeper Murray McDermott could only parry a ferocious free-kick from Murdo MacLeod and Mo Johnston swept in to fire the rebound into the net. However, in the thirty-sixth minute, the Celtic defence allowed Jim Gillespie, a lumbering, one-paced centre-forward, the opportunity to bundle the equaliser beyond the unprotected Pat Bonner. Seven minutes from time, Gillespie exposed alarming gaps in the Celtic defence with a close-range header. It must have been an interesting phone call from Connor to Hay later that evening.

Hay and his players tried to ignore the remarkable shenanigans of their European opponents Rapid Vienna the previous midweek in Glasgow. Celtic had won 3-0 for a 4-3 aggregate success and could now look forward to the quarter-final draw. Or so we thought. More on this unbelievable happening in the club's career is covered in depth in the following chapter. Be warned, it makes for grisly reading.

Three days later, Dumbarton, who had nicked a point in the earlier game at Boghead, provided the opposition and Celtic won 2-0 with goals in each half from Frank McGarvey and Mo Johnston. That's the story of the scoreline, but it fails to inform the reader that Celtic hit the woodwork four times and forced sixteen corner-kicks in a lop-sided encounter. Gordon Arthur, the opposition goalkeeper, had the game of his life and one Sunday newspaper noted, 'But for him, Dumbarton's first-ever Premier League game at Parkhead might have ended in a defeat of embarrassing proportions.'

In the next three games, Celtic began scoring goals for fun as they racked up the victories and the points. On November 17, Brian McClair claimed a hat-trick in a 5-1 triumph over Hearts at Tynecastle, which was the Edinburgh side's first defeat in seven games. Mo Johnston and Tommy Burns hit the others. A week later it was Frank McGarvey's turn to claim the match ball after hammering in three against St Mirren in a 7-1 hiding for the Paisley club at Parkhead. Ironically, that was McGarvey's second hat-trick against his old team. Paul McStay, Tommy Burns, Davie Provan and Brian McClair joined in the revelry. The goal feast continued on the first day of December when Dundee were dismissed 5-1 in Glasgow. Astonishingly, Mo Johnston became the third Celt to claim a hat-trick in successive Saturdays. Burns and McGarvey also netted in the jamboree. McGarvey could even afford to have a penalty-kick saved by overworked Dundee keeper Bobby Geddes.

It was all being set up nicely for Celtic's trip to Aberdeen the following Saturday. The Glasgow club's directors were still reeling from UEFA's decision to order them to replay their Cup-Winners' Cup-tie against their Austrian opponents at a ground at least one hundred and fifty kilometres from Glasgow. The board finally decided on Manchester United's Old Trafford after ruling out Pittodrie. Before the game against the Dons, Celtic announced they had already sold 40,000 tickets for the tie. It was hardly ideal preparation for a tussle against Alex Ferguson's team who were five points ahead at the top of the league. A capacity 23,000 crowd squeezed into the Dons' ground for what was already being described as a 'make-or-break' situation for Celtic.

It was a game that was played in a frenzy. Referee Hugh Young booked eight players - six from Celtic - as Aberdeen stretched their lead at the pinnacle with a storming 4-2 win. Celtic, after scoring seventeen goals in three matches, had forgotten how to defend. Three of the four goals they conceded came from simple, straightforward crosses into the box. The sign of things to come arrived in the thirty-third minute. Peter Weir threw a free-kick into the danger area and Eric Black scored with a header from twelve yards. Celtic were clearly rattled just on half-time as the Dons doubled their advantage when a thirty-yard shot from right-back Stewart McKimmie touched off Tom McAdam and flew into the net.

Strong words were said at half-time as Hay tore into his team. Anyone's belief that the Celtic manager's main outlook was that of a laidback bloke would have had a drastic rethink if they had been a fly on the wall of that dressing room. There was a response just before the hour mark when Black flattened McAdam and Mo Johnston slammed the resultant penalty-kick away from Jim Leighton. But, only moments later, the Celtic defence was caught napping again when Weir flighted in a near-post free-kick and Black raced in front of Danny McGrain to glance a header beyond Pat Bonner. Hay could hardly believe what he was witnessing and it didn't help matters when McAdam had to be helped off with a shattered cheekbone, Willie McStay taking his place.

The action came close to torching the playing surface as the game hurtled along at a frantic, hectic pace. There was a glimmer of light for Celtic when Frank McGarvey pulled one back with a header from a Davie Provan cross in the eighty-fourth minute. Celtic still had hopes of salvaging something, but their aspirations were torpedoed two minutes later when Frank McDougall rammed in a header after yet another cross had created alarm. And as the ball rippled behind Bonner, Celtic had to accept defeat. Not particularly graciously, it must be admitted. McGrain, Aitken, McAdam, McClair, McGarvey and sub McStay found their way into the referee's little black book, a fate that also befell Dons duo McQueen and McLeish.

Celtic then had their date with misfortune in Manchester to face up to in midweek and they attempted to overcome that trauma by the time they travelled to Easter Road to face Hibs. There was a definite hangover from two back-to-back losses that left the team's morale at zero level. Before the turn of the year, Celtic were out of Europe and the League Cup and were trailing Aberdeen by seven points in the title race. The Scottish Cup now appeared to be their most realistic venue to claim silverware in what was becoming a harrowing campaign. All that was forgotten momentarily when a Mo Johnston header in the seventy-eighth minute gave the team a 1-0 success at Easter Road.

Three days before Christmas, Rangers arrived at Celtic Park with only two wins from their previous eight league games. They had been dismissed as serious title challengers even before the first greetings cards had dropped through the letterbox. However, they still proved to be competent enough to be nuisance value to their oldest rivals. Pat Bonner was fated to be both the hero and the villain in a 1-1 draw in front of a 43,748 crowd. Graeme Sinclair lined up in the defence after Billy McNeill returned him to Celtic following the player's brief loan spell at Manchester City.

Celtic led at half-time with an excellent goal deservedly scored by the industrious Brian McClair. Only nine minutes had gone when Danny McGrain surged down the right playing a quick ball to McClair. He switched it on to Mo Johnston whose direct shot was parried by Peter McCloy. McClair, to his credit, had followed up his pass and latched on to the rebound to fire it into the inviting rigging. Rangers had the opportunity to equalise five minutes after half-time when referee Brian McGinlay awarded a penalty-kick after Mark Reid's clumsy challenge on Davie Cooper. With one half of the crowd cheering and the other half jeering, midfielder Cammy Fraser strode forward to belt an effort at goal only to be thwarted by an athletic diving save from the Celtic keeper.

With only five minutes remaining, it looked as though the combined efforts of McClair and Bonner would be good enough to give Celtic victory. Then came Bonner's awful moment as Ted McMinn, an ungainly, awkward outside-left, sent over a teasing cross. The goalie immediately looked in trouble. He was indecisive as he stayed on his line before opting to try to cut out the danger in mid-air. He never got enough purchase on the ball as it swirled over his head and, to the despair of the Celtic legions and delight to the visiting supporters, he presented a gift to Cooper. The Rangers player stroked it home; Christmas had come early.

Celtic, despite the dropped point, were not out of the pursuit of the Championship. Aberdeen, without warning, started to shed points after their 4-2 win over Davie Hay's side. They drew 0-0 with Dundee at home, lost 1-0 to Dundee United at Tannadice and were involved in a 2-2 deadlock with St Mirren at Love Street.

The door that had creaked open just a little was forcefully slammed in Celtic's face two days before 1985 made its presence known. Davie Hay watched in horror and dread and his side threw away a half-time lead over Dundee United to lose 2-1 at Parkhead. To make matters worse, Mo Johnston passed up a penalty chance just after the interval that would surely have buried Jim McLean's team. Celtic were on the rampage in the opening forty-five minutes and Hamish McAlpine made heroic saves from Paul McStay and Brian McClair before Tommy Burns left him helpless with the twenty-second minute opener. McClair left defensive stalwarts Paul Hegarty and David Narey in his slipstream before sending over a low cross. Paul McStay missed and the ball broke to Burns who cleverly and calmly stroked it low into the net.

Then came Johnston's opportunity to add to United's woe. John Holt clearly handled a McClair header and referee Jim Duncan unhesitatingly awarded the penalty. Mo joined the list of Celtic sinners from the spot when McAlpine plunged to his left to stop the effort. The outcome of a contest can alter so swiftly in such an inspirational or depressing instant. Paul Sturrock drove in the equaliser in the sixty-fourth minute and Richard Gough capitalised on more uncertainty in the heart of the home defence when he rose to head in an Eamonn Bannon free-kick eight minutes later. There was no way back for Celtic and the turning point was undoubtedly the squandered penalty by Johnston. United snatched the lifeline and took the points home.

One Sunday newspaperman summed it up perfectly. 'Celtic blew it in the last game of a year they will be glad to forget.'

CHAPTER SEVENTEEN
GOODNIGHT VIENNA

If you ever wish to witness a scowl on the features of Davie Hay, you only have to mention one name; Rapid Vienna. That'll hit the target every time. We were demolishing a late breakfast of outsize bacon butties at my place as we went over some new material for this very book. I broached the subject of the Austrian team with my usual trepidation. It got the expect reaction. 'Cheats!' exclaimed Hay.

No-one who witnessed the incredible, sickening scenes involving the Austrians would even attempt to argue. It's clear that the former Celtic manager is as infuriated today as he was back in 1984 after having the misfortune of drawing the Viennese team in the Second Round of the European Cup-Winners' Cup. No-one could have foreseen what was around the corner. Celtic had ambled through the first stage with a 3-1 aggregate win over Ghent. A goal nine minutes from time by Hubert Cordiez gave the Belgians an unlikely 1-0 win in the first leg at their place, but they were turned over 3-0 in Glasgow with Frank McGarvey scoring two and Paul McStay adding the third.

The ballot paired Celtic with Rapid Vienna with the first leg at the

Weststadion on Wednesday October 24. On a purely footballing front, Rapid won 3-1 with Peter Pacult getting the opening goal eight minutes after the turnaround which was nullified by a Brian McClair strike four minutes later. Substitute Alan McInally, on for the injured Frank McGarvey, was sent off as the Austrians scored two late goals through Leo Lainer and Hans Krankl. The game had been a roughhouse almost from the start and a weak Bulgarian referee didn't appear to possess a semblance of authority.

Celtic won the second leg 3-0 at Parkhead a fortnight later with goals from Brian McClair, Murdo MacLeod and Tommy Burns while Peter Grant failed to hit the target with a penalty-kick. A thug masquerading as a footballer, Richard Keinast, was sent off in the stormiest scenes ever seen at Parkhead. A missile had been thrown onto the pitch during yet another blow-up and substitute Rudi Weinhofer went down as though he had been hit by an invisible express train. After fifteen minutes, order was restored. Celtic thought they were through on a 4-3 aggregate, but UEFA, after an appeal from Rapid, wiped out the second leg result and ordered a third game one hundred and fifty kilometres from Parkhead. Dame Fortune continued to snarl in Celtic's direction and a solitary breakaway effort from Pacult was the only goal at Old Trafford.

Here is how Davie Hay recalled it when I co-authored his autobiography, 'The Quiet Assassin', in 2009.

'What is it about European competition that can transform apparently normal, sane individuals into a bunch of lying, cheating scumbags? I will never in my life be able to recover from the recollection of the outrageous antics of Rapid Vienna when they played at Parkhead in the second leg of our European Cup-Winners' Cup second round tie back on October 24 1984. Who could forget that night? The warning signs were flashing in the first game in Vienna two weeks beforehand. They had a particularly vicious midfielder called Reinhard Kienast and he was doing his best to get sent off with his wild lunges. Frank McGarvey and Alan McInally took a couple of dull ones, but the referee, a Bulgarian named Yordan Zhekhov, didn't want to know. McGarvey, in fact, went off injured after another reckless lunge from Kienast.

'Shortly after the restart, they went ahead, but Brian McClair equalised. Then they got another before their most famous player, Hans Krankl, completed the scoring three minutes from time. In between those goals, McInally was ordered off for a challenge that was nowhere near any of the continual assaults perpetrated by the Viennese throughout the game. Would they resort to underhand tactics in front of a packed house in Glasgow? It got even worse.

'We were 2-0 up at the interval with goals from McClair and Murdo MacLeod and were coasting. Krankl was never far from the Swedish match official, Kjell Johansen, during most of the game, moaning about this, that and the next thing. He did not enhance his reputation as a world-class sportsman in the eyes of anyone who witnessed this prima donna performance. We got a third goal when their keeper, Herbert Feurer, fumbled a shot from McGarvey and Tommy Burns slid in to toe-poke the ball over the line. The shotstopper rolled around while his team-mates went through their routine of having a go at the ref. The goal was perfectly good and, of course, it stood. At last justice caught up with Kienast when he was spotted punching Tommy on the back of the head and off he went. Not before time.

'It was real powderkeg stuff now and the mood of the Austrians didn't get better when we were awarded a penalty-kick after poor Tommy was booted by their keeper. Rapid Vienna's version of the Elephant Walk, led by Krankl, descended once more on the beleaguered official. They surrounded him and pleaded with him to consult his linesman. Johansen, probably fed up with the constant bickering from their players, booked Krankl before agreeing to go over to the touchline in front of the old Jungle, the area that housed the more boisterous among the Celtic support.

'There was the usual pushing, shoving and jostling and, in the midst of all this, one of their players, a sub called Rudi Weinhofer, suddenly collapsed to the ground holding his head. He lay prone on the turf for almost ten minutes. He was holding his head and eventually he came off, swathed in bandages, claiming to have been struck by a bottle. It was all nonsense, of course. The game restarted with the penalty-kick being given and Peter Grant smashed it past the post! Television pictures later showed that Weinhofer hadn't been hit by a bottle or anything else for that matter. It was all a phoney act in an effort to get the game abandoned.

'At one stage, it looked as though Krankl was going to lead the players off the pitch which would have brought automatic expulsion by UEFA from the competition. He thought better of it and played on. Unfortunately, someone in the crowd had thrown a bottle, but it was at least twenty yards away from Weinhofer or any other Austrian player. UEFA's official observer was a West German named Dr Hubert Claessen and he said in his report that he had seen a bottle come onto the pitch, but it had not hit any of the Rapid Vienna players. I didn't believe for a second that would be the end of the matter. I was proved right. Celtic were fined £4,000 and the Austrians £5,000. Kienast was suspended for four games and their vociferous coach, Otto Baric, was banned from the touchline for three matches. Rapid Vienna immediately appealed, changing their story to say that Weinhofer had been struck by a coin and not a bottle. By the way, the Austrian was examined by an ambulance man in Glasgow and, needless to say, there was no sign of a cut.

'The committee that sat on the appeal didn't check any television evidence for reasons known only to themselves. They doubled Rapid Vienna's fine, but, in a remarkable U-turn that suspended belief, they ordered a replay which had to be one hundred and fifty kilometres away from Celtic Park. How they reached such a diabolical decision is anyone's guess. Rapid were delighted, as you might expect. They had been fined a total of £10,000 and they would receive half the gate receipts when the tie took place at Manchester United's Old Trafford. They would actually be punished by making a profit.

'We were angry at being ordered to play that third game. We had won fair and square only to have it binned because some moron threw a missile onto the pitch. I was interviewed on TV later that night and tried to play down the entire situation. I said, "That might turn out to be the most expensive half-bottle of vodka in history." I didn't realise how apt those words would turn out to be. We made our way to Manchester on December 12 and I think we had 40,000 fans inside the ground long before the kick-off. The mood was grim. The supporters, like everyone else, were convinced they had been robbed. I was angry, too, for we had played well against Rapid Vienna, almost as good as the 5-0 romp against Sporting Lisbon the previous year. We never did get the praise we deserved for overturning the Austrians.

'The Celtic party stayed at a hotel in Haydock near the racecourse as we didn't want to get caught up with the emotions of our huge following in Manchester city centre. Old Trafford was heaving with seething Celtic fans by the time the kick-off arrived. There was a lot of venom and poison about. It was an extremely tense occasion, a highly-charged evening, to say the least. We were not fated to book our place in the quarter-finals that season. We came out the traps at a fair old toot and we were so unlucky when Roy Aitken struck the post in the seventeenth minute. We had been attacking en masse and they hit us with a classic sucker punch. They raced straight up field with my team disorganised and their centre-forward, Peter Pacult, swept an effort wide of Pat Bonner.

'We were now 4-1 down on aggregate and we had to claim three goals to push the game into extra-time. We tried. Oh, how we tried, but it wasn't to be. It ended 1-0 for them and cheats had been allowed to prosper. There were another couple of incidents as two fans wearing Celtic colours raced onto the pitch and one of them got involved in a tangle with their goalkeeper. The other had a go at the goalscorer Pacult as he overdid the celebrations at the final whistle. The police lifted them both and I knew we would be in line for some more punitive action from Europe's governing soccer body. The offenders were both from England, but had turned up to support us. We had no jurisdiction over them, but once more we were in the firing line. UEFA acted once again to put the boot into us. We were ordered to play our next home European tie - against Atletico Madrid, as it turned out - behind closed doors.'

Hay still shakes his head at the memory. 'One stupid action from a so-called fan actually cost us two seasons in Europe. I'll always be convinced we beat Rapid Vienna by fair means. They got all the way to that season's Final, which was held in Rotterdam. Their opponents were Everton and, thankfully, the English club won 3-1. Do you know something, though? I would have fancied Celtic's chances against the Merseyside men that year. Genuinely, I believe we would have had a chance - and a good chance at that. It's all conjecture, I realise, but I just happen to believe it. And before you say it, no, I am not a wild optimist. Atletico Madrid? We got a great scoring draw at their place and could you imagine the atmosphere that would have been generated at Celtic Park for the second leg? I've no doubt we would have won that, too. I was desperate to get Celtic to make an impact in Europe again, but we kept getting dealt terrible hands.'

CHAPTER EIGHTEEN
MAZE OF MISTAKES

Davie Hay watched Celtic storm to the perfect start to 1985 with a well-merited 2-1 triumph over Rangers at Ibrox on January 1. He insisted, 'I meant every word of it when I said the time for Celtic sob stories was over.' The manager was determined to move on from the Rapid Vienna affair and dump it in the past. It still hurt like hell, though.

The Parkhead side, with 45,000 fans in attendance, were caught in a maze of mistakes during the first-half of the traditional Old Firm New Year's Day fixture. Mo Johnston squandered a seventeenth-minute penalty-kick with a feeble attempt - his second failure from the spot in four days. Hay's reaction was instantaneous. 'Maybe twelve yards is too far out for him. He won't be taking another.'

A quarter-of-an-hour after Johnston's miss, Celtic were a goal down. A sweet passing movement between the two Fergusons - Derek and Iain - carved open an opportunity for Davie Cooper and he tucked the ball behind Pat Bonner. Hay had harsh words to say to his players at the interval. 'We just weren't playing well. Forget the penalty miss from Mo; we were second best all over the park. I've always insisted a manager gets paid to think quickly and you've got to use the precious minutes in the dressing room at half-time to get your thoughts across.'

Whatever the Celtic manager spelt out to his team deep in the bowels of Ibrox Stadium, it had a desired effect. Johnston atoned for his spot-kick blunder and the Hoops were level within sixty seconds of the restart. Frank McGarvey provided the cross and the darting striker sent a header flashing away from Peter McCloy. Johnston then ran towards the celebrating Celtic followers in the Broomloan Stand and embraced a supporter who had spilled onto the touchline. The player was booked and the fan was led away by the police. Nine minutes later, Brian McClair shot Hay's side ahead following a good run and pass from John Colquhoun. McClair took aim and fired a low eighteen-yard drive past McCloy, the ball getting a nick off the challenging Hugh Burns on its way.

So, Hay, still in a reflective mood afterwards, admitted he was happy enough with the win and the points, but it was time for Celtic to concentrate on what was ahead and not what lay in the past. He also added drily, 'Mo did better with his head than he did with his feet on this occasion.' Rangers boss Jock Wallace didn't participate in the bon homie of his opponents. Brusquely, he summed up, 'We were rubbish in the second-half. My view may hurt feelings, but it is the truth and I believe in honesty.'

Jack Frost made another of his unwelcome intrusions on sport during a shivering, freezing January and Celtic's next competitive Premier League game was on February 2 against a curiously defensive-minded St Mirren at Love Street. The home side erected a barricade in front of Campbell Money and invited Celtic to take the game to them. It worked fine until three minutes from an hour of stifling play, John Colquhoun unlocked the Paisley padlock with a wonderfully accurate corner-kick that picked out Tom McAdam. His header clattered against the base of the post and Mo Johnston, with his lightning reflexes, was the first to react in the packed penalty area. The ball was in the net before the Saints keeper could move. With sixteen minutes to go, Johnston sent Tommy Burns through and the smooth midfielder guided a lob over Money and the points were heading to Glasgow.

A week later, Celtic's title aspirations lay in tatters after a remarkable smash-and-grab act from Dundee at Dens Park. Davie Hay's side controlled a huge percentage of the possession and the manager must have found it difficult to accept it was still goalless with the arrival of the eighty-first minute. He would have been even more puzzled nine minutes later when his opponents had scored twice for a 2-0 win. Ray Stephen claimed the first and, astonishingly, Bobby Connor blitzed in a penalty-kick two minutes from the end. A newspaper noted, 'Dundee battled as if their lives depended on this result. And in so doing probably finished off Celtic's championship hopes.'

Ten days later on February 19, Jock Stein was in the Celtic stand to watch several of his Scottish international contingent against Morton. Paul McStay, Frank McGarvey and Davie Provan were scorers in a 4-0 victory, but Big Jock may have been even more interested in the marksman of the fourth goal - a young lad by the name of Paul Chalmers, who came on as a substitute for Mo Johnston. Paul, of course, was the son of Stevie Chalmers, Celtic's history-making striker with the winner against Inter Milan in Lisbon in 1967. Davie Hay promoted the youngster to the top team squad after being impressed by his twenty-eight goals in twenty-four reserve games. Ironically, his effort against the Greenock side was his only goal in Celtic's top team and, after another three appearances, he was loaned to Bradford City the following year and then agreed a permanent deal with St Mirren.

The biggest league crowd in Scotland for season 1984/85 turned out at Parkhead four days later when Aberdeen were in town. A total of 48,824 generated a stupendous atmosphere and Paul McStay responded with a Man of the Match performance. It was heading for a goalless draw until Davie Hay made a match-winning switch. He said, 'Aberdeen always flooded their midfield against us and I wanted to combat that by matching them man for man. We were nullifying each other when I decided to go for width. I sent on Davie Provan for Peter Grant and, as luck would have it, our substitute was instrumental in the game turning in our favour when he began stretching their defence.'

In the sixty-eighth minute, Provan delivered a perfect corner-kick, Roy Aitken powered it goalwards and Mo Johnston, practically on the goal-line, flicked the ball into the net. Celtic had to wait until the last minute to get their second clinching goal and the manager was as good as his word. The penalty-taking duty had been removed from Johnston and the responsibility handed to McStay. Provan sent another inviting cross into the danger area. Johnston was involved when Neale Cooper knocked him over from behind and McStay lashed the award beyond Jim Leighton.

Bizarrely, though, McStay didn't take a crucial penalty-kick a week later against Dundee United at Tannadice. It was 0-0 with ten minutes to go when referee Mike Delaney gave the award. Defender John Holt dived to push away a shot from Provan and Jim McLean's players couldn't argue when the match official pointed to the spot. McStay stepped back and allowed Peter Grant to take the kick. Unfortunately, the young midfielder battered it straight down the middle and it hit the astonished Hamish McAlpine before bouncing to safety.

Celtic drew a blank again on March 16 against Hibs at Celtic Park. Even worse, they lost 1-0 to a struggling Edinburgh side with Paul Kane hitting the only goal in the twenty-first minute. A Sunday newspaper scribe made these observations, 'Any thoughts I had that being a football manager was a good job disappeared after watching Davie Hay suffer through this game. Look at it this way. At 3pm he was happily in charge of a team in the semi-final of the Scottish Cup and pushing hard for the Premier League title. They were playing a side struggling to keep their head above water. If Celtic have turned in a poorer performance this season, I'm glad I was elsewhere at the time.'

The astute scribe concluded, 'The Celtic back lot looked shame-faced at the goal they conceded. They had every right to. They were tailor's dummies to a man when Ralph Callachan swung in a corner from the left. Willie Irvine had no trouble reaching the cross. He nodded the ball down in the six yards box where Paul Kane could have stopped to tie his laces before shoving it over the line.'

'A real sickener,' declared Hay. 'But don't dare write us off. Aberdeen may be in pole position, but there is still a bit to go. Strange things can happen in this game. Who would have thought Hibs would beat us today?'

So, Celtic and their manager were still clinging to hope on a bitterly cold evening when Hearts arrived in the east end of Glasgow for a midweek fixture. Hay must have wondered if he had walked into a re-run of his worst nightmare. The Tynecastle men were 2-0 ahead inside half-an-hour through efforts from John Robertson and Andy Watson. 'Situations like these are a test of your players' courage,' said Hay. 'Some may just fade into the background, they don't want to know. But, if you were being positive, you could say we had a full hour to get three goals against Hearts and that was not an impossible task.'

Mo Johnston started the fightback with a header eight minutes before the interval and it was all-square when Murdo MacLeod scored with a raging shot in the seventy-eighth minute. Even a draw at this stage would have been unacceptable to the Celtic boss. Brian McClair responded with the winner a minute from time. Celtic, after twenty-eight matches and a game in hand over Aberdeen, were now on forty points, six adrift.

'We had eight games to play and that's when you tell your players every single one of those games is a Cup Final,' said Hay. 'Yes, I know it's a cliché, but it helps focus the minds of everyone. We had to keep winning and hope Aberdeen would slip up and, remember, we still had a game at Pittodrie where we might be able to do some damage to them.'

Once again, the Celtic players were listening to their gaffer. They had four 'Cup Finals' coming up before they travelled north to face Alex Ferguson's team on April 27. They won all four and scored fourteen goals into the bargain. Brian McClair went on a scoring spree with four in a 7-2 win over Morton at Cappielow. Frank McGarvey (2) and Owen Archdeacon chipped in with the others. McClair netted another in a 2-0 victory over doomed Dumbarton at Boghead. Mo Johnston also got his name on the scoresheet. Next up was Hearts at Tynecastle and McClair hammered in the killer second after Paul McStay had opened the scoring in the tenth minute. On April 27 at Celtic Park, Roy Aitken rammed home two penalty-kicks as St Mirren were dismissed 3-0 with McGarvey getting his customary goal against his former side.

Unfortunately, for Davie Hay and Celtic, Aberdeen had won their four games - Hibs (5-0), Dundee United (4-2), Rangers (2-1) and Dumbarton (4-0). They had even scored a goal more than their Glasgow rivals. All eyes were on Pittodrie with only four league games left to play. The situation was simple - a win for the Dons would give them the flag while a draw would still see them as clear favourites. However, as Davie Hay would say, 'You can't celebrate anything until it is mathematically impossible for you to be caught.'

In front of a sell-out 23,000 crowd, Roy Aitken gave Celtic the best possible start with a rocket-like penalty-kick six minutes from half-time after Billy Stark had floored Mo Johnston. However, the Dons got their equaliser from a most unusual source - defensive rock Willie Miller, who normally complained of a nosebleed if he ventured into the other team's half. However, he did just that in the sixty-second minute to great effect. He was left unguarded by the Celtic rearguard as Ian Porteus fired over a free-kick from the right wing. The Dons captain simply raced forward, got his head on the ball and Pat Bonner was beaten. The home players and fans celebrated a 1-1 draw and they were in no doubt where the flag would be flying in the new season.

The inevitable happened four days later when a nine-man Rangers side took a point in a remarkable 1-1 draw at Celtic Park. Winger Davie Cooper and defender Ally Dawson were ordered off by referee Bob Valentine in separate flashpoint incidents. It was a collision of unrelenting action, punishing tackling and astounding occurrences. Even before the double sending-off, Celtic had been awarded a penalty-kick in exactly two minutes and five seconds when Dave McPherson was adjudged to have got a hold of Mo Johnston's jersey. Roy Aitken, who had been successful with his last three spot-kicks, thought he had made it four out of four when he blasted one past Peter McCloy. The match official ordered a re-take because he believed the ball had moved off the spot. Aitken took it again and this time smashed the ball off the legs of the Rangers goalkeeper. It was just a taster of what was around the corner.

It was still goalless six minutes after the turnaround when Cooper was sent off for a retaliatory challenge on Peter Grant. Celtic took the lead on the hour mark when McCloy failed to hold a low drive from Mo Johnston and Alan McInally knocked in his first Premier League goal for the club. Seven minutes later, as the torrid action enthralled the 40,079 paying customers, Johnston and Dawson clashed. The Celt was booked for his part in the incident and, after consulting his linesman, the referee red-carded the Rangers full-back. Unbelievably, Rangers, with two men absent, drew level when they were granted a penalty-kick in the seventy-seventh minute. Aitken appeared to handle and Ally McCoist bashed the award beyond Peter Latchford. It was all breathless stuff and Davie Provan cracked a shot off the Rangers upright near the end. The Ibrox side celebrated as though they had won the league. In fact, the honour had now most certainly been presented to Aberdeen; there were no more technical options open to Davie Hay's team.

It was no surprise when the league season fizzled out with two games still to play. Three days after the stalemate against Rangers, Dundee won at Celtic Park for the first time in a decade when John Brown, a future Rangers player, got the only goal with a well-judged free-kick in the fifty-second minute. It wasn't quite exciting fare for the 8,815 who attended and a journalist stated, 'Try as I might, I can't disguise the fact this was pretty dreadful.'

Celtic, at least, went out on a winning note when 6,514 fans watched them dump Dumbarton 2-0 with two late goals from Brian McClair and Willie McStay. One scribe wrote, 'I learned two things from this game. Firstly, I didn't realise Celtic's form slump was quite so bad. And, secondly, I had no idea ninety minutes could last so long.' Aberdeen won their last two league games against Hearts (3-0) and Morton (2-1) to complete their thirty-six match programme on fifty-nine points, seven more than Celtic.

But Davie Hay still had his eyes on winning his first trophy as Celtic manager. There was the little matter of the Scottish Cup Final to be addressed on May 18 at Hampden.

CHAPTER NINETEEN

THE CELEBRATING CENTURIANS

Davie Hay admitted frankly that defeat was 'unthinkable' as he prepared his team for the historic 100th Scottish Cup Final against Dundee United on May 18. There was awesome pressure on the young Celtic manager.

'My first season had drawn a blank,' he said. 'I didn't need any reminding that it was the first season since 1978 the club had not won a trophy. And now I was ninety minutes away from rectifying that situation, ready to take on a team a lot of people were calling our 'hoodoo side'. With a fair justification, too, I have to concede.

'We had met Dundee United nine times over the two seasons I was in charge at Parkhead and won only once, a 3-1 triumph in the league at Tannadice on October 20 1984. That was our solitary success from eight league head-to-heads. They had beaten us three times and the remaining four matches had ended all-square. There wasn't much between the teams, but they had also knocked us out of the League Cup at the quarter-final stage, winning 2-1 at their place. I felt it was appropriate that we do something about it. It was time for the Celtic support to celebrate again.'

The entertainment value wasn't confined to the action. Someone at the SFA hit on the bright idea of inviting Prime Minister Margaret Thatcher to be the Guest of Honour at the spectacle. The Iron Lady agreed to a rare visit north and didn't bat an eyelid when she was greet by a huge percentage of the 60,346 attendance brandishing red cards in her direction before the kick-off. Unions had distributed the cards to the fans to show their general displeasure at her presence. If she was even remotely embarrassed by the show of unity among the supporters she hid it well.

Thankfully, the sideshow was forgotten when the action got underway. Hay realised everything would have to be earned against a cagey United team with wily old fox Jim McLean in control. And, for a moment nine minutes after the interval following a stuffy first-half that fateful day at the national stadium, it looked as though the Tannadice manager had got his tactics spot on again. Davie Dodds, who might have been lining up in the green and white hoops that day, got free of Roy Aitken and fed a pass through to Stuart Beedie, who found a lot of grass in which to work. He rolled the ball wide of Pat Bonner for a simple and effective goal.

Hay recalled, 'As usual, United sat back and allowed us to come at them while they went through their cat-and-mouse routine. They would suck you in and then hit on the break. We had encountered it nine times in two seasons and here we were at Hampden going through it all again. I warned my team about keeping their wits about them at all times. "Take your eye off this lot and they will punish you," was one of the last things I said to my players in the dressing room. I was reasonably pleased with the first-half. However, the second period was only minutes old when we found ourselves a goal down. They had done it again. I couldn't believe it. Our defence was left exposed, Roy Aitken couldn't match the speed of Stuart Beedie and the United frontman got through to squeeze the ball low past Pat Bonner.

'That's the way it stood with around fifteen minutes to go. Managers are paid good money to make instant decisions and I made two monumental ones that afternoon. If they hadn't worked, I would have had to pay the consequences of leading the team through another trophyless campaign.

I took off Paul McStay and Tommy Burns and put on Pierce O'Leary and Brian McClair. The Celtic fans must have thought I had lost the plot. Paul and Tommy were two excellent midfielders who could pass the ball well and I was putting on a centre-half in Pierce to take one of their places. I knew what Brian could give the team in midfield and he was also a goalscorer.

'Tommy was far from happy about being removed from the action. He muttered something as he walked past me on the touchline and I said, "Just shut up and sit on your backside." The tension was beginning to tell. It was all or nothing now. I put O'Leary into the middle of the defence alongside Tom McAdam and freed Aitken to get forward on the right. I thought his running power might unsettle the United back lot. The switches worked a treat, I am happy - and relieved - to tell you.'

In the seventy-sixth minute, time stood still for everyone at Hampden. Eamonn Bannon had just clattered Murdo MacLeod about twenty-five yards from goal. Davie Provan eyed up the situation as Hamish McAlpine screamed frantically at his defensive wall to get into position. Provan took it with his right foot, the ball flew up tantalisingly and over the United barrier and then there was the exquisite sight of the free-kick beating the United keeper, pawing helplessly at fresh air, at his top left-hand corner of the goal.

In fact, it was an award Provan should never have been allowed to take. He revealed, 'We used a different ball for that match from the one we used for league games and it flew about all over the place. I had actually been practising my free-kicks with Murdo MacLeod and I must have missed the target with every kick. So, we agreed, if the opportunity arose, Murdo would take the kicks. But, with time running out - and at 1-0 down - we were awarded a free-kick at the edge of the penalty box and I fancied it. It was as well as I ever struck a free-kick and it was probably my most important goal.'

Billy McNeill, sitting in the Scottish Television gantry alongside commentator Archie Macpherson, said excitedly, 'Celtic were looking for inspiration and now they've got it. This is what they wanted. Dundee United are in for a very hectic fourteen minutes or so.'

Roy Aitken was revelling in the role of being freed of his defensive shackles and was creating havoc every time he surged forward. With six minutes to go, Paul Hegarty, the harassed United central defender, dived to head a ball away as it dropped menacingly on the edge of the box. It sped off to Celtic's right wing where Aitken was bulldozing into attack again. He caught up with the ball and whipped in a cross that came off his right boot like a meteor. It might have gone out for a shy on the other side, but somehow Frank McGarvey corkscrewed his body into position, got his head to the ball and, from about ten yards, his blurred effort thundered between McAlpine and his left-hand post. The 100th Scottish Cup was about to be bedecked in green and white ribbons. There was no way back for the Tannadice team.

Remarkably, not only was it McGarvey's last goal for Celtic, it was also his last game. Controversially, years later, he said, 'Davie Hay took over when Billy McNeill left and I always feel I was unfairly treated by him. Although I played well for him, he wanted his own players. I was twenty-nine years old and wanted to spend the rest of my days at Celtic, but he sold me on though my Cup Final goal made his job safer.'

Hay replied, 'I've often been asked why I transferred Frank McGarvey to St Mirren that summer. I also read somewhere that Frank had said his goal against Dundee United saved me from the sack. I can tell him, I saved myself from getting a P45. Actually, I think he should have thanked me for allowing him to stay on the pitch that afternoon. I made HIM a hero. While I was mulling over my substitutions, I admit I did think of taking off McGarvey. Even he might admit he wasn't playing particularly well against United. But something popped into my head that my old Motherwell gaffer Ally MacLeod used to say, "Don't take off a goalscorer." Ally would repeat over and over, "When you need a goal, keep on your goalscorer." That stuck with me and, boy, did we need a goal against Jim McLean's team that day.

'Frank was coming out of contract that summer and I decided to offer him an extension. I duly did so and I presented him with a deal that was identical to the one that was about to expire. I could see he was distinctly underwhelmed by my gesture. Frank believed he was worth more and I disagreed. I thought he was on reasonable money and I told him so. I asked him to go away and think about it. However, I detected more than just a slight rumbling of discontent from Frank and I didn't want a dissatisfied player in my dressing room.

'I already had Mo Johnston, signed for £400,000 from Watford in October that season, and Brian McClair to lead the attack. I was already planning in making them my regular partnership up front in the new term. Brian had completed the season with twenty-four goals and Mo chipped in with nineteen. I had also signed Alan McInally for £90,000 from Ayr United and the bustling hitman was scoring on a regular basis, too. Frank, Cup hero or not, was expendable. I actually accepted a reduced transfer fee from St Mirren for the player to enable him to get a more lucrative signing-on fee. I'm still waiting for him to say thanks.'

Any rumblings of future disharmony between manager and player were undetectable at Hampden that May day where even the dreadful conditions, wind and rain pouring almost from the kick-off, could dampen the joy of the Celtic support. One newspaper reporter put it succinctly, 'I can't vouch for all of the previous ninety-nine Scottish Cup Finals, but I'll say this for the one hundredth. Never, surely, has it been surpassed for drama and passion, especially late on.'

And, yet, Celtic were staring into the abyss of oblivion a mere one hour into their Scottish Cup campaign. Unbelievably, they were trailing 1-0 to the part-timers of Hamilton Accies in front of an all-ticket 10,000 crowd at Douglas Park on January 30. Davie Hay's men were heading for the competition's quicksand when the home side scored through veteran Alex Forsyth, who had sampled considerable success against Celtic as a Partick Thistle player in the 1971 League Cup Final where, ironically, Hay was in the opposition team. Now Forsyth was on the verge of another unforgettable Cup triumph at Celtic's expense. Twenty-seven minutes had gone when the defender sent a header from a John Brogan cross soaring past Pat Bonner.

It looked only a matter of time before Celtic retaliated with the equaliser, the Accies upstarts punished for their impertinence. However, the mood on the terracing was distinctly fidgety when an hour came and went and the Parkhead side were still struggling to detect a loophole. No-one could have guessed then what the Scottish Cup competition held in store four months later.

Davie Hay had decisions to make as the clock ticked. He took off Brian McClair and sent on substitute Frank McGarvey to give the opposition something else to think about. In the sixty-first minute, McGarvey embarked on a solo run which was completed with the home goalkeeper Rikki Ferguson, who had been heroic, fishing the ball out of the back of the net. That signaled the siege of Ferguson's goal, but, with only four minutes remaining, the Accies were hanging on and looking at the distinct possibility of a replay at Celtic Park. McGarvey ruined their dreams with the winning goal in the fading moments when he snapped up a rebound from a Danny McGrain drive. Accies would have to console themselves with club record gate receipts of £19,672.

There was no such anxiety when Inverness Caley Thistle, then a Highland League club, visited Glasgow for the next round on February 16. Paul McStay scored his one and only hat-trick for the club against the first non-league outfit to play at Parkhead since Elgin City in 1967 in the same competition. Celtic coasted to a 6-0 victory with Frank McGarvey, Mo Johnston and Murdo MacLeod also weighing in with net-bulging strikes. The Highlanders' sixteen year old goalkeeper Les Fridge was the most overworked man on the park as he valiantly attempted to keep the scoreline respectable. It could have been a lot worse for the game teenager - Johnston hit the woodwork on three occasions.

Dundee had knocked out Rangers at Ibrox in the previous round and were rewarded with a home tie against Celtic on March 9. After a tough and towsy goalless first-half, Davie Hay must have thought his men had cracked it when Mo Johnston got the opening goal in the sixty-seventh minute when he finished off a marvellous run by Brian McClair. However, a replay was required when John Brown equalised with a header five minutes later.

So, it was back to Glasgow in midweek for a good, old-fashioned, rollicking Cup-tie that threatened to boil over on occasion. Bobby Glennie, a no-frills defender, was expelled a minute into the second-half for what one reporter described as an 'injudicious lunge' at Murdo MacLeod. No doubt the Celtic midfielder would have come with a different term altogether as he hobbled around for a few minutes. The Hoops were already leading by a thirty-fourth minute goal from Frank McGarvey after he headed in a fine cross from the right wing from Willie McStay.

However, the home fans in the 37,390 crowd were stunned into silence only two minutes after the removal of Glennie when the Dens Park side equalised as a cross from John Brown was deflected by Pierce O'Leary into the direction of Ray Stephen and he cutely lobbed the stranded Pat Bonner. The ten men took great heart and, suddenly and inexplicably, the tie had turned. Davie Hay, once again, realised impact surgery was required, but no-one could have predicted that he would take off captain Danny McGrain, who had been playing at left-back, and replace him with Tommy Burns in the sixty-fourth minute. It was a bold move that could have back-fired spectacularly. Four minutes later, Celtic were heading for the Scottish Cup semi-final. Davie Provan provided the cross and Mo Johnston supplied the swivel and shot that booked a Hampden spot.

One impressed newspaper reporter wrote, 'Davie Hay's inspired substitution taking off McGrain and putting on Burns turned this encounter. Hay will know after this that his team have truly earned their place in the last four from an enthralling game which managed to surpass the weekend draw.'

Motherwell, managed by Hay's former Rangers foe Tommy McLean, stood in their path to the Cup Final. The game on April 13 ended in a 1-1 deadlock and would never go down as a classic in the memory banks of any of the 30,536 fans who witnessed it. One scribe haughtily observed, 'It's a long time since I saw a good Cup semi-final. Sadly, nothing happened here to alter that state of affairs. Certainly, First Division Motherwell deserve praise for matching Premier League Celtic in fitness, organisation and effort. However, there was little finesse, flair or firepower on show. All the ingredients the fans want, in fact.'

Celtic lived dangerously against the Fir Park side and were a goal adrift in the twelfth minute when future Scotland World Cup captain Gary McAllister turned in a cross from Ray Blair. Tommy Burns equalised in the twenty-third minute, stylishly completing a move that was far above the mundane fare offered throughout most of this confrontation. Danny McGrain struck a crisp pass to Paul McStay who lofted a peach of a pass over the defence in front of Burns. The midfielder, with the ability to sum things up in a heartbeat, didn't hesitate as he lobbed the ball over keeper John Gardiner. That brought a halt to the scoring as the game got sucked into mediocrity. Celtic's moment in the sun at Hampden would have to wait.

Four days later in the replay, Celtic claimed a 3-0 win over stubborn opponents, but the score does not do justice to the efforts of the Lanarkshire men. It was goalless until the seventy-third minute when Roy Aitken swept a low shot wide of the keeper. The effort was met with massive relief by those of the Celtic persuasion. In truth, Davie Hay's men toiled to take control of the situation and their discomfort was manifesting itself in some untidy challenges with McGrain, McStay and Tom McAdam all being booked by referee Davie Syme. There was the distinct whiff of nervous tension around Mount Florida until Mo Johnston finished off the resistance of Motherwell with two goals in the last nine minutes.

On the same evening in Edinburgh, Dundee United beat Aberdeen 2-1 in their semi-final replay after a goalless draw in the first tie. Davie Hay would come to face-to-face with 'nemesis' Jim McLean at Hampden in his quest for his first trophy victory as Celtic manager.

Turned out nicely, didn't it?

CHAPTER TWENTY
POOR FORM

Paul McStay might just have won Celtic the 1985/86 Scottish Premier League title with virtually the last kick of the ball on the FIRST day of the new season. As it was, the campaign went all the way to the wire with Davie Hay's team pipping Hearts on goal difference following one of the most thrilling and dramatic climaxes in Scottish football history.

However, let's go back to the season's kick-off on August 10 when, as fate would have it, Celtic travelled to take on Hearts at Tynecastle. The day didn't start well for the Hoops without a ball being kicked. Hay had been desperately trying to arrange a new left-back during the summer. He used the old boys' network to get in touch with his former international colleague Eddie Gray, who had quit as manager of his ex-club Leeds United in the summer. Eddie's brother Frank had been at Elland Road, too, but the jungle drums were beating that he would also soon be on his way from the Yorkshire club. Hay believed the Glasgow-born Celtic fan would be ideal to solve his problem position. The proposed deal fell through and Gray moved to Sunderland, instead.

So, Tommy Burns, a skillful midfielder, was in at left-back for the game in Edinburgh with veteran Danny McGrain, a naturally right-sided defender who had had covered in the position for a few games the previous term, on the bench. Hay had also tried to utilise Murdo MacLeod, Graeme Sinclair and Mark Reid in the No.3 berth as he sought, mainly in vain, for a solution. It wasn't an ideal situation in which to enter the fray of a new and challenging season.

Hay had sold outside-right John Colquhoun to Hearts with Davie Provan making the berth his own with some fabulously consistent displays. Possibly, Colquhoun thought he had a point to prove that afternoon, but he gave Burns a torrid time. He topped a superb performance by giving his new club the lead just before the half-hour mark when he finished off a John Robertson corner-kick by stabbing the ball wide of Pat Bonner. Hearts stubbornly retained that advantage until there were only thirty seconds remaining.

Willie McStay then launched a pass to his brother Paul on the edge of the penalty area and the midfielder struck a sweet shot low past Henry Smith. Moments later, the referee blew for full-time and Celtic returned to Glasgow with a point. For Hay's team it was certainly a point gained; for Hearts, equally, it was one dropped. It would make an enormous difference to the destination of the title just under nine months and thirty-five games later.

Desmond White, the Celtic chairman who clashed so frequently with Jock Stein and Billy McNeill, had died suddenly of a suspected heart attack while on holiday in Crete on June 21. There was a perfectly observed one minute's silence for the man who held the office for fourteen years before the next game against Motherwell at Parkhead. Davie Hay recalled, 'Yes, I had my run-ins with Desmond, but I actually got on quite well with him. He was an honest gentleman. You always knew where you stood with him.'

It took until just before the hour mark before the Celtic fans in the 20,189 crowd witnessed their first goal of the new season at Paradise. Davie Provan and Murdo MacLeod combined and Brian McClair tucked away a header with a fair amount of aplomb. Provan, who had an inspired afternoon on the touchline, scored a sublime second after racing onto a long pass from Paul McStay, twisting and turning his way towards the edge of the box before finishing in devastating fashion with an unstoppable right-foot shot. Ray Blair got a consolation effort for the Fir Park side with an effort that Pat Bonner failed to hold as it rolled out of his grasp and over the line.

The opening League Cup-tie took Celtic to Palmerston for the first time since 1963 where 6,404 fans saw them overwhelm Queen of the South 4-1. Mo Johnston scored two - his first goals since April 17 constituting a barren run of eight games. Brian McClair and Alan McInally claimed the others while Tommy Bryce gave the home fans hope with an effort that made it 1-1 at the interval. Hay said, 'These were always dodgy games, away ties on grounds you haven't experienced before. But these games weren't showpieces, they were there simply to win, get through and the so-called glamour occasions would come later.'

Celtic were on their travels again the following Saturday as they went to the less-than-salubrious surroundings of Kilbowie Park to face Clydebank. The result was never in doubt, but Hay would have preferred a more convincing winning margin than 2-0, the goals coming from Mo Johnston in each half. So, the manager may have been happier four days later when Brechin City were dismantled 7-0 in Glasgow at the next stage of the League Cup. As anticipated, it was one-way traffic with Johnston again claiming two goals for his third successive game. Roy Aitken, with a penalty-kick, Paul McStay, Alan McInally, Davie Provan and Tommy Burns joined in the scoring spree. The Celtic players actually used Brechin's penalty area as a meeting place that evening.

The target practice set up Celtic nicely for the opening encounter of the season against Rangers at Parkhead on August 31. The game attracted a massive crowd of 58,635 where honours were shared in a 1-1 draw. Ally McCoist gave the Ibrox side the lead against the run of play when he turned in a right-wing cross from Hugh Burns in thirty-five minutes. Paul McStay replied with a fine effort seven minutes after the turnaround when he took the ball for a stroll along the eighteen-yard line before stopping and turning sharply. Goalkeeper Nicky Walker never got near the whizzbang effort.

Davie Hay was clearly frustrated afterwards. 'Celtic should have won easily. We were the better side, in command for most of the match. But we failed to take our chances and we still need to work on our sharpness.' His opposite number, Jock Wallace, wasn't overjoyed, either. 'We played for only twenty minutes. Our best player was our goalkeeper.'

The Celtic manager was apoplectic with his team's performance four nights later after an extraordinary League Cup exit to Hibs at Easter Road. As was the case the previous season against Dundee United at Tannadice, the tie went to extra-time. This time, though, it was still level after the added period and the Parkhead men blew it in the penalty-kick shoot-out. Hay said, 'That was a game we should have won in regulation time. There should never have been any need for an extra half-hour or penalties. We've only got ourselves to blame for this defeat.' I was in attendance among the support in Edinburgh that evening. Certainly, I wouldn't disagree with Hay.

Celtic took the lead through Mo Johnston in the third minute, but then found themselves trailing to efforts from Steve Cowan and Gordon Durie. Davie Provan levelled matters before the interval. Colin Harris put John Blackley's side ahead again in the fifty-eighth minute and it appeared any time Hibs had an effort on target it magically and improbably produced a goal. Mo Johnston equalised a minute later and the tie was dragged into extra-time. Roy Aitken hammered Celtic into the lead only for Danny McGrain to put through his own goal to bring it back to stalemate. When it went to penalty-kicks, no-one should have been surprised that the visitors continued to be so charitable.

Aitken and Peter Grant failed to score with their efforts as did two Hibs players. It went to sudden death and Cowan converted his penalty comfortably. Pierce O'Leary, a lanky centre-half who never looked too comfortable with the ball at his feet, stepped up nervously and, from twelve yards, sent his wretched attempt hurtling over the bar. The streaking ball was probably more of a threat to the statue of Walter Scott sitting in his monument in Princes Street than it was to Alan Rough.

Hay had more to say to his players about their shambolic display, but he kept it private. It wasn't a pleasant journey back to Glasgow late that night. Coincidentally, Celtic were back at the same ground on league business three days later. The players' attitude had changed somewhat. They eased to a 5-0 win with Brian McClair netting two, Mo Johnston, Owen Archdeacon and an own goal from Mark Fulton completing the dramatically changed scoreline from the earlier meeting. It was all too much for Hibs' vigorous defender Gordon Rae who was sent off. One reporter put it rather wittily, 'Rae went for impersonating a magician's assistant. He tried to cut Brian McClair in half!'

Sadly, as there had been for Desmond White the previous month, there was a perfectly executed minute's silence for Jock Stein before the game against Aberdeen in Glasgow on September 14. The legendary Celtic boss had died, of course, four nights earlier while, as Scotland's manager, he had just plotted a 1-1 draw with Wales in Cardiff during a tense World Cup qualifying tie. Everyone was left in a state of shock at the passing of a true football giant at the far-too-early age of sixty-two. Alex Ferguson, the Aberdeen gaffer, sat beside Big Jock that eventful evening at Ninian Park as his assistant. Four days later, Ferguson, as Dons boss, was standing grim-faced on the touchline at Celtic Park paying his own silent tribute to the man he always referred to as 'Boss'. Davie Hay, head bowed, stood only a few feet away. The 39,450 supporters said their farewells, too, in the hushed stadium. It was a solemn moment in the harsh east end of Glasgow.

When the action got underway, Brian McClair gave a masterclass in striking while Paul McStay ruled the midfield, no easy task against an Alex Ferguson team. McClair got the opening goal just after the half-hour mark, but Frank McDougall, so often the scourge of Celtic, thought he had earned his side a point with the equaliser in the eighty-fifth minute. However, McClair, as Jock Stein had always insisted, played to the final whistle and got the winner in the fading moments.

Interestingly, one Sunday newspaper journalist had this to say, 'I think I have just spotted a side which might just go on and win the Premier League. No, not Aberdeen, but Celtic. Davie Hay's team were a nice mixture of power and skill which seemed to surprise Alex Ferguson's men. In fact, the most surprising thing of all was the Dons actually scored an equaliser. Up to that point, they never looked like getting anything.'

Four days later, Celtic travelled to the Spanish capital to play Atletico Madrid in the opening round of the European Cup-Winners' Cup. The teams, of course, had become involved in the infamous brawl in the European Cup semi-final in 1974 when Davie Hay had been playing for Celtic. The game had descended into anarchy when the Spanish club had three players ordered off in a spiteful, savage scoreless stalemate. They won the second leg 2-0, but the meeting of the teams will never be remembered for football. Atletico were desperate to wipe out that shameful memory. This was a different team with a different manager. They wanted the two games to be spectacles.

Celtic officials also pleaded with their support not to travel to Madrid. They were fearful of reprisals after UEFA banned English clubs from European competition in the wake of the Hysel Disaster. There were only a hundred of so Celtic fans in the 55,000 crowd at the Vicente Calderon Stadium to witness a creditable 1-1 draw in a surprising and welcome incident-free ninety minutes. Atletico were, indeed, a transformed unit and played attractive football and forced Pat Bonner into one of his finest evenings. The Irishman was outstanding and his gallery of breathtaking saves included one from a penalty-kick by Juan Jose Rubio with only fifteen minutes to go.

Enrique Setien had given the Spaniards a deserved first-half lead when Mo Johnston celebrated his first appearance in a European tie with a memorable goal in the sixty-ninth minute. The striker, working tirelessly, accepted a pass from Peter Grant and spread it wide to Davie Provan on the right. He then sped into the penalty area to dive full-length to get his head to the measured cross from his team-mate and Argentina's World Cup-winning goalkeeper Ubaldo Fillol had no chance as the ball tore past him high into the net.

Davie Hay commented, 'I was so proud of the players. It was a superb performance and Johnston scored a great European goal. Pat Bonner's penalty save was terrific. I thought we would do well, but a draw is marvellous. What we do now is up to us.'

It was a delighted Celtic party that flew home the following morning. Little did they know that their European adventure only had another ninety minutes to go. In one of the strangest games in the club's history, they lost 2-1 a fortnight later in Glasgow where the official attendance at Parkhead was given as nil. The European rulers had ordered Celtic to play behind closed doors as a punishment for the misbehaviour of some misguided folk the previous season at Old Trafford. The spectre of Rapid Vienna refused to go away. Club officials reckoned the ban cost them in the region of £250,000 in gate receipts. The game also had a 2pm kick-off and was played throughout in ghostly silence.

Celtic's best chance came early on when Murdo MacLeod, only six yards out, rattled a shot off Fillol's crossbar. Setien collected his second goal of the tie before the interval and Quique Ramos netted a second in the seventy-first minute. Roy Aitken became unique two minutes later - the only Celtic player to score a European goal at Celtic Park and not arouse a single cheer from the terracings. Celtic just couldn't rise above the eerie, motivationless surroundings that afternoon and slipped out on a 3-2 aggregate.

'The players were badly affected by the flat atmosphere,' observed Davie Hay. 'It shows how much the supporters mean to this club. We just did not play at all. If you can't string passes together it's obvious what will happen.'

Four days beforehand, 15,387 fans watched Celtic win 2-0 over Dundee at Dens Park with Brian McClair and Mo Johnston, gelling nicely as a profitable pairing up front, shared the first-half goals to pick up another two points. Celtic were now unbeaten in their first seven league games of the campaign, winning five and drawing two. It was title-winning form.

Three days after the Atletico Madrid 'experience', Celtic must have enjoyed playing in front of a crowd of 25,651 as they overcame St Mirren 2-0 with the normal vocal atmosphere returned to their own ground. Danny McGrain took a bow before the game in recognition of his 600th appearance for the club. He would go on to make another fifty-nine outings before leaving Celtic at the age of thirty-six. At his best, McGrain had no superior. The Jungle also had an extra cheer for Frank McGarvey, playing his first game in front of his old fans. McGarvey waved cheerily, but the mood of the crowd switched early in the encounter when the striker felled Roy Aitken. The fickleness of the football supporter neatly encapsulated in a matter of minutes. The fans went home happy after a solid 2-0 win lit up by the goals of Brian McClair and Paul McGugan, his first for the club. McClair's effort was a smart scissors kick in the twenty-fifth minute and McGugan slammed in a low shot before the interval.

Celtic got a rude awakening a week later when they lost 1-0 at home to Hearts with John Robertson striking just after the half-hour mark. A newspaper journalist summed up the proceedings, 'Hearts must have been blushing all the way back to Edinburgh after the most blatant snatch of the season. Celtic scorned so many opportunities while Hearts made their one real chance count. The defeat moves Celtic off top spot by the merest of margins. They share the same points and goal difference as Aberdeen, but the Dons have scored more goals. I daresay target practice will be this week's remedy for that.' Davie Hay summed up, 'It was a wasteful performance.'

Two goals from Paul McStay got the Hoops back on track in a hard-fought 2-1 victory at Motherwell where Celtic fans got their first glimpse of the striking ability of a young Andy Walker. McStay, already picking up the tag as 'Maestro' from his adoring legions, got an early opener after working a neat one-two with Murdo MacLeod before stroking the ball past John Gardiner. However, Walker, who would become one of Billy McNeill's first signings when he returned to the club in the summer of 1987, took advantage of some slack defending to knock the ball in at the back post after a cross from Ray Blair wasn't cleared. The game ended on a stormy note when referee Ian Cathcart awarded Celtic a penalty-kick ten minutes from time. Gardiner went down at the feet of Mo Johnston who toppled to the ground. The keeper was booked for protesting before McStay made a masterful job from twelve yards.

What occurred over the next three games still has Davie Hay shaking his head in disbelief almost three decades later. Celtic contrived to lose three crucial confrontations to Dundee United, Aberdeen and Rangers while conceding ten goals in the process and scoring with one solitary effort.

The agonising run kicked off on October 26 when Dundee United, without a league victory in seven weeks, arrived in Glasgow's east end. Remarkably, they returned to Tannadice with the points after an embarrassingly easy 3-0 win. Jim McLean's side were undoubtedly inspired by a sixth-minute opener from Davie Dodds and thereafter Celtic stumbled and blundered to defeat. Eamonn Bannon got two opportunities before he netted a second just before the interval. He raced through the defence onto a raking pass from Richard Gough, but it looked as though he had squandered the opening when he battered the ball off Pat Bonner. It bounced back to him and, unhindered, he delivered a shot of more accuracy.

Celtic's ability to get back into the game weren't helped by Mo Johnston being stretchered off just after the hour mark after a fairly hefty challenge from Paul Hegarty. It was all over in the sixty-eighth minute when Bannon, in acres of space, sent a header past Bonner. One newspaper called the outing for the United players as 'a guided tour of Celtic Park.'

It didn't get much better a week later when Frank McDougall went on a one-man rampage and claimed all of Aberdeen's goals in a one-sided 4-1 win at Pittodrie. The stocky forward was bereft of pace and polish, but as someone pointed out, 'All he does is score goals.' And how well he demonstrated the most efficient execution of his career to leave Celtic humiliated, but, amazingly, the score was level at 1-1 at half-time. McDougall got his first with a header, but that was nullified by an excellent free-kick strike from Davie Provan two minutes from the break.

McDougall then switched to destruction mode and hammered in a hat-trick in sixteen devastating minutes. The Celtic defence fell apart as he got his second with another header in the forty-eighth minute, then knocked in one at the far post and volleyed in his fourth to complete his whirlwind act of finishing at its most potent. It had been an ill-tempered affair and referee Brian McGinlay booked eight players - six from Celtic. The McStay brothers, Paul and Willie, Danny McGrain, Roy Aitken, Tommy Burns and Provan were yellow-carded and, just for good measure, the overworked match official added the names of Dons duo Willie Miller and Brian Mitchell.

The hat-trick from hell was completed at Ibrox where Rangers, who had been in indifferent form, romped to a 3-0 success. Davie Hay had signed Mark McGhee from SV Hamburg for £150,000 during the week and the striker made a quickfire debut. It would have been more memorable if the chunky raider had enjoyed better fortune in the sixty-sixth minute when he slammed a low twenty-yard shot past Nicky Walker only to see his effort thud against the woodwork and bounce clear. At that stage Rangers were a goal ahead after Ian Durrant ended an almighty scramble in the six-yard box by bundling the ball beyond Pat Bonner on the half-hour mark.

With ten minutes to go, Celtic were still in with a chance, but their hopes disappeared when Davie Cooper scored with a neat lob and Ted McMinn drove in the third four minutes later. A newspaper stated, 'The long-suffering Ibrox fans couldn't believe their luck as Rangers pulverised Celtic with their finest display of the season.' It's worth noting that Jock Wallace's team had failed to win any of their previous four games before meeting their ancient foes. They had lost to Hibs

(1-2) and St Mirren (1-2) and drawn with Dundee United (1-1) and Clydebank (0-0). The next two matches after beating Celtic saw them hammered by Hearts (0-3) and then Dundee (2-3).

Davie Hay was magnanimous in defeat. 'The better team won and they showed all through that they wanted to win much more than we did.' Mark McGhee reflected on his Old Firm baptism, 'The pace surprised me after a spell in West German football. And I had certainly forgotten about experiencing tackling like that.' The loss dropped Celtic to third in the table.

Hay can now look back and say: 'You find out a lot about yourself in adversity. That was a dreadful period, hammered three times on the bounce and conceding so many goals. You need to be strong within yourself. Back then, I think that's what kept me going. I never had any thoughts about chucking it. It was just a question of being able to transfer your determination and spirit to your players. They had to show they had backbone, too.'

Davie Provan had been substituted during the second-half against Rangers after signaling to Hay that he was feeling somewhat out of sorts. As he went straight up the Ibrox tunnel, it would have been beyond the comprehension of everyone that the end of his footballing career was only twenty minutes away.

Provan was later diagnosed with ME (Myalgic Encephalomiyietis), also known as a post-viral fatigue syndrome. The entrancing winger who had pranced and pirouetted along the touchline and won the hearts of Celtic - and neutral - fans sadly discovered he didn't even possess the energy to complete the pre-match warm-up. He was thirty years old and had performed in two hundred and eighty-seven games contributing forty-two goals in eight memorable years at the club. It had been fairly well known that Provan had been brought up as a Rangers supporter, but by his own admission he didn't hesitate when he received the call from John Clark, Billy McNeill's assistant, who asked him, 'Look, we know about your background, but would you come to Celtic?' Without a moment's hesitation, Provan replied,

'Yes, in a minute, not a problem at all.' Seven honours - four titles, two Scottish Cups and one League Cup - bear only scant testimony to the player's allegiance, determination and devotion to Celtic.

In fact, one of my favourite football stories concerns Provan. Alex MacDonald was always a snarling, little terrier who thrived in the frantic action of an Old Firm game. The sparky enforcer was adored by the Rangers hordes. During a typical no-holds-barred Glasgow derby, MacDonald had been snapping at the heels of the artistically-talented Provan for most of the confrontation before the graceful winger came up with an unanswerable and classic put-down. 'I could keep a beach-ball off you in a phone box,' Provan told his Ibrox adversary. Peter Grant overhead the remark and could barely finish the game for laughing.

After three consecutive losses, perhaps luckily, Celtic's next game was against Clydebank at Celtic Park. Mark McGhee got his first goals for the club in each half and the best that could be said about the display was that it was deserved if not decisive. Worryingly, though, for Hay was the fact that Mo Johnston was misfiring up front and had now gone seven games without a goal. That miserable run came to a halt against Hibs a week later in Glasgow, but Celtic still had to be content with a 1-1 draw in a game they dominated. Liverpool's legendary manager Bill Shankly would have looked at this performance and after an hour declared it as 'a 1-0 massacre.' Colourful, maybe, but fairly apt.

Mark McGhee set up Johnston's first goal since September 28 when he put him through with a flick on the thirteenth-minute mark. Johnston couldn't miss as he tucked the ball past Alan Rough. Celtic controlled proceedings after that, but try as they might, they couldn't add to Johnston's goal thanks to some excellent goalkeeping from Rough and some wayward finishing. They were punished in the seventy-sixth minute when the defence was undone with a simple, straightforward move. Iain Munro crossed from the left, Gordon Durie nodded it goalwards and Pat Bonner, who had been so inactive, actually looked alarmed to be brought into play. He failed to control the ball and it fell in front of Gordon Chisholm who prodded home from almost under the crossbar.

Davie Hay commented, 'We were throwing away points in games we were dominating and I knew that couldn't all just be down to bad luck. We were passing up chances, but we had guys such as Brian McClair, Mo Johnston and Mark McGhee with proven goalscoring pedigrees. It would be something we would work on.'

A week later, Celtic dropped another point in a 1-1 draw with Hearts in the capital. It was a far better performance, but a point was the same reward. On this occasion, though, Davie Hay's side displayed a spirit and vigour that had been mystifyingly absent in recent outings. John Colquhoun was still menacing his old team with sharp raids on the right always with the promise of a more-than-decent delivery as an end product. So, it was no surprise when the diminutive flanker set up the ninth-minute goal for John Robertson. A good ball across and Robertson, one of the smallest players on the pitch, buried a header behind Pat Bonner.

There was the usual inquest at half-time - especially at the gift of another goal scored by unmarked opposition in the penalty box - and there was more urgency about Celtic in the second period. The equaliser came from Mark McGhee in the sixty-seventh minute after being teed up by Mo Johnston. However, another reverse was only a week away and, once again, Celtic were fuming after being on the receiving end of a controversial refereeing decision. Two days before Christmas, Bill Crombie was extremely generous in awarding Dundee United a crucial penalty-kick with the game goalless and heading for half-time.

Even the United fans in the 15,400 crowd at Tannadice must have been surprised when the match official pointed to the spot after a mid-air clash between Paul McGugan and Paul Hegarty as the two tall centre-backs went for a ball slung into the box by Ian Redford. Hegarty, fairly theatrically, somehow managed to fall into the net and Crombie indicated he had been pushed. That sparked a posse of Celtic players protesting, but as ever, there was no changing the referee's mind. He wasn't interested, either, in consulting his linesman. Once the furore died down, Eamonn Bannon stepped forward and drove the ball high into the net. Kevin Gallacher, grandson of Celtic legend Patsy, played one of his first games for United. Tommy Burns earned the only booking of the encounter for a foul on the youngster. So much for the season of goodwill to all men.

Three days before 1986 was ushered in, Celtic beat Clydebank 2-0 in front of 13,822 shivering supporters at Celtic Park. The game had been switched from ice-bound Kilbowie and Mo Johnston netted the opener in the eleventh minute. Paul McStay brought down the curtain on the action in a highly-intriguing year with an unstoppable penalty-kick shortly after the turnaround. With a fair degree of alarm, the Bankies were the only team Celtic had beaten since October 19 - and they had managed the feat twice. Over that period, though, there had been losses to Dundee United (twice), Aberdeen and Rangers with draws against Hibs and Hearts. Ten points dropped and two gained.

Davie Hay, even at his most positive and optimistic, would have been hard pushed to agree it was championship winning form.

CHAPTER TWENTY-ONE
ON THE VERGE

Unless gifted with the powers of clairvoyance, the Celtic management, players and support hadn't an inkling of the extraordinary events which were about to unfold in 1986. However, for the time being, anyway, they left Parkhead on January 1 with smiles on their faces after witnessing their third win out of the past four New Year's Day games against Rangers. A crowd of 49,000 saw Davie Hay's men in cruise control, rarely being unduly troubled in their 2-0 success.

Paul McGugan, maturing into the centre-half role on a game-by-game basis, headed the opening goal from an Owen Archdeacon centre in the ninth minute. Jock Wallace had switched Davie Cooper from the left wing to the right to play directly against thirtysomething Danny McGrain, but it was a ploy that backfired with the so-called veteran defender so much in command of the situation that the Rangers 'secret weapon' was removed from play and replaced by the equally-ineffective Ted McMinn. Any meagre resistance from the Govan outfit was obliterated in the forty-ninth minute when the McStay brothers, Paul and Willie, combined down the right with the final delivery being tucked away with expert ease by Brian McClair.

Three days later, it was an entirely different story as Celtic slumped 4-2 to Dundee United at Tannadice. Davie Hay was so strapped for fully-fit players that he was forced to draft in Ronnie Coyle to a central defensive position. The twenty-one year old had only made one fleeting appearance as a substitute against Dundee in May the previous year. However, the absence of Paul McGugan and Pierce O'Leary through injury catapulted the youngster into the first team fray. Hay was also preparing to oppose extremely dangerous opponents without the services of Murdo MacLeod, Mo Johnston and Davie Provan, who, at that stage, had still to discover the full extent of his debilitating illness.

Celtic were mercilessly pulled apart and trailed 4-1 at the interval. Davie Dodds scored two in three minutes, Eamonn Bannon claimed another penalty-kick and Kevin Gallacher snapped up his first Premier League goal. What would his legendary grandfather have thought of that? Brian McClair was the Hoops' marksman, the second coming in the fading moments with the game over and an icy gloom settling on Tayside.

If the Celtic manager thought for a moment critics might have offered a sympathetic viewpoint considering his extensive injury list, he would have been disappointed. One newspaper reported, 'This was devastating stuff from United and ample proof they are the most exciting team in the country. Celtic were outclassed in skill, imagination and perception as the home fans revelled in the excess of riches. This was Celtic's third successive Premier League defeat against the class of Jim McLean - and that's not the form of potential champions.'

An eighteen-year-old winger who didn't look old enough to cross the road on his own made a huge impact when Aberdeen came to town a week later. His name was Joe Miller, a Glaswegian who had been pinched from under Celtic's noses and whisked off to the north when he was probably still in his nappies. Persistent rain and a vicious wind awaited to greet Alex Ferguson back to his native Glasgow. And for fourteen minutes it looked as though it was going to be an enjoyable return for the Govan man.

Miller jinked through the back-tracking Celtic rearguard and suddenly found himself on a one-on-one situation with Peter Latchford, deputising for the injured Pat Bonner. The popular Englishman managed to block the first effort, but, unfortunately, the rebound went straight back to the precocious winger and he tucked the second opportunity away. However, it was a lead that would last only five minutes. Danny McGrain and Brian McClair combined on a mazy manoeuvre on the right and Peter Grant finished the enterprising move with a superb shot. Both sides had chances, but, in the midst of the punishing gales, it finished 1-1.

The following Wednesday, Celtic won 3-2 against Motherwell, but it was an occasion that will now be remembered by many as a melancholy circumstance. It was the last time Davie Provan would be seen in the green and white hooped jersey in competitive action. And the man who had always been a class act from the first day he walked through the front door at Parkhead almost signed off with his usual panache. Although 2-1 ahead, Celtic were toiling against the Fir Park side with 11,402 fans growing impatient for the decisive goal to ease the tension on the terracing. With twenty minutes to go, Davie Hay sent on Provan for Owen Archdeacon. The smooth operator hadn't been seen for two months and received a hero's welcome back.

Without preamble, Provan set about making the points secure. With four minutes remaining, the debonair Celt thumped in a shot that bounced off goalkeeper John Gardiner's chest to arch-predator Brian McClair and he knocked the ball home from close range. If future circumstances had been known at the time, McClair would no doubt have been happy to gift that goal to his colleague of three years. It turned out to be the winner and that's how Davie Provan will always be remembered by football followers who ever witnessed him at his tantalising best - a winner.

Celtic made heavy weather of their win against the Lanarkshire outfit and were a goal down in only twelve minutes when John Reilly scored a simple effort. Mark McGhee responded in kind just after the half-hour mark and Mo Johnston got in on the act four minutes after the interval. Provan then helped set up McClair for the goal that made the difference with Jamie Doyle smashing home a free-kick a minute from the end. It was more about perspiration than inspiration, but the points were in the bag.

Three days later, the championship once more was looking like a forlorn hope. Celtic dropped a point in a 2-2 draw with Hibs at Easter Road while

Hearts overcame Aberdeen 1-0 at Pittodrie. A bleak picture needed a splash of colour. Davie Hay's men once again were careless and derelict in their duties of protecting an advantage. A crowd of 13,512 saw Gordon Durie give the Edinburgh men a half-time lead, but that was nullified by Owen Archdeacon just after the hour mark. Tommy Burns placed one behind Alan Rough in the seventy-third minute and Celtic now had to attempt to shut up shop. The lead endured for four minutes when Steve Cowan rolled in the equaliser. Another point squandered against a team that would complete the season in third bottom place.

The title race was put on hold for ninety minutes when Scottish Cup action got underway on January 25 and Celtic eased to a 2-0 triumph over St Johnstone at Celtic Park. First-half efforts from Peter Grant and Mo Johnston made the difference, but it was far from an impressive performance in front of 15,000 supporters. One newspaper summed up, 'Holders Celtic strolled through their first defence of the Scottish Cup doing enough to win, which was nowhere near enough to warm the fans on a chilly day.'

The loudest cheer of the afternoon came when the tannoy announcer informed the departing supporters that Rangers' interest in the trophy was over, Jock Wallace's side losing 3-2 to Hearts at Tynecastle.

Back on the league trail, there were some dramatic unfolding of events before, during and after the 3-1 victory over Dundee at Dens Park as February was ushered in. Davie Hay was aware that there would be a parting of the ways between himself and his assistant Frank Connor. The manager had known for three days about the decision to remove Connor. Now it was all down to timing. As Celtic travelled to Tayside, a radio report broke the news that Celtic were about to sack their assistant boss.

Hay said, 'I had no quarrel with Frank, but, remember, he was not my choice and had been appointed by the board and before I had been offered the vacant manager's job. I discovered Frank and I were on different wavelengths. We looked at things in different ways. We approached things from different directions. And, gradually, we began pulling against each other in a football sense. Frank wanted us to play one way and I favoured another. Or Frank wanted one player bought and I didn't. Or else he would disagree with my team selections. It simply wasn't working and the directors, too, had been concerned at Frank's behaviour in the dug-out.

'When I admitted that things were not going well between us, they agreed that they should work out a financial package for Frank and that they would speak to him and make the break as kind as possible. I left that to them, thinking it would be best if a decent financial settlement could be organised. For three days I worked with Frank having the uncomfortable knowledge gnawing at me that he was going to be leaving. As we were heading for Dundee, the thing I feared most happened - the story leaked. Not from me, but from a board member, because no-one else knew what was going on. The radio station carried the news item and after the game reporters asked me questions about it. So did Frank and, unfortunately, I could not give him a proper answer. We travelled back to Glasgow on the team bus in silence. I was furious. It was wrong that Frank, a good servant to the club, in spite of our own falling-out on a personal level, should have discovered the news from the media.'

It wasn't all plain sailing on the pitch that Saturday afternoon, either. In front of a crowd of 12,295, who had also picked up on the story about Connor's imminent dismissal, Dundee took the lead through a ninth-minute penalty-kick from Ray Stephen. Paul McStay then contrived to miss from the spot when Bobby Geddes saved from his peculiarly weak and badly-placed effort. Mo Johnston managed to grab a leveller in the forty-second minute, but the rocks were in plain sight and Hay had to keep a steady hand on the tiller. The tension in the dressing room at the interval was close to unbearable, but Hay got his message across. 'Forget what you've heard. All that is for later. Your job is the next forty-five minutes, so concentrate on that and play like Celtic players.' McStay atoned for his awful spot-kick by scoring a glorious headed goal just before the hour mark and Brian McClair made certain near the end. But the stressful events of the day were far from over for Hay.

'I made phone calls to each member of the board that night,' he said. 'The next morning, all denied they had said anything at all to anyone outside the club. But I knew one of them must have. Then they came up with another suggestion to cover the embarrassment of the leak. "Let's forget about it," they said. "Let's just continue as we are." I knew, though, that was impossible now. Frank knew there was a background to the stories. Trying to re-establish a working relationship which had already been falling apart was out of the question.

'None of the board would take any decisive action. I had to do it myself. I went to one of the groundsmen's homes, collected the keys to Celtic Park, opened it up and met Frank there - just the two of us - and told him that he was sacked. I apologised to him for the way the business had been handled. It was a shambles. He had done nothing wrong, he was a single-minded kind of person and the partnership wasn't paying off the way I had hoped. And so it was better to end it.'

Once the club eventually went public, Connor, who at forty-nine was ten years Hay's senior, said, 'I'm shattered. I knew nothing at all about this. I loved Celtic Park and my job. I had no idea this was about to happen. It comes as a tremendous blow.'

In a prepared statement, Hay said, 'After discussing the matter with my board and been given full approval, I have decided to carry on working without the assistance of Frank Connor. This unpleasant step was taken after much deliberation in the best interests of Celtic.'

Chairman Tom Devlin went on record supporting Hay. 'This is a matter for the manager who has full say in the running of the dressing room. Mr Hay has my complete confidence and also that of the other directors.'

It had been a rocky few days in the history of Celtic Football Club and in such situations focuses can become blurred. The following Saturday, in front of a crowd of 18,102, Celtic dropped a point in a 1-1 draw with St Mirren at Celtic Park. It wasn't quite as dramatic as distress flares lighting up the skies above the east end of Glasgow, but Celtic were clearly lacklustre against the Paisley side. Hay still had to keep his mind on purely football-related matters. Paul McStay, by now a darling of the support, was hooked at the interval after an off-colour display throughout a goalless first-half. Hay always had the courage of his convictions. He put on Paul's brother Willie at right-back, switched Danny McGrain to the left and freed Tommy Burns to play in midfield. It worked, to a certain extent. Burns scored three minutes after the turnaround, but some woeful defending at a corner-kick - becoming a worrying trait - enabled Saints full-back Steve Clarke to hit a seventy-fifth minute equaliser from six yards. There were dark mumblings among the supporters as they made their way to the exits.

They weren't exactly performing cartwheels, either, the following Saturday when Celtic continued their defence of the Scottish Cup with a scrappy 2-1 win over the amateurs of Queen's Park, playing their first game at Celtic Park since they lost 5-3 in the same competition in 1967. A deathly hush among the 11,656 spectators descended on the stadium when the Hampden side took the lead five minutes after the interval with a penalty-kick strike by Jimmy Boyle. Thankfully, Brian McClair delivered a quickfire response with the equaliser four minutes later and Roy Aitken claimed the winner shortly afterwards. Once again, though, it must be admitted it was far from a vintage performance from the Hoops.

This unremarkable game brought down the curtain on the Celtic career of Tom McAdam just short of his thirty-second birthday. With Hay looking more and more at youngsters such as Paul McGugan and Derek Whyte, he granted a free to a player who was a valued servant to the club and will always be remembered as one of the heroic ten men who won the league on that glorious Monday night in May 1979.

Hearts' title challenge was now being taken so seriously that Davie Hay whisked his players off to Seamill Hydro to prepare for the visit of the Edinburgh team on February 22. He said, 'It was obvious they were going to last the course. They were achieving some excellent results and the focus was shifting from ourselves, Aberdeen and Dundee United to the Tynecastle men. They had gone twenty games unbeaten before they were due to play us in Glasgow and I was giving them the respect they certainly deserved. I wanted to give us any advantage I could because I had what the newspapers were calling an "injury crisis" and they weren't far wrong.

I would be without Pat Bonner, Paul McStay, Murdo MacLeod, Owen Archdeacon, Peter Grant, Pierce O'Leary and Davie Provan. Normally, we would used Seamill for preparation for big European ties or Cup Finals, but I thought this was an extremely important game for us and I wanted us completely tuned up for it.'

A massive crowd of 45,346 agreed with the Celtic manager and they were in attendance by the time referee Alan Ferguson blew for the kick-off. Derek Whyte, only seventeen years old, made his league debut against the leaders at left-back. Mo Johnston put Hearts' unbeaten record under serious threat when he scored just after the half-hour mark following a typical electrifying burst of speed as he raced between Sandy Jardine and Craig Levein, the future Scotland manager, onto a wonderful through pass from Danny McGrain. Henry Smith hadn't a chance as Johnson whipped his shot low and true. Unfortunately, Celtic couldn't hold the lead and John Robertson made it all-square virtually on the half-time whistle.

It remained a stalemate, but Mark McGhee passed up a glorious chance near the end to take the points. Roy Aitken rattled his way down the right wing before driving in a vicious low cross. McGhee was unmarked in front of goal, but fluffed his kick completely and as the ball flew to safety, with it went the hope of a well-deserved win. One newspaper reporter commented, 'Perhaps McGhee's miss is the one that could end Celtic's title hopes.' It also spurned the opportunity of re-introducing Hearts to defeat. Imposingly, they had now gone twenty-one games without a loss.

Another scribe declared, 'Hearts have never won a harder point this season. Celtic's spirit, passion and effort to tear apart the championship was impressive.' At the end of the day, alas, mere praise does not win championships.

Davie Hay had seen Celtic knocked out of the League Cup by Hibs at Easter Road earlier in the season and fate, with that odd sense of the ridiculous, decided to send them back to the same venue for the Scottish Cup quarter-final on March 8 as they continued their defence of their trophy. Having scored four goals in the previous tie, they might have expected to progress, but of course, they didn't. Now, after scoring three in the national competition, you might believe that a semi-final place beckoned. Wrong again. Unbelievably, the Edinburgh side won by the odd goal in seven and Celtic's grip on the trophy was prised free with under a minute to go.

It was a frantic game that must have taken most of the 20,000 crowd by surprise. It was heading for a goalless scoreline at half-time until Brian McClair popped in the opener in the forty-second minute. It may have been slow to ignite, but, once the fuse was lit, there was an explosive end with a bewildering three goals - two penalty-kicks - in the last six minutes. Cruelly, for the holders, they led twice before conceding three in a dreadfully inept fourteen-minute spell. Steve Cowan cancelled McClair's effort six minutes after the turnaround, but Mark McGhee restored Celtic's advantage on the hour mark. Gordon Chisholm levelled sixteen minutes later and then the floodgates burst. Cowan hammered Hibs into the lead with a spot-kick with only six minutes to go. The home team thought that was the winner, but they would have to put their joy on hold. Referee Hugh Alexander then awarded a penalty-kick to the visitors and McClair made his usual tidy job to tie the game at 3-3. A replay at Parkhead the following Wednesday looked inevitable until Eddie May scrambled in the winner.

One Sunday newspaper had sympathy for the Parkhead side's plight. 'The agony of Celtic manager Davie Hay this morning must be considerable,' it stated. Today, Hay can now offer a wry smile. 'Aye, that would be putting it mildly. We had now gone out of three Cup tournaments in the oddest of circumstances. Beaten in the Cup-Winners' Cup in a deserted stadium after getting a great result in Madrid. Beaten in the League Cup after scoring four goals away from home while being the superior team. And beaten on the same ground in the Scottish Cup after scoring three goals and, once again, showing we were the better team. However, we had the lead twice and gave it away. Their winner was a real sickener. Hibs were wiped out 3-0 by Aberdeen in the semi-final. Interestingly, the Dons' goals were scored by Billy Stark, Eric Black and Joe Miller - two, Stark and Miller, went on to play for Celtic and one, Black, had a spell as coach. Maybe we got our revenge, after all!'

Celtic were hoping to beat Dundee United at the fourth time of asking in the Premier League when Jim McLean's team arrived in Glasgow on March 15 with 22,965 turning out to see if the Bhoys could indeed turn the tide. It appeared Canute could have offered little to repel the Tannadice side against the Hoops during that campaign. Disturbingly, in a high wind on a bumpy pitch, the defenders were still operating their free-gift scheme when they allowed United to open the scoring from a corner-kick just before half-time. Kevin Gallacher floated it in, Tommy Burns left it to Pierce O'Leary, Pierce O'Leary left it to Tommy Burns, and Davie Dodds took the responsibility to score from six yards. McLean was edging closer to breaking into a smile at the thought of taking all eight points from Celtic in a season after their Scottish Cup Final defeat. The grin was put back on cold storage when Murdo MacLeod first-timed an equaliser eight minutes from time. The United manager's humour wouldn't been helped, either, when defender John Holt was sent off after picking up two bookings.

Where would Celtic go from here? The quick answer was to Ibrox a week later when they took part in one of the most spectacular, rumbustious Old Firm games in history. Davie Hay watched as his side, with only ten men for almost an hour, thumped four goals into the Rangers net. Unfortunately, his extremely generous back lot allowed the Govan side to help themselves to four of their own in a confrontation played in monsoon conditions in front of 41,006 spellbound fans. The wet and wild conditions were so bad that there was the tale of Roy Aitken, captain for the day, winning the toss of the coin and telling referee Davie Syme Celtic would play towards the deep end in the first-half.

At one stage, Celtic led 2-0, but Willie McStay saw red and Rangers took full advantage of having the extra man. McStay had the unenviable task of trying to defend against Ted McMinn, an erratic, ungainly, leggy outside-left who raced along the wing with his elbows jutting out like a glider coming down to land. On his day, McMinn could be a handful. He was having one of those days. McStay was booked after only fifteen minutes for a clattering challenge on the Ibrox man. Shortly afterwards, McMinn went into the book for something similar on McStay. It looked as though it was going to be a long day for the two combatants. Referee Syme had other thoughts. McStay flew into another tackle and that was his exertions cut short for the day in the thirty-third minute.

At that stage, Celtic were 2-0 up and in those watery conditions it could be said they were coasting. Mo Johnston thumped the first behind Nicky Walker in the twenty-first minute after some good lead-up play from Paul McStay and Owen Archdeacon on the left. Eight minutes afterwards it was Brian McClair's turn to rattle the rigging behind the Rangers keeper. However, four minutes later Willie McStay was banished and, within thirty seconds, Cammy Fraser had pulled one back. That was the score at the interval and Davie Hay had to change things around to compensate for the dismissal of McStay. He took off winger Archdeacon and put on midfielder Peter Grant to strengthen his rearguard.

Hay said: 'Strangely enough, I was thinking of substituting Willie before he was ordered off. I could see he was having an uncomfortable time against an awkward opponent and I had it in mind to make the change at the interval. Davie Syme took that opportunity away from me. Maybe I should have acted more quickly.'

Two minutes into the second period and Tommy Burns, with a well-timed run and clever shot, restored Celtic's two-goal advantage. Ally McCoist then took Pat Bonner completely by surprise by scoring with a right-foot belter from twenty-five yards, the shot skidding through the mud before nestling behind him. No-one in living memory, could ever remember the Rangers player attempting a shot from such a distance. It didn't get any better for the big Irishman as he conceded another seven minutes later to Robert Fleck and four minutes after that he was helpless as Fraser headed in from just about under the crossbar. Rangers had scored three goals in eleven minutes and their fans were singing in the downpour. Murdo MacLeod, with an almighty whack from twenty-five yards in the seventieth minute, gave Celtic a deserved point and brought the end to a breathtaking Glasgow derby.

Rangers manager Jock Wallace was enthusing about the game afterwards. He believed the fans had just witnessed an 'all-time Old Firm great game'. Not so impressed, though, were his board of directors who were far from enthusiastic in allowing a team with only ten men for almost two-thirds of the game to get a point and score another two goals while doing so. It was to be Wallace's last Glasgow derby; he was sacked a month later and the club announced Graeme Souness, the Scotland international skipper, would be leaving Italian side Sampdoria to take over as their new player/ manager the following season.

Concerns across the city mattered not a jot to Davie Hay as he steadfastly refused to accept Celtic had no chance of silverware. Like last season, he would be prepared to go all the way until the very last day of the league season to make his wish come true.

Celtic beat Clydebank 5-0 at Kilbowie in front of only 7,969 fans on March 29. The score was not heralded with any fanfare of trumpets, but it transpired to become one of the most significant results for the Parkhead side in a momentous season. It was the first of seven successive wins that would set up the memorable last-day title showdown at St Mirren while Hearts travelled to Dundee.

Surprisingly, though, the first-half of the Bankies encounter was scoreless and Hay reckoned, 'I had witnessed such things happening after an Old Firm game, especially one as exciting as the 4-4 draw. Ibrox was heaving and raucous whereas Kilbowie was almost tranquil and serene. I took my time at the interval to remind the players we would only get the same points for beating Clydebank as we would have had if we had beaten Rangers. The rewards were identical.' Brian McClair smashed in two penalty-kicks within five minutes of each other at the start of the half on his way to a hat-trick, Tommy Burns hit another and Alan McInally collected the fifth. The result hardly created a ripple, even among the Celtic support.

Davie Hay had to lift his troops again for the midweek game against Dundee with a lot of atmosphere missing in the ground while the traditional Celtic End of Paradise was closed for reconstruction. A crowd of 12,506 witnessed a 2-1 victory over the Dens Park side. The result was never in doubt with Mo Johnston getting the opener in the eighteenth minute and Tommy Burns adding a second two minutes after half-time. Ray Stephen made the scoreline tighter than it should have been with a consolation effort four minutes from the end. The win left the Hoops in joint third position with Aberdeen, both having played thirty games and on thirty-eight points. Hearts led with forty-five points, but, interestingly, had played two more games. Sandwiched in between were Dundee United with forty points after thirty games. Rangers, with Jock Wallace heading out the door, were a massive thirteen points behind the leaders.

Celtic kept the momentum going with a 2-1 win over St Mirren at Love Street on April 5 with 11,284 watching the action. The highlight of a fairly dour first-half, performed on a pitch that gave the appearance of taking a direct hit after another terrible winter, was a typical whizzbang twenty-yard effort from Murdo MacLeod that almost burst the net. There was a jolt, though, for Hay's men ten minutes after the interval. Yet again the defence failed to deal with a direct corner-kick and Peter Mackie, the former Celt who had created problems while at Dundee, struck again, taking advantage of some alarming dithering from Pat Bonner and Co to net at the back post. Paul McStay appeared to have dropped into a mysterious air pocket and was largely anonymous until three minutes from time when he steamed into the box to get on the end of a Brian McClair cross and lash an unstoppable drive past Campbell Money. Better late than never.

The acid test awaited Celtic the following week as Davie Hay took the team to Pittodrie for another high-octane duel with Alex Ferguson's Aberdeen, who were still eyeing a late surge for the championship. On the same afternoon, something had to give at Tannadice where Dundee United played hosts to Hearts. A crowd of 22,500 watched the sparks fly as the two great protagonists locked horns in the Granite City. Hay's men were up for the skirmish right from the off. It was scoreless when referee Bill Crombie blew for half-time, but Mo Johnston made a startling impact four minutes into the second period.

No danger immediately threatened when he accepted a throw-in from Tommy Burns some thirty-five yards from goal. Without warning, he switched on the afterburners and withstood two desperate challenges before firing the ball beyond Bryan Gunn. It was a spontaneous burst of invention and execution by the fiery forward, channeling all his energy in the right direction during this confrontation. Possibly, he was given extra impetus by the fact that Alex Ferguson, preparing Scotland for the World Cup, continually overlooked him for international squads. Whatever the reason, it was still a superb individualistic fusion of skills by Johnston.

There was a flashpoint later in the contest when, with the Dons beginning to sag, Johnston had the ball in the net for a second time. His celebrations were cut short, however, when a linesman flagged for an offside decision against Brian McClair, who was not interfering with play. Unfortunately, referee Crombie took the word of his assistant and nullified the valid effort. Fortunately, it made no difference to the outcome. The Celtic fans remained in the stadium well after the final whistle to acclaim their team's exceptional performance. Even those who had previously doubted were beginning to believe their favourites just might be on the brink of something special.

A scribe summed up, 'One impressive quality kept Celtic in hot pursuit of the championship - commitment. It showed on every sweat-stained face at the end.' Hearts pounded Dundee United 3-0 and the title tussle was becoming a little more clear-cut. Hearts were top after thirty-three games and on forty-seven points. Jim McLean's side had blown a great opportunity and were now five points adrift, but with a game in hand. Celtic also sat on forty-two points, but they also had a crucial game in hand over the Tynecastle side. United had a superior goal difference of plus nine on Hay's team. Aberdeen were just about out of it, trailing seven behind the leaders and running out of matches.

The Celtic fans travelling home were in joyous form and their spirits were given an extra spur with the news that Rangers' new era had kicked off with a 2-1 defeat from Clydebank at Kilbowie. Walter Smith, recruited from Dundee United, was in charge while Graeme Souness honoured his playing commitments in Italy.

Celtic were involved in another 'no goal' storm in the next game against double Cup conquerors Hibs in Glasgow. Mo Johnston almost picked up where he left off at Pittodrie and had an effort cleared off the line with Alan Rough beaten in the first minute. In the thirteenth minute, the international keeper was left helpless again by his former Partick Thistle team-mate and the 15,966 cheering fans were settling back for an onslaught with the margins of goal difference now very much on everyone's mind. Johnston had swooped like lightning after a shot from Brian McClair had bounced of the post. Remarkably, a linesman raised his flag and referee Don McVicar raced over for a confab. The assistant, like his chum the previous week, had eagle-eyed some mysterious infringement. Again, the effort was chalked off much to everyone's consternation and puzzlement.

Conspiracy theories abounded and it didn't get much better with only ten minutes remaining and the Edinburgh outfit stoutly holding out after wave after wave of Celtic attacks came to nothing. Then there was a moment of optimism as Owen Archdeacon slammed a left-foot drive past the scrambling Rough. Cheers were stifled with the sight of a linesman furiously waving his flag. McVicar raced over seeking an explanation for a second time that day as to why he should disallow a goal he originally thought was valid. There was a hush around Parkhead while the two officials had their meeting on the touchline. The referee turned, put his whistle back to his lips, it shrilled loudly and was drowned by the relief and cheers of the fans as he pointed to the centre spot. With three minutes to go, there could be no doubt about the second goal when Roy Aitken fired over a cross and McClair hurtled a header over Rough's shoulder. It was a very big 2-0 win for Celtic.

Davie Hay deserved praise again for his tactical nous. At 0-0, he changed things around as he pushed Aitken into midfield, brought on Derek Whyte to take his place in central defence alongside Paul McGugan and moved Tommy Burns into the left-back position. Burns' promptings were getting little dividend against Hibs and Hay elected to go for Aitken's power, instead. The final result vindicated his decisions. But, modestly, at the end the Celtic manager merely said, 'There is no doubt that Roy Aitken is an inspiration to everyone around him.'

Celtic didn't need a helping hand in the following midweek fixture against Dundee in Glasgow, but they got it, anyway. Quite literally. Ray Stephen, who had developed the habit of snatching a goal or two against the Hoops, only completed twenty-two minutes before he was invited to leave proceedings by referee Dougie Hope. The 14,511 fans couldn't believe the actions of the opponents' striker after he was brought down by Danny McGrain. Stephen gave the Celtic captain a back-hander in full view of the match official and it was early bath-time for the hothead. Dundee regrouped, but their barrier was breached twice after the interval by Brian McClair in the fifty-sixth minute and Mo Johnston five minutes from the end.

Now there were two games to go. Cracks were beginning to appear at Hearts. In their third last game of the campaign, they dropped a point at home to Aberdeen. In fact, if it hadn't been for ex-Celt John Colquhoun they would forfeited double that amount. The Dons were leading 1-0 through a seventy-third minute penalty-kick from Peter Weir when the little winger wriggled through to hammer in an equaliser with only three minutes left on the clock. On the same weekend Celtic were easing past ten-man Dundee, Alex MacDonald's side looked decidedly nervy in their match against a rock-bottom Clydebank team that was only rescued from relegation by league reconstruction with two more teams being added to the Premier Division for the forthcoming term. A shot from Gary Mackay in the thirty-fourth minute gave them a 1-0 victory, but they looked far from comfortable in achieving their target.

Now it was up to Davie Hay's men to apply the pressure in a thrilling war of nerves. Who would blink first? Hearts were left with only their fixture against Dundee at Dens Park to fulfill, Celtic were still playing catch-up. They were due the tricky trip to Firs Park in midweek. Brian McClair must have been working on the theory that he would never receive an invitation to too many Motherwell Old Boys' Reunions in the future. He set up the amazing grand finale with both goals in Celtic's 2-0 victory and showtime was just around the corner. A crowd of 10,540 watched the striker knock in a cross from Owen Archdeacon in the thirty-fourth minute. Just after the hour mark, Archdeacon, proving to be a thoughtful, energetic wide player, was hauled down in the box and referee Jim McCluskey had little alternative but to point to the spot. McClair stood on no ceremony as he rammed the ball past Ally Maxwell. Celtic had now claimed a maximum eight points against Motherwell and McClair had pitched in with four goals.

One newspaper scribe spelled out the situation clearly for the readership, 'Celtic kept alive their Premier League title hopes with two Brian McClair goals which means the destination of the crown won't be decided until Saturday. The Parkhead side must beat St Mirren 3-0 at Love Street and Hearts must lose 1-0 to Dundee at Dens Park to ensure the flag flies in Glasgow. Celtic would then be champions on goal difference.'

Davie Hay, doing remarkably well to contain his emotions, said, 'I feel we should have scored a few more goals as we certainly made the chances. However, I know we will win against St Mirren and the way we are playing we are capable of making enough chances to get the target we need.'

The scene was next. Next up, Judgement Day.

CHAPTER TWENTY-TWO
HIGH FIVES

Celtic were a mere seven minutes away from completing their Premier League programme for season 1985/86. They were pummeling shattered St Mirren 5-0 following a power surge that took them to a four-goal advantage at half-time. Alas, it looked like being a glorious failure after completing the run-in to the campaign without a defeat in their last sixteen games while racking up eight successive victories. They desperately needed Hearts to lose against Dundee and, at that stage, it was goalless at Dens Park.

Davie Hay recalled the moment vividly. 'We were coasting at Love Street to what might have been an impressive, but ultimately meaningless, win. Then something quite amazing happened. I remember their goalkeeper, Jim Stewart, had the ball in his hands and was about to launch it downfield when a huge roar came up from the terracings. He looked startled for a moment. Our fans were going doolally. The transistor radios had imparted a gem of news and we all knew what had happened - Dundee had scored. I knew there were two players named Kidd on the pitch that afternoon, Hearts' Walter and Dundee's Albert. I was told Kidd had scored and, judging by the reactions of our support, I didn't have to enquire which one.

'There was unconfined joy as the fans danced jigs everywhere and then there was another massive cheer. Dundee had scored again. The title was ours! Albert Kidd, a player I had at Motherwell during my days as manager, had netted a second. Love Street was bouncing, the entire place was heaving. Then came the final whistle from referee Andrew Waddell and suddenly fans were on the pitch, scarves were being thrown at me and the players and it was just one big happy carnival. I allowed myself a moment. I was just so proud of what my players had achieved. I admired their spirit, their courage, their belief, their fortitude. Oh, call it what you like. They just refused to be beaten and they merited the accolades. The fans, too, deserved to join in the party. They had been our twelfth man and so many never gave up hope. On a personal level, I massively appreciated that.'

And yet, with seven minutes remaining, the Premier League championship was on its way to Tynecastle. It was as close as that. 'There are defining moments in football and in life when you realise the gods are smiling on you,' added Hay. 'This was undoubtedly such an occasion. I had watched a sports programme on TV the night before and I was left with the impression that the silverware was as good as already in the Hearts trophy cabinet. Celtic were being written off by just about everyone. Believe me, that can raise the hackles. The following morning I picked up all the daily newspapers. Sure enough, they followed the same route. It appeared we were wasting our time bothering to fulfill our remaining fixture, the trophy was already bedecked in maroon colours. Oh, really?

'All the way to this deciding day I had been optimistic about winning the title. I'm not being smart after the event because I was quoted at the time. People may have thought I was trying to get a psychological advantage over the Edinburgh team. Maybe subconsciously I was. But the fact of the matter remained that I genuinely felt we could achieve what a lot of folk were tagging "Mission Impossible." Really, a lot of them should have known better. We had won seven consecutive games - four away from home - to set up the big finale. To simply dismiss us was as insulting as it was stupid.

'My reasoning was simple. In the run-in, I believed Hearts would slip up somewhere along the line. I had witnessed it countless times before and I had to believe that they might not get the bounce of the ball in at least one game. To be absolutely fair to them, they kept on going. But I still persisted with the thought that we would get a break. Obviously, to a certain extent, it wasn't in our hands. All we could do was keep on winning and hope the pressure would get to them.

'I could detect they were creaking a little bit during the run-in. On that fateful day, I gave one of the shortest team talks I have ever given any team. I asked one of the backroom staff to cut out all the articles from the newspapers relating to ourselves and Hearts. The cuttings were pinned to the walls in the Love Street dressing room. When we arrived, I simply said to the players, "Go and read those notices." I could see the steam coming out of some ears. They got the drift okay. Apparently, they were to be no more than bit-part players in Hearts' day of celebration. That's not Celtic's style.

'Once the players had settled down and, just minutes before they took the short walk down the tunnel at Love Street, I merely said, "It can be done. We can win this title." I looked around the dressing room and all I could see were determined expressions. I had never any doubts whatsoever that we would beat St Mirren in this game. I had said so often enough after our win the previous Wednesday at Motherwell. Now I knew we would not only win, but win well. In fact, win in the Celtic manner.'

The players went at St Mirren in whirlwind fashion, snapping into tackles, spraying passes hither and yon, sweeping around the playing surface at full pelt, attacking through the middle and on the flanks and only too eager to keep Saints keeper Jim Stewart from wearying. Brian McClair knocked in the opener in the sixth minute and Mo Johnston added two within a minute while Paul McStay almost took the net away with a first-time effort from the edge of the box.

'I was standing on the touchline in awe of my own team,' said Hay. 'Everyone remembers Brazil's fourth goal against Italy in the mesmerising World Cup Final in Mexico in 1970. I'm talking about the one where it seems every Brazilian gets at least three touches of the ball before Pele nonchalantly rolls a pass across to the right where the rampaging Carlos Alberto comes thundering in to first-time an almighty effort low past the bewildered and beaten Enrico Albertosi, the Italian goalkeeper. It was a fitting end to a glorious and memorable World Cup.

'Take it from me, Celtic scored a goal against St Mirren that was every bit as good and it was just a pity the planet wasn't tuned in to witness it. Danny McGrain, a truly world-class right-back, started it on the edge of his own penalty area. He moved the ball to Murdo MacLeod who gave it back to Danny as we were swiftly building a move down our right-hand side. Danny shifted it inside to Paul McStay who switched it to Roy Aitken and once again the ball landed at Danny's feet. He touched it on to Brian McClair and he flashed a ball across the face of the Saints goal. Mo Johnston, lurking in the danger zone as usual, came sliding in at the back post to nudge the ball into the net. It was all done at bewildering speed and it is right up there with any goal I have ever seen scored by any side. It was good enough to win the title on its own.'

Eighty-three minutes were on the clock with Davie Hay, arms crossed, standing on the touchline and admiring his team's flawless performance. No-one could have blamed him for just a momentary thought that possibly the TV and newspapers had got it right; Hearts were going to win the league, after all. And then came the unforgettable moment when the fans raised the roof at Love Street and Hay knew the championship was coming home to Paradise. In three years as Celtic manager, he had delivered the Premier League title and the Scottish Cup.

'We had no champagne to toast the triumph because no-one had pre-empted anything,' added Hay. 'Imagine that? We've just won the title and there was no bubbly to celebrate with. Well, actually, that's not quite true. Someone produced a solitary bottle of champagne from somewhere - I think it might have emerged from the magic bag of masseur Jimmy Steele - and I got a wee taste. I made up for it later that evening.'

Davie Hay was already planning for the new season. He had identified players he wanted to bring to Celtic. 'I knew Rangers would be stronger under Graeme Souness,' he added. 'I was also made aware they were about to spend big money. They had completed the campaign in fifth place, fifteen points behind us. They hadn't actually been serious title contenders for a few years. Their best performance had been runners-up to Celtic in Billy McNeill's first season back in 1978/79. They had shown their hand by bringing in Souness and I, for one, realised he would never have accepted the job if he hadn't been assured of money to spend. And, by that, I mean serious money. I was looking forward to the challenge.'

One year and fifteen days after the emotional scenes at Love Street, Hay was out of a job.

CHAPTER TWENTY-THREE
LOOK ON THE MONEY SIDE

Davie Hay's desire to strengthen his Celtic first team squad wasn't met with quite the same enthusiasm as the club's board of directors. 'I tried to emphasise the importance of buying when we were at the top, but, unfortunately, my words were falling on deaf ears,' said the frustrated manager, with a title to defend, as he prepared for the dual assault at home and in Europe in the 1986/87 season.

The Premier League champions' only cash acquisition was Anton Rogan, a twenty year old left-back from Irish side Distillery. Hay, looking to the future, had also brought in a promising young outside-right by the name of Mark Smith from Queen's Park. Across Glasgow, new Rangers player/manager Graeme Souness had spent a remarkable joint £1.35million on England internationals Terry Butcher, the central defender from Ipswich Town, and Chris Woods, the goalkeeper from Norwich City. For good measure, he signed a further cheque to the value of £200,000 for Watford's top scorer Colin West. Rogan had cost Celtic £20,000 while Smith, as an amateur, arrived for free.

Celtic, though, had the swagger of champions and, after twenty league games, had suffered just one reversal - a late strike from Ian Durrant giving Rangers victory at Ibrox in August. The so-called new era at their Old Firm rivals hadn't dawned as anticipated. Rangers had been beaten five times over the same period while the volatile Souness had to endure the embarrassment of an opening-day ordering-off in a defeat from Hibs.

Three months into the season, Alex Ferguson, redoubtable and much-decorated manager of Aberdeen, resigned. Manchester United, searching for a replacement for Ron Atkinson, had their eyes on the Pittodrie side's European Cup-Winners' Cup-winning gaffer and, on November 6, he was unveiled as the Old Trafford side's new boss. Things would never be the same at that club. Ian Porterfield, then in charge at Sheffield United, was named as Fergie's successor. Meanwhile, Davie Hay concentrated on steering the good ship Celtic on a consistent course. However, there are always rocks hidden beneath the murky depths.

The Celtic manager led out his victorious team to receive the Premier League trophy on the sun-kissed afternoon of August 9 before battle commenced with a game against Dundee, the team who had beaten Hearts at Dens Park only three months beforehand to play their role in the unfurling of the flag. Chairman Tom Devlin did the honours and the home support in the 35,443 crowd incessantly chanted the name of a rival player for the first - and only - time in history. 'Albert Kidd...Albert Kidd' reverberated around the stadium in an atmosphere of grand bon homie.

The fans were cheering joyously only four minutes into the contest when Mo Johnston demonstrated his goalscoring expertise with a delightful lob that completely transfixed goalkeeper Bobby Geddes before gliding towards its intended destination. Kenny Dalglish, newly-appointed manager of Liverpool, watched from the stand and applauded. That proved to be the only goal of the game, but, at least, Celtic had got off to a winning start. Rangers, for all their lavish spending, couldn't echo that sentiment. They folded to a 2-1 loss in a brutal, bad-tempered encounter against Hibs at Easter Road where Souness saw red following a sickening stud-raking assault on former Celt George McCluskey, who had to be carried off with blood pouring from his ankle wound. It was going to be an interesting season.

Johnston looked as though he had a point to prove after being snubbed by Alex Ferguson, Scotland's caretaker boss, for the World Cup Finals in Mexico that summer. New international managerial double-act Andy Roxburgh and assistant Craig Brown were at Fir Park in midweek to watch the busy little striker hammer in two during a 4-0 mauling of Motherwell. Brian McClair just couldn't stop scoring against his old team and he chipped in with two, one a penalty-kick to open the scoring just before the half-hour mark. Johnston was on a roll and he came to Celtic's rescue at Kilbowie where the modest Clydebank were only two minutes away from a shock point with the game heading for a goalless draw. Then McClair slung over a cross and Johnston was the quickest to react with a bullet-like header.

Davie Hay observed, 'No-one will find it easy to score goals at Kilbowie this season. They made life extremely difficult for us and fought for every scrap. However, to our credit, we just kept plugging away and hoped that a gap would appear. With a natural goalscorer such as Mo Johnston in the team, you've always got a chance and so it proved again this afternoon. I would have preferred a wider winning margin, but, at least, we are still top of the league - so far so good.'

No-one felt like reminding the Celtic manager of the joke about the world's most optimistic man who fell out of a window from a top-floor flat in the Empire State Building and was heard to say, as he passed window after window on his way to the pavement below, 'So far so good.'

Alex Ferguson took his place in the dug-out at Celtic Park for the last time as Aberdeen's manager on August 23. As ever, he had been busy in the summer transfer market and had brought in Davie Dodds, the former Dundee United striker who had a brief flirtation with soccer in

Switzerland at Neuchatel Xamax, and Bobby Connor, a hard-working midfielder from Dundee. Both were plucked from the bargain basement. In years to come, Ferguson would be dealing in multi-million pound transfer deals at the other end of the market. A crowd of 46,073 turned out to watch a fast-paced 1-1 draw with Murdo MacLeod netting for Celtic while Joe Miller, once again, breached the champions' rearguard.

Davie Hay said, 'I enjoyed my tussles with Alex Ferguson. He was as committed to winning as I was and I could respect that. His enthusiasm for football never waned throughout his phenomenal career. Yes, he could snarl with the best of them, but that never bothered me. Some may be surprised to discover that, after a particularly tense match against the Dons at Parkhead where Alex and I appeared to be constantly at loggerheads, I drove him in my car to a function in the old Albany Hotel in Glasgow while the Aberdeen team headed north by coach. I would have much preferred to spend time in his company than a few other managers I won't bother naming. So, in a way, I missed our individual jousts when our teams met.'

The Celtic manager sampled defeat for the first time in the opening Glasgow Derby encounter of the campaign. Apart from the Hibs debacle, Rangers had been turned over 3-2 by Dundee United in Glasgow a fortnight before Graeme Souness' baptism at Old Firm level. The game was deadlocked at 0-0 with nineteen minutes to go when Terry Butcher launched himself into a reckless, full-length charge on Brian McClair on the right touchline. The Celt was sent spinning into mid-air as the Ibrox skipper arrived far too late to make a legitimate challenge. 'Off! Off!' was the enraged chant from the Celtic followers, but referee Kenny Hope showed stunning leniency by merely brandishing a yellow card. The Englishman had got away with it and he knew it.

Two minutes later, Ian Durrant netted the only goal of the game. Davie Cooper set up the youngster with a neat backheel and Durrant, with exceptional composure, tucked the ball under the exposed Pat Bonner. Celtic's best chance to gain a point came a couple of minutes from time when Murdo MacLeod swung in a free-kick from the left. Chris Woods came for it, hesitated and McClair, coming in at speed at the far corner, had a glorious opportunity to put the ball in the empty net. Instead, his header raged over the crossbar.

'One little flash of inspiration won the game,' said Hay. 'We weren't under too much pressure and, equally, Chris Woods wasn't asked to do too much, either. Both attacks seemed to be pushed back and that led to a congested midfield. I don't like losing to anyone, but we've got a long way to go and that includes another three games against Rangers. We'll see what happens in these matches. Nobody wins league titles in August.'

Happily, the Celtic players were picking up win bonuses the following week with a solid 4-1 victory over Hamilton Accies at Celtic Park. The earnest Douglas Park side would complete a torrid season by being relegated along with Clydebank. In doing so, they conceded ninety-three goals and Alan McInally helped himself to three of them that particular afternoon. 'Rambo On The Rampage' was the headline most newspapers chose as the powerful striker collected his first hat-trick for the Hoops, all his goals coming in a blistering twenty-two minute spell in the first-half. Mo Johnston added the other while Kevin McKee got his side's consolation.

Old warhorse Danny McGrain made his first top team appearance against Accies. Ironically, McGrain would bring down the curtain on his memorable playing career with Hamilton the following year and lead them back to promotion. In fact, the incomparable right-back looked as though he was heading out of Parkhead in May even before the championship was clinched. Airdrie were poised to announce him as their new player/manager before a boardroom split of 5/4 vetoed the move. They had even got round to salary talks with local firm Dalziel covering McGrain's £30,000-plus wages. Then came the last minute inexplicable change of mind within the boardroom and the thirty-six year old resumed playing duties with Celtic after signing a twelve-month extension.

Controversy raged in the next game, a 2-2 draw with Dundee United at Tannadice. Celtic had been firmly in control and leading 2-0 inside half-an-hour and were then denied a clear-cut penalty-kick that would surely have ended any doubt about the destination of the points. There was also uproar when referee Don McVicar allowed United's late equaliser to stand when it was obviously offside. Don't take my word it, here's how the Glasgow Herald reported it at the time.

'Two incidents turned this game on its head and twice Celtic were the victims. Just before the interval, when Celtic were leading 2-0 and looking so far ahead in every aspect of the game that no-one would have put money on United avoiding a hammering, Paul Hegarty blatantly pushed Tony Shepherd inside the box and referee McVicar turned a blind eye to the incident. Even worse was his decision to allow United's eighty-fifth minute equaliser to stand. When substitute Ralph Milne collected the ball deep on the right before crossing into goal he was yards offside.'

Celtic were coasting before McVicar's uninvited intrusion. Brian McClair thumped in the opening goal in the third minute and Paul McStay added a second in the twenty-fourth minute. Davie Hay's side were superior all over the pitch as harassed United players, harangued from the dug-out by fuming boss Jim McLean, chased shadows. Hegarty had had enough as half-time approached and flattened Shepherd. There seemed no doubt to anyone in the ground - and that included the United contingent on and off the field - that it was a stonewall penalty-kick. McVicar waved play on to the collective astonishment to all witnesses. McStay was booked as he protested about the match official's bewildering decision. He would later be joined in the little black book by team-mates Roy Aitken, Paul McGugan and Derek Whyte.

Iain Ferguson threw his side a lifeline in the sixty-fifth minute and, with time running out, a long ball found Milne unguarded on the touchline. It was such an obvious infringement that the Celtic defence didn't bother with the time-honoured arms-in-the-air gesture to attract the match official's attention. Milne realised there was no flag and once more McVicar, incredulously, waved play on. The winger duly sent in a cross and Kevin Gallacher squeezed the ball behind Pat Bonner. Afterwards, Davie Hay, mindful of the SFA's policy to slap fines on anyone willing to dare to have their say, would only comment, 'We're playing Shamrock Rovers in Dublin on Wednesday - thank goodness the referee is from Holland.'

The European Cup First Round first leg encounter with the resilient Irishmen passed without incident as 19,750 squeezed in to watch the action. Celtic hit woodwork twice with efforts from Brian McClair and Mo Johnston before Murdo MacLeod sizzled in the winner with only eight minutes remaining. Jody Byrne, the Rovers keeper, had a night to remember, spoiled only by the awesome shooting power of the Celtic midfielder. Two weeks later Davie Hay's side completed the job with a 2-0 win in Glasgow. Mo Johnston scored the goals in each half and was serenaded by the Celtic songsters throughout with 'Mo Can't Go'. Maybe it could have done with a little polishing of the lyrics, but it got the message across. Johnston had been quoted in a national newspaper as saying he would like to join Manchester United. Later, it appeared he had been 'misquoted'. Mind you, it would have been interesting when Alex Ferguson walked through the doors as the new United manager just over a month later. There never seemed much likelihood of these characters exchanging Christmas cards.

On September 20, there was a minute's silence before the game against Hibs at Celtic Park. The players of both clubs wore black armbands in respect of the sudden passing of Tom Devlin, who was in office for only fifteen months after succeeding Desmond White. Devlin had been in poor health in recent months. Jack McGinn, founder of the Celtic View, became the club's new chairman.

During the game, there was the merest hiccup when Stuart Beedie scored an equaliser, but, in the end, Celtic strolled off with a 5-1 win. Brian McClair (2), Paul McStay, Alan McInally and Mo Johnston were the marksmen. However, Davie Hay wasn't entirely convinced about the attitude of his players. 'When they score, they seem to think that the job is finished,' he said. 'We suffered because of that outlook against

Dundee United and it cost us a point. There may have been mitigating circumstances at Tannadice, but we should never have been in a position where we could get caught. We got away with it against Hibs because the players seemed to realise what was happening and they stepped things up again.'

A week later, Celtic bridged a thirteen-year gap by playing a league game at Brockville, the dilapidated, derelict home of Falkirk. The ground gave the alarming impression that it might have been one the last pieces of construction work completed by F. Flinstone and Son. Thankfully, the foundations weren't put to the test too often by the excited leaping up and down from the 17,500 fans and Celtic were content to grind out a 1-0 win courtesy of Mo Johnston bundling a Murdo MacLeod corner-kick over the line eight minutes from the end. The visitors could even afford the luxury of a first-half penalty-kick miss from Brian McClair, who hit a tired-looking effort wide of the target.

However, the same player executed a more professional touch in the midweek fixture on October 8 when Celtic beat Hearts 2-0, their first league win over the Edinburgh side in five meetings. As ever, it was a close-run thing with Hearts now operating Dundee United-style peek-a-boo tactics. Mo Johnston seized the barrier-breaking goal in the sixty-fourth minute for his fourteenth strike of the campaign. His peroxide-blond hair was shimmering like a beacon under the Celtic Park floodlights, but the Hearts defence failed to detect his whereabouts when Henry Smith pushed out a drive from McClair. As they dithered, Johnston was onto the scraps in a flash and blasted the ball into the net. It was still edgy until a minute from time when referee Douglas Yeats spotted what everyone else in the ground - all 35,382 of them - witnessed at the same time, Sandy Jardine handling a netbound effort from Alan McInally. McClair, after his aberration against Falkirk, sent the penalty-kick soaring high past Smith.

'That was an important win for us,' said Davie Hay. 'Some players tend to be a wee bit superstitious and you'll see them going through little routines before kick-off. So, when you continue to fail against a team, there will be some who believe they have an Indian Sign over you. The best thing to do is expel these notions at the quickest opportunity and that made this win so important. Well, that and the two points.'

Celtic had another four league games to play in October as well as the first leg of a European Cup Second Round tie against the soccer aristocrats of Dinamo Kiev and the little matter of a League Cup Final against Rangers. Hay conceded, 'It was a punishing schedule, but, of course, I wouldn't have had it any other way. No-one wanted to be idle and no-one was complaining.' Dundee, St Mirren, Motherwell and Clydebank were the teams who provided the competition for the much-prized Premier League points. In rapid succession, they were dismantled in impressive fashion with Hay's men collecting eight points and fourteen goals with the concession of one.

On October 11, Celtic cemented their place at the top of the Premier League with a vital 3-0 victory at Dundee with all the goals coming after the interval. Mo Johnston struck two minutes following the break and Brian McClair knocked in the second in the sixty-ninth minute. Possibly, Johnston was thinking of the importance of goal difference at the end of the season and he claimed a third in the final minute. The deadly double-act were up to their penalty box tricks in the 2-0 win over St Mirren at Celtic Park. Again, the first-half passed without the nets behind the goalkeepers being required to participate in the action. However, Johnston, always on the look-out, hit the breakthrough goal when he followed up a shot from Tony Shepherd that had struck a post in the fiftieth minute. McClair doubled the advantage near the end.

Johnston and McClair were dovetailing superbly. McClair said, 'We seem to have hit it off well. I don't think a striking partnership is something you can work on. It just clicks and I hope ours can continue for a long time. Mo is an excellent finisher. In fact, he's a great player. I think the difference in our styles complements each other. We are vastly different players who help each other equally.'

Could any team put the brakes on Celtic's goal twins? Motherwell provided the answer when they shackled the menaces, but that left space for Alan McInally who rifled in two efforts in a 3-1 triumph in Glasgow. Tony

Shepherd claimed the other and Steve Kirk was the man who spoiled Pat Bonner's shut-out displays with the visitors' effort. Dinamo Kiev Head Coach Valeri Lobonovski was in the stand that evening and he must have left more than slightly perplexed. Were Johnston and McClair disguising their true form? Was this part of the Celtic master plan? Hay can answer today. 'No, it was just one of those performances when the star men continually fluff their lines. There was no great secret. Which manager in his right mind would send out players to mask their best form? Players can do that without any instructions!'

The October league season was completed with a perfect ten when Celtic dismissed Clydebank 6-0 at Paradise. The Kilbowie side offered stern resistance in the first-half and kept the scoring down to two - efforts from Murdo MacLeod and Brian McClair. The roof fell in on veteran goalkeeper Jim Gallacher - father of future Scotland international No.1 Paul - after the break. Alan McInally hit two, Mark McGhee, back after injury, got his first league goal of the season and McClair hit his second and Celtic's sixth with fifteen minutes to go. Mo Johnston's name was missing from the scoring roll of honour for one very good reason - he watched the action from the stand after picking up a suspension for accumulating too many yellow cards. A crowd of 10,161 had been well entertained, but they didn't realise they were also witnessing the last hurrah for the popular Peter Latchford, brought in by Davie Hay for that final game.

'I've absolutely no doubt Peter would have been a regular first team goalkeeper at any other club outside Celtic,' said Hay. 'Pat Bonner was just so consistent that it was difficult to see past him. But I liked Peter and I knew that he was more than reliable when he was called upon. He may have been born and brought up in the Midlands and, of course, had signed for us from West Brom. Big Jock bought him in 1975 and he became a huge Celtic fan; not just a player, but a supporter. I thought he deserved the opportunity to go out there one last time.'

Four days before the Bankies stroll, a crowd of 48,000 watched Celtic face Dinamo Kiev, who were the European Cup-Winners' Cup holders at the time. They were also tipped as dark horses to go on and win the major tournament. Their pedigree was obvious - they possessed nine of Russia's World Cup squad that travelled to Mexico for that summer's Finals. And Head Coach Lobonovski was a well respected tactician. The Celtic fans anticipated a treat, but what they didn't expect was the thuggish treatment meted out by a team that could all too easily mix beauty with brutality. Poor Tommy Burns had his ankle snapped by a wicked late challenge from Aleksandr Zavarov. An observer noted, 'The tackle was so late it was almost in the return match.' The Celtic midfielder would be out of football for the next six months.

Evidently, it wasn't Celtic's night. In the fifth minute, Roy Aitken pitched over a free-kick, Murdo MacLeod nodded down and Alan McInally, with a half-volley, smacked the ball off the junction of bar and post. Thirteen minutes later, the Russians scored and Pat Bonner, normally so efficient, presented them with the gift. The keeper got his angles all wrong at a left-wing corner-kick and Vadim Yevtushenko, from six yards, couldn't believe his good fortune as he rolled the ball over the line. Parkhead went deathly silent. Celtic attacked and Dinamo soaked up the pressure and came back with their own questions.

However, they were beginning to upset the support with their over-vigorous challenges. One player who appeared to be provoking the ire of the supporters more than most was a flame-haired defender. His name? Oleg Kuznetsov, who, of course, later became part of the Souness Revolution at Rangers. Spanish referee Emilio Aladren seemed remarkably reticent to take action and the Celtic players received no protection from the match official. Johnston deserved a goal when he wriggled clear to get to a Roy Aitken pass and chipped keeper Viktor Chanov. The ball dipped and swerved before bouncing off the base of the post. Ten minutes from time, Johnston did get the ball in the net and Celtic got the goal their patient play deserved. Murdo MacLeod launched over an angled ball from the left, Johnston was first to it, but Chanov blocked his initial effort. The striker made no mistake from the rebound, lashing the ball into the roof of the net.

It finished 1-1, but the Celtic supporters had been amazed at what they had just witnessed. This was not a world-class group of sportsmen fit to grace arenas throughout the globe. The Russians smiled at the final whistle, but they won no friends in Glasgow. They were confident they were as good as in the quarter-finals. Alas, it was difficult to mount a reasonable argument; Dinamo had never lost in Kiev in more than twenty years of competing in Europe. Davie Hay said drily, 'There's a first time for everything.'

The second confrontation with Rangers was played on a crisp afternoon at the beginning of November and, watched by 60,000, it proved to be a frustrating affair for Celtic. It finished tied at 1-1, but the champions realised they had passed up the opportunity to put added pressure on Souness and Co. Rangers had dropped a point in a goalless draw against Dundee United at Tannadice the previous Wednesday and had received some criticism for their lack of enterprise in a dull ninety minutes. Now Celtic could add to the misery and it looked good, too, in the twenty-fifth minute when Brian McClair pounced on a Mo Johnston flick to thrash the ball behind Chris Woods. Unfortunately, Davie Hay's men didn't apply the coup de grace and Ally McCoist snatched the equaliser in the second-half.

Celtic didn't have too much time to reflect on a missed opportunity as they prepared to fly to Russia for the second leg of their European Cup Second Round tie against Dinamo Kiev. The game was being played in the aftermath of the Chernobyl Nuclear Disaster the previous spring. Davie Hay said, 'Yes, some of the players were a bit hesitant about travelling, so the board decided to send chief scout John Kelman to check out the area and report back. If he passed a Geiger Counter Test we knew it would be okay to go ahead with the game! Seriously, everything was fine. There were no problems.'

As ever, Celtic are at their most dangerous when they are arrogantly dismissed and there is little doubt Kiev believed the result in Glasgow had already propelled them into the quarter-final. 'There was a crowd of 100,000 in their vast stadium, but my players were hardly intimidated,' said Hay. 'Most of them had performed in the intensity of Old Firm games, Cup Finals and the like, so we weren't likely to go weak at the knees in

Kiev. Anyway, as Big Jock would often say, "The supporters can make as much as noise as they want, a fan has never scored a goal." I always thought that was a valid observation.'

Mark McGhee, in fact, struck the Ukrainians dumb when he scored four minutes after the turnaround to wipe out former European Footballer of the Year Oleg Blokhin's twelfth-minute free-kick goal. Murdo MacLeod and Brian McClair combined to set up McGhee for his first Euro strike for Celtic. In fact, Celtic could have equalised in the thirty-first minute when Paul McStay curled a delightful left-foot effort away from Viktor Chanov only to see the ball strike the post and rebound straight into the grateful keeper's arms. Pavel Yakovenko looked marginally offside as he raced onto a ball that had been misjudged by Derek Whyte and the pacy striker stuck the ball past Bonner in the seventy-second minute to restore the Russians' advantage. Hay though, realised that one more strike from his team would put Celtic through on the goals away rule. Kiev ditched the silky skills to begin hoofing clearances all over the place and, with Austrian referee Leonard Braummier warning them about time-wasting tactics, Vadim Yevtushenko, scorer in the first leg, netted the killer goal bang on full-time. Celtic were out, the sixth year in succession they had failed to reach the last eight in Europe. They were far from disgraced, though.

Afterwards, Davie Hay said, 'Valeri Lobanovski actually told me we were the best foreign team to have played them on their own ground in twenty-one years. Nice words, but I would have preferred him spitting blood with Celtic in the next round. However, considering we had youngsters such as Paul McStay, Tony Shepherd, Peter Grant, Brian McClair and Derek Whyte playing in such an intimidating atmosphere and performing well, there is plenty of reason for optimism. And Roy Aitken and Murdo MacLeod are hardly in their dotage. I think the experience will do my players the world of good.'

As Hay flew home with the party the following morning, he could never have known he would never again manage Celtic at that level.

Three days after Kiev, an understandable reaction set in among the players as they toiled at Douglas Park against Hamilton. They were trailing 1-0 with only nine minutes remaining and a huge setback looked on the cards. John Mailer, who had just been signed from the Juniors and was playing only his second game, gave Accies the lead in the seventy-fifth minute. The signs looked ominous until referee Dougie Hope awarded Celtic a penalty-kick after defender Graham Mitchell hauled down Mo Johnston. Brian McClair tucked it away with authority. The conspiracy theorists could have had a field day - Johnston and Mitchell were the best of friends. Johnston pushed the friendship to the extreme when he claimed the winner in the dying moments after Alan McInally had nudged on a free-kick from Derek Whyte.

Around about the same time Johnston was scoring the winner against Accies, Ray Farningham was doing likewise for Motherwell against Rangers at Ibrox. Saturday November 8 could have become a pivotal date in the destiny of the Scottish Premier League title.

Mo Johnston scored his thirteenth league goal of the season and it proved to be unlucky for Dundee United, who had received a large slice of good fortune in the corresponding fixture at Tannadice earlier in the campaign. Billy Thomson was turning in a Man of the Match performance in front of 34,319 fans at Celtic Park until the will-o'-the-wisp marksman displayed his penalty-box predatory instincts once more when he raced onto a Peter Grant pass to slide the winner away from the keeper with only ten minutes remaining.

Davie Hay reckoned, 'The way things are turning out, we only have the league games to concentrate on between now and the turn of the year. We have eight to go and we are in the driving seat. There is no point in looking too far ahead because all sorts of things can happen to knock you off course; injuries, suspension and the like. A player can be unstoppable one month and virtually unrecognisable the next. Consistency is a tricky customer.'

Falkirk were beaten 4-2 at Celtic Park with Mo Johnston again hitting two. Alan McInally and Peter Grant got the others with Kenny Ashwood and Jimmy Gilmour replying in the second-half. After nineteen games, Celtic were four points ahead of Dundee United with Rangers in fourth position eight points adrift. Hay wasn't entirely satisfied, though. 'I didn't feel we were imposing ourselves enough on our opponents. It was goalless at half-time in the game against Falkirk when we really should have been a couple of goals ahead. My players were performing like they knew, eventually, they were going to win. That's a dangerous assumption in football. A good team will keep their foot on your throat and do damage for ninety minutes. Not too many teams have the ability to pick and choose when they are going to go up a gear.'

Celtic were involved in an extraordinary 1-1 stalemate with Aberdeen at Pittodrie on Wednesday November 26. Alex Ferguson may have gone, but his determination and fighting spirit lived on. The drama kicked off in the eleventh minute when Pat Bonner made an excellent penalty-kick save from Jim Bett. It was a well-placed shot to the keeper's right, but Bonner catapulted across his line to push the ball to safety. However, he had no chance when Alex McLeish scored with a header three minutes after the turnaround. It remained that way until only eight minutes remained. The Dons had beaten Rangers at the weekend and were eyeing an Old Firm double.

Referee George Cumming had little hesitation in pointing to the spot when McLeish, with a badly-timed tackle, dumped Alan McInally in the penalty box. Brian McClair triggered off an astonishing quickfire series of incidents when he thrashed the ball high past Jim Leighton. His elevation was slightly out and his effort crashed against the underside of the crossbar and came flying back out. Mo Johnston, with those remarkable instincts, was first to the rebound to head the ball back towards goal, but this time his attempt thumped against a post. An almighty melee ensued and McClair tried again with a hook shot. Stewart McKimmie handled on the line and the match official gave Celtic their second penalty-kick within seconds. This time McClair, after recovering his composure, fizzed the ball past Leighton.

It wasn't quite so dramatic in the next game, but Celtic were still happy to collect two points in a 1-0 win over St Mirren with centre-half Pierce O'Leary scoring his only goal for the club. It was a cracker, too, in front of a crowd of 16,233 at Love Street. In the sixty-third minute, Paul McStay sent in a cross and O'Leary instinctively took a swipe at the ball with his right foot to send an effort swerving past Campbell Money. It was a worthy match winner.

How Celtic could have done with such impromptu heroics in the next game, a 1-0 defeat from Hearts at Tynecastle on a bleak Wednesday evening in the capital. Davie Hay's men had gone into the fixture with an unbeaten run stretching to sixteen games. The Edinburgh men, for their part, hadn't lost at home for twenty-eight games. The only goal arrived just after the half-hour mark and once again emphasised Celtic's need for a commanding force in the penalty area while defending a set-piece. John Robertson worked a short corner with Sandy Clark before flighting the ball to the back post. Defender Neil Berry scored goals with the frequency of snowstorms in the Sahara and, unchallenged, he couldn't miss from two yards.

A piece of breathtaking individualism from Mo Johnston got Celtic back to winning ways against Dundee in Glasgow three days later. Johnston had already given the hosts the lead with a typical opportunistic effort two minutes after the break, but his second in the 2-0 win, sixteen minutes from time, was a thing of beauty. Owen Archdeacon sent in a cross from the left and, in an instant, Mo, on the edge of the penalty area, flicked the ball up into the air, steadied himself and then volleyed an exquisite right-foot drive past 'keeper Bobby Geddes.

The goal wasn't in keeping with the ordinariness of the football on display that afternoon. One newspaper reporter stated, 'If there is an art to winning while playing badly, Celtic - on this display - have perfected it. The league leaders had one of those days when nothing, except the result, went right for them.'

Without warning, Celtic dropped three out of six points in their remaining league fixtures against Motherwell, Aberdeen and Clydebank as they edged to the close of 1986. The first of three consecutive 1-1 results materialised at Fir Park where, before the start, the visiting fans burst into a chorus of 'Jingle Bells' as the snow drifted gently around them. They were in an even better mood two minutes before the interval when Brian McClair netted once more against his former team. Alan McInally whipped over a cross and McClair nipped in to direct a close-range effort away from John Gardiner. Despite the merry ditties from the terracing, Motherwell weren't in the mood to hand out Christmas gifts and they grabbed a point five minutes after the turnaround when there was a mix-up between Pat Bonner and Piece O'Leary and Paul Smith equalised.

Alan McInally gave Celtic a third-minute lead against Aberdeen in front of 35,624 fans on a piercingly crisp afternoon in the east end of Glasgow. Things were going the champions' way when the Dons passed up a penalty-kick opportunity in the fourteenth minute. Derek Whyte brought down Stewart McKimmie and referee Jim Duncan couldn't fail to see the infringement. Joe Miller's drive was too close to Pat Bonner and the keeper parried the ball and Mo Johnston, of all people, completed the clearance. Miller atoned three minutes from half-time when he headed in a left-wing cross from David Robertson at the back post.

Two days after Christmas there was little Festive Cheer around Kilbowie where Clydebank battled to a tenacious deadlock. The struggling Bankies gave Celtic a fright when Lex Grant opened the scoring when he exposed the persistent Achilles Heel and got in at the back post to score with ease. A lacklustre Celtic equalised eight minutes after half-time, but even then it was twinged with a bit of desperation. A handball was detected in the penalty area, the award was given and Brian McClair's shot was pushed onto the post by Jim Gallacher. Unluckily for the home custodian, McClair kept his wits about him and followed up to bash in the rebound. The scrappy goal seemed to sum up a Celtic performance impoverished of guile, class and invention.

Still, Celtic remained at the top of the league and were sitting on forty-one points, five ahead of Rangers. An intriguing second half of the Premier League campaign was assured.

CHAPTER TWENTY-FOUR
HAMPDEN FIASCO

Hampden was in uproar. Referee Davie Syme had just ordered off Mo Johnston during a volcanic encounter with Rangers and, within seconds, he flashed another red card at young Celtic midfielder Tony Shepherd. Davie Hay, standing yards away from the flashpoint incident on the touchline, had the match ball in his hands. 'For a split-second I thought about volleying it as powerfully as possible in the direction of the ref,' admitted the Celtic manager. 'Thankfully, though, I had a swift change of mind. I guessed it would be an action that would send an already powderkeg confrontation into utter chaos.'

The 1986 League Cup Final on October 26 was as volatile a confrontation against Rangers as any in history. Match official Syme had already given the Ibrox side a hugely controversial penalty-kick - from which Davie Cooper scored the winner - and the fans in the Celtic end were still seething at the award. Only four minutes remained when Johnston was banished after an off-the-ball clash with defender Stuart Munro. Syme didn't see the incident, but the linesman eagerly flagged and that was enough to see the Celtic striker ordered off. Then the ref dramatically delivered another red card to Shepherd whose only misdemeanour appeared to be standing in the vicinity wearing a green and white jersey. Remarkably, Syme admitted afterwards he believed the young Celt had punched him on the back of the head. When it was pointed out that no such action had taken place, Syme changed his mind and ushered the befuddled player back onto the pitch.

'The referee told me he had made a mistake,' recalled Hay. 'I replied, "You're a mistake!" It was the best I could offer in the circumstances as I felt my blood boil at the injustices I had witnessed all day. The referee booked seven Celtic players - Johnston, Pat Bonner, Roy Aitken, Alan McInally, Derek Whyte, Peter Grant and Owen Archdeacon. Had we suddenly become a dirty team overnight? It was some of the most outrageous refereeing I had ever seen. I have to admit I cracked up during that 2-1 defeat. I think the referee simply lost the plot. The penalty-kick he awarded to them was just ridiculous. I only saw footage of that spot-kick recently when I was doing an interview for Celtic TV. It was worse than I thought first time around and, believe me, that is saying something!

'As I recall, there were only six minutes to go and a corner-kick came in from the right. Roy Aitken and Terry Butcher went for it at the back post. These are two big guys we are talking about and both were extremely passionate captains of their respective clubs. They were jostling with each other and it looked to everyone that it was a case of six of one and half a dozen of another. Well, everyone apart from Syme, who was, by the way, positioned at the near post and would have required x-ray vision to see through the crowd of players to witness what was going on between Roy and Terry. I couldn't believe it when he pointed to the penalty spot. To be fair, even the Rangers contingent looked more than a little surprised by this absurd decision. I was furious, absolutely livid. It was an outrageous bit of refereeing and it cost us the game and the trophy.

'Afterwards, I still couldn't prevent myself from showing my anger. I just could not calm down. "I think we should take Celtic to England," I said, a bit ahead of my time. "At least, we'll get a fair crack of the whip down there." I meant every word of it, too. How could I think otherwise after that performance from Syme? There seemed no logic to his decision-making, as far as I was concerned.'

Celtic were denied the opening goal five minutes before the interval when Aitken set up Johnston who rattled a low drive away from Chris Woods only to see the ball thud against the upright and bounce clear. It was the Ibrox side who struck first in the sixty-second minute after some lamentable defending by Celtic. Cammy Fraser flighted in a free-kick and Ian Durrant was allowed time and space to turn the ball beyond Bonner. Once again, the woodwork rescued Graeme Souness' team when McClair sent a free-kick over the defensive wall and away from Woods. The ball didn't dip quickly enough, though, and it smashed against the crossbar.

Just when Celtic thought they were fated not to score, McClair netted an absolute belter in the seventieth minute. Aitken and Johnston combined and their team-mate hit a shot on the run from the edge of the box that simply flew into the top corner of the net. It was a marvellous strike and set up the game for a nerve-tingling finale. Then Syme intervened and, even to this day, his penalty-kick decision mystifies Davie Hay. 'It doesn't matter now,' he said, 'but nothing will ever change my mind. That was NOT a spot-kick in any shape or form.'

And yet the League Cup competition started so innocuously on a bright August evening in Paradise when Airdrie were dismissed 2-0 in front of 15,000 fans. The supporters got their first look at Mark Smith, Davie Hay's summer capture from Queen's Park. 'I had received good reports about the player, had a look myself and decided to give him a chance,' said the manager. 'When you've played behind Jimmy Johnstone for a few years you realise the importance of having width in your team.' Brian McClair got the show on the road with the opening goal in the third minute, but, curiously, it wasn't until three minutes from the end that the same player put the game to bed with the clincher.

A week later, Dumbarton made life slightly more difficult for Celtic in Glasgow. Mo Johnston snatched the opening goal just before the interval and, although Celtic were hardly stretched, it wasn't until the seventy-eighth minute when Paul McStay struck that the 11,390 fans could settle a bit. Johnston made it 3-0 with another strike six minutes from the end. The part-timers from Boghead had made their illustrious opponents work hard for their victory.

Celtic had coasted into the quarter-final, but they found the waters a lot more choppy when they were drawn against Aberdeen at Pittodrie on September 3. It was a highly-charged and emotional evening that left Davie Hay fuming at referee Bob Valentine. A series of decisions by the match official set Hay's pulse rate racing, not least the ordering-off of substitute Tony Shepherd, who had picked up two dubious bookings. The tie roared along at a pulsating pace and was deadlocked at 1-1 after extra-time. Penalties would be called for to decide the winner. Earlier, the Dons must have thought they were heading into the last four when Bobby Connor gave them the advantage with a header in the thirteenth minute. However, in the sixty-ninth minute, Mo Johnston dragged the tie into the additional half-hour when, at the second attempt, he managed to nudge a Paul McStay cross over the line. Johnston and Owen Archdeacon were also booked by an over-fussy referee before the spot-kicks came into play.

Roy Aitken didn't give Celtic the best of starts when he hit Jim Leighton with a blaster that went as straight as an arrow. Jim Bett then side-footed a neat effort past Pat Bonner. Johnston tucked his attempt away before Bonner saved from John Hewitt. Peter Grant and Peter Weir both netted with their efforts. It was reaching the strenuous stage, but Archdeacon commendably held his nerve to slot his shot wide of Leighton. Captain Willie Miller then held his head in his hands as he saw Bonner save his badly-placed attempt. Brian McClair was given the opportunity of sealing it 4-2 during the sudden death period and he walloped his drive into the net.

Hay, though, barely attempted to conceal his contempt for the performance of the match official. 'I will be writing to the SFA asking that Mr Valentine never again handles a Celtic game. I've done so before and no doubt I'll do so again with the full backing of my club. It's for his own good as much as anything. It's terrible to say things like this after such a tie, but I think it's necessary.'

Celtic came close to blowing the opportunity of a Hampden Final when they let slip a two-goal advantage over Motherwell in their semi-final. Davie Hay's men were cruising on the hour mark and the Fir Park side had rarely threatened. Brian McClair headed the Hoops in front when he turned in a Willie McStay cross in the thirty-eighth minute and Roy Aitken added to that when he finished off a breathtaking solo run by rounding keeper John Gardiner and sliding the ball home. However, a mistake from Willie McStay allowed substitute Andy Walker to pull one back in the seventieth minute and, with Celtic hanging on, Paul Smith netted the equaliser with a header from a John Gahagan cross. Hay's side seemed to have perfected the inability of making life easy for themselves.

It finished in a 2-2 stalemate and once more it went to penalty-kicks. Celtic won 5-4 with a one hundred per cent record from the spot with McClair, Mo Johnston, Derek Whyte, Paul McStay and Tommy Burns converting. Tommy Boyd and Walker were among the Fir Parkers to beat Pat Bonner, but John Philliben was the villain who missed. It had been and enthralling, exciting tie.

However, it had nothing on what was to follow in the same arena just over a month later.

Davie Hay still insists, 'Sadly, that Old Firm Hampden Final will be remembered for all the wrong reasons. There were a lot of good players on the park that afternoon, but one man managed to spoil the occasion – referee Davie Syme. I will never change my mind.'

CHAPTER TWENTY-FIVE
COUNTING THE COST

To this very day, Davie Hay is unshakeable in his belief Celtic would have won the Premier League in the 1986/87 campaign if the board, when he needed their backing most, had displayed more ambition and commitment in the transfer market. 'I have absolutely no doubt we would have been champions for the second successive season,' insists Hay, adding almost wistfully, 'and I wouldn't have lost the job I loved.'

No-one should get the notion Hay is seeking sympathy. Far from it. Anyone misguided enough to take that trail of thought clearly does not know the man. Or his qualities. 'If we had to have the opportunity of picking up silverware at the end of the day, I realised in October that the squad needed strengthening and I knew the areas we had to target. These wouldn't have been mere additions to the pool, these were urgent replacements. I'm talking about players who would have gone directly into the first team. No disrespect to either Paul McGugan or Pierce O'Leary, two excellent youngsters, but neither was the dominant centre-half I was looking for. Joe McLaughlin wanted out at Chelsea, I knew of his feelings for Celtic and I thought he would be ideal.

'Davie Provan's right-wing position had never been filled since his retirement and I liked the look of Pat Nevin, the former Clyde player who was also at my old club Chelsea. Nevin was a tricky winger, a bit of a crowd-pleaser and, after the likes of Jimmy Johnstone and Davie Provan, the Celtic fans had become accustomed to such a player. The right-back role had been a headache with Danny McGrain in his last season at the club and it was obvious, at the age of thirty-seven, he would need to be replaced. I tried Willie McStay in there and he gave it his best shot, but I believed we could still take it up a notch. I knew Steve Clarke, of St Mirren, could step comfortably in to that slot. I was aware all three players were available at the right price. I didn't think they would have broken the bank and, while we were on top of the table, they would have strengthened the team at the right stage.

'I continually warned the board to look at the bigger picture and see what Rangers were doing across the city. Our age-old rivals were investing heavily in their playing resources and were bringing in quality from England. In the summer, they had signed Terry Butcher and Chris Woods and around about Christmas time they paid a reported £450,000 for Graham Roberts from Spurs. That was the sort of financial backing I needed from the board. The turn of the year is an ideal time to give your team an extra bit of impetus. A new face or two can lift the place and, of course, it boosts the fans, too. They know we are attempting to give them a superior product and they respond accordingly. We were all in it together. But the board wouldn't budge from their stance no matter how many times I went back to them to point out the folly of their ways. Our squad was fragile, wafer-thin, and I knew - even if they didn't - that it could prove costly at the end of the day.

'In fact, I should point out that I made the plea to add to the pool at the end of the previous season after we had won the title. Even at that stage, I was far from satisfied with the depth of our squad. Or, more accurately, the lack of depth. I repeated this throughout the summer and, alas, no-one was listening. However, two or three months into the new season, I knew something had to be done.'

1979 – TEN MEN WON THE LEAGUE!
On a dramatic Monday evening in May 1979, Celtic against all
odds emerged triumphant against a Rangers team in pursuit of a
treble. Billy McNeill's team, reduced to ten men after Johnny Doyle
was sent off early in the second half, roared back to score 4 goals
with ten men to win the league in splendid style. There were large
huddles in the Jungle on that wonderful Monday night!

1980 – SCOTTISH CUP FINAL – the match that ended the drinking culture inside the grounds in Scottish football. Celtic deservedly won the Cup, thanks to a deflected Danny McGrain shot that George McCluskey touched to get the extra-time winner. That should have been that but with a lack of police in the ground, some Celtic fans spilled onto the park to celebrate and the response from the other end was much more aggressive. Shameful scenes followed, although the Celtic support made light of the riot in song over the next year or so singing "We chased them all over Hampden!"

1981 – CHAMPIONS! Dundee United were possibly the hardest team in the eighties for Celtic to beat. Although we enjoyed two very notable Scottish Cup Final successes against the team from Tannadice, they always managed to frustrate Celtic and regularly sneaked a result. Not on this wonderful midweek evening, as Celtic travelled to Dundee and played some outstanding football inspired by Tommy Burns. Celtic won 3-2 and were worthy champions.

1982 - CHAMPIONS once again in May with a 3-0 win over St Mirren at Celtic Park. "We've won the League again, fly the flag!" was the song from the Jungle. Then Celtic became LEAGUE CUP WINNERS in December– the Celtic team by this stage was beginning to look special and this was being billed as the first step on the way to a treble. Celtic played Rangers off the park in the December rain in the first half and should have been more than two goals to the good. Rangers pulled one back early in the second half thus avoiding a hammering, and Celtic settled for what they had: the trophy that just seems so tricky for us to win. It was all relatively simple that day with Nicholas and MacLeod both scoring lovely goals.

1985 SCOTTISH CUP WINNERS. This was the 100th Final and it just seemed appropriate that the Celtic fairytale would continue at Hampden. A goal behind and frankly not playing that well, it was all beginning to look rather unlikely. Davie Hay made some significant tactical changes and after Davie Provan scored a wonderful free-kick these changes saw Roy Aitken released on the right to fire in a cross to the rubber man, Frank McGarvey to score with a stunning header. The ball seemed slightly behind him and it was a remarkable effort from the Celtic striker to put the ball into the net and send the Celtic support wild with delight.

1986 CHAMPIONS – against all odds! Hearts had released their song as a single and had printed their Championship winning t-shirts. Celtic had hung in there but on the last day Hearts had to avoid defeat at Dens Park and Celtic had to score a handful at Love Street. In an unforgettable afternoon the transistor radios at the ears of the anxious Celtic support brought the brilliant news from Tayside that Kidd had scored! When Davie Provan signalled to the players that Kidd had done it again it was all over – Celtic had scored their goals and were once again worthy champions.

1988 – CENTENARY CHAMPIONS! The fairytale once again continued and the league was won at Paradise against Dundee. The crowd that day was enormous, rather like the numbers back in 1980 when Real Madrid came calling. Late goals were a feature in Celtic's league campaign as this Celtic team simply refused to accept defeat. Having got their first trophy in Celtic's Centenary year it was on to Hampden for some more late, late drama. Frankie bhoy…

1988- OUR BIRTHDAY PARTY!

Happy Birthday, to you, happy Birthday to you.
Happy Birthday dear Celtic. Happy Birthday to you!

1988 – CENTENARY CUP WINNERS! – Once again Celtic found themselves a goal behind in the Scottish Cup Final with the clock ticking away. When Frank McAvennie grabbed a late equaliser neutrals watching on TV would have expected extra-time. We didn't. We had been at the semi-final against Hearts and celebrated late, late goals by Andy Walker and Mark McGhee to get us to this Final. We knew the script. A poorly hit corner at the Celtic end rolled through to Frank McAvennie and he placed the ball in the Dundee United net to set off the wildest Celtic celebrations since Lisbon. Later, watching Tommy Burns being interviewed on TV, was very special. But that was much later!

WE ARE CELTIC SUPPORTERS! Circa 1988 courtesy of Lawrence Monaghan from CQN. Some young supporters, who will be in their mid thirties now, are pictured playing football in Maryhill. The image on page 10 is from the Glasgow Garden Festival 1988 (on the site where BBC Scotland is now located) and is the city's tribute to our very special football club on our Centenary. Other images of the Celtic support in Janefield Street come from a match against Aberdeen on 17th September 1988 where the champions were unfortunately defeated by 3 goals to one by the Dons.

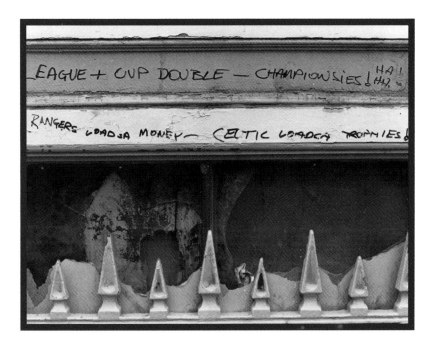

1989 – TREBLE BUSTERS! – It took 101 years for Celtic to get the benefit of an "honest mistake" but when Roy Aitken "stole" a throw-in just inside the Rangers half in the 1989 Scottish Cup Final and Joe Miller nipped in to take advantage of a short pass back, we had one of our own. A refereeing error in Celtic's favour! This was the only goal in a very tense match thus Celtic had retained the Scottish Cup! So the eighties ended on a high with silverware in the Parkhead trophy room. Remarkably for years later when "honest mistakes" were topical, this throw-in would be brought up as an example of decisions going against Rangers and for Celtic.
Maybe that's what Caesar is laughing about in that photograph with Alex Gordon earlier in the book?

Hay travelled south to watch McLaughlin and Nevin in action against West Ham at Upton Park. McLaughlin was so eager to leave the Stamford Bridge club he had asked for a transfer every week for a month. He made no secret that a move to Celtic would be more than welcome. When the newspapers broke the story that the Parkhead manager had been at the game, Jack McGinn, the new Celtic chairman, made the preposterous statement that if 'Hay wants to bring those players to Celtic, then he will have to pay for them himself.' It was a ludicrous remark of Everest proportions.

Hay could only shake his head in wonderment. He knew Desmond White, oft-criticised former chairman, would never have gone public with such a statement. 'Yes, Desmond had his critics, but I know he would have been better equipped to assist me when Graeme Souness arrived at Ibrox and was given what appeared to be a blank cheque book,' said Hay. 'Desmond was careful with money, as we were all aware, but, importantly, he understood what Celtic were all about.' No elaboration was required from Hay.

The manager's words should have echoed around the Celtic boardroom after the New Year's Day meeting with Rangers at Ibrox. Celtic lost 2-0 and, in truth, were outclassed for most of the game. Graeme Souness took part for the first time on the field in a Glasgow derby and he virtually strolled through the proceedings, played in driving sleet throughout. The match turned into a personal disaster for keeper Pat Bonner who turned in one of the worst performances of his career. The dreadful conditions certainly didn't aid the Irishman, but his judgement calls in the space of four first-half minutes went a long way to gifting Rangers their victory.

Bonner was caught in no man's land when Robert Fleck scored the opening goal in the twenty-eighth minute. Davie Cooper nonchalantly lifted over a left-wing corner-kick to the near post where Terry Butcher posed an obvious threat. As the ball swirled in the air, the keeper came for it far too late. The England international skipper flicked it on, Bonner was eliminated completely and Fleck was handily placed six yards out to blast the ball into the net.

Unfortunately, it got worse for the goalie moments later. Once again, Cooper was the provider as he hung up a diagonal left-wing cross. It looked like the keeper's ball, but, to the horror of his team-mates, Bonner's timing was out as he got under the cross. He fumbled the ball, dropped it behind him and there was Ally McCoist, totally anonymous beforehand, ramming in the gift from a handful of yards. Bonner looked aghast; his colleagues mirrored his emotion. Davie Hay watched his team toil throughout the first-half and Souness actually seemed to be enjoying himself as he cut a swathe with acres of room in which to manoeuvre in the middle of the park. Put starkly, he was bossing the event and no-one in Celtic's colours that day appeared to have the gumption or the ability to do something about it.

Souness had the Ibrox fans cheering wildly when he went in combustibly on Roy Aitken. The Celtic midfielder was flattened and it was an obvious 'marker' from the Rangers player/manager. It was about as subtle as an earthquake and referee Kenny Hope booked a grinning Souness. Aitken recovered after treatment, but contributed little to proceedings after that.

Over on Celtic's left wing, Graham Roberts, who obviously revelled in his tough guy image, was whipping up a storm of adulation from the Ibrox hordes as he hammered into the slender Owen Archdeacon. Roberts left the youngster writhing on the sodden turf after only four minutes. The match official merely gave him a warning and the bulky Roberts realised it was open day on his unfortunate opponent. Not long afterwards, he administered something of the same on Archdeacon and one newspaper likened the tackle to an 'assault'. Referee Hope was satisfied with another friendly word in the Englishman's ear. However, when he clattered Archdeacon in the second-half, Roberts did eventually get a booking. It was well after it mattered to Celtic.

Hay watched in a fair degree of discomfort from the touchline. Paul McGugan, an earnest performer, was making journeyman Robert Fleck look world class at centre-forward and Peter Grant was clearly a midfield player performing as an emergency right-back as the wily Davie Cooper went through his full repertoire on the left flank. Brian McClair and Mo Johnson were feeding on morsels and Paul McStay had too much retrieving to do in his midfield role to even contemplate being creative. He left Souness in his wake at one point in the second-half as he surged forward, but Chris Woods showed a clean pair of hands as he plucked his twenty-yard drive out of the air. The only other time the Ibrox No.1 was remotely troubled was near the end when he got down to his right to push a McClair shot round the post.

The fastest some Celtic players moved all day came at the full-time whistle when at least three seemed to be in a personal race as they sprinted for the sanctuary of the dressing room. A grim Davie Hay, who realised his team's flaws had been mercilessly exposed, said, 'I expected better from my players. We surrendered areas of the pitch where I thought we should have been competing strongly. It's too easy to point the finger at Pat Bonner and he knows only too well himself that he should have done better at the goals. But you have to have a bigger viewpoint. We didn't play well and we must now go away, re-group and come back stronger than ever.'

Rangers were now three points behind with a game in hand. If Hay hoped the deficiencies of his team, cruelly exposed time and again in Govan, might provoke a reaction from his new chairman and the board he was to be sadly let down. He would have to toil on with what he had. Souness had what turned out to be a Rolls-Royce, Hay had a moped.

Two days later, Celtic papered over the cracks by beating Hamilton Accies 8-3 at Parkhead. The goal avalanche may have fooled the Celtic board into believing the Ibrox result was merely a bad day at the office, but Hay was adamant they would have to dust the cobwebs off the cheque book before it was too late. 'We are strong in obvious departments,' said Hay. 'This game underlines it perfectly. In Mo Johnston, Brian McClair and Alan McInally we've got three of the most prolific strikers in the country, but there are other departments that need to be addressed with a fair degree of urgency.' The board members weren't listening.

Curiously, there was no sign of Johnston against Accies, but sidekick McClair nailed four in his absence while McInally grabbed two. Murdo MacLeod joined in the frolics with a pair while the valiant Accies replied with goals from Albert Craig, John Mailer and Kevin McKee. A crowd of 13,380 welcomed in the New Year at the home of their favourites as the cold wind shrieked around the ground. The supporters must have wondered if their team could weather the storm.

Pat Bonner conceded his eighth goal in three games as Celtic lost 3-2 to Dundee United on January 10. Remarkably, Jim McLean's men had tasted defeat only twice in their past sixteen games against the Parkhead outfit although this was another close-run encounter. Brian McClair thought he had hauled the champions back into the contest when he netted two goals to wipe out United efforts from Iain Ferguson and Kevin Gallacher. The winning goal came thirteen minutes from the end and was supplied by Eamonn Bannon. On the same afternoon, Rangers strolled to a 5-0 home win over Clydebank, in a state of collapse and in obvious freefall.

Celtic had two games still to play in January and Davie Hay was left in no doubt he would have to see out the remainder of the season with the squad at his disposal. There were no transfer windows back then, but that made no difference to the men who held the purse strings at Parkhead. Their mantra was simple. The team that won the league last season would just have to be good enough to hold onto their crown. Hay had also identified another centre-half he thought would make the difference to the spine of his team. He was a big, raw defender at Norwich City, but the Celtic manager was never given the green light to move for him, either. Steve Bruce ended up with Alex Ferguson later that year and played almost ten trophy-laden years at Manchester United.

Hibs arrived at Celtic Park on a grim Wednesday evening and Hay urged his team to make no mistakes; a win would put them a point ahead of Rangers. A crowd of 21,583 witnessed Anton Rogan scoring his first goal for the club with a spectacular eighteen-yard drive past Tom Carson, on loan from Dundee, for the only strike of the game. It hadn't exactly been magical football on a flint-hard surface, but the Hoops fans accepted the two points with glee. It was the same story three days later at Brockville where Celtic had to fight back from a first-half Kenny Ashwood strike to overcome Falkirk 2-1. Mo Johnston snatched both goals in the second-half. The travelling support also had a special round of applause for a Falkirk player - Albert Kidd had joined the club from Dundee and the fans let him know they hadn't forgotten his actions of the previous season. There was an extra roar at the end when it was announced Rangers had dropped a point in a goalless draw with Aberdeen at Ibrox. The dream was still on.

As February made its arrival, so, too, did the Scottish Cup and Celtic were about to embark on a three-game marathon with Aberdeen. Twenty-four hours before the fans travelled to Pittodrie for the Third Round tie, they had been pleasantly surprised by events at Ibrox. Little Hamilton Accies, courtesy of a seventieth minute strike from Adrian Sprott, had eliminated Rangers in Govan. The part-time Douglas Park side, where the players earned fifty quid a week, were no-hopers until Sprott blasted the ball beyond Chris Woods, the first time the keeper had conceded a goal in 1,196 minutes.

So, there was a lot of optimism in the frozen north where there was far too much fiasco football on a frost-bound pitch. One reporter noted, 'No-one would have been surprised if ice-skating champions Torvill and Dean had appeared at any stage.' The tie ended 2-2 after Celtic had led by two goals at half-time. Alan McInally got the opener in the fourteenth minute with a raging header from a Mo Johnston centre and Brian McClair notched the second when he banged a penalty-kick past Jim Leighton after David Robertson had upended Paul McStay. However, the Dons got a spot-kick of their own in the sixty-eighth minute when Danny McGrain pulled down Paul Wright and Jim Bett buried his effort behind Pat Bonner. John Hewitt forced a midweek replay in Glasgow with the leveller five minutes later.

Rain tumbled down from grey, leaden skies the following Wednesday, but it didn't prevent a crowd of 55,405 turning out for the second installment. But it, too, ended in stalemate; this time goalless. Incredibly, the teams had ended all-square in their last five outings and even extra-time couldn't prise a winner. A third game was arranged for Dundee's ground at Dens Park the following Monday. Celtic prepared with a 3-0 victory over St Mirren watched by 20,143 fans at Paradise. Davie Hay fielded Mark Smith, his summer signing from Queen's Park, and the young winger looked lively while that pair of penalty-box plunderers were in action again. The game was balanced at 0-0 after a stale first-half, but Mo Johnston netted two and Brian McClair added another. The double-act was now on twenty-seven goals each during a prolific campaign.

And it was McClair who proved to be the difference in the epic Scottish Cup power scrimmage with their Pittodrie foes. New boss Ian Porterfield had yet to sample a loss in his previous sixteen games since taking over from Alex Ferguson. Something had to give on a chilly evening in the City of Discovery and McClair had the answer in the sixteenth minute when he scampered onto a through ball from Paul McStay and left Jim Leighton helpless. The Scottish Cup draw hadn't been particularly kind in the Third Round and that was mirrored in the Fourth with a tie against Hearts at Tynecastle. If Davie Hay was going to enjoy success in the national competition for the second time in three seasons he was going to have to do it the hard way.

Before the Cup-tie in Edinburgh on February 21, Celtic were due to face Hearts on league business in Glasgow a week beforehand. Celtic were held to a 1-1 draw and looked weary. No wonder - this was their fifth game in fourteen days with a threadbare squad pushed to its limit. Brian McClair hit his thirtieth goal of the campaign in the sixteenth minute when Henry Smith could only push out a rasping drive from Alan McInally. With tiredness and fatigue setting into the limbs, the defence dropped its guard and John Colquhoun, proving to be a real thorn in the side since his move from the Hoops, set up Wayne Foster for an equaliser eleven minutes from the end.

So, a late goal had cost Celtic a crucial point in the league race and an even later effort removed them from the Scottish Cup a week later. It was scoreless with only ten minutes remaining when the Edinburgh side were awarded a free-kick twenty-five yards out. John Robertson sized up the situation before hitting a right-foot drive at goal. Pat Bonner moved confidently to his right to deal with the danger, but was left with no chance whatsoever when the ball struck Paul McStay on the left shoulder, altered its course and flew into the opposite corner. And that was the end of the hopes of a return to Hampden.

Davie Hay hoped for a change of fortune as he tried to revive the sagging spirits of his team. 'I always tried to put a positive spin on things,' said the Celtic manager. 'The players looked absolutely shattered in the dressing room that day. I wasn't far behind them. We had one fixture to fulfill in February, a game against Dundee at Dens Park, and then I hoped we had the legs to carry us through March and April. We had two games in May, but I knew they would take care of themselves, the impetus would get us there.'

Dundee had yet to win in 1987 when Celtic arrived on February 28 and the Tayside outfit's miserable run looked like continuing when Brian McClair gave the visitors the initiative in the twenty-first minute with 12,455 looking on. The second-half metamorphosed into Celtic's most shambolic forty-five minutes of the campaign. The mood on the terracing turned decidedly ugly and the Celtic directors, in an exposed area in the stand, were pelted with coins as well as being subjected to a torrent of verbal abuse from raging supporters. Clearly, the patience of the fans had snapped at the lack of investment in the team and the obvious imperfections in the squad.

Dundee, hardly the most dynamic opposition in the Premier League, exposed every flaw as they trampled all over the Parkhead side, every shortcoming highlighted, every weakness uncovered. It was embarrassing and humiliating for Davie Hay and his drained players. Astoundingly, Dundee scored four goals as the dog-tired opposition disintegrated in front of them. Vince Mennie kicked off the torment with the leveller a minute after the turnaround and Rab Shannon, John Brown and Ross Jack hit three in a whirlwind twenty-three minute period of punishment for Hay's Celtic side.

The cave-in allowed Rangers to go on top on goal difference although they had struggled the same afternoon to draw 1-1 with Hibs at Ibrox. But events on Tayside shook Celtic, from top to bottom. Hay recalled, 'The reaction from the fans was hostile. It had been like a ticking time-bomb, the pressure had been growing week by week as we tried to manoeuvre our way through the many problems. We had gone out of the Scottish Cup the week before and now they had just witnessed Dundee scoring four against us in one half. I didn't blame them one bit. I felt their pain.

'Having said that, it's a fairly long walk from the Dens Park dug-out to the tunnel and I knew I would be on the receiving end. The fans pay their money and they have a right to voice their opinion. Mind you, it's not pleasant being the focal point of the abuse, that's for sure. A lot of vitriol came in my direction. I decided I would walk the gauntlet on my own. Tommy Craig, my assistant, and a couple of other backroom guys were about to accompany me along the track, but I told them to hang back. I didn't want them to face the insults; I was the manager and I would deal with it. In that horrible situation, you just can't react. There's no way you should make eye contact. Do that and you're a dead man. I stared ahead as I walked towards the tunnel and I could hear all sorts of stuff from the fans, obviously at the end of their tether. I was being pilloried from all sides.

'Eventually, after what seemed about ten minutes, I got to our dressing room. The players looked done in, absolutely shattered. There was no need to say anything. I do recall Jack McGinn, our chairman, looking completely ashen-faced. The fans had turned on the board and they had never experienced anything like that before. I went over to Jack and put my hand on his shoulder and said, "Be strong." I wanted to try to reassure him, but deep down, I wondered if we had reached a turning point in the season. Had we lost the trust of the people who always mattered most to me, the supporters? Well, after what I had just been through, I didn't think it would be too difficult to work out the answer.

'There was little point in reminding the board that all this could have been avoided if I had been allowed to bring in some new players. You can't guarantee success in this game, but some fresh legs could have seen us over the line. Let's put it this way, we would have had a better chance of achieving something if new players had been signed. The directors decided not to shell out and now we were struggling. Also, I realised our fans were never comfortable with having Rangers' riches rammed down their throat just about every day. It was clear our rivals were the princes and we were the paupers. Who could be satisfied in that environment?'

Almost 15,000 supporters braved the swirling snow as Motherwell visited Celtic the following week and this time the centre for the wrath from the terracings was Mo Johnston. A newspaper had leaked the story that the player, the fans' favourite not so long ago, had rejected a new £2,000-per-week contract and had made it clear he wanted to leave Parkhead. His agent, Bill McMurdo, a well-known Rangers follower, was seen as a destabilising influence on his client. It was all too much to bear. The fury among the support was evident even before the kick-off. Although this was the first time the Celtic fans would find him guilty of being disloyal to the jersey, it wouldn't be the last. He hadn't helped his cause, either, by failing to score in his last five games.

The Parkhead powderkeg was poised for ignition again, but, thankfully, the attention of the supporters was attracted to the action and there was relief when Roy Aitken scored in the sixth minute. The tension was cranked up again when Steve Kirk levelled with a free-kick in the twentieth minute. Shortly afterwards, old Celtic favourite Tom McAdam, now with Motherwell, turned the ball into his own net and Tony Shepherd rifled in the third in the seventy-second minute. That ended the scoring, but not the cacophony that still came Johnston's way every time he kicked the ball. One sports scribe observed, 'Mo Johnston should get his agent to fix him up with ear plugs!'

Events were turning against Celtic and on March 14 they toppled 1-0 to Aberdeen at Pittodrie while Rangers turned the screw with a 2-0 win over their Scottish Cup tormentors Hamilton Accies in Glasgow. Defender Brian Irvine gave the Dons their first victory over the Parkhead side in eight games with the only goal in the sixty-third minute. The smallest and quietest crowd of the season, a miserly 13,092, bothered to witness the visit of Clydebank the following week. There was no sign of Mo Johnston as Celtic won 3-0 with two goals from Brian McClair, one a penalty-kick, and a single from Alan McInally.

Both were on target again a week later in a 3-2 victory over Hamilton Accies at Douglas Park. McInally struck in the tenth minute and, sixty seconds later, McClair did likewise. Gerry Collins, Tommy Burns' best pal, pulled one back on the half-hour mark before Owen Archdeacon restored the two-goal advantage just before the interval. Davie Hay, with the fourth Old Firm league game against Rangers only a week away, decided to give Mo Johnston the opportunity get some much-needed match practice and sent him on for Archdeacon. Johnston saw Kevin McKee score for Accies as the game petered out at 3-2 for the champions.

Davie Hay had been left raging at the woefully timid performance from his team in the New Year's Day defeat against Rangers. He demanded improvements this time around. 'This was a must-win game for us,' said Hay. 'If you have to motivate players for an occasion like this, then they are in the wrong profession. Old Firm games were always special and players can become heroes with the fans forever for doing something special in these encounters. I asked the players if they wanted to be remembered for the showing back in January. They knew they had let themselves, the club and the fans down. You could say we were well up for the task by the time kick-off came around.'

Mo Johnston, now without a goal in eight games, came the closest to breaking the deadlock early in the conflict with a cute back-flick that beat Chris Woods, but carried just over the crossbar. With the troublesome wind prevailing, Johnston then attempted an audacious effort from wide left and Woods had to scramble back to his near post to grasp the ball as it wickedly changed direction in flight. Rangers thought they had scored the opener when a Davie Cooper right-wing corner-kick sailed over Pat Bonner straight into the net, but referee Bob Valentine spotted an infringement by Robert Fleck on the keeper.

There was a curious moment in the first-half when Graeme Souness was awarded a free-kick while being persistently challenged by Mo Johnston. The strutting Rangers gaffer grinned theatrically at the fans in the Jungle and made the gesture that he had Johnston in his back pocket. That triggered the obvious response from the vocal Celtic support. Eleven minutes from half-time, Souness' smile became a scowl as the referee awarded Celtic a penalty-kick. There was no arguing with the decision. Wood flapped at a high ball as Derek Whyte nodded into the congested penalty area. The ball dropped to Brian McClair, who swivelled to fire a snap-shot towards the top left-hand corner. Left-back Stuart Munro showed excellent goalkeeping reflexes to punch the effort over the bar.

McClair blitzed the ball to Woods' right as the keeper took off for his left. And McClair staged an action replay only moments later when Valentine again pointed to the spot. On this occasion, the lumbering Terry Butcher was almost comically slow in his challenge on Johnston as he bowled over the quickfire striker. Inevitably, the ref gave the award and McClair thrashed the ball past Woods, hitting it to the identical area as the previous one. An invader managed to get onto the field to remonstrate with the Celt who was asked afterwards what the fan had said. McClair, totally non-plussed, answered, 'I don't know. He doesn't speak my language.'

A belligerent Souness glowered at referee Valentine and his linesmen as they came off at the interval. He was going through the motions of shepherding his own players towards the tunnel, but his glare didn't waver from the match official. He wasn't smiling, either, in the second-half when the ref booked him for a bad-tempered barge into the back of Peter Grant. However, Rangers did momentarily show they could yet threaten Celtic's unbeaten home record when, eight minutes into the second period, they pulled one back. Davie Cooper breezed past Danny McGrain and picked out Ally McCoist on the six-yard line. McCoist couldn't miss. Johnston was in a similar situation shortly afterwards, but managed to blaze the ball wildly over the bar with only Woods to beat. It was an uncharacteristic miss from a player, who, although in dispute with the club, was putting himself about with a fair degree of zest.

Davie Hay sent on Owen Archdeacon for Alan McInally as he went for the killer third goal. Near the end, Johnston got clear again and raced into the box where he was flattened by a crude, foot-up challenge from Woods. The striker writhed in agony as the Celtic fans stuck up the chorus of 'Mo, Mo, Super Mo.' They would be using an entirely different adjective when he next stepped onto Celtic Park in an Old Firm confrontation two years later.

The scoring came to an end in the fading moments after an almighty mix-up between Woods and Jimmy Nicholl, the Northern Ireland international right-back who had been brought back to Ibrox by Souness from West Brom that season. Woods and Nicholl deliberated over the deadball effort and got their wires well and truly crossed. The keeper knocked it forward and that was all the speedy Archdeacon required to nick in and propel the ball goalwards and, with a fair degree of delight, follow it into the net. It ended 3-1 and Davie Hay said, 'That was a lot more like it. The players got in about it, made their presence felt and competed. We moved well up front, stretched Rangers and I don't think anyone can argue we deserved to win.'

Rangers, though, were still favourites to lift the title for the first time since 1977/78. Celtic simply had to push them all the way to the wire. Mo Johnston at last got on the scoresheet when Celtic overcame Hibs 4-1 at Easter Road a week after the win over Rangers. Ex-Celt George McCluskey fired the Edinburgh side into a third-minute lead, but Alan McInally wiped that out two minutes before the turnaround and Johnston, Paul McStay and Brian McClair struck with three goals in a devastating fifteen-minute spell at the end.

The torch became a flicker a week later when Celtic dropped another point in a 1-1 draw with Dundee United in Glasgow. Once more, a late goal undid the champions. Brian McClair scored a clever solo effort in the sixty-seventh minute when he anticipated a long kick-out from Pat Bonner, gathered a flick, rounded Billy Thomson and rolled the ball home. Two minutes from the end, the Celtic defence was static when Paul Hegarty headed on David Bowman's straightforward throw-in and John Clark was in isolation as he steered in the leveller. On the same day, Rangers beat Clydebank 3-0 at Kilbowie.

On April 25, Celtic were due at Love Street, the venue of last season's title party. They turned up still looking for some divine intervention. Two goals from Brian McClair and one from Mo Johnston made certain of a 3-1 victory. Davie Hay had now seen his team hit a domestic total of one hundred goals for the season with McClair notching an incredible forty. Frank McGarvey got some mild applause when he scored Saints' consolation with his old club already three goals ahead. Rangers didn't falter against Hearts, winning 3-0 at Ibrox. It was getting tight.

Disastrously, Celtic handed the championship on a platter to Rangers a week later. In their last game of the campaign at home, they were expected to take care of Falkirk without too much fuss. They lost 2-1 and, unbelievably, the winning goal in the dying moments came from Jimmy Gilmour, the legendary Jimmy Johnstone's nephew. You couldn't make it up. Johnstone had said to his relative before the game, 'Noo, don't ye dae anythin' daft, ye hear?' Clearly, he wasn't listening to the advice from his uncle. Celtic were well warned there was a tremor in the vicinity when they conceded the opening goal in forty seconds. Crawford Baptie, a skyscraper of a centre-forward, nodded the ball into the path of Sam McGivern and he leathered it beyond Pat Bonner. Brian McClair equalised with a penalty-kick on the hour mark and Celtic pushed forward frantically for a winner.

With four minutes to go, Gilmour dragged the ball forward and tried a speculative effort from outside the box. It looked Bonner's ball all the way as he dived to his left. It dipped in front of the keeper and spun past his left hand. The 14,238 fans inside Celtic Park couldn't believe their eyes as the ball crossed the line, barely possessing enough steam to touch the net.

News was emanating from Pittodrie that Graeme Souness had been sensationally sent off in the first-half against Aberdeen. Indeed, the Rangers player/manager had been banished after two savage tackles each earned yellow cards. He walked in the thirty-third minute, but, shortly afterwards, Terry Butcher put the ten men ahead. Celtic fans, listing to their transistors, cheered when Brian Irvine equalised before half-time. Could they dare to hope for a Dons winner in the second-half? Joe Miller gave them hope with a drive that took a looping diversion and smashed against the post with Chris Woods helpless. Around the time Gilmour's tame attempt was bouncing past Bonner, Miller, from just about under the crossbar, headed over after a flick-on from Alex McLeish. Minutes later, Rangers celebrated their newly-won championship.

As their deliriously happy fans staged an impromptu pitch invasion, fuming Celtic supporters threw scarves onto the pitch in outright dejection. It was over. Celtic lost 1-0 in the last game of the campaign when Hearts' John Robertson cracked an eighth minute penalty-kick past Pat Bonner in Edinburgh.

Mo Johnston, Brian McClair, Danny McGrain, Alan McInally and Murdo MacLeod all bowed out of Celtic at the same time. Their contracts had expired and they were moving on.

So, too, was Davie Hay. He just didn't know it at the time.

CHAPTER TWENTY-SIX
FAREWELL, DAVIE...
HELLO AGAIN, BILLY

'We have decided that we must get rid of you as manager of the club. You can either resign or you can be sacked, but we would like you to resign. There will be compensation from the club.'

Davie Hay stared in disbelief at Jack McGinn, his chairman. Had he heard correctly? On the morning of May 20 1987, Hay had been at Parkhead to tidy up a few things after an admittedly disappointing season. He was looking at contract issues concerning Mo Johnston, Brian McClair and Alan McInally. He also informed the players that the proposed summer tour of Australia had been cancelled. He then discussed possible signing targets with chief scout John Kelman.

'Just the night before I had gone over to Brian McClair's house,' recalls Hay today. 'I made him the same offer that was on the table for Mo Johnston. Brian practically told me he would stay. At that stage, I had no idea that Mo was heading for France to sign for Nantes. I still wanted the opportunity to sit down with him and have a frank discussion. I had brought him to Celtic and I wanted him to remain at the club. An agent was at work, though. Obviously, I was keen for Brian to stay, too, because they had struck up a fabulous partnership and I could see us progressing with these guys in the team.

'The board had given me some money to spend and I immediately paid £450,000 for Manchester City centre-half Mick McCarthy. He was a no-nonsense type of defender and it was obvious we had required someone like that in the previous season. The board allowed me to negotiate his wages and, after a half-hour meeting in a hotel in Carlisle, he had agreed to £1,000-per-week as his basic pay. It was as easy as that. So, after signing Big Mick, I turned my attention to Mo and Brian. Alan McInally, too. He was undecided and I thought he would stay if I could get the chance to talk to him. I realised I wasn't going to get much time for relaxation in the summer.'

Then came the thirty-eight little words, delivered in hesitant tones from a clearly embarrassed chairman, that changed Davie Hay's life forever. 'My immediate emotion was that of disbelief,' said Hay. 'Why had nothing been said in the morning? Why hadn't there even been a hint of such action? Disbelief gave way to a feeling of being let down by the board I had gone out of my way to protect when the going got tough and the supporters were demanding answers about the lack of new signings and investment in the squad.'

Graeme Souness hadn't hesitated when he was asked about the reason for Rangers' turnaround in fortunes. Only minutes after the title triumph at Pittodrie, he faced the TV cameras and, without a pause, responded, 'The key feature was being able to go out and buy quality players. I was allowed to sign Terry Butcher and Chris Woods in the summer and add Graham Roberts at the turn of the year. I knew these guys were winners and I wanted them at Rangers Football Club. They were better professionals than the players who were at the club when I arrived.' Souness added ominously, 'There is no point in being successful and the money that comes with it goes into a bank just to collect interest. We're going to strengthen the team for the new season.'

Hay had been ready to meet the challenge head-on. Until the interruption of Jack McGinn and the Celtic board. 'After the initial setback, I have to admit bitterness set in. I couldn't help it, ' said Hay. 'I looked at the chairman and he was obviously uncomfortable with what he had just said. I had been very publicly betrayed. I had lost the job I loved.

'Celtic prided themselves in never having sacked a manager in their history and they didn't want to do so with their Centenary Year in 1988 coming up fast. They wanted me to quietly walk away and let everyone think I had quit. I stared back at the chairman and said, "No chance. If you want me out you will have to fire me." There was a long silence and I added, "Who's got my job? Who are you going to replace me with?" Jack was now looking distinctly ill at ease. He didn't want to answer that one. I wasn't about to drop to my knees and plead for my job. They had made a decision and, only a year after winning the championship, I was no longer the Celtic manager. Could you blame me for feeling bitter?

'I said at the time that it was like a death in the family. That, of course, was a gross exaggeration. I was hurt, though; badly hurt and humiliated by a board I had continually urged to look at the bigger picture and see what Rangers were doing and achieving across the city. Our age-old rivals were investing heavily in their playing resources and were bringing in quality from England.'

Hay, it should be remembered, underlined his loyalty to Celtic in 1986 when he knocked back a move to Hibs that would have just about doubled his Parkhead wages. Kenny Waugh, the millionaire chairman of the Edinburgh club, made the offer in the summer after the championship success, but Hay said thanks, but no thanks.

Looking back at the fateful day in May, Hay continued, 'No-one could ever accuse me of lacking ambition and there was no-one at Celtic Park more single-minded than me when it came to keeping Celtic at the pinnacle. However, when I needed the board to back me, they back-stabbed me, instead. Listen, I am a great advocate of nurturing your own talent and building for the future, but there are other times when you need a quick fix and you can only do that through sound purchases in the transfer market. And that costs money.

'There was a period when I didn't talk to Jack for about fortnight. That was after he said I would have to shell out from my own pocket to buy players such as Joe McLaughlin, Pat Nevin and Steve Clarke. Upon reflection, I realise a chairman and his manager should always have dialogue. But relations were strained at that stage and that didn't help. We should have been singing from the same hymn sheet, after all. However, on that May day I realised my four-year stint as Celtic manager was over. Once I had taken it all in, I asked the chairman about compensation. He told me the board hadn't worked that out yet, but he would get in touch. I reaffirmed that I would not resign and I left Parkhead in a bit of a daze.

'Remember, please, this was the same board of directors who allowed me to spend a club record £450,000 on a player just one week beforehand while also giving me a wage increase from £33,000 per year to £40,000 during the season. Those decisions surely suggested they had not lost faith in me. None of it made a lot of sense. I drove home and broke the news to my wife Catherine and she was clearly distraught. We talked things over with daughters Allison and Caroline and we were all emotionally drained, to put it mildly. I was in the public eye and, suddenly without warning, I was out of work. At first, I didn't want to leave the house. In those sort of circumstances, you don't want to meet anyone because there is nothing more to be said.

'My sacking was completely unexpected and, even now, I don't think too many of that particular board of directors can be proud of the way it was handled.'

Chairman McGinn didn't help when he revealed, 'Davie Hay is too nice for a manager.' Hay can laugh at that sentiment today. 'How would Jack know? Was he ever in the dressing room when I was having a go at the players? Was he a fly on the wall when a player was invited to have a "wee talk" in the manager's office? Oh, it happened, alright. Paul McStay, Tommy Burns, you name them and I would have a private chat with them if I didn't think they were performing as I expected a Celtic player should. I may have been perceived as being laidback, but there is an edge to me that is on display when I think the time is right. Too nice? Go and ask the players who played for me. They'll tell you a vastly different story.'

Davie Hay was left astounded by the suddenness in the change of his circumstances. In the morning, he was the manager of Celtic. In the afternoon, he was the ex-manager of Celtic. 'Just like that,' he said. 'I was shattered and I sat down in the early evening to watch the news on TV. I wanted to see how Celtic were handling the situation. Would they admit they had sacked me? Or would they attempt to fudge the issue? I switched on the TV and it was then, and only then, that I discovered Billy McNeill would be returning to Celtic as manager. I stared at the screen in disbelief. I was out, Billy was in and it all seemed to be done in a matter of hours.'

CHAPTER TWENTY-SEVEN
CAESAR IN PARADISE

Billy McNeill admits he was at the lowest point of his life. A proud man, he had just lost the manager's job at Aston Villa. And, for the first time in his life, he was in a dole queue and preparing to sign on at the Labour Exchange in Altrincham. The man known as 'Caesar' had joined the ranks of the unemployed and, at the age of forty-seven had little idea of what he would be doing to earn a living in the future.

Then the telephone rang at the Queen's Park apartment of McNeill's good friend Mike Jackson, his former Celtic team-mate of the late fifties and early sixties. McNeill was in Glasgow for a brief visit and was staying with Mike and his wife Pat. Only a few people had the knowledge that McNeill would be at the Glasgow south side residence of his pal. 'It's for you, Billy,' said Mike as he handed over the telephone receiver. Puzzled, McNeill accepted the instrument. The caller was Jack McGinn, the Celtic chairman.

'Answering that call would dramatically change the course of my life,' said McNeill. 'Jack asked briefly if he could see me for a chat. He didn't say why and I didn't ask. I told Jack I had only one thing left to do before I returned south and that was to take part in a recording session about the Lisbon Lions at Radio Clyde. So, when I was contacted, I told him of the arrangement and he hit on the idea of us meeting in the car park at Clydebank, near the radio station and not far from his home in Dumbarton. Nobody would ever suspect two men sitting in a car discussing something which would soon be banner headlines in all the newspapers.

'Jack immediately asked me if I would like to return to Celtic as manager. I had hoped this was his reason for wanting to talk to me. But I couldn't be sure. The way my luck had gone that year there was no sense in anticipating anything. He then began to detail what Celtic would offer me. I replied, "Jack, I'm not really interested in the details. You've asked me a question and the answer is, Yes. The next problem was that I had to meet the rest of the board and it had to be done secretly the next day. In a city like Glasgow, nothing in football can be kept quiet for long. I suggested that we assemble at the Jackson home. Mike and Pat were at work, so this wouldn't cause them any bother. The meeting went off just fine.

'The directors then had to face a situation with Davie Hay in which they had to say, "Sorry, but we have to make a change." The chairman had to speak to Davie, but the whole board were quite genuinely distressed about having to sack the manager. For my part, I had feelings for Davie as well. The easy thing for me to say was, "Thanks and, yes, I'll take the job". But I had just been booted myself, so I knew exactly how Davie would be feeling. He had my sympathy, but there was nothing more I could do.

'When I left the manager's job at Celtic I phoned to wish Davie Hay good luck. And when I moved back, I called him at his home to say I was sad about what had happened to him. He understood my position perfectly. I liked Davie as a person. Still do, as a matter of fact. I never had any argument with him. It's not the easiest thing in the world to accept you are out of a job. I also realised the board didn't find it straightforward while making the change. The fact that Davie is such a likeable man added to their discomfort.

'In truth, I could never see myself returning to Celtic, but I always hoped it would happen. Lots of friends said I would eventually get the job again, but I thought it was wishful thinking. When it did happen, it was so quick it was scarcely believable that my dream had come true. A lot of fans may have been confused by the fact that Davie was allowed to spend £450,000 on Mick McCarthy so soon before parting with the club. I never questioned the reasoning behind the move. I was simply happy at the way it had turned out for me. The decision leading up to Celtic offering me the job was momentous, as far as I was concerned. Many may think my move was well planned, but, believe me, it wasn't so. My return was exactly as I have said.'

There were still surprises in store, though, for the returning McNeill. 'When I arrived for the Press Conference when the news was announced, I realised right away the place had changed. Nothing material at that stage, but I felt it wasn't buzzing. I always believe that stadiums talk. Parkhead was saying nothing to me. It was dull, dreary and depressing. Part of the reason for this may have been the fact that a manager had just departed. There were also problems with players who were making noises about their contracts. There was an air of despondency.

'Later, I spent several hours talking to Tommy Craig, John Kelman and Neilly Mochan trying to get to grips with the problems. That was a long drawn-out period. Tommy, of course, was already with Celtic when I joined. He was worried about his position as assistant manager. One of the first things I did was to ring him to explain I was the manager. I arranged a chat and it was quickly apparent that Tommy would liked to have been a player at Parkhead, but never had the opportunity. Now he was delighted to be on the staff.

'Tommy was disillusioned. The Celtic that he had encountered in a short spell under Davie Hay was not the one he had visualised. I told him that, because of the speed of my switch back, I had not been able to consider what changes I should make at the club. However, I informed Tommy that if we could quickly develop an understanding, I saw no problems about him staying and working with me. Very quickly, we found there was a rapport between us.'

McNeill stressed, 'I knew the first season back was very important for me. It was necessary to achieve something. I'm not saying winning the league, but it was important to demonstrate to everyone that Celtic were on the way up. I also needed to reinforce my confidence. I had taken a hard knock at Aston Villa. I needed to show that I had recovered from it.'

CHAPTER TWENTY-EIGHT
STRIKING BACK

Celtic had been linked with a dramatic move for Charlie Nicholas as Billy McNeill attempted to put the jigsaw together before the club's Centenary Year in 1988. With the greatest of urgency, he needed to get at least one new striker in place. Frank McAvennie, at West Ham, had also been mentioned. Mo Johnston had quit for French club Nantes, Brian McClair had signed for Manchester United and Alan McInally joined him across the border after agreeing a deal with Aston Villa. The heart had been ripped out of the forward line.

McNeill eventually paid £350,000 to Motherwell for a youngster by the name of Andy Walker, who, with the greatest of respect, didn't quite match the star quality of Nicholas or McAvennie. Obviously, though, the Celtic boss was fighting the clock with the August 8 Premier League kick-off looming. He needed a new right-back, too, with evergreen Danny McGrain, at the age of thirty-seven, moving on a twelve-month contract to newly-relegated Hamilton Accies. A fee of £125,000 tempted Sheffield Wednesday into selling Republic of Ireland defender Chris Morris. Murdo MacLeod was on his way to Borussia Dortmund and McNeill found himself light in the midfield area. He bought Billy Stark from Aberdeen for £75,000.

In truth, the three signings - still well short of what Graeme Souness had paid for Terry Butcher alone a year ago - were not viewed as ticket-sellers.

Morris, Stark and Walker made their first appearances for their new club at Paradise in a friendly against Arsenal on August 1. Mick McCarthy, signed by Davie Hay, was sidelined with a stomach muscle injury. He was the lucky one. The London side romped to a one-sided 5-1 win in the glorious sunshine and, to make matters worse, Charlie Nicholas got the opening goal. Earlier in the day, McNeill had been likened to the Messiah, the man who had come back to lead Celtic out of the shadows cast by their Glasgow rivals. The task that lay ahead of him couldn't have been put more sharply in focus. It would be a long, hazardous journey back to glory.

McNeill said, 'Mick McCarthy is an important man now. There is no doubt that we need an experienced and dominant centre-half.' Ironically, McNeill was echoing the very words of Hay twelve months earlier.

Now it was time to get down to real business. Mark McGhee was handed the opportunity to annex a regular first team place with the striking department emptying at an all-too-hasty rate. The stocky forward, looking toned and slimmer after the summer break, underlined his determination with the first goal in the opening league fixture, a 4-0 victory over Morton at Cappielow. McGhee netted in the twelfth minute to settle the nerves and the Celtic fans were delighted to see Andy Walker add two more after the interval. With perfect timing, Billy Stark, viewed as a makeweight, notched the fourth goal. There was further good news when it was announced Rangers had drawn 1-1 with Dundee United at Ibrox.

Teeming rain cascaded around the east end of Glasgow when Billy McNeill made his return to competitive action the following Wednesday. Hearts, always dangerous and tricky customers, were in town and McGhee smashed in the only goal of the game three minutes from time. The Edinburgh side complained bitterly that referee Kevin O'Donnell had overlooked their claims for a penalty-kick when John Robertson went down after a challenge from Anton Rogan. Mysteriously, O'Donnell disappeared from the big-game rota shortly afterwards. Once more, there was a mighty cheer when the news came through from Easter Road that Souness and Co had lost 1-0 to Hibs with a young midfielder called John Collins netting the goal.

'It was absolutely crucial we kept the feelgood factor at a high level,' said Billy McNeill. 'Rangers had slipped up in their two games, but it was obvious they would come back off the ropes. No-one was being lured into a false sense of security at Celtic. After all, we had played only three hours of league football. It was nice to be three points ahead, though.'

Andy Walker hammered in another two goals as Celtic overwhelmed Motherwell 4-1 in Glasgow. Mark McGhee got the opener just after the half-hour mark and, whether by accident or design, the two new strikers were dovetailing as though they had been team-mates for years. Billy Stark may have been on the wrong side of thirty, but he, too, had been re-energised. He contributed another goal while Steve Kirk was the lone marksman for the visitors. It was a stroll for the Hoops against a Fir Park side who were left with only ten men with twenty minutes still to play after centre-half Craig Paterson was expelled. News came through from Pittodrie that Rangers had lost 2-0 to Aberdeen. There was joy unconfined among the Celtic support. There had been a shift in power of seismic proportions no-one could have predicted.

The League Cup interrupted the collection of league points on Wednesday August 19 when Forfar played their first game at Parkhead since 1951. Amazingly, Andy Walker hit his third double in four games as Celtic won 3-1 against their Angus opponents who had former Rangers goalkeeper Stewart Kennedy doing his best to repel Walker and Co. Billy McNeill's men hit their goals in the first-half. Stark, proving to be an absolute steal, added to Walker's brace while Kenny McDonald got the Station Park side's consolation via the penalty spot.

Celtic didn't see the next one coming as they lost 2-1 to Dunfermline at East End Park. That hadn't been in the script. The warning lights were flashing in only two minutes when Craig Robertson thumped in the opening goal in the second minute. Andy Walker levelled with a penalty-kick before the interval and then had cruel luck with a shot that crashed against the underside of the bar. Eric Ferguson claimed the winner just before the hour mark and Billy McNeill realised Mick McCarthy would have to swiftly overcome his injury and get into the backline to shore up a wobbly defence. Rangers got back on track, beating Falkirk 4-0 at Ibrox with new boy Mark Falco, bought from Watford for £400,000, netting one of the goals.

'It was imperative, absolutely imperative, that we got back to winning ways as quickly as possible,' said Billy McNeill. 'The Dunfermline result was sore, but I had to make sure it didn't knock the confidence of a team still gelling together.'

Dumbarton in the League Cup at Boghead Park was an obvious banana skin, but Celtic neatly side-stepped it with the guidance of Tommy Burns who ran the show as he opened the scoring just before the half-hour mark while Billy Stark, with two, Andy Walker and Mark McGhee chipped in with the others. David Martin spoiled Allen McKnight's debut in goal. The future Northern Ireland international, signed from Distillery the previous year, got his chance after Pat Bonner pulled out with a virus.

The twenty-three year old was still in charge of net-minding duties when the first Glasgow derby game of the season took place at Celtic Park on a sunny, windless afternoon on August 29. Rangers, with Graeme Souness in midfield, hardly got a chance to settle into proceedings when Chris Woods was being invited to drag the ball from the back of his net. Only four minutes were on the clock when Celtic scored a goal of exquisite quality. Tommy Burns, that most casual of craftsmen, slid a cunning pass to Mark McGhee, running clear on the right. He delivered an excellent pass that was dummied by Andy Walker and fell perfectly for Billy Stark, who imperturbably glided a low side-foot effort away from the Ibrox keeper from the edge of the box.

That acted as the catalyst for a bad-tempered encounter and referee

Davie Syme booked Souness on the half-hour mark. It didn't get much better for the impulsive Rangers player/manager in the fifty-fourth minute when he was ordered off after a reckless assault on Celtic's goalscorer Billy Stark. One report stated, 'His late, high tackle almost removed Stark's body from his legs.' Celtic came close to doubling their advantage when Ian McCall, just bought by the Ibrox side for £150,000 from Dunfermline, directed a cross onto his own post. That might have taken some explaining afterwards. Graham Roberts endeared himself to no-one by refusing to shake hands with any of his opponents following the final whistle.

Celtic's interest in the League Cup ended abruptly in midweek when a sixtieth-minute shot from Aberdeen midfielder Jim Bett exploded behind Allen McKnight for the only goal of the game at Pittodrie. 'We'll just have to concentrate on a league and Cup double,' said Billy McNeill, without the trace of a smile. He meant it.

The manager continued to keep faith in McKnight although Pat Bonner was now fit for selection. The agile shotstopper and his counterpart Billy Thomson were the main reasons the next game against Dundee United at Tannadice was completed without a goal. McKnight was unbeatable and made a handful of fine saves, one, in particular, from a header by John Holt. Billy McNeill commented, 'It was a great game although there were no goals, but this could be partly due to the tough programme both sides have had in recent weeks.'

McNeill had now seen his side score only one goal in three games and there was the fear that the contribution from Andy Walker and Mark McGhee could dry up. The Celtic manager didn't have an excess of riches in this department and there were persistent rumours he was about to sign Charlie Nicholas, who wasn't getting a consistent start from manager George Graham at Arsenal. McNeill denied the speculation, but he did admit: 'We have to look at strengthening up front, that's obvious. We can't continue to rely on the same players to score the goals for us. I am working towards a solution.'

The lack of firepower was again in evidence a week later as Celtic relied on a strike from Tommy Burns to give them a 1-0 victory over Falkirk at Brockville. 'We seemed to want to walk the ball into the net rather than just have a go,' said McNeill. 'I thought we had a terrific first-half and the goal was first class, but I have to admit we were disappointing after the interval. I don't really know the reason for that, but it could have been caused by several things. I think the awkward wind had some effect, but we also had several young players who may have been looking ahead to their first experience of European competition with Borussia Dortmund due at our place in a few days' time. I also think the players allowed frustration to get to them. Having said that, I'm happy to take two points from a fixture which is never an easy one.'

Burns' goal was a rare right-footed effort and the smooth midfielder commented, 'I suppose the law of averages dictated I would eventually get one with that foot.'

Celtic's interest in Europe was short, sharp and, ultimately, painful. Murdo MacLeod, returning to Celtic Park for the first time since penning a deal with the German giants, was given a standing ovation by the 41,404 fans before the UEFA Cup First Round first leg tie. When it got down to the serious stuff, McNeill's youngsters gave a reasonable account of themselves. Andy Walker, who along with Allen McKnight, Chris Morris, Anton Rogan and substitute Owen Archdeacon, was making his debut at this level, opened the scoring from close range in the fourth minute.

A momentary lapse in concentration by Roy Aitken had disastrous consequences in the sixty-fourth minute. Aitken, making his fortieth European appearance and playing in central defence with Mick McCarthy still sidelined, was caught in possession by the nippy Frank Mill, who raced through to lash the ball wide of the exposed McKnight. Celtic actually had a copious amount of possession, but failed to convert it into goals. However, defender Derek Whyte managed to force home the winner a minute from the end when an Archdeacon cross caused alarm in the Borussia Dortmund penalty area. A fortnight later, Celtic were out, but there was no shame in the team's display.

They were ahead on aggregate until the seventy-second minute when the defence failed to pick up Norbert Dickel at a Mill corner-kick and his header flew past McKnight. Celtic, with Mick McCarthy making his belated debut, piled forward in the knowledge they were facing the exit on the away goals rule. They left the back door open and Dickel netted a second four minutes from time. The 3,000 travelling fans remained behind after the full-time whistle to applaud the efforts of their emerging side at the Westfalen Stadium.

Earlier, on September 19, Celtic threw away a two-goal lead to draw 2-2 with Aberdeen in Glasgow. Joe Miller, yet again, punished his boyhood heroes by sizzling an angled drive past Allen McKnight for the equaliser in the last minute. Celtic had been coasting with an effort from Tommy Burns eight minutes before the break and another from Billy Stark shortly after the turnaround. But Peter Nicholas hauled one back on the hour mark before Miller, born in the shadow of Celtic Park, hammered in the point-saver for the Pittodrie outfit. Billy McNeill liked the look of the youngster.

Celtic struggled to overcome St Mirren at Love Street a week later. Their inability to capitalise on their opportunities was highlighted once more. It was left to defender Derek Whyte to get the only goal of the game with a well-placed shot following a Tommy Burns corner-kick only fifteen minutes from time. On the same afternoon, Rangers ran amok against Morton at Ibrox, winning 7-0 with a pair of hat-tricks from Ally McCoist and Mark Falco. Robert Fleck contributed the other goal. They weren't going to give up their title without a fight.

Billy McNeill realised it was essential to add to his team's goal threat and on Friday, October 2 he finally persuaded West Ham boss John Lyall to sell Frank McAvennie. The Celtic board didn't have too many options when it came to haggling with the London side; Rangers were in the throes of completing the Scottish record transfer of £1million for Richard Gough from Spurs on the same day. The directors had to dig deep to fund McNeill's ambitions and they signed the biggest cheque in the club's history, £750,000 being required to prise the charismatic striker away from Upton Park.

McAvennie, at twenty-seven, was realising his dream later than anticipated and he said, 'I am absolutely delighted. Celtic, more than any other, are the club I have always wanted to play for. I can't wait to get started.'

McNeill, who had flown south with chairman Jack McGinn to make sure the deal was sealed and delivered, added, 'Frank is exactly what we need and I can tell you he had no hesitation in signing. My only regret is that we did not manage to sign him earlier.'

West Ham manager Lyall, who paid £340,000 to St Mirren for the forward only two years earlier, lamented, 'We didn't want him to go and we're sorry to lose Frank, but he wanted so much to play for Celtic and that outweighed everything else.'

McAvennie was pitched into the first team twenty-four hours later, but his arrival failed to spark a victory with Celtic being held to a 1-1 draw at home by Hibs. A crowd of 31,805 turned out to welcome McAvennie and Mick McCarthy, who, at long last, was making his debut at Parkhead. McAvennie, who had scored twenty-six goals in his first season in England, but had struggled with only seven a year later, was eager to make up for lost time. With the score standing at 1-1, he thought he had hit the winner when he blazed a drive past Alan Rough, but his effort thundered against the underside of the crossbar and bounced to safety. Andy Walker got the one that mattered with a glancing header in the fourth minute. However, that was nullified when Andy Watson struck with eleven minutes remaining.

Celtic had to be content with another 1-1 draw a few days later against Dundee at Dens Park. Frank McAvennie teamed up with Andy Walker again to spearhead the attack and there were signs they were beginning to understand each other's style of play. However, in treacherous conditions with the rain pouring down incessantly, there were few opportunities for them to shine. Walker got Celtic's goal in the seventieth minute to equalise an effort from Ian Angus just before the interval. The game turned when Billy McNeill sent on substitutes Owen Archdeacon and Tony Shepherd for the toiling Peter Grant and Billy Stark after the hour mark.

'Nothing changes,' said the Celtic manager. 'I always seem to get it tough up here.' Possibly, his thoughts were drifting back to an ill-fated game in 1979/80 when his big friend Tommy Gemmell sat in the opposite dug-out.

However, McAvennie's big moment was merely delayed another three days when he notched one in a 3-1 victory over Morton in Glasgow. It was a storming start by Celtic who were three goals ahead in the first nineteen minutes with Andy Walker and Derek Whyte also on target. Walker could even afford the luxury of a dreadful penalty-kick miss as he cleared the target area with a wayward effort. Alex O'Hara gave the small pocket of travelling Cappielow fans something to cheer just before half-time. Once again, the tannoy announcer sent the home fans heading for the exits with outsize grins on their faces with the news that Rangers, with big-money Richard Gough making his debut, had lost 1-0 to Dundee United at Tannadice. Four defeats in twelve games was not part of the Ibrox master plan for total dominance of Scottish football.

On October 17 at Ibrox, there were some of the most remarkable scenes ever witnessed in a Celtic v Rangers engagement as Rangers came from two goals behind to secure a last-gasp draw. However, the actual football was almost brushed aside during an explosive, outrageous derby in front of 44,000 baying fans. Hell was unleashed in the eleventh minute when Ibrox keeper Chris Woods, picking up a pass-back from Jimmy Phillips, reacted angrily to a challenge from Frank McAvennie. They squared up, Woods grabbed the Celt by the throat and referee Jim Duncan raced to take action. Terry Butcher needlessly joined in to barge McAvennie to the ground and, unfortunately, the match official missed Graham Roberts' sneaky involvement. Woods and McAvennie were banished, Butcher was booked and Roberts escaped completely. He took over in goal from Woods and was picking the ball out of the net in the thirty-third minute when Andy Walker sent a low angled shot under his collapsing body. Butcher, not having his happiest day, lobbed the ball over the emergency keeper two minutes later as he was put under pressure from Peter Grant chasing a through ball from Walker.

Celtic were well in control and Butcher, in the midst of throwing the world's longest tantrum, was red-carded following a swipe at Allen McKnight during a skirmish after a high ball had dropped into the box. A newspaper noted, 'Butcher flattened McKnight with a fist. Quite rightly, he was sent off.'

In the midst of the carnage, Celtic should have pressed home their advantage. Remarkably, they didn't and they paid the price. Rangers tried to bolster their backline by taking off Mark Falco and putting on Avi Cohen, the Israeli international recently recruited from Liverpool. It was a damage-limitation exercise by Graeme Souness who must have been as amazed as anyone when a sixty-fifth minute effort from Ally McCoist glanced off a post and into the Celtic net. He would have been even more astonished when Richard Gough scrambled in a last-minute leveller. McKnight was badly at fault as Ian Durrant delivered a right-wing cross into a packed penalty area. A safe pair of hands would have solved the problem in an instant, but the keeper hesitated, was slow to react and Gough forced the ball home.

Billy McNeill was livid. The Celtic manager rarely criticised his players in public, but I knew McKnight, in his eyes, was the culprit for a dropped point. I met the Hoops boss a couple of days later for lunch and, as you might expect, we were chatting about the game. He was still furious. McKnight was immediately dropped and played only three more league games that season, ironically one of them was against Rangers while Pat Bonner was injured. Football can be an extremely harsh game.

The fall-out of the Ibrox skirmish was just as remarkable. McAvennie, Woods, Butcher and Roberts were charged with 'conduct likely to provoke a breach of the peace.' A special referee's report was also ordered by the SFA. All four players denied the charges and were present during their trial in April the following year. There was a not guilty verdict for McAvennie while Roberts was not proven, Woods was fined £500 and Butcher £250. A newspaper reporter commented, 'I wonder if these players, especially those who have come from England, fully understand the powderkeg situation they are in every time they take part in an Old Firm game. If not, then it is time for someone with a sense of responsibility to spell it out in full.'

A week after the Ibrox catastrophe, Billy McNeill suffered his first competitive defeat at Celtic Park since returning as manager. He gave a first team opportunity to young Dugald McCarrison in place of the suspended Frank McAvennie and the gamble didn't pay off. Dundee United left Glasgow with the points after a 2-1 win. All three goals arrived in a dramatic ten-minute spell at the end of what had been a fairly dull encounter. John Clark and Iain Ferguson netted for the Tayside men while Tony Shepherd struck for the Hoops in the last minute. McCarrison played only three more first team games and eventually moved to Kilmarnock.

Falkirk visited the east end of Glasgow on a bleak autumn evening on October 28 and Celtic had to scrap all the way for a 3-2 win with Billy Stark scoring twice after Owen Archdeacon set the ball rolling on the half-hour mark. Billy McNeill's side continued to give away late goals and Ray Stewart and Roddie Manley netted for the Brockville side in the last five minutes. 'All sorts of questions were being asked about the team,' said McNeill. 'The fans were making their demands. This was when I had to exercise the determination to do what I thought was right. There had been loud and persistent chanting from the crowd during the last couple of games demanding that I sign Charlie Nicholas. I realised that this was the classic time for a weak manager to surrender. I stood firm.'

Importantly, though, Celtic had moved to within three points of leaders Hearts. Three days later it was the Hoops' turn to grab a vital late goal when Frank McAvennie pounced to score in the 1-0 win over Aberdeen at Pittodrie. Chris Morris crossed from the right and McAvennie cracked the ball past Jim Leighton in the seventy-second minute.

It was a vital victory with a visit to Hearts next in the hectic schedule. It was a 29,000 sell-out for the November 7 clash and Celtic gained an extremely creditable 1-1 draw after seeing Mick McCarthy sent off ten minutes after the interval. They were already trailing to a curling effort from John Colquhoun five minutes before the break. McCarthy, earlier booked for handball, was deemed to have body-checked John Robertson and referee Jim McCluskey flashed the red card at the Republic of Ireland international defender. It seemed harsh treatment and possibly justice was done twelve minutes from the end when Roy Aitken picked out Mark McGhee with a splendid cross and the striker sent a header flying towards its destination.

Billy McNeill, as he had proved in his capture of McAvennie, was nothing if not persistent. He had been knocked back three times by Aberdeen in his pursuit of Joe Miller, but he still viewed the nineteen-year old as an enterprising player who had the capacity to supply crosses for Frank McAvennie, Mark McGhee and Andy Walker. He knew Miller could add goals, too. In fact, the Dons had mainly utilised his skills playing off the main striker through the middle. His strike-rate against Celtic alone proved his ability in this role. On November 13, McNeill slapped in a £650,000 bid for the player and was delighted when the Pittodrie board decided to accept. Not so happy was Alex Ferguson at Manchester United who believed he had a 'gentleman's agreement' in place with his former club to be allowed the first opportunity to sign Miller. The Dons hierarchy denied all knowledge of such an arrangement and Miller was on his way back to the east end of Glasgow.

Like McAvennie before him, Miller didn't have too long to wait to make his first team debut. Billy McNeill put him straight into the team for the league game against Dundee at Parkhead the following day. It proved to be a sound decision. A crowd of 31,466 turned out to see the player who had given their favourites so much grief in recent seasons. They weren't disappointed. Andy Walker had Celtic 2-0 up inside five pulverising minutes and Miller took centre stage on the hour mark when McAvennie set him up for his debut goal. McAvennie then added two more and one Sunday newspaper immediately nicknamed the attacking trio as the Three Musketeers.

Miller thanked team-mate Chris Morris for his help during his baptism. He said, 'I was nervous at first, but Chris told me to keep talking to him during the game and that relaxed me. He really helped me get over that first hurdle and I owe him.'

A beaming Billy McNeill said, 'Joe Miller will prove to be a good buy for this club, I have no doubt about that. None whatsoever. Very quickly he confirmed that Parkhead was the place for him to play. His enthusiasm spread throughout the team and his presence will give us all a lift at an important stage of the campaign. He'll be money well spent.'

Joe Miller dazzled again in midweek as Celtic beat Motherwell 2-0 at Fir Park. A good run down the right in the thirty-third minute was completed with an impeccable cross and Andy Walker scored with a header against his old club. Derek Whyte got the second shortly after the break with a twenty-yard screamer past Cammy Duncan. On the same evening, Rangers suffered their first defeat at Ibrox in twenty-five matches when a goal from Willie Miller gave Aberdeen a 1-0 win. Terry Butcher, back after his three-game suspension, was carried off after eight minutes with a broken leg.

Celtic indulged in a bit of shooting practice in the next game as they beat Dunfermline 4-0 at Celtic Park. Andy Walker rattled two penalty-kicks beyond the overworked Ian Westwater while Billy Stark and Frank McAvennie also got on the scoresheet. 'That's eleven goals scored and none lost in the past three games,' said Billy McNeill. 'I've got to be happy with that. The forwards are scoring goals, the midfield is ticking over and the defence is doing its job. We're looking very settled and we've come a long way since the start of the season in August.'

Peter Grant scored his first goal of the campaign in a 1-0 win over St Mirren on a cold and misty evening on November 25 in Glasgow while Frank McAvennie took over the marksman's duties in a single-goal victory over Hibs in Edinburgh three days later. The blond striker accepted a pass from Paul McStay to hammer a twenty-first minute shot past the Easter Road side's new goalkeeper, Andy Goram, recently purchased for £325,00 from Oldham.

On a bitterly cold evening on Monday November 30, a crowd of 42,464 turned out to say farewell to Davie Provan. Nottingham Forest provided the opposition and won 3-1, but the scoreline was irrelevant. The popular former Celt came out to a tumultuous welcome and, after eight minutes of action, he handed his jersey to Joe Miller, the new pin-up on the right wing. Kenny Dalglish turned out for the Hoops after an absence of ten years and Brian Clough even took time to plant a kiss on Provan's cheek. It was a special occasion for a special player.

Frank McAvennie must have been inspired by playing alongside his boyhood idol Dalglish against Forest because he was on fire against Morton a few days later. Celtic won 4-0 in freezing cold conditions in barren Greenock and McAvennie rattled all four behind Davie Wylie. It was a sparkling performance from McAvennie and Billy McNeill enthused, 'When he's playing like that, there's nothing anyone can do to stop him. He sniffs out goals. His movement all along the line is extraordinary, his first touch is good, he's brave and he's not afraid to have a go at goal.'

Celtic had four league games left to go in December and Hearts, Aberdeen and Dundee United were three of the teams waiting for them before the turn of the year. Falkirk were also in the mix. A crowd of 44,000 at Parkhead thought their favourites had blown it against the Tynecastle side who were leading 2-0 through goals from John Robertson and Mike Galloway, who would later be signed by Billy McNeill. However, there was a never-say-die spirit about the team and they came back to score twice through Andy Walker and Paul McStay, in the last minute. 'As long as I score the important ones, I'll be happy,' said McStay. Celtic could have done with McStay, or anyone, to hit the target when Aberdeen provided the opposition on December 19. The game ended goalless and Celtic found it impossible to penetrate the defiant Dons back-line of Stewart McKimmie, Alex McLeish, Willie Miller and David Robertson.

Celtic extended their unbeaten run to twelve games when they beat Falkirk 2-0 at Brockville. Andy Walker claimed his twentieth goal of the season just before the hour mark. Paul McStay made certain a minute from time with a glorious shot that left Gordon Marshall without an earthly. The opposing goalkeeper was the main reason the Hoops didn't rack up a few goals and, four years later, he would sign for Celtic.

The Boxing Day meeting with Dundee United at Tannadice was the one that caught everyone's imagination. Celtic hadn't beaten the Tayside team on their own pitch since October 1984 and Billy McNeill said, 'It's time we did something about that. If we are going to win this league, then this is one of the games from which we have to get both points.' Andy Walker netted with a penalty-kick and Iain Ferguson claimed one for Jim McLean's team. However, with only a minute left to go, Chris Morris, who had been putting in a good shift throughout the afternoon, hammered down the wing one last time before slinging over a deep cross. Joe Miller, with immaculate timing, took off Superman-style and bulleted in the winner.

'We're looking good,' said McNeill, 'but I'm too old and experienced to take anything for granted. We've got a huge year ahead of us and, quite simply, we have to deliver. Celtic don't do second-best and particularly not during our Centenary Year. If we apply ourselves properly, remain focused and committed, then we might have something to celebrate. But there's a long way to go.'

CHAPTER TWENTY-NINE
CONGRATULATIONS, CENTURY BHOYS

'Happy birthday Dear Celtic...happy birthday to yoooooooooou.' Arms aloft, Frank McAvennie spun away after tucking the ball into the Rangers net for the second time and the delirious Hoops fans in the 60,800 crowd burst as one into booming voice. Never has the age-old anniversary ditty been warbled so thunderously out of tune by so many at the same time. But it was sweet music all the same.

'When I scored to make it 2-0, the whole stadium erupted,' said McAvennie. 'Everyone seemed to be singing and if there was anyone who did not know this was a special year for the club, they certainly knew at that moment.'

Winning the first Glasgow derby encounter on January 2 was the ideal way for Celtic to kick off the Centenary Year. The triumph put Billy McNeill's men seven points ahead in the league although Rangers had a game in hand. However, to many onlookers, the New Year victory was the one that made the Celtic supporters believe that history was in the making. Graeme Souness had once again reinforced his squad with the £500,000 signing of Aston Villa winger Mark Walters, adding him to other English imports such as Trevor Francis and Ray Wilkins who had arrived earlier in the season.

All were in attendance to be assailed by the Celtic fans' clamorous rendition of the feelgood jingle. They didn't join in. Billy McNeill said, 'I told my players before the game this was the ideal opportunity for us to move further ahead in the title race and I warned them that the exact opposite would be said in the Rangers dressing room. They would want to claw back the deficit and they would see this as an ideal opportunity. But I reminded the players of the fact that we had already beaten them at our place and drawn with them at Ibrox when we really should have won. Victory in this one could very well have a demoralising effect on them.'

Celtic opened the scoring a minute from half-time when Paul McStay dispatched a long, raking pass into the tracks of the raiding Chris Morris on the right. The full-back lashed a low cross into the penalty area and McAvennie, with precision timing, found a pocket of space as he fired the ball behind Chris Woods. It remained that way until eight minutes from the end. Shortly beforehand, Woods had injured a shoulder in an accidental mid-air collision with Lex Baillie, ironically, the son of former Rangers centre-half Dougie. Graham Roberts, as he had done in the 2-2 draw at Ibrox after his team-mate had seen red, went into goal. Moments later, McAvennie sent a header spiraling past him and victory was secure.

'I felt that was one of the more convincing wins that Celtic had over Rangers,' viewed McNeill. 'I believed from then onwards that winning the league was in our own hands. I never at any time said to the players during the season that we would be champions - even when this was being shouted by others from the rooftops. But, privately, I was sure it was in the bag if we kept our cool. I adopted the style of discussing only our next game and never projecting any farther than this. All we needed to do was keep winning and nobody could touch us. The victory over Rangers, and the style of it, was the biggest morale boost we could have had.'

A week later, Celtic were strangely subdued at Love Street where St.Mirren keeper Campbell Money gifted them their goal in a 1-1 stalemate. Chris Morris whooshed over a cross from the right and the normally-reliable Paisley custodian palmed the ball into his own net. However, Celtic swiftly got back on track with a 2-0 victory over Hibs at Celtic Park where two first-half strikes from Paul McStay and Joe Miller left Andy Goram helpless. On February 6, Celtic struggled against Motherwell at Fir Park, but still managed to chip away for a 1-0 win. Andy Walker hit his first goal since Boxing Day to end his personal drought.

'No-one will do us any favours on the league run-in and Motherwell typified that,' said Billy McNeill. 'They are involved in a battle of their own at the other end of the table and it was evident they came to Parkhead looking for a draw. They have a very solid defence and I was pleased that we still made several chances although we only took one of them.'

The 25,035 crowd groaned in unison when, only minutes into the action, Fraser Wishart passed the ball back to his goalkeeper - the Motherwell defender was about five yards inside the Celtic half at the time. 'That told us what to expect for the rest of the game,' added McNeill. 'They certainly weren't at our place to add to the entertainment value.' The only goal arrived just after the hour mark when Frank McAvennie nodded down a long throw-in from Roy Aitken and Walker applied the killer touch.

Celtic were gaining a reputation as a team which would fight tooth and nail until the last shrill of the referee's whistle and so it proved again in the 2-1 victory over Dundee at Dens Park on February 13. It was scoreless in the first-half before Chris Morris struck his first goal for the club four minutes after the break. The Cornish-born defender curled a magnificent free-kick round the Dundee defensive wall from twenty yards. Goalkeeper Bobby Geddes could only stand and watch in admiration. Two minutes later, it was all-square again when Ian Angus knocked one in from close range. Only two minutes remained when

Morris flighted over another dangerous deadball and Frank McAvennie snapped a header past Geddes. Another two points were in the bag.

Billy McNeill's men left it even later before claiming a 1-0 win over Morton at Parkhead in front of 23,170 frustrated fans. Celtic had battered away at the Cappielow side's goal all afternoon without luck. Then, with only thirty seconds left on the clock, McAvennie swept through and was upended by goalkeeper Davie Wylie. Referee Brian Miller pointed to the spot and was immediately surrounded by angry Morton players. After booking three of the protesters, he blew for the kick to be taken and Roy Aitken smashed a vicious effort into the net. Strangely, it was to be Aitken's only goal of the league campaign.

'The single-mindedness of the players was brilliant,' said McNeill. 'At this point, I was realising the full extent of the progress Celtic had made since the start of the season. Young players had matured and we were now a hardened crew.'

Frank McAvennie netted twice in the 4-0 stroll past Dunfermline at East End Park in the next game. 'If there's a better front player than Frank in Scotland this season, I have yet to see him,' offered Billy McNeill in an obvious side-swipe at Scotland manager Andy Roxburgh who had snubbed McAvennie for an international get-together. Roxburgh named forty-three players in the squad, but somehow managed to overlook the player who had scored thirteen goals since signing from West Ham in October. Andy Walker and Billy Stark joined McAvennie on the scoresheet in Fife.

Celtic were now four points ahead of Rangers with both teams having played thirty-four games. McNeill added, 'We didn't play at all well in February, although we did get the results. Now we've started March with a good performance and a victory, so I couldn't be more delighted.'

Decision Day was beckoning and on Sunday March 20, with an enormous TV audience tuning in, Billy McNeill took his players to Ibrox for the fourth and final league meeting of the campaign against the most bitter of rivals. Graeme Souness was still making optimistic noises, as he had every right to do, but his words were beginning to ring a little hollow. After this set-to, they sounded as though they were bouncing around an echo chamber. Celtic triumphed 2-1 to take their seventh out of a possible eight points from the Ibrox side and the championship was surely heading towards the east end of Glasgow. Rangers, as expected, expended a lot of energy into attempting to delay the inevitable.

However, a magical moment from Paul McStay shattered their resistance and drew admiring gasps from a noisy visiting support in the 43,650 audience. The strutting midfielder hit a shot of such power and accuracy from twenty yards that Chris Woods had no entitlement to even attempt to keep the ball out of the net. The Rangers keeper stretched to his fullest extent, but his Celtic-inflicted misery continued as the shot sped past him in the sixty-seventh minute. It was a fabulous left-foot strike, but, astonishingly, Rangers dragged themselves back into the game seven minutes later. Full-back Jan Bartram pounced on the edge of the box after a right-wing free-kick from Derek Ferguson had only partially been cleared by Lex Baillie. The header, admittedly under pressure, went straight to the Dane. He swung a foot at it, made excellent contact and Pat Bonner was beaten low down at his left as the ball bounced past him.

The winning goal came in the seventy-ninth minute after some aerial ping-pong in the Ibrox penalty box ended with the quick-thinking Andy Walker chesting the ball beyond a startled Woods. Tommy Burns swung in a delightful left-footed corner from the right, Anton Rogan came in powerfully to direct the ball goal-wards and nimble Walker improvised to direct it home from six yards. They all count. A delighted McNeill said, 'I am particularly satisfied with this victory as Rangers played so well. We had to work hard throughout and I thought my players were immense.'

Celtic then had to be content with a goalless draw with Dundee United in Glasgow, but McNeill was not too despondent about the loss of a point to menacing opponents. 'That's twelve games we've played and had nine clean sheets,' he pointed out. 'We've conceded only three goals over that period. I think we have learned how to become hard to beat.' McNeill had set about re-organising his back-lot immediately after they shipped five against Arsenal even before the official start to the season. His endeavours were proving worthwhile.

Celtic's relentless march towards the championship took them north on March 30 where an old friend was waiting to line up against them. Charlie Nicholas had, indeed, returned to Scottish football, but not to the east end of Glasgow as so many had anticipated and forecast. Instead, he had swapped Arsenal for Aberdeen. Could he prevent his old chums from racking up their twenty-eighth game without defeat? Could he derail the title charge? The answer to both questions was a resounding 'No'. The only goal of the game arrived on the hour mark and it was an effort straight from the Barrowfield training ground. Joe Miller swung over a corner-kick, Anton Rogan met it solidly with his head and Andy Walker volleyed an unstoppable drive into the net. It was nervy stuff as the Dons, with Nicholas trying as hard as anyone, attempted to get a share of the points. Frank McAvennie and Paul McStay twice put the ball behind Jim Leighton, but referee Alan Ferguson ruled them both out for offside. It finished 1-0 and Celtic were now seven points ahead of Rangers with only seven games left.

Celtic overcame Hibs 2-0 at Easter Road with goals from Peter Grant and Andy Walker in each half and one newspaper scribe believed the title should have been handed over there and then. He wrote, 'Celtic are going to be worthy champions. They ARE the best team in Scotland and their fans can start celebrating now, even though there are still five games to go. No-one is going to catch Billy McNeill's team.' There were more cheers at the end with the announcement big-spending Rangers had lost 2-1 to Hearts at Ibrox.

A crowd of 45,465 watched Celtic take on St Mirren in their attempt to move to within two points of the Premier League title. What a way to celebrate one hundred years in the entertainment business. Understandably, the players looked anxious and there was to be no relief when Andy Walker smashed a first-half penalty-kick straight at goalkeeper Campbell Money. However, the elusive forward atoned just before the hour mark when he finished off a speedy move between Joe Miller and Mark McGhee. The excellent Paul McStay made certain eleven minutes from time with an eighteen-yarder that flicked off Brian Martin on its way into the net.

Celtic had the opportunity to win the flag in the capital when they took on Hearts at Tynecastle, but their old foes refused to follow the script. Pat Bonner presented them with the opening goal in the twenty-fifth minute when he fumbled a long, high free-kick from Malcolm Murray at the feet of Mike Galloway. His future team-mate couldn't miss from only six yards out. Frank McAvennie beat Henry Smith with a low drive, but Kenny Black booted the ball off the line as Billy McNeill's men fought back. It just wasn't Celtic's evening when a shot from Gary Mackay in the seventy-first minute was deflected past Bonner. Mark McGhee pulled one back three minutes later, but the champagne would have to wait for another day. The celebrations were merely temporarily halted.

'Happy birthday Dear Celtic...happy birthday to yoooooooooou.' The Celtic fans had been practising and they were in full throttle when Dundee arrived at Parkhead on Saturday April 23. The record books show an attendance of 60,800, but there are those in the know who say you could add at least another 15,000 to that total. The Celtic board, for reasons known only to themselves, decided not to make the game all-ticket and fans were queuing up overnight to make sure they got in to join the party. Nothing and no-one was going to spoil this day. Referee Alister Huett blew to kick off the carnival and three minutes later he was re-centering the ball - Celtic had scored.

Chris Morris and Andy Walker sliced through the Dens Park rearguard and the adventurous right-back, a worthy successor to Danny McGrain, slammed the ball past the helpless Tom Carson. It remained that way until Walker hit two in a scintillating sixty-second spell. Frank McAvennie set up the first with a neat through ball in the seventy-fifth minute and the lithe attacker rounded the keeper before slamming into the unprotected net. And, within a minute, Walker, thoroughly enjoying his first season in the green and white hoops, squeezed one between Carson and his near post. Job done. Break out the champagne.

'The game every Celtic fan in the world wanted to see was that meeting with Dundee,' said Billy McNeill. 'The victory gave our supporters something to remember for a long, long time. There seemed to be fans everywhere and it was a smashing birthday party afternoon. The crowd chanted "Happy Birthday" throughout and refused to leave until I came out with the players fifteen minutes after the game had ended. I was still wearing a tracksuit and hadn't been in the bath, but nobody cared about such details. This was the first time the fans were seeing the team on home territory as the 1988 champions. It was a record thirty-fifth championship for Celtic and my fourth as a manager plus nine previously while playing. A proud moment, indeed.'

A week later, Celtic continued on their winning ways when Anton Rogan, playing to the final whistle as usual, got the winner against Motherwell at Fir Park. A long ball from Paul McStay created havoc in the home side's defence and it fell to the Irish full-back who belted a left-foot shot into the net a minute from the end. Now for the party to end all parties.

The sun shone radiantly in the pale blue sky, the flags and scarves rippled in a vivid sea of green and white and the 44,482 fans sang heartily and lustily. The noise was deafening as gallant Dunfermline, relegated after a gruelling campaign, lined up alongside manager Jim Leishman to applaud the champions onto the field on Saturday May 7. It was a fine gesture by the Fifers. They may have wondered if they were in for another punishing session when Paul McStay released the adventurous Chris Morris and he slashed a stunning, curling shot away from Dave McKellar in only eleven minutes.

'The game died after that,' said Billy McNeill. 'But, having said that, I realised that my message about the standards required at Celtic Park had been driven home. There was never any danger of Dunfermline scoring, but when the players came into the dressing room at the end they were flat and disappointed. They hadn't turned on that final bit of style for the customers. I had to say to them, "Hey, you've won the league. Would you have settled for this at the start?" However, that's when I knew they had set the highest standards themselves and that they were annoyed personally when these dropped. We had been on such a high against Dundee. Then we beat Motherwell and had only the Fifers to meet before the Scottish Cup Final a week later. The fact that Celtic won those last three games with the Cup Final looming spoke volumes for the professionalism of the players. Remember, too, we had won the championship with a record amount of seventy-two points.'

Celtic had ninety minutes to complete a memorable and outstanding league and Cup double in their Centenary Year. Dundee United, at Hampden on a sunny afternoon in May, had no intention of joining the celebrations.

In truth, the three signings - still well short of what Graeme Souness

CHAPTER THIRTY
OH, HAMPDEN
IN THE SUN

The champagne flowed - courtesy of Queen's Park. Billy McNeill's men had just beaten Dundee United in an extraordinarily dramatic climax to the Scottish Cup Final in front of 74,000 hyperactive fans at throbbing Hampden Park. Celtic had completed a remarkable Double in their Centenary Year. And a bemused manager said, 'I believed we had thought of everything, covered every eventuality. The only mistake we made in our preparation was forgetting to bring champagne. So, we had to borrow some bottles from Queen's Park. Thank goodness the amateurs had a few in stock.'

Saturday May 14 was another sun-drenched afternoon in Glasgow, the glorious climate matching the mood of the cavorting, dancing Celtic fans. No-one thought back to a perishing afternoon at Parkhead on January 30 when the Scottish Cup adventure was almost lost in the icy mists of winter at the first hurdle. The part-timers of Stranraer, second bottom of the Second Division, were the opponents and, of course, they were mere cannonfodder. And when Frank McAvennie diverted a cross from Chris Morris past goalkeeper Martin McLafferty in the sixth minute, it appeared everything was going like clockwork. And then someone at the Stair Park side produced a spanner.

Referee Louis Thow had no option but to award Stranraer a penalty-kick after Lex Baillie had tripped Keith Knox. Bruce Cleland was given the opportunity to put the frighteners on the celebrated opponents. Cleland took aim and fired. Pat Bonner managed to beat the ball back to the player who had followed up. It looked as though he must score from the rebound, but he snatched at the effort and ballooned the ball wildly over the bar. The bulk of the 21,625 attendance sighed with relief. Four minutes from time, Cleland found himself staring at an empty net again. A cross from substitute Joe Coyle left Bonner and Baillie in a tangle. The ball dropped at the part-timer's feet only ten yards from goal. He could have rolled the ball home, but he elected to go for power and blazed an effort against the crossbar. Celtic were through.

'I phoned the Samaritans when I got home and they were engaged. It was that type of day,' said Cleland, who, at least, proved he hadn't misplaced his sense of humour. It helped, also, that he would be emigrating to Canada a few weeks later.

Billy McNeill wasn't smiling, though. 'The players are disappointed and they realise they let themselves down. Perhaps the early goal lulled us into thinking that more would follow no matter how we played. Our finishing was abysmal and some of our misses rivalled those of our opponents. On that form, we could just about escape relegation, but it might be the best lesson our players have had in a long time. Stranraer's away record is appalling and we scored our goal when they only had ten men on the field with a player off getting treatment. A replay at Stair Park in midweek certainly didn't appeal.'

The Scottish Cup trail appeared to be littered with obstacles when Hibs arrived at Celtic Park for the next round. The game, watched by 30,537 at the ground while being televised live on the Sunday afternoon of February 21, limped to a goalless conclusion. The nearest Celtic came to scoring was a Peter Grant shot that cannoned off the woodwork. Fortunately, with only a minute remaining, Chris Morris booted a

Graham Mitchell effort off the line with Pat Bonner hopelessly stranded.

'It was particularly disappointing because the game was watched by millions on live television,' observed McNeill. 'I had previously thought that this would present a fine opportunity for my skilled players to show a watching public just how fluent Celtic can play. Sadly, it just didn't come off and credit to Hibs. They quelled the threat carried by our more inspirational players, especially Paul McStay and Joe Miller. I'm confident we can go and get a good result at Easter Road. Despite not playing well, we still created several clear-cut chances. If we had drawn Hibs away from home in the first instance, I would have fancied our chances to progress further. Nothing has changed now as far as that is concerned.'

The Celtic manager's faith in his players was not without foundation. They dominated the midweek replay in Edinburgh, but had to be patient before getting the breakthrough goal. That arrived eleven minutes from time after Joe Miller and Tommy Burns had worked a clever free-kick to present Peter Grant with a shooting opportunity. The midfielder cracked the ball high past Andy Goram, his attempt hammered off the underside of the crossbar and, in the midst of a crowd scene, Billy Stark rose the highest to head home. Sitting in the Easter Road stand that evening was Liverpool manager Kenny Dalglish. He was watching Hibs playmaker John Collins, who was a player also much admired by Billy McNeill.

The quarter-final draw took Celtic across Glasgow to Firhill to face part-time First Division outfit Partick Thistle on March 12. Billy McNeill said, 'I warned the players that there was a potential upset on the cards. I didn't want Celtic getting a custard pie in the face.' The players listened to the boss. Frank McAvennie turned from goal-taker to goal-maker as he set up a 3-0 victory. The tie was in its infancy when the zestful striker pitched over a cross and Andy Walker headed past Archie McLean. Six minutes after the interval, a McAvennie chip found Tommy Burns in space and the gifted midfielder hit a ferocious shot on the drop for No.2. Just after the hour mark, the dynamic attacker did it again with a blistering drive that smashed against the crossbar and Billy Stark did the needful when the rebound came his way. Thistle completed the contest with only ten men after Eddie Gallagher decided to demonstrate his pugilistic skills on Anton Rogan fourteen minutes from time. Referee George Smith was far from impressed with the Thistle player's impromptu change of sporting professions and pointed to the dressing room.

Billy McNeill was reasonably satisfied after Celtic had booked a semi-final spot in the national competition for a record fifty-fourth time. He said, 'Tommy Burns deserved his Man of the Match award. He worked very hard, but also backed up many of his team-mates. We didn't quite hit peak form, but the professionalism shown by the players was pleasing. We accommodated Thistle's threat well, despite being hindered by a heavy pitch and our opponents' up-and-at-'em tactics. The goals, too, were magnificent. Each of them had a stamp of quality about it. We were able to curb Thistle's enthusiasm in the first-half and then enjoy the second-half more than just a little. And Billy Stark once again showed that when there is even a sniff of a chance he'll be there at the kill.'

Celtic and their manager were ready for the last four. McNeill said, 'When I looked at the semi-final draw - Aberdeen versus Dundee United and Celtic against Hearts - I said that whatever happened it was going to be a good Final. Remember, too, Celtic hadn't lost a goal in four ties. I wanted my strongest team available, so we brought forward a fixture against St Mirren because it allowed Frank McAvennie to work off a one-game disciplinary ban. That enabled him to play against Hearts.'

Celtic were establishing a remarkable capacity for rescuing what appeared to be lost causes throughout a strenuous and momentous campaign. That was never more emphatically highlighted than in the rousing semi-final against Hearts at the national stadium on Saturday April 9. The Tynecastle side were leading 1-0 with only two minutes to go. The league and Cup Double dream was fading fast. Then came one of the most stirring, impassioned fightbacks ever seen at the grey, old football fortress. Hearts had taken the lead in the weirdest of circumstances just before the hour mark. Brian Whittaker, the former Celtic defender, hit a hopeful punt downfield and Pat Bonner went for the high ball with Dave McPherson acting as a distraction. There was a mighty intake of breath as the ball cleared both the goalkeeper and the Hearts player and sailed into the back of the net. It was a complete freak, but referee Kenny Hope didn't see the clear infringement and signaled a goal.

McNeill sent on Mark McGhee as substitute for Joe Miller in the sixty-ninth minute to add more power to the central attack. The eighty-eighth minute arrived as Celtic took a corner-kick on the right. Goalkeeper Henry Smith came for the swirling ball, didn't make a proper connection and the ball bounced around wildly in the packed penalty area. Roy Aitken had a frantic shot blocked before McGhee had a go. Astoundingly, his effort weaved its way through a forest of legs on its way to the back of the net.

'The easiest thing to do when we equalised was hold out for a replay,' said McNeill. 'But my players didn't want to know about a draw. They still believed they had time to finish the game.'

In the fading seconds, Frank McAvennie hurled in a cross from the right and once again Smith, looking decidedly unsure and nervous, came in an effort to catch the ball. McGhee challenged him, the keeper fumbled and Andy Walker reacted with haste to bash the winner into the net just as the match official was looking at his watch. Even Billy McNeill had to shake his head in disbelief, but, once he had recovered his composure, the proud manager said, 'This game showed my players' appetite for winning. The determination of the team is as good as or better than any I have come across. I said to the players at half-time that we weren't playing as well as we could. It was up to us to put it right. I urged them, "If we want to get to the Cup Final, let's go out and do it." We lost a goal in controversial circumstances, but then, I'm happy to say, we took over.'

Dundee United, frustrating, awkward opponents, awaited Celtic in the

Scottish Cup Final on May 14. Once again, the setting was in spectacular technicolour, explosions of green, white and gold streaming down the Hampden terracings with splashes of tangerine. Everything looked poised for a very pleasurable and eventful occasion. United, managed by curmudgeonly Jim McLean, had a disturbing habit of bringing grey to proceedings. The 74,000 fans were given a surprise even before the kick-off when Pat Bonner failed to turn out and Allen McKnight was in his position. McNeill explained, 'Pat had a calf muscle injury. On Friday, I told Allen he had to prepare as though he was playing the next day. I told Allen I would let him know in the morning. Possibly, it was unfair to leave him wondering all night, but there was no other way. Pat's injury was camouflaged from everybody as physio Brian Scott tried to get him fit. I worked Pat quite hard in the morning and then asked how he felt. He told me he wasn't one hundred per cent and I replied that he had taken a hard decision. So, Allen was in. But Pat's attitude was so typical of the team. He didn't want to risk letting anyone down. I know all of them would have done precisely the same in Pat's situation.'

The first-half passed without any real incident, both sets of players anxious not to make a mistake. However, the situation changed dramatically only four minutes after the turnaround. The Celtic defence was stretched as Eamonn Bannon sent a searching pass in the direction of Kevin Gallacher, a genuine speed merchant. He raced onto the ball and kept going before lashing a drive wide of McKnight. McNeill recalled, 'It was a very good goal from Gallacher. Roy Aitken was running beside him, but, having had his name taken shortly before, the risk of a tackle was too great. Roy tried instead to jockey him on the run, but Gallacher was going fast and was in no mood to lose the ball. Now we were a goal down.'

With fifteen minutes to go, Celtic were surging forward in torrents while being ever mindful about their rivals' keen ability to break at pace, especially with Gallacher roaming into danger areas. Then Anton Rogan, Davie Hay's £20,000 bargain buy from Distillery, surged forward on the left and slung in a magnificent cross. Frank McAvennie, as courageous as ever, threw himself at the ball and sizzled a header beyond goalkeeper Billy Thomson. 'Even when we were a goal down, we knew we could make something happen,' said the marksman. 'We also knew if we could score one goal they would collapse.'

McAvennie practised what he preached with only a minute to go. Joe Miller didn't connect with his right-wing corner-kick properly. It swept low across the surface where Billy Stark fed it back to his team-mate. This time his elevation was better, there was a scramble in front of Thomson and McAvennie hit an effort sweetly into the net. 'We had to finish the game in ninety minutes because we couldn't handle extra-time,' admitted Celtic's match-winner. 'It had been a really hard season and we felt the effects of the tiredness in the last couple of weeks as we wrapped up the league title.'

McAvennie wasn't surprised at Celtic's late, late show. 'Billy Connolly did a sketch about Celtic at that time because we always left things so late. He used to say to his friend, "How long to go?" His friend would reply, "A couple of minutes." And he would go, "Och, plenty of time! I'm away for a coffee."'

Chris Morris, the only player to perform in every game for Celtic throughout their historic season, paid homage to his gaffer. 'Billy McNeill was crucial to that success. I got on really well with him and enjoyed his company. He could also be absolutely charming. But, boy, was he a sore loser! I can remember him coming into the dressing room after a defeat and kicking a boot that was lying on the floor. It bounced around the walls before landing squarely on Anton's head. When he spoke, we listened.'

Billy McNeill deserved the accolades. He said, 'Big decisions had to be made when we went a goal down. I was prepared to leave Celtic short at the back. I said to Tommy Craig, "Right now we've lost the Cup...we've got to go and win it." That's why I brought on Billy Stark for Derek Whyte to give Joe Miller freedom on the other side. Andy Walker had probably been asked for too much during the season, so I changed him for Mark McGhee's strength and determination. We stretched United while stretching ourselves. While the players were

---

out on the pitch celebrating at the end, I went to the dressing room. I was alone there with my thoughts. The players deserved their moment of triumph because they had won the Cup, not me. It is unlike me to want to be by myself, but for once I did. Eventually, Jack McGinn came in and said, "I think they want you out there, Billy." Later I reflected on the past twelve months. I had gone from one extreme to another as a manager - booted by Aston Villa and now lauded by Celtic. That Centenary Double will go down in the rolls of Celtic history.'

Davie Hay, deposed manager but still a Celtic fan, was at Hampden that afternoon. 'I had to laugh at the end when a Dundee United supporter was passing me in the stand. He recognised me and said, "If you had still been their manager, we would have won." I shot straight back, "Aye, just like you did in 1985!"'

The Centenary script had been skillfully written, flawlessly delivered and perfectly followed. Now for the hard bit.

CHAPTER THIRTY-ONE
WHEN THE CHEERS BEGIN TO FADE

It's a long way down from the top. Celtic, unfathomably and improbably, were never competent enough to even achieve second place in the Premier League during the remaining three years of Billy McNeill's reign.

Despite the manager's inspirational leadership qualities, he was unable to apply the brakes to a disastrous downward spiral. Celtic, alas, were in freefall. A 2-1 defeat from Rangers in the 1991 League Cup Final was as good as it got in that competition. Europe was a wasteland.

However, there was a solitary nugget buried amid the rubble of mediocrity. Thank goodness for the Scottish Cup success in 1989.

Billy McNeill, like Davie Hay three years before him, had beseeched his chairman, Jack McGinn, and the directors to strengthen the squad while they were at the pinnacle during the summer of the Centenary Year. 'I asked the Celtic board for £5million to combat Rangers' investment in players. They offered me £1million. I wanted three players - a defender, a midfielder and another striker. Winning the Double should have been the springboard to even greater achievements, but not everyone at Celtic Park appreciated the need to consolidate our position from a base of strength. I was aware that Rangers would not simply sit back and accept the situation. It was evident that they were prepared to spend big in a determined effort to regain the upper hand.'

Apathy in the boardroom will undoubtedly lead to anxiety in the dug-out. Frustratingly, McNeill was forced to spend £300,000 of his transfer cash on a goalkeeper. Pat Bonner was struggling with a back injury and the club had sold Allen McKnight to West Ham during the break. McNeill moved quickly to sign Ian Andrews from Leicester City. Alas, it did not prove to be money well spent.

Andrews, in fact, played only five league games after his confidence was battered beyond repair in a dreadful 5-1 defeat from Rangers at Ibrox on August 27. It was the Parkhead team's worst result against the Govan side for twenty-eight years. The former England Under-21 international played only two more games before being loaned to Leeds United in December. He left Glasgow on a permanent basis when Southampton bought him for £200,000 the following February. McNeill was left with a major goalkeeping headache and eventually turned to former Scotland international Alan Rough, who had been playing in the States with Orlando Lions after quitting Hibs in the summer. The thirty-five year old answered the SOS and performed in five league outings - two of them defeats against Dundee and his former Easter Road club - before Bonner returned at the end of October.

McNeill was being asked to manoeuvre another season out of Centenary heroes Tommy Burns, Billy Stark and Mark McGhee, none of whom would see a thirtieth birthday again. There was also talk of Frank McAvennie finding the lure of a return to London and its nightlife irresistible. His obvious unrest was creating friction with his manager while the continual conjecture about his future was also unsettling his team-mates. Eventually, he was sold back to West Ham for £1.25million in March 18 1989 only hours after playing in an explosive 2-1 Scottish Cup quarter-final win over Hearts at Celtic Park. Leaks of the imminent transfer had reached the ears of the support and, for the first time, McAvennie was booed by the fans who had showered him with adulation the previous season. McNeill had become increasingly fed up with the entire business and was happy to put the whole affair behind him. Uncannily, the situation imitated Mo Johnston's final months at the club when he was coming out of contract in 1987. Interestingly, both players employed the same agent, Bill McMurdo.

McAvennie moved while the sparks were still flying following a bad-tempered encounter with Hearts that saw three players sent off in a turbulent first-half. Mark McGhee and Roy Aitken, with a penalty-kick, had put Celtic two goals ahead by the thirty-sixth minute when Tynecastle defender Alan McLaren was first to be dismissed by referee Davie Syme for talking out of turn. Then Tosh McKinlay was extremely late with a tackle on Billy Stark and Mick McCarthy took up the cudgels on behalf of his stricken team-mate. He threw a punch at the Hearts defender who tried to fight back. There was a flurry of blows and players from both sides got involved. Once order was restored, to a certain extent, the match official expelled both of the principal combatants. Eamonn Bannon, who had joined the Edinburgh outfit from Dundee United, sent a free-kick hurtling beyond Pat Bonner eighteen minutes from time, but Celtic held on to reach the semi-final.

Billy McNeill was far from impressed. He said, 'As far as I am concerned, any semblance of football finished at half-time. Passions definitely have a place in football, but here they clearly carried too far.'

Thankfully, the semi-final confrontation with the other half of Edinburgh's big two, Hibs, was a more sedate affair. Celtic were three goals ahead in the first half-hour with Mick McCarthy, Mark McGhee and Andy Walker on target. An effort from Stevie Archibald, back in Scotland after his lucrative spells with Spurs, Barcelona and Espanyol, pulled one back, but nothing could prevent Celtic heading for their forty-fifth Scottish Cup Final. Rangers had struggled in their semi-final tie against St Johnstone and had been held to a goalless at Celtic Park. They won 4-0 in the replay and Graeme Souness was making noises about his team completing the Treble. Celtic appeared to be mere nuisance value to Rangers on their triumphal trek.

A vociferous crowd of 72,069 made their presence known on a beautiful sun-kissed afternoon at Hampden on May 20. Rangers, after beating Celtic three times in their four league games, were huge favourites. Joe Miller had been asked by Billy McNeill to play through the middle alongside Mark McGhee in the previous two matches against Hibs and St Mirren. With Frank McAvennie plying his trade elsewhere, Tommy Coyne, recently signed for £500,000 from Dundee Cup-tied, and Andy Walker injured, the Celtic manager had no alternatives. Miller proved to be the match-winner in the last two league outings of the season, scoring the only goal in each game. The big question was, could he complete the hat-trick at Hampden?

The slight but tenacious player provided the answer three minutes from the interval. Peter Grant pushed a speculative pass forward, but his radar was faulty and the ball was headed clear by Richard Gough. It was returned by Paul McStay and went straight to Rangers full-back Gary Stevens. Miller, though, didn't give up the chase. 'I had noticed that Stevens was short with three passbacks before that,' he said. 'He was forcing the keeper to sprint off his line to clear the ball. I took a chance he would do the same again. I read the pass and sprinted onto it.'

Stevens was shockingly short with the ball back to Chris Woods and Miller, anticipating it perfectly, seized on the wayward pass and stroked it low past the startled goalkeeper. 'Where's your Treble gone?' was the gleeful serenade from the Celtic end as Rangers toiled to get back into the contest. Derek Whyte cleared a Mark Walters shot off the line, but Stevens, attempting to atone, did likewise at the other end with a Tommy Burns header. The final whistle from Bob Valentine, Davie Hay's old adversary, brought the game to a conclusion with Celtic claiming their twenty-ninth Scottish Cup.

In the midst of the cheering, singing and hollering, Billy McNeill said, 'I was not one bit concerned about stopping Rangers from winning the Treble. My commitment is to Celtic. We are now in the European Cup-Winners' Cup next season and we have done it through our own efforts. That's what this victory is all about. It's nothing to do with Rangers. I thought we deserved to win. The players in the back four were excellent and Joe Miller finished off magnificently for the winning goal. Now we can have a break and prepare for a new campaign. This Cup victory can send us all away on our summer holidays with a smile on our face.'

Celtic's aspirations immediately dropped into a black hole and it would be 1995 before they lifted silverware again. Once more, it was a 1-0 Scottish Cup triumph with Pierre van Hooydonk heading the only goal against Airdrie. The years in between could be filed in the insufferable category for those of a Celtic persuasion. After the splendour of the title success to mark one hundred remarkable years, Celtic finished third in the league on forty-six points, ten behind Rangers and four short of Aberdeen the following season. The fallen champions suffered eleven losses as opposed to only three the previous term. Dundee United knocked them out of the League Cup at the quarter-final stage and Werder Bremen did likewise in the second round of the European Cup.

There was also an emotional Sunday afternoon on March 4 when Celtic hosted Liverpool in the Hillsborough Memorial Game to honour the ninety-six Merseyside supporters who had lost their lives in such tragic circumstances in the FA Cup semi-final against Nottingham Forest at the ground of Sheffield Wednesday. A crowd of 60,437 turned out in an astonishing show of unity. Never has 'You'll Never Walk Alone' been rendered with such feeling.

The smile on Billy McNeill's face in the summer of 1989 was erased fairly quickly with the news that the expected return of Mo Johnston had hit a snag. Celtic thought the deal was as good as done and dusted with the striker returning from Nantes in a £1.2million move. The Parkhead club, in fact, had already shelled out £400,000 as a deposit for their former player. 'I was pleased,' said McNeill. 'Johnston was younger than McAvennie and he was at the top of his form, scoring six goals in Scotland's successful World Cup campaign. He was also a more complete player than the one who had left Celtic two years earlier. But, suddenly, the rumours started flying around. The word on the streets was that Rangers had stepped in to try to sign Johnston.'

McNeill wanted to get to the truth of the matter before he took his family to the States on vacation. Scotland were in their Troon HQ, the Marine Hotel, as they prepared for international games against England and Chile in the Rous Cup. The Celtic manager met Johnston and was immediately dismayed. 'My suspicions were confirmed. He was both evasive and, I think, embarrassed.' At this stage, FIFA, football's world governing body, agreed with Celtic that a letter of agreement, signed by all parties, was legal and binding. It was not a contract, as such, but a letter of intent. FIFA told the Celtic board Mo Johnston was their player. If someone else wanted to sign him, they would have to deal with Celtic. It would have been highly unlikely that Rangers would have chosen to travel that route. McNeill also implored his board to pay the outstanding £800,000 to make absolutely certain the deal was cemented and remove any contractual loopholes.

Absurdly, Johnston was now saying he wouldn't complete the deal. It hadn't been too long beforehand that he was captured on film, beaming brightly, holding a Celtic jersey in front of him, while announcing, 'Celtic have come in for me and I'm delighted to be rejoining them.' No-one detected his nose growing at that stage.

McNeill was clearly more in touch with the real world, or, at least, the legalities of the situation, than his board of directors. Publicly, he maintained praiseworthy decorum when he was told Johnston had changed his mind. The manager, realising the power of FIFA, was quite prepared to call the player's bluff. Privately, he told close friends, 'If he doesn't play for us, he won't play for anyone.' McNeill was quite prepared to put the player out of football. He was also astute enough to understand how Johnston would react to such a prospect. It seemed a bit late for Wee Mo to seek alternative employment. The Celtic manager knew the player would be forced to relent, bite the bullet and get on with business on a football field. There weren't too many other employment opportunities on the horizon.

McNeill told the board of his thoughts. Unfortunately, and not for the first time, the Parkhead power brokers failed to heed the advice of their manager. While he was in the States, the directors issued a statement to the effect that they would not pursue the transfer 'on a matter of principle'. In doing so, they opened the door to Ibrox. Johnston was unveiled as a Rangers player on July 10. It was the most remarkable transfer in Scottish football history and created a furore within both sets of fans. The Celtic support immediately labelled him 'Judas' while an army of Rangers fans were furious at their club signing a Roman Catholic. And a high-profile one into the bargain. Rangers scarves, flags and even season ticket books were burned outside the front door of Ibrox Stadium when the news broke.

The clandestine move for Johnston was done under the noses of the Celtic board, but, as Sports Editor of the Sunday Mail at the time, I find it inconceivable that those in power within the Celtic Park boardroom never got a whiff of the impending defection.

Certainly, I received enough information myself, long before Johnston, with a smug smile on his face, was being paraded in front of the press as a Rangers player. As a newspaper, the Sunday Mail had done everything to uncover the story. We hit a wall of lies and denials. My colleague Don Morrison, our excellent Chief Sports Writer, pinned down his agent Bill McMurdo and asked him directly, 'Is Mo Johnson signing for Rangers?' Don told me McMurdo laughed and replied, 'It's a complete fabrication – you could run that story for ten years and it still wouldn't be true.'

I used the quote in the newspaper. A few days later Johnson was unveiled as a Rangers player.

Davie Hay also recalls vividly the day his former player signed for Graeme Souness. 'I was preparing to leave Norway after winning the league with Lillestrom when I received news Mo was signing again for

Celtic. I telephoned him to wish him all the best on his return to the club. There was a pause before Mo came back on the line. "Davie, the deal's not done," he told me. "I haven't signed a contract." I asked him if there was a problem. Again, there was silence. "Not sure," he replied. I told him good luck again and thought no more about it. You can get all sorts of hitches before a contract is finally done and dusted and I simply thought they had encountered a wee hiccup; nothing that couldn't be sorted out.

'I came home to Scotland and a friend picked me up at Glasgow Airport. "You'll have seen that Wee Mo has signed, then?" He asked. "Aye, good," I replied. He almost drove the car off the road. "What do you mean? He's signed for Rangers!" I could hardly believe it. To put it mildly, I was astonished. From what I knew of Mo, I believed he was a big Celtic man. Obviously, a revision of my thoughts was required. I watched Mo playing for Rangers and I'll tell you something. Mo Johnston was a lot happier playing for Celtic than he ever was for Rangers.'

Billy McNeill still had much work to do as he prepared his team for season 1989/90. 'There was nothing more I could do in the Mo Johnston situation,' said the Celtic boss. 'So, I looked elsewhere. I paid £600,000 to Pisa for centre-half Paul Elliott after Mick McCarthy had joined French side Olympique Lyonaiss at the end of his contract. I also brought in the versatile Mike Galloway from Hearts for £500,000.' McNeill, though, realised he had to strengthen his attack, especially with Mark McGhee, who couldn't be promised a regular place in the starting line-up, returning to former club Newcastle United.

By this stage, the Celtic board either refused or didn't have the nous to embrace the acceptance that players' wages had spiraled out of control. They wanted Celtic to be a big club, but were far from acting like one. Adding to McNeill's frustrations was what was happening across the city at Ibrox. Their board appeared to have grasped the reality of the situation and were willing to pay the going rate as they continued to attract big-name players. McNeill, consequently, had to lower his sights and search elsewhere. He paid £500,000 for Legia Warsaw striker Jacki Dziekanowski and most fans were intrigued when they were informed he was 'Poland's answer to George Best.' McNeill also shelled out £400,000 for his team-mate Dariusz Wdowczyk, a dependable defender. Souness, meanwhile, dealt in millions. The outcome, sadly, was inevitable.

Celtic finished fifth in the Premier League behind Rangers, Aberdeen, Hearts and Dundee United. The Parkhead side were beaten twelve times in the new thirty-six game set-up. It was a disastrous fall from grace. Aberdeen sunk them 1-0 at the quarter-final stage of the League Cup and they didn't get past the first stage of the Cup-Winners' Cup, exiting the competition in an imagination-stretching scenerio. They drew 6-6 on aggregate with Partizan Belgrade and went out on the away goals rule. Poor Dziekanowski. He scored four goals in the 5-4 win in Glasgow, but a dozy defence allowed the Slavs to score in the last minute and his good work was obliterated. There was a spirited run to the Scottish Cup Final that included a 1-0 victory over Rangers in the Fourth Round. The Final against Aberdeen ended in a goalless draw after extra-time and Wdowcyzk and Anton Rogan missed from the spot in the penalty shoot-out as Celtic lost 9-8.

If it could go wrong, it most assuredly would. Even Mo Johnston scored two goals against Celtic that season. He netted the only goal of the game at Ibrox on November 12 and was booked by referee George Smith for overdoing the trackside celebrations with his 'new' fans. He scored the second in a 3-0 victory at the same venue five months later.

Allegiances to Celtic were being stretched to the unbearable. Could it get any worse than this?

CHAPTER THIRTY-TWO
AND, NOW,
THE END IS HERE

Behind the scenes at Celtic Park, Billy McNeill was well aware a conspiratorial mood was developing. The team were struggling to make an impact during the 1990/91 season and McNeill admitted, 'It was obvious that certain elements in the boardroom wanted me out.'

Many thought the manager's days were numbered when Rangers won 2-0 at Ibrox on January 2. It was Graeme Souness' side's third successive win over Celtic in ten weeks, including a League Cup Final victory in October. The Parkhead men were now a massive fourteen points behind their rivals and for a lot of exasperated followers it was not the last straw. It was the one after it. The rumblings were not lost on McNeill. He disagreed with the thought process that he had been put in front of the firing squad after the New Year loss. 'I believe my fate was sealed the previous month with the appointment of the board's hatchet man, Terry Cassidy,' said McNeill. 'Cassidy was given the title Chief Executive. A more appropriate title would have been Chief Executioner.'

There was friction between McNeill and Cassidy from day one. 'I found him to be a thoroughly unpleasant, untrustworthy, overbearing, offensive individual,' said McNeill. Cassidy was at the club for twenty-two months before the axe fell on the hatchet man, but, by then, it was too late to save McNeill. The Press got wind of a hush-hush meeting of the Celtic board shortly after the January defeat to Rangers. If it was their intention to relieve their manager of his duties around that period, they were well and truly scuppered. McNeill, astonishingly when everything is taken into consideration, managed to turn things around. The team went on an eleven-game unbeaten run, including two back-to-back wins over Rangers at Parkhead in March. Celtic knocked the Ibrox side out of the Scottish Cup with a 2-0 win in a free-for-all that saw Rangers' Mark Hateley, Terry Hurlock and Mark Walters sent off along with Celtic's Peter Grant. The following week, Celtic won 3-0 and Ibrox defender Scott Nisbet saw red on that occasion.

The league was blown, but there was a chance of a piece of silverware to prevent the board from following through with their initial thoughts to rid the club of an individual whose loyalty to the cause was boundless; a fact that was transparently obvious to all, with the sad exception of some members of the club's board. Celtic faced Motherwell in the Scottish Cup semi-final while Dundee United met St Johnstone in the other last four tie. On April 3, McNeill saw his team held to a goalless draw by Tommy McLean's Fir Parkers. Six days later in the replay, Celtic led twice before capitulating 4-2 in shocking, unacceptable circumstances. Tommy Coyne and Anton Rogan scored, but their efforts were wiped out by a double from Motherwell's fiery little raider Dougie Arnott. In the sixty-seventh minute, Colin O'Neill hit a happy-go-lucky strike at goal from fully thirty-five yards and the ball arrowed straight into Pat Bonner's top left-hand corner. O'Neill had never hit, nor would ever hit again, a shot that accurate. It was all over four minutes from the end when Steve Kirk rolled in the fourth.

The following morning, Billy McNeill could only say, 'I can't remember ever feeling as flat after a semi-final defeat, either as a player or a manager. I was debating whether to come in today, but you just have to get on with it. The players are very low, as you would expect. We've got to get over this disappointment very quickly because it is difficult to contemplate another year without Europe for this club.'

The first two games of the Premier League programme set the ball in motion for what McNeill and his players would have to endure in an excruciating campaign. Dariusz Wdowcyzk was sent off in the first-half of the opening fixture against Motherwell where strikes from Bobby Russell and Dougie Arnott after the break gave the Lanarkshire side a 2-0 victory. Seven days later, Celtic conceded three goals in fourteen minutes to Aberdeen in Glasgow as the pattern was set for an alarmingly dire campaign. It didn't matter that Paul Mason's opening goal in the fifty-third minutes looked yards offside or that the defence was asleep when Bobby Connor and Hans Gillhaus added the others. Celtic, in front of a crowd of 45,222 fans, looked very ordinary, lethargic and bereft of sparkle. Charlie Nicholas was given a hero's welcome, but a less than rapturous farewell. The magic had dimmed. John Collins had been bought at a cost of £1million from Hibs, but he was slow to ignite.

The League Cup offered hope, but Celtic matched the bleak conditions at Hampden on a grey afternoon on October 22 as they toppled to a 2-1 extra-time defeat to Rangers in the Final. Again, they had no excuse for their failure. Paul Elliott gave Celtic the lead with a smart header after a Collins corner-kick seven minutes after the interval. But the defence was too easily shredded when Ally McCoist set up Mark Walters for the equaliser in the sixty-sixth minute. The winning goal arrived in the one hundred and fourth minute and, once again, Richard Gough was the beneficiary of some lamentable Celtic defending. Trevor Steven swung in a straightforward free-kick from the right that shouldn't have created a problem. Disturbingly, Pat Bonner and Chris Morris got into a terrible fankle and the Rangers skipper merely had to prod the ball home from close range.

If any goal starkly illustrated the deficiencies in the porous Celtic defence it was that one. A lack of communication, awareness, bravery and positivity all combined to surrender a trophy. Throughout the error-strewn term, the Celtic rearguard was an accident waiting to happen. Ultimately, it would cost Billy McNeill his job.

Celtic won their last four league games against Dunfermline (5-1), Hearts (1-0), St Mirren (1-0) and St Johnstone (3-2) to claim a place in Europe in the forthcoming season. But McNeill admitted, 'I knew deep down that winning those four matches and getting a place in the UEFA Cup would not be enough to save me.'

Quite apart from what McNeill was experiencing with his players on the field, he was forced to look over his shoulder to keep a wary eye on Cassidy. An indication of the running interference with which McNeill was expected to cope came in a tart seven-word sentence from the Chief Executive. Cassidy asked McNeill to tell him what salary he believed the manager of Celtic should be given. Cassidy, in fact, had done this with all the other executives and, apparently, he hoped to have contracts and terms of employment clarified before the start of the new financial year in June. He was asked what would happen if McNeill did not provide the information requested in time. Cassidy blithely replied, 'He will get whatever I give him.'

'Whenever I attempted to seek clarification on my position from the board, I was continually stonewalled,' said McNeill. 'But I only had to pick up a newspaper to discover what was going on behind my back. A prominent sportswriter friend of mine quipped at the time, Celtic had so many leaks if it had been a ship it would have been renamed The Titanic.'

On Wednesday May 22 - eleven days after the final league game of the season against St Johnstone - McNeill, as he had been previously tipped off by friends in the Press - was summoned to Celtic Park for a 10am meeting with the directors. He was sacked moments after arrival. Jack McGinn expressed deep regret that the board had been forced to take such a 'painful' decision. A short statement was passed onto the waiting newspapermen, alerted to attend a hastily-convened Press Conference, to the effect that the club had decided to terminate Billy McNeill's employment.

'That day was the lowest point of my life,' admitted McNeill. 'I had no qualms about the directors deciding I was no longer the man for the job, but I don't think I deserved to be sacked in that manner. The fact is, if a manager fails to produce the results then he deserves to be kicked into touch. If the board wanted shot of me, all they had to do was come up and say to my face that my time was up. All the manipulation and conniving was so unnecessary.

'I was very disappointed by the directors' treatment of me, but I was not surprised. I felt the people running Celtic at that time had lost the ability to behave with dignity.'

It was a cruel, sad and pathetic end to a career that had spanned eighteen years as a player and nine as a manager. Afterwards, Billy McNeill broke the news to his wife Liz. He returned to the family home in Pollokshields, on Glasgow's south side, closed the front door behind him and, in private, shed a tear.

EPILOGUE

It seems a long distant winter now since two proud, decent and honourable men lost their jobs at Celtic Football Club.

Time will neither dim nor demean the achievements of Billy McNeill and Davie Hay, two natural leaders who have an immoveable place in the club's heritage.

As two highly-motivated individuals, Billy McNeill and Davie Hay never wavered in their pursuit of excellence. As players and managers, they represented the heart and soul of a proud club. On and off the field, they inspired loyalty. Neither was slow to march towards the fury of the guns on behalf of their club. Nor were they forelock-tuggers, ready to bow to anyone. Football is a flawed sport run by people who are hardly infallible. Harsh decisions are made in a results-driven business. There are often casualties.

But Billy McNeill and Davie Hay have proved to be strong and sensitive individuals who have steadfastly refused to be crushed by bruising experiences. Robustly, they have continued to support Celtic to an unrivalled degree.

Criticise Celtic at your peril when McNeill is in the vicinity. Nowadays, the Official Ambassador of the club will tell you, 'Looking back, I can say there were many more highs than there were lows in my playing and managing days at a club with the status of Celtic. Nothing will ever obscure the enjoyment factor of being associated with this club.'

In a private moment, Hay confided to me, 'You know, I have a greater fondness now for the club than ever. Even as a player and a manager. I enjoy my games at Celtic Park purely as a supporter. I've grown stronger over the years and, yes, there was bitterness at first. That's long gone. Whatever has happened in the past will remain there. Today, without any pressure, I can roll up to the ground and watch Celtic. Why not? I've always considered them my team. They'll always be special to me.'

Both McNeill and Hay have enriched the Celtic tapestry. They have presented us all with oceans of memories to wade through. They can bask in the glowing satisfaction they were unstinting in their endeavours on behalf of the club closest to their hearts. They deserve their moment in the sun after such distinguished service.

Billy McNeill and Davie Hay captured the very essence of Celtic Football Club.

Celtic Football Club, somewhere along the way, may just have captured the very essence of Billy McNeill and Davie Hay.

MORE FROM CQN BOOKS

Thank you for reading Caesar & The Assassin – it is quite a story!

If you have enjoyed Caesar & The Assassin you will be pleased to know that the story will continue in the next book from CQN where we will feature the period in Celtic's history taking us from Liam Brady being appointed as manager to Martin O'Neill leaving the club. In the meantime if you haven't checked out these earlier books from CQN there's always time!

Yours in Celtic

Paul Brennan
Founder
Celtic Quick News

SEVILLE
The Celtic Movement

Jim McGinley

Published March 2014 (Hardcover)

SEVILLE - The Celtic Movement is the story of over 80,000 Celtic supporters who travelled to Seville in May 2003 for the UEFA Cup Final. Most didn't have tickets and over 50,000 Celtic supporters watched the final in various parks and bars around Seville. Inside the Estadio Olimpico the Celtic support filled over 80% of the stadium and produced an amazing atmosphere roaring the team on in the intense early summer heat in Seville. This book is over 400 pages and tells the stories - some hilarious, some very sad indeed - of what happened during those few days in Seville in 2003. This is the collective tale of the Celtic support in Seville and is perhaps the definitive book on what It means to be a supporter of this grand old team. It is packed full of supporters stories - and these are reflected in words, photographs and even specially commissioned cartoons. SEVILLE - The Celtic Movement captures perfectly the very special relationship that exists between Celtic Football Club and her wonderful support. **RATING*****

TOMMY GEMMELL
All The Best

Tommy Gemmell and Alex Gordon

Published: May 2014 (Hardcover)

Tommy Gemmell scored perhaps the most significant goal in the history of Celtic FC on that beautifully sunny day in Lisbon on 25th May 1967. Here in his final book Tommy looks back with Alex Gordon, on a lifetime in the game and selects the players he rates as the best he's played with or watched. Tommy recalls in a chapter from his first book from 1968, called The Big Shot, the events in South America when Celtic participated in the Inter-Continental Cup against Racing Club of Argentina. From the beauty of Celtic's attacking play in Lisbon to the farce of facing these cheats from Argentina - Tommy tells us about every kick, and not just of the ball! This emotional book concludes with Tommy answering questions from Celtic supporters on his career at Celtic. All The Best from Tommy Gemmell is a book that every Celtic supporter will want to own. Lisbon Lion, Celtic legend and the man who scored for Celtic in not one but two European Cup Finals – no wonder he was called The Big Shot! **RATING*****

WILLIE WALLACE
Heart of a Lion

Willie Wallace and
Jim McGinley (BRTH)

Published: May 2013 (Hardcover)

Join Willie Wallace on a journey of a lifetime. And a trip it has been, as you'll find out in Heart of a Lion. This is Willie's own story, from boyhood in Kirkintilloch, to the life of a professional footballer criss-crossing Scotland and Europe as part of the all-conquering Celtic squad of the late 1960s, to the decision to make a post-retirement home under the warm Australian sun. While there are plenty of football recollections to relish, Heart of a Lion is about much more: it is about Willie's devotion to his family; it is about the irrepressible enjoyment of life that allows him to find humour in almost any situation and it is about his special relationship with – and respect for – the fans who made the game truly great. Scotland has had two famous men named William Wallace. Heart of a Lion reveals the journey of today's Wallace to be no less colourful, courageous and loyal than his predecessor. **RATING****

These books from CQN Books and many other Celtic books are available now from www.CQNBookstore.com and are sold at all good bookstores including Waterstones, WH Smith, HMV and of course Celtic stores. You can also order the Kindle version.

EXTRA TIME
CONTENTS

EXTRA TIME - CHAPTER 1

FORGET ELVIS! KING KENNY HAS LEFT THE BUILDING!

To understand the extent of the task faced by Billy McNeill when he first became Celtic manager we have to go back to the summer of 1977and remember that the Celtic support was left all shook up by the loss of our best player…

Elvis Presley died on 16th August 1977. Millions around the world mourned. However many Celtic fans like myself were still in mourning for something that had happened a week earlier. Kenny Dalglish – the "King" – had left Celtic for Liverpool. For me the news of his departure was devastating. It was the only time I felt like giving up Celtic and indeed football. Looking back that may have seemed an over the top reaction but at the time I genuinely felt that way. I was probably a bit disillusioned over many aspects of Scottish football at that time. The standard of play did not seem to be as good as it was in the "Lisbon Lions" years and there was a dullness about many of the games. Celtic were no longer a team who would be expected to reach the latter stages of European competition. Rangers were not much better and there seemed to be no challenge offered by the likes of Hibs or Aberdeen who had come close to Celtic in the latter 9 in a row years. The Old Firm Cup Final played a few months earlier had attracted a crowd less than 55,000. Even allowing for the weather and the game being televised live it was an attendance less than half of what it would have been a few years earlier. The Scottish International side was doing well but for me anyway a lot of the enthusiasm was tempered by the fact that there were players such as Masson and Rioch, whose connection with Scotland seemed tenuous and mercenary.

And yet amidst all this Celtic had 2 of their greatest ever players - Danny McGrain and Kenny Dalglish. I had seen nearly every game Kenny played for Celtic from his debut as a substitute at Douglas Park in 1968. In December 1974 at Dens Park I saw the best individual performance from a Celtic player (apart from possibly Jinky's famous second half against Red Star Belgrade). On that dark afternoon in Dundee Kenny scored a hat trick and set up 3 other goals in Celtic's 6-0 win. It reminded me of the story my uncle John used to tell me when I was wee boy. Apparently on the way to Pittodrie in the 1950's the Celtic team bus broke down and the players had to make their way to Aberdeen by grabbing lifts from passing motorists. At kick off only goalkeeper John Bonnar and Charlie Tully had arrived. So not to forfeit the points the 2 of them started the game. Celtic were 1-0 up when the remaining players arrived at half time. The whole team played in the second half and Aberdeen won 2-1! Charlie Tully was my Uncle John's favourite player and that joke story was used to emphasise the Irishman's importance to the team. For the couple of years before his departure Kenny Dalglish was just as vital to Celtic. I had been worried he might leave in 1975 but possibly because of Jock Stein's car crash he stayed. And he was one major, though not the only, reason why we won the double in 1976/77. Enjoyable as those domestic triumphs were we were no great threat in Europe. Our only game in European competition that season was a 2-4 aggregate loss to Wisla Krakow. If we were to re-establish ourselves in Europe we needed to bring in better players. Instead on the eve of the new season we were selling our best player.

One of the saddest aspects for me was that I understood why Kenny was leaving. Some fans accused the Celtic management of penny pinching and while there may have been some truth in that I felt there was really no amount of money that would have made him stay. He needed a bigger challenge than Celtic and Scotland could provide. At that time I was still staying occasionally with my parents in Bellshill and Thursday nights would see me in the Snug bar in Mossend to catch up with mates and have some craic. Most of my friends were Motherwell fans so did not share my concerns over Kenny's departure. So the following week when I called into the Snug I was glad to see Walter Ingles. Walter was at least an occasional visitor to Parkhead but he was also a musician and music teacher. He was more concerned about the death of that other king- Elvis. In fact he chided me in that school teacher way. "Mike, he said, "you seem more upset about Kenny Dalglish than Elvis." Well of course I was. I replied to Walter "No disrespect but the world will get another Elvis. Where are we going to get another Dalglish?" In view of the amount of Elvis impersonators I have had to endure over the years there was obviously some foresight in my statement!

The Saturday before that night in the Snug I had been at Celtic Park to see Celtic and Dundee United open the season with a scoreless draw. In keeping with the gloom of the day Pat Stanton and Alfie Conn, 2 players who were capable of bringing experience and skill to the team, were injured and effectively out for the season. We would now see how much Celtic had needed Kenny Dalglish. That point against the Tannadice men was the only one Celtic picked up in the first five games of the League campaign. On the last Saturday of September fellow strugglers Clydebank came to Celtic Park. I remember some of the dark humour of the day talking about Celtic's relegation battle! That game was won 1-0 and although relegation was never an issue we hovered around the lower reaches of the League before finishing 5th out of 10. Meanwhile of course Liverpool and Dalglish were going from strength to strength. Especially in the early part of the season it seemed as if every Saturday we trudged home after another defeat to see a great goal from Kenny. The English media were busy telling us about this great "new" player and seemed to forget – or did not care - about what he had already achieved.

The Cups did not bring any relief either. We did get to the League Cup final but lost in extra time to Rangers in an untidy game. The Scottish Cup saw us exit in the 4th Round to lower division Kilmarnock in a replay. I had been at the first game when a late Roddy McDonald goal gave us a draw but did not go to Rugby Park a week later. Transport problems and work commitments were the reasons I gave but this was the first Scottish Cup game I had missed in 12 years - in previous seasons I would have found some way of getting there.

Europe of course was where our shortcomings really showed up. Luxembourg outfit Jeunesse d'Esch were disposed of in the first round of the European Cup but we exited in the next round to S.W.W Innsbruck. After a 2-1 win at home we were thrashed 3-0 in Austria. Apparently Jock Stein went straight to bed after that game. Normally the big man was a bit of an insomniac, staying up to go over the game just played and plan for the next one. Now it seemed as if even he could not stomach the task of coping without Dalglish.

And inevitably Dalglish and Liverpool were taking Europe by storm. At that time I was playing amateur football in the quaintly named Saturday Morning Civil Service League. (Most of the games were anything but civil!). On the night of the European Cup Final between Liverpool and Bruges at Wembley we had a catch up game at Espieside Park in Coatbridge. After the final whistle most of the players from both sides showered quickly to get to a pub to watch the game. Myself and a couple of others took our time in the changing rooms. There was no point in hurrying. The script for this game had been written about 9 months previously. I eventually got to the Forge bar in Whifflet but I had not finished my first pint when the inevitable happened. Kenny Dalglish scored. As he leapt the advertising hoardings to celebrate I downed the rest of the glass and headed home. I don't think the game was even on the TV at my parent's house. Neither my father nor brothers seemed to want to talk about it. For once I was glad to see the end of a football season. Fortunately things would pick up over the next few seasons with the arrival of Billy McNeill as manager but it was many years before I got over the Dalglish departure and its repercussions for Celtic's ambitions.

Earlier I mentioned how I had considered stopping attending Celtic games. Well that did not happen – but up until the Saturday of the first game of the season I was still swithering. Late morning my father asked me if I was going to the game – Well he asked in a way that presumed I was so I answered in the affirmative. "I fancy going too" he said "if you can pick me up". I was a bit surprised. The last game I could remember him going to was the Aberdeen Cup Final in 1967. No matter - for the first time I took my father to a Celtic game. Normally I would have gone to the Celtic End to meet my friends but on this occasion we stood at the Rangers End not far from the spot where he took me to my first games some 17 years previously. Why did he decide to go that day? To show his support at a difficult time? Or did he suspect I was wavering and wanted to make sure I "kept the faith"? Whatever the reason that was the last time I stood with my dad to watch our team. So despite the sadness of Kenny's departure I do have one happy memory from that time!

Written by Mike Maher for CQN Magazine

EXTRA TIME - CHAPTER 2
THEY DON'T LIKE MONDAYS...

Thursday 24th April 2003. It's dinner time in our Auckland house for myself, wife Christine, daughter Nichola and boys Stephen and Sean. Tomorrow is a public holiday so no work for me and Christine and no school for the kids. However the boys and myself still have an early rise as we will be heading to the Newmarket RSA Club in Auckland to watch the second leg of the Boavista v Celtic UEFA Cup semi-final. Naturally conversation round the dinner table is mainly focussed on the game. Nichola and Christine don't quite share the enthusiasm of the boys but at one point Christine puts in her opinion on some matter on the game. Both boys roll their eyes and sigh! I know they are thinking what could their Kiwi born mother could possibly know about football. And sure enough Sean pipes up in what is a statement rather than a question- "Mum, what do you know about it?" Her reply is simple – "well I was at the 4-2 game". Both boys are silent. There is even an indication of jaw dropping and envy! They were both born and brought up in New Zealand and have never been nearer than 18000 kilometres from Celtic Park but they know about that game. A game that was played almost a quarter of a century earlier, before the boys were born, before I was even married.

As I think back over the years I have to admit that that game sort of crept up on me. The previous season, 1977/78, had been a disaster. Kenny Dalglish had gone, Celtic had finished halfway down the division and had not qualified for Europe. During the close season Jock Stein had been replaced by Billy McNeill but I had the feeling that Caesar would need some time to get things righted.

We did get off to a good start. The first 4 league games were won including a 3-1 victory over Rangers at Parkhead. The second Old Firm encounter produced a 1-1 draw at Hampden (Ibrox being under reconstruction). However I still felt we were a bit short of Championship material. Big Billy must have thought so too and bought Davie Provan and Murdo MacLeod. Even then I still had my doubts and I also now had other distractions. My Kiwi girlfriend was now living in Scotland. She actually came to a couple of games with me but we also sought other ways of spending Saturday afternoons. While Celtic were losing at Tannadice in October we were with friends on a beer festival weekend in Belgium. In December we were at Murrayfield watching the All Blacks (not that either of us knew much about rugby) while Celtic played out a scoreless draw with Aberdeen at Celtic Park. Christmas was spent with Christine's family in Connemara and so I missed Celtic's defeat at Cappielow on 23rd December.

We were now at the halfway stage and Celtic were in 6th place. Although that may seem a lowly position we were only 1 point behind Morton, Rangers and Aberdeen, 2 points behind second placed Partick Thistle and 4 points adrift of league leaders Dundee United. The Ne'erday game with Rangers would obviously be vital.

At this time I was often going to games in company of an old work colleague, Terry Crossan, who had returned to Glasgow after some time working in England. We decided to splash out on stand tickets for the New Year clash with Rangers and I went into Celtic Park one afternoon to purchase a couple of tickets from Jim Kennedy. However the tickets would end up in my drawer for a while as wintry weather caused postponement of the game. Indeed after our defeat to Morton on 23rd December we did not play a league game until 3rd March when Alfie Conn's goal gave us a victory over Aberdeen. By now I had another distraction. An old school friend, John Fagan, was managing an amateur team in Coatbridge. He had asked me to assist with training and I was enjoying the Tuesday evening work-outs. John asked me to help out on a Saturday and I even made a couple of substitute appearances despite being a bit older than most of the players. I was beginning to think that I could spend Saturdays without Celtic. Then one day we arrived at the game to discover there had been a management "coup". John was asked to stand down. The new manager was happy for me to stay as trainer but my loyalty was to John so I resigned and headed off to Celtic Park to watch a 2-0 win over the Jags. I still had my reservations about Celtic's Championship credentials though. The following midweek saw an important trip to Tannadice. It was a late decision to go with my brother Jim so it was 7.20pm when we got to the ground. We could tell by the crowds milling round the turnstiles at the away end that we would miss the start of the game. Then on the spur of the moment I stuck my head in the office door and asked if any stand tickets were left. The answer was positive so a few minutes before kick-off Jim and I took our seats. At that stage we were still usually 'terracing Tims" but this occasion was a bit of an eye opener. At half time I went to the toilet and came back to tell Jim almost incredulously that there were wash-basins, soap and towels there! That was to be a turning point in how I viewed facilities at football grounds. On the field though my reservations seemed to be vindicated as United won 2-1. The feeling was reinforced a few weeks later when we lost 1-0 to Rangers at Hampden. I viewed that game from the old North Stand using Terry Crossan's ticket. He was now back in England. However one positive that came from that occasion was meeting some of Terry's mates who were regulars at Heraghty's Bar. For the next few seasons they would be my companions on trips around Scotland following the Bhoys. However on that day all I knew was that were a point behind Rangers with only 4 games to play.

We won the next 2 games away to Partick Thistle and St Mirren and then had a must win home game with Hearts. Nowadays there is despair on Celtic websites when crowds drop below 40,000. Well for that game against an admittedly poor Tynecastle side (they were relegated that season) only 18,000 turned up. Mike Conroy scored the only goal which set up a league decider the following week. Celtic now had a 1 point lead over the Ibrox men, the other teams having fallen by the wayside. However Celtic only had that last game at home to Rangers while the Ibrox side had a game in hand. It was quite simple. A Celtic win would give us the title while any other result put Rangers in the driving seat. Where were those tickets I had bought 5 months ago?

Terry was still in England and the other guys had their terracing tickets so I decided to ask Christine some important questions. Would she marry me and did she want to come to the game with me! Yes was the answer to both so on Monday 21st May 1979 we both headed off to Paradise.

It was quite a warm night and the atmosphere was electric. Christine had been to a few games before but none as tense as this. An early Bobby Russell goal gave the visitors the advantage. 10 minutes after the break things got worse. Johnny Doyle kicked a prone Alex McDonald and was sent off. I was despondent and annoyed. From our vantage point in the stand we could see that the red card was justified. I turned to Christine – "he could have cost us the League!" Sometimes a team down to 10 men is inspired to get a result but that inspiration usually comes from a feeling of injustice. This sending off was justified. However that does not matter tonight. The crowd's passion, emanating from the Jungle gets behind the team. In those days we did not need Ultras or cheerleaders or canned music. We responded to what was happening around us. You could almost touch the tension and the passion. We were literally on our feet, including Christine. Roy Aitken equalises and in 74 minutes George McCluskey puts us ahead. The joy is short lived as a couple of moments later Rangers equalise. I am deflated for a moment but then we are all back on our feet roaring on the team. Davy Provan, socks down by his ankles, is everywhere. Roy Aitken spurs on his mates. With 5 minutes to go a cross is knocked into his own net by Colin Jackson. Christine is now standing on her seat. We are kicking every ball. In the dying seconds Murdo McLeod breaks away. All he needs to do is keep the ball for a few moments. Instead he thumps the ball towards Peter McCloy's goal. "Aw naw "I yell "you should have kept the ball ya...beauty! – Goal!" The ball is in the Ranger's net - 4-2 and it is all over. We have won the League. I hug Christine. We won't forget the night we decided to get married! As we spill joyously out into the streets the fans have already adapted the words of Boney M's hit 'Brown Girl in the ring" to "10 men won the League". We get home to discover that there are no TV highlights but that disappointment is minor as we were there. And all these years later we can still remember that game and that night.

As a postscript I should mention that Christine's memories of that occasion go beyond the actual game. At that time she was working in an office in Maryhill. One of her workmates was another New Zealand girl. However that girl, Bonnie, although not a great football fan herself came from a family whose sympathies were with the "other side". Despite their common nationality they were not great friends, especially as Bonnie could be a bit bossy. Christine was friendlier with another girl in the office – Anne Marie- a strapping red head of Donegal stock. A couple of days after that game Christine and Anne Marie were at their desks when Bonnie came in and started to complain about some aspect of their work. Christine still recalls the smug smile on Anne Marie's face as she looked up and responded with "4-2 ya ***!"

Written by Mike Maher for CQN Magazine

EXTRA TIME - CHAPTER 3
MONDAY 21ST MAY 1979...
OH WHAT A NIGHT

The best and most memorable Celtic game I've attended, and unless you were at the 7-1 game or in Lisbon, the 4-2 has to be your all time best Celtic game, surely!

At the time, I was going to the games with my mates on the Edinburgh & District bus, despite my dad, uncles and brother going separately by car. It cost me more, but at that age (18) there was something magical about going to Celtic games by bus with your pals.

The bus would leave Midlothian (Bonnyrigg/Gorebridge) and pick up at a couple of points in the town. Most of the town guys like myself would get on at Ryrie's Bar, Haymarket. I remember the actual bus itself because it was green, with the bus company name "Lintons" emblazoned across it.

Anyway, there was a bit of hassle between the club committee and Lintons - I don't know the details – but without forewarning, the bus just did not turn up that night of all nights. There were no mobile phones, so no message saying the bus was a no-show...we waited and waited...most guys hopped on to other buses that were turning up late (there must have been around 7 or 8 Celtic buses that picked up at Haymarket in those days). Stupidly we waited too long and eventually had to get the 7pm train from Haymarket, getting into Queen Street at 7.45pm (the game kicked off at 7.30pm). We jumped in a taxi. We had no way of knowing the score (the game was not even on the radio) and we got into the Jungle just after 8pm to find out that we were 1-0 down, and just as wee Johnny (God rest him) was getting sent off for booting Alex Macdonald. It was demoralising.

Down 1-0 - I had a sudden yearning to see my family. My dad and uncles always stood near the back of the Celtic End, the right hand side looking down. I left my mates and made my way there, totally devastated.

If there's been a better second 45 minutes watching Celtic, then I have not seen it. It was, and is, the stuff of legend. It was Roy Aitken's finest hour in a Celtic jersey. He would never – could never – better this display, and he was only about 2 years older than me at the time – about 20. He drove us and we willed that ball into the Celtic End net below us. The level of euphoria, when we went 2-1 up, then utter dejection when Bobby Russell equalised was palpable. When we made it 2-1 I was hugging my Dad and we both fell on the ground, suffering a bit of trampling, but ecstatic. The sickening micro-second of silence after their equalizer and before the roar from the Rangers End was unbearable.

Thank God for big Colin Jackson who then popped up with an OG, but we celebrated it a bit different from chicken George's goal that had made it 2-1…we half expected another equaliser from them.

I can still see Murdo's winner, screaming into the net. I would give anything to see - not the actual goal again - but that thing that TV companies do nowadays, when they have cameras permanently trained on fans, and then show their reaction to a goal. I would love to see the ecstatic, euphoric, joy on the faces of the Celtic support for the second or two it took to sink in that we were the Champions, and that we had beaten the other mob, coming from behind, and with only 10 men, to do so. It was beautiful.

My Dad always parked in London Road – as we do now, but unlike most Celtic fans who parked there for normal home games, he still did that when they came (rather than go the Gallowgate side) which always bugged the hell out of me. It meant being heavily outnumbered and hiding scarves etc. The atmosphere as we walked along London Road through their support and back to the car was poisonous. I remember waiting to cross at the lights at Springfield Road. I must look like a Tim, or maybe I just looked too happy to be one of them, but this guy waiting beside me winked, and lifted his jacket slightly to show me his Celtic scarf. I did the same, we had a quick mini hug and off we went, delirious into the Glasgow night.

We got back to our house in Edinburgh in time to see the highlights on TV – or so we thought. But nothing could deflate us that night. My mum had an old clapped out mini car at the time. I had passed my test a few months before. I told her I was nipping out in it to get a chippie. Me, my 16 year old brother and 17 year old cousin headed for Princes Street in the car – no pubs open after 11pm in Edinburgh in those days. We just drove up and down Princes Street 5 or 6 times with our Celtic scarves out the windows shouting to everybody that Ten Men Won The League. (Written by Tully57)

As a 15 year old this was my first ever Glasgow derby as my dad would let me go to any game bar against them. My brother and I told our mum we were going to the library but instead went on the Johnstone No.1 bus. The game is to this day one of the highlights of my life. After the game our bus did not turn up so 75 of us had to walk back into town for a bus from Anderston Cross bus-station. I will never forget our bus convener asking for 75 singles to Johnstone. The singing on the way home was incredible and in particular coming down the hill past the railway station and into the town past the Orange Lodge and Masonic. (Written by Catman)

21st May 79. THE 4-2 game. My last ever day at school. I finished my Modern Studies Higher, ditched the green blazer and set off to get the Busby and Eaglesham Celtic supporters bus to the game ! Our bus had its window smashed in by some brick hurling Rangers supporters on Springfield Road. I was saved from glass injury by my tricolour. I got off the bus with no concern at all about how I might get home, only aggravated butterflies in my stomach. Indeed I was even more determined to shout myself hoarse in the cause of supporting a mediocre Celtic team to fulfill their destiny against them.

I took up my place in the Jungle and shared the emotions of it all. If ever the team and crowd were united it was that night. Folk forget we were 7th in the league when we played Aberdeen in March. A very mediocre team needed all the support it could get and even more after we went down to 10 men. Still the rest is history and the journey home was the next challenge when I came back down to earth. A bus legend Charlie Sharkey took me under his wing and the double celebration of leaving school and winning the league with ten men commenced.

A half and half pint in what seemed like every pub from Celtic Park to Glasgow Cross. I have still got no idea how I got from there back to Eaglesham that night though! Great memories. (Written by Burnley78)

Wee anecdote from the 4-2 game. I was chatting to Colin Jackson a couple of years ago. He said at the end of the game he shook Murdo's hand and said that he would now be on his Christmas card list – for obvious reasons! (Written by Billy Bhoy)

I listened to the 4-2 game sitting on the step of my close. I could tell the score by the volume of the celebrations, loud for them and bedlam for us. It was a very emotional time for a young boy still short of his twelfth birthday, my mother had passed away exactly three months earlier, so although I was delighted when a neighbour confirmed the score that feeling of real sadness was still very raw. Also that night I was heading to London, on the overnight sleeper, with the rest of primary seven year. Buick Makane who posts on CQN was also on that train, we had an exchange on here about it a while back but it's worth repeating. We suffered a lot of abuse from Rangers fans who got on the train, our head teacher was a nun and she got a really hard time from them. There were five of us in our compartment and when a particularly ugly group opened our door and threatened us it was extremely frightening. However one of the boys in our group and my friend at the time was able to extract revenge, he had to wait ten years but scoring the winning goal for Celtic in a Cup Final against them in 1989 was worth the wait. (Written by borgo67)

I was serving my time at a now defunct engineering firm in Clydebank, along with another few bhoys we headed on to the District Bus at the bottom of Whitecrook Street and set off for Celtic Park. We were soon into the ground and decided that the Celtic End would be our best bet for the night as the Jungle was already pretty full. I don't have the best memory but I think it was a particularly pleasant evening weather-wise.

Anyway, the game started and it ebbed and flowed until the fateful moment when Johnny Doyle got sent off. I was among a crowd of guys which included the Edmonds brothers from the Mill Road flats, as JD was running off, Peter (Pa Bear) and Billy started fighting with each other about the merits of Johnny's actions that had brought us down to 10 men! It was full on and took about 8 of us to separate the two maniacs and I think it was Billy who wanted to get onto the pitch to have a word with the referee who had just sent off Johnny Doyle, this above everything else was my most abiding memory of that game. We knew we were home when Murdo sent in his screamer and like one or two others have mentioned on CQN, one of our bus windows got tanned in the East End on the way home.

The next day at work, I would have been untouchable, the place was full of them and I was a bit of a wind-up merchant, happy days indeed.

I remember sometime later, Celtic Films bringing it to the old Unity Club, probably the worst footage I have ever seen but still mightily enjoyable all the same. (Written by Antipodean Red)

I wasn't at the 4-2 game – was a student at the time and had some wimpy excuse like a Degree exam the next day! My experience of trying to find out what was going on at Celtic Park throws today's world of Internet, live everything, dodgy feeds and social media into sharp relief.

The auld hands will remember that there were all sorts of strikes on including the technicians who worked for the TV coverage – hence not even the highlights exist. I can testify that the game wasn't even on the radio! As I searched I found Radio Clyde DJ (I think it was Paul Cooney) offering updates during his show. Talk about agony! I heard the early goals, Johnny being sent off and eventually Jackson's OG. At 3-2 we win the league – I am in a state of nervous exhaustion when the DJ cries – 'there's been another goal at Celtic Park'…"I'll tell you who scored it after this next record!"

I don't remember the record but it took for ever, I'm sure I rattled off a few decades and a lot of promises never to do certain things ever again – at 4-2 we are Champions, at 3-3 we are done for. As the record faded there was another agonising delay before – 'It's Murdo MacLeod who puts Celtic 4-2 up!' There is another agonising wait broken only by prayers, promises and dodgy music before full time is announced and we are Champions! I lost it – grabbed what drink I had and went visiting – proceeded to break all the promises – don't remember getting back to my place.

And I passed the exam! Oh I remember the record – 'Oh what a night' (Written by jinkyredstar)

A selection of contributions to the discussion on the 4-2 game on www. celticquicknews.co.uk

THE FINAL WHISTLE
CELTIC QUICK NEWS

SPECIAL THANKS TO MIKE MAHERS, TIMMY BLETHERS and the contributors to this section from www.celticquicknews.co.uk

Want to talk about Celtic and just about anything else you can think about?

Why not join the conversation and chat to South of Tunis * Kdc * NegAnon2 * Monaghan1900 * THE EXILED TIM * Brogan Rogan Trevino and Hogan * Vmhan * Mild mannered Pedro Delgado * The Battered Bunnet * !!Bada Bing!! * kikinthenakas * Hamiltontim * Thunder Road * blantyretim * tobagostreet * connaire12 * roy croppie * corkcelt * 16 roads – Celtic über alles…* BOBBY MURDOCH'S CURLED-UP WINKLEPICKERS * Nye Bevan's rebel soldier * timbhoy2 * Neustadt- Braw * eddieinkirkmichael *oldtim67 * leftclicktic * IGC * jamesgang * martybhoy59 * TBJ * Burghbhoy * jinkyredstar * A ceiler Gonof Rust * gordybhoy64 * the unthank road * Greenpinata * Turkeybhoy * What is the Stars * Lennybhoy * Parkheadcumsalford * Tallybhoy * Jobo Baldie * 67 Heaven * bankiebhoy1 * twist n turns * Frantic07 * stevo * Maestro * Margaret McGill * Tom McLaughlin * FFM * Delaney Dunky * Macjay * The_huddle * Celticrollercoaster * Dallas Dallas where the heck is Dallas * Lilys grandpa * BGX * petec * pedrocaravanachio67 * ticwaewin * The Spirit of Arthur Lee * Stephenbhoy1 * Gordon64 * praecepta * Hrvatski Jim * Can I Have Raspberry * Big Georges Fan Club * Awe_Naw_No_Annoni_ Oan_Anaw_Noo * Fieldofdrams * bognorbhoy * sipsini * Doc * voguepunter * Morrissey the 23rd * Clashcitybhoy * setting free the bears * Auldheid * itscalledthemalvinas * timbhoy2 * prestonpans bhoys * neilbhoy * Troontim * BIG-CUP-WINNERS * whitedoghunch * celticbhoy73 * KevJungle * RobertTressell * ernie lynch * 'GG * Cathedral View * Jonny the Tim * weet wee tweet (GBWO) * greenyin * EKBhoy * Geordie Munro * gearoid1998 * lennon's passion * SELF DOUBT AND SELFISM * Philbhoy * michaelj * bournesouprecipe * Supersutton * Moonbeams * TootingTim * LiviBhoy * timaloy29 * williebhoy * Imatim * innishcolly * starry plough * Cathal * Clink\o/ * gordybhoy64 * McCourt For 7 * Looks a lot like Che Guevara * ChippyBhoy * Jonny the Tim * niallo83 * Blooter It! * Tom Molach * topkat *

BigYinMilan * Mullet and co 2 * pintaguinness * excathedra44 * boondock saint * Snake Plissken * coolmore mafia * Cowiebhoy * dksglen * iki * DownForSam * themightyquinn * dessybhoy * m6bhoy * antipodean red * jc2 * Saint Stivs * tommytwiststommyturns * Tricolour Ribbon * Jimmynotpaul * johann murdoch * Hoop doggydog * fleagle1888 * cliftonville celt from belfast * Joe Filippis Haircut * Booker T * saltires en sivilla * Emerald \ o/ still proud to be an internet bampot * overseasbhoy * Snake Plissken * mighty tim supporting wee Oscar * Summa of Sammi * hebcelt * Dear reader *guernica * mncelt * Toor A Loo * Paddybhoy88 * Dontbrattbakkinanger * hankray * beatbhoy * weebobbycollins * glendalystonsils * Zico-Maltese Bhoy * Zbyszek * CultsBhoy * dena29 * justshatered * ElDiegobhoy * Ron Bacardi * Pogmathony aka Laird of the Smiles * scullybhoy * weeminger * An Tearmann * PeteTheBeat * may67 * An Tearmann * Minceyheidman * timhorton * h@n skelper * a light insanity * Markjig * Burnley78 * Fred Colon * The Comfortable Collective * sixtaeseven * smoke and mirrors * Gary67 * JimmyQuinnsBits * Melbourne Mick * ruggyman * paolosboots FC before PLC * nally81 * Sannabhoy and 2000 kids say thank you to bucketeers and donator * Hoops_Neil_Lennon_diditagain * Marrakesh Express * tonydonnelly67 * senga * time for change * Ray Winstone's Big Disembodied Heid * martybhoy59 * Captain Beefheart * FAVOURITE UNCLE * LivornoBhoy * googybhoy * TroonTim * paulloantony * the glorious balance sheet * PFayr supports WeeOscar * soukous * foghorn leghorn * Jackie mac * derbyshirebhoy * Stringer Bell * BigMike * Blindlemonchitlin * Celtic Mac * el flaco * 50 shades of green * mighty tim * viewfaethewidae * Papa John * skyisalandfill * Fess19 * westies * ger57 * Taurangabhoy * Monaghan1900 * Sandman * foghorn leghorn * seanoc * and many other Celtic supporters? You will be guaranteed a very warm, Celtic welcome.

Join the conversation every day on www.celticquicknews.co.uk

For Jock Stein, Johnny Doyle and Tommy Burns. Celtic men.